Families Across Time

A Life Course Perspective

Readings

Sharon J. Price
The University of Georgia

Patrick C. McKenry
The Ohio State University

Megan J. Murphy
The University of Georgia

New York   Oxford
OXFORD UNIVERSITY PRESS

Oxford University Press, Inc., publishes works that further Oxford University's
objective of excellence in research, scholarship, and education.

Oxford   New York
Auckland   Cape Town   Dar es Salaam   Hong Kong   Karachi
Kuala Lumpur   Madrid   Melbourne   Mexico City   Nairobi
New Delhi   Shanghai   Taipei   Toronto

With offices in
Argentina   Austria   Brazil   Chile   Czech Republic   France   Greece
Guatemala   Hungary   Italy   Japan   Poland   Portugal   Singapore
South Korea   Switzerland   Thailand   Turkey   Ukraine   Vietnam

Published by Oxford University Press, Inc.
198 Madison Avenue, New York, New York 10016
http://www.oup.com

Oxford is a registered trademark of Oxford University Press

ISBN 978-0-19-532989-6

Printed in the United States of America
on acid-free paper

This book is dedicated to. . .

        Sylva and Glendyn Price
        Reba and Frank West

        . . .those who supported and directed us in our passage across the life course.

Contents

Section I:
Introduction
Sharon J. Price, Patrick C. McKenry, and Megan J. Murphy
The editors provide an in-depth historical and conceptual overview of the development of the life course of families and a rationale for adopting this approach.

Section II:
Structural Variations Across the Life Course
Kimberly J. M. Downs, Marilyn Coleman, and Larry Ganong,
Unlike other normative events related to family life, the authors argue that there are few social norms for guiding appropriate divorce time and behaviors over the life course.

Margaret Crosbie-Burnett and Katrina McClintic
In this piece, the transitions stepfamilies experience in their various stages of development and the natural tensions between the individual's and the family's development are addressed.

Katherine R. Allen and Karen L. Wilcox
Allen and Wilcox discuss the multiple life-course context of same-sex partnerships and romantic relationships, lesbian mothers and gay fathers, and children of lesbian and gay parents.

Section III:
Processes Through the Life Course of Families 91

Julie K. Kohler and Shirley L. Zimmerman
This essay stresses the interconnections between families and political systems. The authors argue that understanding these complexities and the way in which policies affect families would help avert possible adverse consequences for families.

Acknowledgments

The support, advice, and encouragement of colleagues and friends were instrumental in the conceptualization and production of this text. In particular, we would like to express our appreciation to the many students who through the years have asked for a book of this type and who contributed to our ideas for this volume, and we would like to thank our respective departments, which have long provided the atmosphere and support needed to enhance our careers. We are very grateful to all the contributors to this book for their impressive, thoughtful, and valuable contributions. Their enthusiasm and timely revisions helped make the project less onerous. We are also indebted to others for their valuable assistance, including Roy Fish and Hyoun Kim, whose contributions to this project were immeasurable.

We also wish to thank the following reviewers for their insights and comments: Linda Ade-Ridder (Miami University), Carolyn Balkwell (San Diego State University), Betsy Bergen (Kansas State University), Gloria Bird (Virginia Polytechnic Institute), Timothy Brubaker (Miami University), Marsha Carolan (Michigan State University), Kenneth Davidson (University of Wisconsin-Eau Claire), William Doherty (University of Minnesota), Bron Ingoldsby (Ricks College), David Klein (University of Notre Dame), Helen Mederer (University of Rhode Island), Shelley McDermid (Purdue University), Kay Pasley (University of North Carolina at Greensboro), and Michael Sporakowski (Virginia Polytechnic Institute). ✦

About the Editors

Sharon J. Price, Ph.D.

Dr. Sharon Price, Professor in the Departments of Child and Family Development and Sociology, has been on the faculty at The University of Georgia since 1973. Prior to coming to The University of Georgia she was a faculty member in the Department of Sociology at The University of Tulsa and an Instructor at Iowa State University, where she earned her M.S. and Ph.D. degrees in Sociology. She was Department Head in the Department of Child and Family from 1989 to 1996, presently serves as Graduate Coordinator in the same Department, and is also on the faculties of Gerontology and Women's Studies.

She has published extensively in professional journals and she and Dr. McKenry have authored and edited *Divorce* (Sage) and *Families and Change* (Sage; 2nd edition forthcoming). Her present research focuses on a qualitative study of widows who live on family farms—which she describes as the "most exciting work of my career."

Dr. Price, a former ACE Fellow, has won several teaching awards including the Osborne Award, presented by the National Council on Family Relations for outstanding teaching in Family Studies. In 1990 she was presented the highest honor for teaching at The University of Georgia, the Josiah Meigs Award. She is active in several professional organizations, and has served in many capacities, including President, in the National Council on Family Relations. She was recently named a Fellow in the National Council on Family Relations.

Patrick C. McKenry, Ph.D.

Dr. Patrick C. McKenry is a Professor in the Department of Human Development and Family Science and the Ohio Agricul-tural Research and Development Center at the Ohio State University; he also is an adjunct professor in the Department of African-American and African Studies. He has served as Visiting Professor at the University of British Columbia and the University of North Carolina-Chapel Hill.

Dr. McKenry received his Ph.D. in Child and Family Studies from the University of Tennessee. He also served as a postdoctoral fellow in the Department of Child and Family Development, The University of Georgia.

Dr. McKenry's research focuses on families and stress with particular interest in family conflict and violence, post-divorce adjustment, and variations in coping by gender and race. He currently is studying the role of conflict and violence in the co-parenting process after divorce. He has published extensively on marriage and family and has co-authored two other books with Dr. Sharon Price (*Divorce* and *Families and Change*).

Dr. McKenry is a member of the American Sociological Association and the National Council on Family Relations where he has held several leadership positions. He has been the recipient of three Ohio State University awards for excellence in teaching and research.

Megan J. Murphy, M.S.

Megan J. Murphy is a Ph.D. candidate in the Department of Child and Family Development (Marriage and Family Therapy) at The University of Georgia. She received her undergraduate degree from State University of New York at Geneseo in psychology and sociology, and her M.S. from Colorado State University in the Department of Human Development and Family Studies with a specialization in Marriage and Family Therapy. Her areas of research and clinical interest include feminist family therapy, therapeutic process and outcomes, and power in the supervisor-supervisee relationship. She has worked as a support group leader with the AIDS Coalition of Northeast Georgia and as a teaching assistant with the Department of Women's Studies. Her work has appeared in *Journal of Family Psychology, Handbook of Family Development: Dynamics and Family Interventions*, and the *Encyclopedia of Parenting*. She is currently working on her dissertation. ✦

Author Profiles

Katherine R. Allen, Ph.D., is Professor of Family Studies (with appointments in Gerontology and Women's Studies) at Virginia Polytechnic Institute and State University. She is the author of three books: *Single Women/Family Ties: Life Histories of Older Women*; *Women and Families: Feminist Reconstructions*; and *Handbook of Family Diversity*. She served as program vice-president in the National Council on Family Relations and serves as deputy editor of the *Journal of Marriage and the Family*. She is chair-elect of the VPI Academy of Teaching Excellence.

Margaret E. Arcus, Ph.D., is a retired Professor of Family Science at the University of British Columbia. Her scholarly work has focused on family life education and values education. She was a member of the NCFR Standards and Certification Committee that developed the Life-Span Framework for Family Life Education and the Certified Family Life Educator Program. She is senior editor of the *Handbook of Family Life Education*. She received the Osborne Award for Excellence in Teaching from the National Council on Family Relations, several teaching awards from the University of British Columbia, and the Canadian Home Economics Association Honour Award.

Suzanne Bartle-Haring, Ph.D., is Associate Professor in the Department of Human Development and Family Science—Marriage and Family Therapy at The Ohio State University. She has published in several professional journals, including *Family Process, Journal of Marriage and the Family*, and *The Journal of Adolescence*. Her research interests include the influence of the family system on adolescents, young adult development, and assessment of families.

Roy A. Bean, Ph.D., is Assistant Professor in Human Development and Family Science at The Ohio State University. He is a clinical member and supervisor-in-training in the American Association of Marriage and Family Therapy; his research interests include sexual abuse, multicultural families, and marital satisfaction.

Tina Bedell, M. A. is a Ph.D. student and graduate administrative assistant in the Department of Human Development and Family Science—Marriage and Family Therapy, at The Ohio State University. Her research interests include marriage and family counseling and African-American families and religiosity.

Gary L. Bowen, Ph.D., is the Kenan Distinguished Professor in the School of Social Work (with a joint appointment in the Department of Communication Studies) at the University of North Carolina at Chapel Hill. He teaches courses on family stress, coping and social support, and the evaluation of programs and practice. His scholarly focus includes the effects of fear and danger on the lives of youth, and he has worked with various branches of the armed services on how structural and dynamic aspects of the military environment influence the adaptation of service members and their families.

Natasha K. Bowen, M. S.W., is a doctoral student in the School of Social Work at the University of North Carolina at Chapel Hill. Her research interests focus on communities and schools and school social work practices.

Thomas L. Campbell, M.D., is Professor in the Departments of Family Medicine and Psychiatry at the University of Rochester School of Medicine. He has written extensively on the role of families in medical practice and the influence of families on health, including co-authoring *Families and Health* and *Family-Oriented Primary Care*. He is co-editor of *Families, Systems and Health: The Journal of Collaborative Family Healthcare* and chair of the Advisory Council of the Bayer Institute for Health Care Communication.

Marilyn Coleman, Ed.D., is Professor of Human Development and Family Studies at the University of Missouri. She is author or co-author of over 100 articles and two books (co-authored with Larry Ganong), including *Remarried Family Relations* and *Bibliotherapy with Stepchildren*. She served as editor of the *Journal of Marriage and Family*, and associate editor of the *Home Economics Research Journal*, and she currently serves on the editorial boards of several professional journals. Her current research focuses on family responsibilities following divorce and remarriage and the development of stepparent roles. She teaches in the areas of divorce, remarriage, and step families.

Margaret Crosbie-Burnett, Ph.D., is Associate Professor and Head of the Department of Counseling Psychology at the University of Miami. Her research, teaching, and writing has focused on the development of theory and policy related to step families and the development of an instrument for the assessment of step family adjustment. She was guest editor of a special issue of *Family Relations* on step families and is co-chair of the Focus Group on Remarriage and Step families in the National Council on Family Relations.

Kimberly J. M. Downs, M. S., is a doctoral student in the Department of Human Development and Family Studies at the University of Missouri-Columbia. Her research interests include divorce and remarriage, family commitment, and the effects of gender in couple interactions.

Jacki A. Fitzpatrick, Ph.D., is Assistant Professor of Human Development and Family Studies at Texas Tech University. Her research interests focus on romantic relationships and adult friendships. She has published on romantic relationships, remarriage, and community/family economics.

Larry Ganong, Ph.D., is Professor of Nursing and Family Studies at the University of Missouri. He has co-authored (with Marilyn Coleman) *Remarried Family Relations* and *Bibliotherapy with Stepchildren* along with over 100 articles. His research interests include postdivorce family relationships, remarriage and stepparenting, intergenerational family responsibilities, and family stereotyping. He teaches in the areas of research methods, family dynamics, intervention, and family theories. He has served on the editorial boards of several professional journals, including the *Journal of Marriage and the Family*, *Family Relations*, and the *Journal of Nursing*.

Richard J. Gelles, Ph.D., holds The Joanne and Raymond Welsh Chair of Child Welfare and Family Violence in the School of Social Work at the University of Pennsylvania. His book *The Violent Home* was the first systematic investigation of family violence; he is author or co-author of 21 books and more than 100 articles and chapters on family violence. His latest books include *The Book of David: How Preserving Families Can Cost Children's Lives* and *Intimate Violence in Families* (3rd ed.). He is a member of the National Academy of Science's panel on Assessing Family Violence Interventions and vice president for publications in the National Council on Family Relations.

Julie K. Kohler, B.A., B.S., is a Ph.D. student in the Department of Family Social Science at the University of Minnesota. Her research interests focus on openness in adoption; she has worked with the Child Welfare League of America and the Children's Defense Fund.

Ronit D. Leichtenbritt, Ph.D., is affiliated with The Bob Shapell School of Social Work, Tel Aviv University, Tel Aviv Israel. Her research interests include attitudes, meanings, and values surrounding the issues of socially assisted dying.

Geoffrey K. Leigh, Ph.D., is Professor in Cooperative Extension at the University of Nevada. His research and teaching interests include adolescents and families, emotional expression in families, and human energy fields in children. His current work in cooperative extension focuses primarily on adolescent sexual behavior and prevention of violence. He has co-edited one book, published a number of professional papers and chapters, and conducted numerous workshops for adolescents, parents, and other professionals.

Stacie A. Leonard, M. S., is a doctoral student in the Department of Family Resources and Human Development at Arizona State University. Her research interests involve children's emotional development and play behaviors. She is currently conducting longitudinal research on internalizing problems in young children.

Debra Madden-Derdich, Ph.D., is Assistant Professor of Family Studies and Marriage and Family Therapy at Arizona State University. Her research focuses on family processes during the postdivorce period. She has published in academic journals that specialize in research on families and family intervention.

Katrina McClintic, M. S., is a Ph.D. student in the Department of Educational and Psychological Studies at the University of Miami. She holds an M. S. in counseling from the University of Georgia.

Patrick C. McKenry, Ph.D., is Professor in the Department of Human Development and Family Science at The Ohio State University (with appointments in African-American and African Studies and the Ohio Agricultural Research and Development Center). He has co-authored or co-edited (with Sharon Price) two books: *Divorce: A Major Family Transition* and *Families and Change: Coping with Stressful Events*, and he has widely published in the marriage and family literature. His areas of research include family stress and coping with particular interests in marital dissolution and family violence.

Megan J. Murphy, M. S., is a doctoral student in the Department of Child and Family Development—Marriage and Family Therapy at The University of Georgia. Her scholarly interests include effectiveness of feminist family therapy, conceptualization of clients' issues in family therapy, and the effectiveness of various theoretical approaches of supervisors on outcomes of therapy.

J. Elizabeth Miller, Ph.D., is Associate Professor of Family and Child Studies at Northern Illinois University. She is active in the National Council on Family Relations, having served as chair of the Religion and Family Life section and vice-chair of the Feminism and Family Life section. She received the Excellence in Undergraduate Teaching Award at Northern Illinois University.

Benjamin J. Perry, M. A., is a Ph.D. student in Human Development and Family Science—marriage and family therapy at The Ohio State University. His research interests focus on family therapy with American Indian families.

Gary W. Peterson, Ph.D., is Professor and chair of the Department of Sociology at Arizona State University. His scholarly interests focus on parent-child relations, adolescent development within a family context, adolescent social competence, and family influences on low-income youth. He has published extensively in academic journals, is author of several book chapters on parent-adolescent and parent-child relations, and is co-editor of *Marriage and Family Review* and the *Handbook of Marriage and the Family* (2nd ed.).

Christine A. Price, Ph.D., is Assistant Professor in the Gerontology Program and the Department of Consumer and Family Studies at Southwest Missouri State University. Her teaching and scholarship focuses on aging families and gender in later life with specific interests in women's retirement experiences and aging parent and adult child relations. She has authored the book, *Women and Retirement: An Unexplored Transition*.

Sharon J. Price, Ph.D., is Professor in the Department of Child and Family Development (with appointments in Gerontology, Women's Studies, and Sociology) at the University of Georgia. She has published extensively in professional journals, and she and Patrick C. McKenry have authored and edited two books, *Divorce: A Major Family Transition* and *Families and Change: Coping with Stressful Events*. Her research interests focus on widows who live on family farms. She has won several teaching awards including the Osborne Award for Outstanding Teaching from the National Council on Family Relations and the Josiah Meigs Award at the University of Georgia; she has served in numerous leadership positions, including president of the National Council on Family Relations.

Kathryn D. Rettig, Ph.D., is Professor in the Department of Family Social Science at the University of Minnesota-Twin Cities. Her research interests include interpersonal justice issues in divorce, decision making integral to relationship-ending transitions, legal-economic and ethical conflicts in families, and family quality of life.

Jack M. Richman, Ph.D., is Professor in the School of Social Work at the University of North Carolina at Chapel Hill. He teaches in the areas of clinical social work practice with individuals, couples, and families. His research focuses on how individuals, couples, and families develop and maintain interpersonal and social processes involved in the interface with their ecological environment. He also is involved with the North Carolina-Israel partnership in which he studies the effect of violence and trauma on children and families.

Hilary A. Rose, Ph.D., is Assistant Professor in the Department of Human Development at Washington State University. Her research focuses on gender development over the life course (she has recently developed a bio psychosocial model of gender development, looking specifically at caregiving) and stereotyping about gender and sexual orientation. She is the student/new professional representative on the board of directors, National Council on Family Relations.

Karen S. Wampler, Ph.D., is Professor and Director of the Marriage and Family Therapy Program in the Department of Human Development and Family Studies at Texas Tech University. She has published on marriage and family therapy research methodology, the impact of families on child difficulties, and attachment processes in couple interaction. She is currently serving on the Commission on Accreditation for Marriage and Family Therapy Education— American Association of Marriage and Family Therapy, and the editorial board of *Family Process*.

Karen Weddle-West, Ph.D., is Associate Professor and Assistant Dean of graduate studies in the College of Education at the University of Memphis. Her research focuses on at-risk African-American adolescents, adolescent pregnancy and prevention, and minority teachers. Her teaching has focused on culturally diverse teachers, infant and child development (with an emphasis on black children), and family relationships. She is currently serving as co-chair of the Equity and Diversity Committee of the

Teacher Education Initiative, National Education Association.

Karen L. Wilcox, Ph.D., is Assistant Professor of Family Studies at Ohio University. She teaches courses on family development, human sexuality, pluralistic lifestyles, death and dying, and family gerontology. Her research interests are in the areas of family diversity, adult sibling relationships, and parent-young adult relationships. She was the recipient of the 1997 Student of the Year Award from the National Council on Family Relations.

Shirley L. Zimmerman, Ph.D., is Professor of Family Social Science at the University of Minnesota-Twin Cities, where she teaches courses on family policy, family policy research, and family policy from an international perspective. She is the author of numerous articles and three books: *Understanding Family Policy: Theoretical Approaches; Family Policies and Family Well-Being: The Role of Political Culture;* and *Understanding Family Policy: Theories and Applications* (2nd Edition). Her research focuses on policy choices that mediate the connections between families and government, factors that influence such choices, and the outcomes of such choices for families. ✦

Preface

It is obvious that families change over time. At family gatherings, you can see these changes as persons and relationships mature. You can observe relationships that evolve and last for decades, as well as those that do not last for a variety of reasons including divorce and death. Family members are born, and most grow to old age; others die at various ages—producing changes in the number, structure, and roles of families and of extended family networks.

Many of the changes that occur in families are influenced by other family members, by each individual's life history, and by events in the family's social context, culture, and time in history. That is the focus of this book. Specifically, it is our hope this volume will demonstrate how families change over time.

Scholarly interest in families over time is not new. Rather, the evolution of this approach of viewing families has a varied and rich history. During the early part of the twentieth century, scholars developed a stage approach to viewing families for the purposes of enhancing research, solving family problems, and developing policies related to family life (e.g., Rowntree, 1901). In addition, it was during this time that scholars shifted from viewing families as closed systems to seeing them as semi-closed systems, characterized not only by internal interaction among family members but also by interaction with other social systems, such as school, work, economy, and government (Burgess 1926).

One could argue that the developmental approach is the only conceptual framework created specifically for viewing families. In contrast, other frameworks (structural-functional, systems, conflict, symbolic interaction) were developed for other pur-

poses, and their application to families evolved over time.

During the last few decades, the life span approach to conceptualizing families appeared to wane. Recently, however, it has experienced a resurgence, with an emphasis on a "life course" approach to family life, including parent-child, marital, and sibling relationships. This perspective encompasses changes in individuals and families as well as other social units over time, with family development being subsumed under the life course approach or viewed as part of life course analysis.

This recent emphasis on a life course approach to viewing families is also evident in the mission statements of Family Science and other social science academic units that focus on individuals and families. Academic units within colleges and universities have acknowledged that individuals and families change over time and are influenced by the larger societal context (which also changes over time). Therefore, *Families Across Time* addresses the needs of a variety of academic units that have incorporated a life course perspective into their conceptualization of families, including human development, child and family development, family medicine, nursing, sociology, public policy, social work, education, and public health.

This text represents an integration of research, theory, and application by including interdisciplinary scholarship in a variety of topic areas. One of the major criticisms of the family development approach is its focus on the typical, intact nuclear family to the exclusion of families that vary from this traditional ideal. Therefore, in this text special attention is devoted to a variety of family forms that exist in today's society. To overcome another weakness in the application of the life course perspective to families, this text covers *all* stages of family life, even though traditional scholarship has focused on the early stages.

This text is intended to serve as a basic or supplementary text for undergraduate and introductory graduate courses that focus on families. It will also be useful to professionals, lay persons, and those with considerable experience working with and studying families.

Each chapter follows a similar outline, with the purpose of providing students with an overview of our current understanding of families over the life course. Each chapter applies a life course perspective to one topic. For example, a chapter on the topic of marital relationships might include information on early marriage, middle-age marriage, and older families. In addition, case scenarios or other examples are extensively used to augment chapter content. The inclusion of cases and other examples should enhance the reader's ability to understand the challenges families face at different stages over the life course. Therefore, a conscious attempt has been made to emphasize transitions and tasks in lieu of an exclusive focus on characteristics of stages associated with family development over the life course.

Consistent with this life course theme, another goal in this project was the involvement of "younger" colleagues and doctoral students; that is, we requested authors to include a younger colleague or graduate student in the development of their chapter. In addition, we included some junior colleagues as contributing authors. We are pleased that these scholars, who are the future of our field, are represented in this text. One of these is the co-editor, Megan Murphy, who worked "elbow to wrist" with the senior editors for several months.

Because of page constraints, not all topic areas that may lend themselves to a life course approach are included in this text. The topics chosen, however, represent those deemed most relevant to the majority of families, the interests of students, and available literature.

In Section I, we begin the text with a conceptual overview of the development of the life course of families and a rationale for adopting a life course approach. We present the history and evolution of this approach, including coverage of stage models of development by selected scholars, as well as the tasks families need to accomplish at each stage. We also discuss models of individual development since one cannot understand the development of families without also looking at the developmental trajectories of individuals who make up the families.

After the introductory chapter (Section I), this text is divided into two sections: Structural Variations Across the Life Course, and Processes Through the Life Course of Families. The authors in Section II address several family forms that have been neglected by life course analysis. For example, Kimberly Downs, Marilyn Coleman, and Larry Ganong examine divorce over the life course. These authors stress the fact that divorce is so common that some view it as a normative event in the life course. Unlike other normative events related to family life, however, few informal social norms are available to guide appropriate divorce timing and behaviors. In addition, there are no established societal rituals through which individuals may celebrate or mourn a divorce.

A life course perspective for remarried families is addressed by Margaret Crosbie-Burnett and Katrina McClintic. In this chapter, the authors focus on the transitions step families experience in their various stages of development throughout the life course and the natural tensions between family members' individual development and the family's development. The latter include family role transitions and realignment of boundaries, individual psychoemotional adjustment of family members, and changes in financial and legal aspects of remarried families. This chapter also emphasizes the diversity and life course complexities of remarried families.

Katherine Allen and Karen Wilcox discuss sexual orientation and family relations across the life span. Although it has been estimated that approximately 10 percent of the population is gay or lesbian, little research has focused on sexual orientation over the life course. In spite of a growing body of literature devoted to same-sex partnerships and romantic relationships, lesbian mothers and gay fathers, and the children of lesbian and gay parents, we know very little about the multiple life course contexts of families in which sexual orientation is relevant. Because education about family diversity is critical to dismantling prejudices and stereotypes, Allen and Wilcox emphasize the important role of schools.

In Chapter 5, Karen Weddle-West addresses trends and issues related to African-American families over the life course. She discusses the challenges that confront African-American families—challenges related to historical origins, continued societal oppression, and the sex-ratio imbalance. In spite of these challenges, however, African- American families have survived by utilizing culturally distinct strengths and resources. These strengths are evident in the socialization of children, variations in family structure, emphasis on work and education, cooperation between family members, egalitarian gender roles, and the role of the church as a source of community organization and support. Weddle-West also notes the importance of within-group variations when looking at the life course of African-American families.

Geoffrey Leigh applies a life course perspective to cohabitation and never-married families. He argues for the need of a model that outlines changes in relationship dynamics or interaction patterns for close relationships (e.g., cohabitation) over time in order to keep pace with the current changes in the population and norms regarding relationships. In addition, he notes the need to focus on the complex development of individuals through a variety of nonmarital relationships.

In Section III, the authors address processes through the life course of families. Jacki Fitzpatrick and Karen Wampler examine marital relationships by focusing on the ways in which identity, networking, and safety tasks are accomplished over the life span of marriages. The authors see these tasks as relevant to all marriages, and although the tasks share similarities over time, each task also has unique aspects as the marriage and partners mature. This approach is in contrast to the traditional emphasis on conflict resolution, social support, and relational cognitions over time. In addition, Fitzpatrick and Wampler stress that it is important to refrain from using only middle-class marriages as the framework for life course analysis.

Richard Gelles discusses the issue of violence over the life course of families. He stresses that age is related to the likelihood of engaging in family or intimate violence or of being the victim of such violence. Unfortunately, while research on the life course and family violence can suggest which stages may have the highest rates of intimate violence, we do not know whether developmental tasks related to these stages play any causal role in the rates of intimate violence. Using a life course approach may, however, aid in the development of interventions, prevention programs, and policies that can ameliorate intimate violence and its consequences.

In Chapter 9, Gary Bowen, Jack Richman, and Natasha Bowen emphasize the interaction between communities and families. Specifically, communities as a resource for families vary over the life course, but studies of the effects of communities on family outcomes have tended to neglect variations in the level of "fit" between family and community at particular stages of the life span. Previous research has focused on community as a constant when, in fact, communities also change over time. Therefore, models of family development are needed that recognize today's diversity of family forms and variation in the timing and sequencing of family statuses, as well as the community context in which family transitions and processes take place. Therefore, these authors present a model for guiding practice and informing research efforts based on the aforementioned interactions.

Thomas Campbell addresses the issue of the interface between families and health over the life span. Specifically, health problems of any individual family member, at all stages of the life cycle, have an enormous impact on other family members. In turn, family members are capable of influencing the development and course of many physical illnesses. Therefore, the challenge for health care professionals is to develop and implement more family-oriented approaches to health care, in contrast to focusing primarily on the individual. Campbell proposes the utilization of biopsychosocial approaches for addressing these issues over the life course of families.

Christine Price and Hilary Rose use an attachment model to discuss issues centering on caregiving throughout the life course of families. Specifically, from birth to death, family members typically care for their loved ones. These authors propose that because of the many life cycle transitions, caregiving should include providing support and exchanging resources at multiple stages of family life. Caregiving thus includes the care parents provide children, adolescents, and young adults; the support exchanged between mature parents and middle-aged children; and the care provided to aging parents by adult children. These authors, like others, also stress the fact that the literature on caregiving has largely focused on intact nuclear families, often to the exclusion of nontraditional family forms.

Kathryn Rettig and Ronit Leichtenbritt discuss family economics over time. Specifically, these authors examine the impact of family and individual decisions made at various points through the life cycle on the economic status of women. Because of the significant effects of these decisions, the authors advocate the development of educational programs for young people regarding family economic issues across the life span. For example, better estimates of the direct and indirect costs of caregiving for children would result in more-informed decisions about family size. In addition, such educational programs would help young people to understand the possible long-term economic consequences of decisions about their allocation of time and to

better balance the demands of work and family life.

J. Elizabeth Miller reviews the role of religion through the life course of families. She addresses both the structural effects and the interpersonal interactions that are influenced by religious beliefs and religious organizations. These influences include rituals, religious education, social support, and community support, which form connections to families and provide meaning throughout the life course. Religion helps families and individuals cope with changes in the family life cycle by providing organizational structure and moral guidance, a sense of community and extended family, and a sense of external authority and internal empowerment.

Gary Peterson, Debra Madden-Derdich, and Stacie Leonard address parent-child relationships over the life course. These authors review literature relevant to the transitions in parent-child relationships over the life course, with an emphasis on the shifting balance between autonomy and connectedness that must continually be defined and redefined. These processes are seen over the life course of all families despite variations across societies, ethnic groups, social classes, family traditions, or individual differences. The choices family members make often shape salient patterns of development within parent-child relationships.

Margaret Arcus discusses the implications of a life course perspective for family life education—whether the focus is on education for the couple relationship or for the parent-child relationship. However, family life education has historically focused on the entry or early stages of family life among traditional families. Arcus argues that greater attention must be given to the family life education needs of later-life individuals and families and nontraditional family forms. If these challenges are met, family life education will be relevant to all individuals and families, regardless of their structure or stage in the life course.

Interventions with families over the life course are addressed by Suzanne Bartle-Haring, Roy Bean, Tina Bedell, and

Benjamin Perry. These authors stress the need for therapists to explore and understand the context in which families and their problems are embedded. By understanding the culture, values, belief systems, and norms that a family utilizes to cope with transitional periods throughout the life cycle, mental health professionals will be better equipped to diagnose problems and formulate culturally relevant ways to help families shift their balance of separateness and connectedness. Thus, these authors suggest that extended family, friends, and religious leaders can and should be involved in the treatment of a family's presenting problem.

Julie Kohler and Shirley Zimmerman discuss policy issues in relation to families over the life course, stressing the interconnections of families and government. This is a complex issue and pertains not only to the federal nature of our political system but also to the institutional framework that involves (a) different branches of government in various aspects of the policymaking process, (b) a multitude of special interest groups that attempt to influence lawmakers, and (c) political elites who have their own agenda to advance. Professionals should be aware of these complexities and the ways in which policies may affect families, whether their family goals are explicit or implicit, in order to avert possible adverse consequences for the families they most directly affect.

Bibliography

Burgess, E. W. (1926). The family as a unity of interacting personalities. *The Family,* 7 3–9.

Rowntree, E. S. (1901). *Poverty: A Study of Town Life.* London: Longmans Green. ✦

Section I

Introduction

Chapter 1 presents a conceptual overview of the development of the life course of families and a rationale for adopting a life course approach. This introductory chapter examines the history and evolution of this approach, including stage models of development by selected scholars as well as tasks families need to accomplish at each stage of development. In addition, the chapter discusses models of individual development, as it is assumed that one cannot understand the development of families without also looking at the developmental trajectories of individuals. ✦

Chapter 1
Families Across Time

A Life Course Perspective

Sharon J. Price
University of Georgia

Patrick C. McKenry
The Ohio State University

Megan J. Murphy
University of Georgia

The Middletons are holding their annual family reunion. They have held this reunion for over 100 years, and approximately 150 people attend every year. A wide variety of family types and ages are represented. Family members arrange vacations and visits with friends around this event. One of the oldest persons attending is the matriarch of the family, Mrs. Middleton, age 85. A direct descendent of the original settlers in this county, she has been a widow for 15 years and has five living children ranging in age from 45 to 60, along with 16 grandchildren and 8 great-grandchildren. Sometimes she is surprised at how family life has changed since she was a young woman. She was expected to marry—and marry young—and to have children. In contrast, several of her grandchildren are not married and are pursuing careers or living in what is now termed an "alternative lifestyle." In addition, her 45-year-old daughter, who has two children in college, just announced she is pregnant with her third child. Two of Mrs.

Middleton's grandchildren are getting divorces, and some family members are a little uncomfortable because one of Mrs. Middleton's sons will be arriving with his male "partner," with whom he has lived for 12 years. All in all, Mrs. Middleton wonders if other families have had similar experiences.

Those of us who have attended family reunions have witnessed firsthand how families change over time. We have watched individuals grow up and grow older, and we have seen their relationships change, evolve, and perhaps last for decades. We have also witnessed relationships that do not last for a variety of reasons including divorce and death. Family members are born and family members die—both producing changes in the number, structure, and roles in each family as well as the extended family network.

For family scholars, the study of such changes over time has been the focus of inquiry during most of the twentieth century. This area of study has been referred to as the family life cycle (Duvall 1957, 1977), family development (Klein and White 1996), family careers (Aldous 1978, 1996), life span (Hagestad and Neugarten 1985), and life course (Bengtson and Allen 1993). The various approaches of this inquiry have been influenced by several disciplines including child development, human development, sociology, home economics, and developmental psychology. The diversity of disciplinary influences have, without a doubt, contributed to the ongoing debate regarding an appropriate concept or term for looking at families across time.

The term *family life cycle* has been discounted because it implies that family life is a "repeated sequence" of events when, in reality, family change over time does not constitute a true cycle (Aldous 1996). Families cannot go back; once they experience a stage, phase of development, or change over time, they must move on. For example, a couple who has children will never again be a "childless couple," and a couple who decide to divorce cannot return to the status of "never married." Also, families, even if they experience the same stagewise program in development, will experience generational variation.

The term *life span* has been viewed as inappropriate because historically it has been limited to "intrapsychic phenomena." Changes over the life span are often viewed as the turning points in an individual's life, which are usually related to transitions based on age (Hagestad and Neugarten 1985).

In an attempt to overcome some of these problems with terminology, Aldous (1978, 1996) used the concept *family career* as another term for family development and focused on the careers of subsystems in families, such as parent-child, spousal, and sibling relationships. Aldous also stressed the need to focus not only on the family system but on individuals and subsystems in the family, as well as on changes in the wider society.

The term *life course* has been used in a broader context. It encompasses changes in individuals as well as in families and other social units over historical time (Bengtson and Allen 1993). Family development has been subsumed under the life course approach (Holman and Burr 1980) or has been viewed as part of life course analysis (Klein and White, 1996). Vern Bengtson and Katherine Allen (1993) have concluded

the "life course perspective" provides important insights about change over time. . . in the lives of individual family members over time, and of families as social units as they change over historical periods. . . [It] involves both the micro-social and the macro-social levels of analysis. (492)

In short, a variety of perspectives are represented in scholarly analyses of how families change over time. However, it is our belief that a life course perspective to family change over time may be the most useful. This approach allows us to focus on individuals and families as well as on subsystems and changes in wider society, thereby providing both a macro and a micro approach.

Types of Time

Three types of time are used in a life course perspective: *individual time, generational time*, and *historical time*.

Individual time, ontogenetic time (Bengtson and Allen 1993), or "seasons of life" (Levinson 1978, 1996) roughly refers to chronological age. The basic focuses of ontogenetic time are the periods of one's life (childhood, adolescence, young adulthood, middle age, old age), or how persons are defined and channeled into positions and roles largely based on chronological age. For example, Mrs. Middleton's 16-year-old grandson is expected to be in school. At the same time, rights, privileges, and obligations are also based on culturally shared age definitions (Hagestad and Neugarten 1985). For example, in most states an individual has the "right" to drive at age 16 and the "right" to vote at age 18; he or she is also expected to be a wage-earner at some time during early adulthood.

Related to ontogenetic time is *cohort time*, which refers to the age categories or cohorts in which people are grouped, based on when they were born. For example, persons born between 1946 and 1964 are referred to as "baby boomers." We often hear about how the "baby boomers" influenced the need for schools when they were children and how they are expected to affect health care as they age. Therefore, it is assumed that members of a particular cohort experience *and* are influenced by similar life events within a defined span of time.

Historical time focuses on societal or macro-level changes over time, assessing how changes in society affect the lives of individuals and families. It is not historical time per se that is of most interest but rather the events that occur with the passage of time (Bengtson and Allen 1993). Families are strongly influenced by geopolitical and economic changes, including, among others, war, fluctuations in the economy, and increased technology. For example, Mrs. Middleton has lived through many such changes during her lifetime. She worked as a domestic during the Depression for $1.50 per week plus room and board; her husband served in World War II; one of her sons was killed in the Korean conflict; and one grandson was killed in the Vietnam War. Some of her children and grandchildren say she still thinks she is living during the Depression because she strongly emphasizes "saving for a rainy day," and the entire family is sensitive to the value of life because of the untimely deaths of family members.

Generational time (Bengtson and Allen 1993) or "family time" (Elder 1975) refers to the rank order of positions that individuals hold in families (grandparent, parent, child) as well as the roles, expectations, and identities associated with these positions. It is assumed that movement into these positions may be related to ontogenetic or individual time, but not necessarily; for example, a woman may become a grandmother at 26 or 62 (Bengtson and Allen 1993; Burton and Bengtson 1985). In both cases, she is in the rank order position of grandmother, yet the significant difference in age on assuming this position/role will affect her family interaction.

The Evolution of Viewing Families Over Time

The developmental approach to studying and working with families over time may be the only theoretical approach specifically developed for this purpose. Many other approaches (conflict, exchange, symbolic interaction) have been used for a multitude of purposes (Klein and White 1996). The developmental approach, however, borrowed key concepts from scholars in other fields, including rural sociology, child psychology, and human development (Hill and Rodgers 1964).

The earliest record of a scholar investigating families over the life course is Rowntree's (1901) three-stage description of the "persistence of poverty." He concluded that families tended to be economically distressed when children were young and an economic liability. In contrast, when children were old enough to be wage earners, they contributed to family resources, enhancing the family's economic well-being. When the children left home, however, the family again suffered economically. More recently, Atkinson, Maynard, and Trinder (1983) replicated this study with the descendants of Rowntree's original sample and found a similar pattern.

As early as 1931, sociologists constructed a four-stage family life cycle model: (a) married couple, (b) family with one or more children, (c) family with one or more self-supporting children, and (d) couples growing older. In l934, Kirkpatrick and others described the family life cycle as dependent on the age and growth of children, and home economists used the concept of the family life cycle in addressing the issue of stress involved in long-term planning of both human and material resources to meet the needs of families (Hill and Rodgers 1964).

During the 1940s and 1950s, several family scholars made major contributions to the development of the concept "family life cycle," and even today their work serves as a foundation for analyses of families across time. For example, in 1947 Paul Glick, a family demographer, published the first of several seminal studies that focused on changes in families at various periods over the life span (Glick 1947). In 1948, Gutheim (cited in Hill and Rodgers 1964) edited a publication resulting from a conference that focused on pressures placed on families by the changing needs for housing over the family life cycle. Evelyn Duvall chaired this meeting. Similar to early rural sociologists, those attending the conference identified four stages of family life: (a) early stages, (b) crowded stages, (c) peak years, and (d) later years. By using the number and ages of children and parents, the attendees were able to address the demands for space and equipment within the home at each stage (Hill and Rodgers 1964).

Also in 1948, Evelyn Duvall and Reuben Hill, prominent family scholars, chaired a committee on the dynamics of family interaction, as part of the National Conference on Family Life convened by President Harry Truman. Their charge was to describe the natural history of families as small groups, through formation to dissolution (Duvall 1957; Hill and Rodgers 1964). This was a pivotal period in the development of the life span approach because the work of this group was integrated with the works of such scholars as George Herbert Mead, Ernest Burgess, and Willard Waller, who viewed families internally as interacting systems

(Mattessich and Hill 1987). Thus, the approach shifted from an emphasis on structural changes that occur in families over time to an inclusion of interaction within families related to structural changes.

It was also about this time that an increased acceptance was given to the idea that families are not closed systems but rather semi-closed and characterized not only by internal interaction between members but also by interaction with other societal systems (e.g., school, work, economy, government) (Hill and Rodgers 1964). The result was an increased emphasis on how individuals interact within families and how families interface with wider society over their history. In addition, the styles and focuses of external interactions change over time. For example, Mrs. Middleton and her descendants have witnessed how interaction between parents and children change as children grow up and parents grow older. Specifically, Mrs. Middleton clearly remembers when her children were small and she took care of them and provided advice; today, in many ways, they take care of her, and she seeks their advice before making financial decisions.

In 1957, Duvall published the first of several editions of her text, *Family Development*. For several years this was the only textbook available whose primary focus was on families over time. More recently, however, numerous authors, including Aldous (1978, 1996), Bengtson and Allen (1993), Elder (1974, 1975), Hagestad and Neugarten (1985), Hareven (1978), Klein and White (1996), Rodgers (1973), and White (1991), have made major contributions to our understanding of the developmental nature of family life. These authors have stressed that viewing families over time is a valuable mechanism for understanding family life. As a result, this approach has been widely accepted by researchers, practitioners, and family life educators as a legitimate and important way of looking at families.

Stages, Tasks, and Transitions

Families have a developmental history characterized by periods of change and periods of stability. The periods of stability are stages. *Stages* are the stable or plateau periods of family life and represent divisions "within the lifetime of a family that are distinctive enough, in its cluster of interaction patterns, from those that precede and follow it to constitute a separate period" (Aldous 1996). Families vary in the length of time they may spend in a stage, and not all families experience all stages in the same sequence or same manner.

The periods of change are referred to as transitions. *Transitions* are those periods when families are shifting from one stage to another and often are times of increased stress. In addition, for families to successfully move from one stage to another, both individual and family tasks must be accomplished at the different stages over the life span (Aldous 1978, 1996; Carter and McGoldrick 1988; Duvall 1957, 1977).

Looking at developmental stages over the life course of families provides us with a wealth of information. For example, depending largely on their stage of development families vary in their structure, composition, and interaction both within the family and with people and institutions outside the family. It may be more important to our understanding of an individual to know where he or she is located in the development of a family than to know his or her chronological age (Klein and White 1996). In addition, families in the same identifiable stage of development share many similar characteristics. For example, families with school-age children often have family members about the same age and engage in many of the same activities (after-school programs, Little League, soccer practice).

A stage approach to viewing families over time is based on the recognition that families experience successive patterns in the addition, growth, and loss of family members. In addition, knowing what stages families will experience provides a sense of predictability about their life course, helping families and others in knowing what might be expected at any given stage.

A major limitation of the stage approach is that it has historically focused on once-married couples with children. Today it is widely accepted that families and family life include many forms beyond the nuclear conjugal family. Although today's families may vary greatly and represent complex systems, in general they have similar functions and goals for their members. A life course approach has therefore been found valuable to our understanding of both traditional and nontraditional family forms (see chapters in Section III).

Because of the increase in life expectancy, it is not uncommon for families to be composed of four or five generations. In one family the "senior" generation could be confronted with the challenges of old age, the next generation characterized by the challenges of the empty nest, retirement, aging, or being part of the "sandwich" generation. The third generation could be in the throes of issues characterized by young adulthood or middle age (and could also be part of the "sandwich" generation), while the fourth generation could range from infants to young adults who are establishing their own families, and the fifth generation could range from preschoolers to adolescents (Rodgers and White 1993). Consequently, families could be confronted with the challenges of addressing the needs and demands of a wide range of age groups and stages of family development.

Models of Families Over Time

Despite the shortcomings of a stage approach, it is valuable when addressing family issues over time. Several authors have proposed stage models of family development. The most elaborate model was proposed by Rodgers (1973), and it includes 24 stages. Other models include fewer total stages but longer periods of time in each stage (e.g., Aldous 1978, 1996; Carter and McGoldrick 1988; Duvall 1957, 1977). Most models, however, include two general stages of family life (Duvall 1957, 1977):

1. **The expanding stage.** This stage includes the period of time when individuals are being added to the family unit—from the formation of the marriage through the birth of children to when

children are adolescents and still at home.

2. **The contracting stage.** This stage includes the period from the time children start exiting their parents' home until the only one of the original couple remains or until the death of both original spouses.

This two-stage approach is too global to be of much value to practitioners, educators, or researchers, as it ignores many of the changes that occur in family life within each of these macro stages. Therefore, stage models were developed to address the need for a more detailed approach to the changes families experience over time. All models, however, contain three key concepts: (a) *positions* (location of each person within the family—i.e., child, parent, spouse, sibling); (b) *roles* (behaviors expected of each member of the family; family members often carry out multiple roles); and (c) *norms* (rules for behaviors that guide conduct of family members).

The Duvall Model of Family Development

Duvall (1957, 1977) proposed an eight-stage model that has been widely used to describe once-married couples who have children; it is based on the addition, age, and exiting of children in families. Although this model has been criticized for its focus on traditional families, her analysis of these traditional families also applies to many other families. The stages in this model include

Stage I: Married couples (couples without children)

Stage II: Childbearing families (the age of the oldest child is birth–30 months)

Stage III: Families with preschool children (age of the oldest child is 2 1/2–6 years)

Stage IV: Families with schoolchildren (age of oldest child 6–13 years)

Stage V: Families with teenagers (age of oldest child 13–20 years)

Stage VI: Families launching young adults (period from the time the oldest child leaves home to when the last child leaves)

Stave VII: Middle-aged parents (period from the empty nest to retirement

Stage VIII: Aging family members (period from retirement to the death of both spouses)

Duvall (1957) introduced the notion of developmental task, borrowed from individual theories of life span development (e.g., Havighurst 1948). *Tasks* are normative expectations of families at different stages over the life course. Duvall contends that if families accomplish the tasks related to each stage of development, they experience greater levels of satisfaction, societal approval, and success with later tasks. In contrast, failure to accomplish stage-related tasks contributes to unhappiness, social disapproval, and increased difficulty with later tasks.

The idea that families should accomplish tasks, however, has been criticized as too value laden, because what is viewed as appropriate tasks at specified stages may change over historical time. For example, Mrs. Middleton was very proud that when her children were small, they were all "potty trained" by the time they were two and one-half years old. Today this norm has changed, and she has several great-grandchildren who are three and four years old who are not toilet trained. Today a wider range of time, often directed by the child, is viewed as appropriate to accomplish this task.

Nevertheless whenever tasks are accomplished, they are important to the successful development of families. They need to be completed to assure that the family members' developmental tasks and societal expectations are fulfilled and that a foundation is laid for the family's continued development. Families that do not successfully accomplish tasks associated with their respective stages of development are often criticized by wider society, and they experience increased conflict among members (Aldous 1996).

In spite of these criticisms, there do appear to be some general tasks that are not generation specific that families need to accomplish throughout the life course. These include (a) physical maintenance of family members; (b) socialization of family members for roles both inside and outside the family; (c) maintenance of social control within the family as well as between family members and outsiders; (d) maintenance of family members' motivation to perform roles inside and outside the family; and (e) addition of family members through adoption or birth and their release when mature (Aldous 1996).

Duvall (1957) also described specific stage-critical developmental tasks that occur when families enter each new stage of development. Critical events, such as getting married, giving birth to a child, launching teenagers and young adults, and retiring from work propel families into and through each successive stage. Therefore, each new stage requires new adaptations and new responsibilities but it also offers new opportunities and challenges. As indicated in Table 1.1, stage-critical tasks change as families change. For example, the tasks specific to Stage 1, the married couple, include establishing a mutually satisfying marriage, fitting into the kin network, and adjusting to pregnancy. This stage has only two positions (wife and husband). In contrast, Stage 6, families launching young adults, could include at least 12 positions (wife-mother-grandmother; husband-father-grandfather; daughter-sister-aunt; son-brother-uncle), and stage critical tasks include releasing young adults into adult roles with appropriate rituals and assistance while maintaining a supportive home base.

The Aldous Model

It is important to recognize that families are often simultaneously involved in multiple stages and accompanying tasks. For example, in the Duvall model, a family could simultaneously be involved in Stage 4 (families with schools age children), Stage 5 (families with teenage children), and Stage 6 (families launching young adults). In addition, all families do not exactly fit into any one stage or model (Aldous 1978, 1996). To compensate for this inadequacy, Aldous (1996) proposed a four-stage family career:

1. *Formation or couples beginning.* During this stage, the legally married couple

Table 1.1

Duvall's Family Development Tasks Through the Family Life Cycle

Stage of the Family Life Cycle	Positions in the Family	Stage-critical Family Development Tasks
1. Married couple	Wife Husband	Establishing a satisfying marriage Adjusting to pregnancy and parenthood Fitting into the kin network
2. Childbearing families	Wife-mother Husband-father First child	Having and adjusting to children, encouraging development of infants Establishing a satisfying home for parents and children
3. Families with preschool children	Wife-mother Husband-father Children-siblings	Adapting to needs and interests of preschool children Parents coping with fatigue and lack of privacy
4. Families with school-age children	Wife-mother Husband-father Children-siblings	Fitting into community of school-age families Encouraging children's educational achievement
5. Families with teenagers	Wife-mother Husband-father Children-siblings	Balancing freedom with responsibility for teenagers Establishing postparental interests and careers
6. Families launching young adults	Wife-mother-grandmother Husband-father-grandfather Child-sibling	Releasing young adults into work, college, marriage, etc., with appropriate rituals and assistance Maintain a supportive home base
7. Middle-aged parents	Wife-mother-grandmother Husband-father-grandfather	Rebuilding marriage relationship Maintaining kin ties with older and younger generations
8. Aging family members	Widow/widower Wife-mother-grandmother Husband-father-grandfather	Adjusting to retirement Coping with bereavement and living alone Closing the family home or adapting it to aging

Adapted from: Duvall 1957.

make changes in ways of doing things in order to satisfactorily live together in an intimate relationship. During this stage, developmental tasks include learning how to live intimately with the spouse, developing competence in engaging in sex with the spouse, negotiating how household responsibilities will be divided, and adapting the relationship to their families of origin or friends.

2. ***Childbearing/child-rearing years.*** This stage is viewed as more critical than marriage, marking an individual's entrance into adult status. Developmental tasks during this stage involve caring for, supporting, and nurturing a child or children while maintaining a spousal relationship. This stage involves significant transitions on the part of both parents, but because of the demands of pregnancy, childbirth, and child rearing, it usually demands a bigger transition on the part of the mother. Parental demands continue for several years, depending on the number of children a couple has. These demands may also have a negative impact on the marital relationship because of less family income per person, less money to support couple-only activities, more demands on time, and a more traditional pattern of domestic roles (Aldous 1996). At the same time, couples may be receiving rewards, including family and societal approval for their accomplishments as parents and the success of their children. Therefore, although the marital relationship may be

stressed, they may receive other rewards for being parents.

3. ***Children leaving home/the middle years.*** Children generally leave their family of origin when the spousal couple is middle-aged. As a result of this transition, parents are alone as a dyad for the first time since the birth of their children. For many couples, this is a positive time in their relationship, as it affords them an opportunity to refocus on their marital relationship and undertake activities they had postponed because of parenting responsibilities. Some couples, however, find the tasks associated with this period to be overwhelming and, consequently, end their marriage. Also, for many couples this stage of family life involves providing substantial help to both their children and their parents; consequently, they find themselves as part of what some term the "sandwich" or "caught" generation.

4. ***The final years (elderly couple and the end of the family career).*** This period generally lasts from the time the spouses retire until one of them dies (Aldous 1996). During the early part of this stage, when one or both spouses retire from the labor force, they are confronted with the task of learning how to deal with both being around the house more than in the past. This stage also provides time when couples can pursue activities such as travel, volunteer work, or hobbies that lack of time may previously have prohibited, and can enjoy the multiple roles associated with being a grandparent. It is during this stage, however, that most couples are confronted with the fact that the family career is ending, and they must deal with the inevitability of death, money issues related to long-term care, physical and possibly mental disabilities, and, in some cases, the disposition of assets.

The Carter and McGoldrick Model

Carter and McGoldrick (1988) departed from the traditional sociological approach to describing the family life course as beginning with marriage and ending with the death of one spouse. Their model emphasizes the interpersonal aspects of families over time. They proposed that the "intact middle-class family life cycle" starts when young adults are coming to terms with their family of origin. This differentiation, or finding a healthy balance in separating from one's family of origin without severing all family ties, is a major task during this period. Young adults need to establish themselves in a work role and make connections with their peers before successfully becoming involved with a future spouse and starting a family. The successful completion of this stage is viewed as profoundly influencing "who, when, how, and whether they will marry, and how they will carry out succeeding stages of the family life cycle" (Carter and McGoldrick 1988, 13).

The second stage proposed by Carter and McGoldrick (1988) is the joining of families through marriage, or establishing the marital dyad as a couple. This task encompasses inclusion of the spouse in the family of origin, inclusion of the spouse's in-laws within their family boundaries, establishment of marital boundaries, and being acknowledged as a couple.

The third stage is families with young children. The major tasks at this stage focus on making room for the addition and inclusion of other family members and adapting roles to accompany the new status of the couple as parents. In addition, roles in families of origin may have to be adapted in order for grandparents to allow the couple to assume parental responsibilities without interference. In addition, both members of the couple must come together in assuming responsibilities for child-rearing, financial, and household tasks.

Launching children and moving on is the fourth stage of development. The general tasks at this time center on the acceptance of family members moving in and out of the family system through the marriage of children, birth of grandchildren, or death of their parents. During this time, the immediate family usually shrinks, leaving the couple alone. Therefore, the couple must renegotiate their relationship as a dyad rather than as a couple with children, and relationships with children change from parent-child to adult-adult. Therefore, successful completion of this stage includes redefining roles in relation to one's partner, children, and, if still living, parents and in-laws.

The last stage in the Carter and McGoldrick (1988) model is families in later life. Completion of this stage includes accepting the shift in generational roles while facing the tasks associated with solidifying the couple relationship in the face of physical decline. Dealing with the loss of one's partner and peers and preparing for one's own death are the major tasks of this stage.

Alternative Models

The models developed by Duvall, Aldous, and Carter and McGoldrick are traditional in their focus on once-married spouses with children. However, we are seeing an increasing recognition of families and family life as constituting a wide variety of family structures. This recognition of multiple family forms has resulted in a need for alternative models of the life course development of families. For example, remarried families may experience several stages at one time, and gay and lesbian families sometimes have two fathers or two mothers; gay families may also resemble remarried families, as they may have a child or children from a previous heterosexual relationship. In addition, different cultures may also warrant variations in the traditional models. For example, African Americans are less likely to marry, may marry at a later age, and are more likely to be single parents, and immigrant families may not expect children to necessarily leave home once they reach adulthood. However, it is assumed that all families, regardless of structure, experience development over the life course of both individuals and the family unit. Some authors have addressed the limitations posed by the traditional models. For example, Aldous (1996) developed a model and applied it to divorced and never-married parents. This model is largely based on one's partner's career history, one's work history, and the age of the children in the family. Therefore, this model could apply to persons who have children and never marry, who have children before they marry, who marry and divorce and do not remarry, or who divorce and remarry. The stages in this model include (Aldous 1996, 40):

Stage 1: The divorce transition and establishment of the single-parent family.

Stage 2: Parents continue, institute, or reinstitute their work life career.

Stage 3: Families with primary-aged children.

Stage 4: Families with adolescents.

Stage 5: Families with young adults leaving home.

Stage 6: Parents in the middle years.

Stage 7: The retirement of parents from work life career or their responsibilities for their parents.

For divorced families, the Aldous model begins with the divorce transition and the establishment of a single-parent family. For never-married women, this model would not include the divorce transition. Rather, it would start with the establishment of the single-parent family. In addition, it would depend on the oldest child's school career and whether the woman marries or cohabits in the future (Aldous 1996).

Carter and McGoldrick (1988) also proposed a developmental model for divorced and remarried families over the life course (Table 1.2). Although many American families experience the "middle-class family life cycle," the largest variation from that model consists of families who divorce. Therefore, these models begin with the *decision to divorce* and proceed to the *postdivorce family* and possibly *remarriage*. These models largely focus on the emotional aspects involved in these major life events while also addressing tasks that must be accomplished for a successful and productive life after divorce and into remarriage. Specifically, the divorce models suggest that divorced families (while also addressing the developmental tasks of intact families produced by changes in family structure, age of children and parents, and outside influences) must go through additional phases and accompanying tasks, including acceptance of one's role in the failure of the marriage; working cooperatively with the former spouse in areas related to custody, visitation, and finances; mourning the loss of one's intact family; and

Table 1.2

Dislocations of the Family Life Cycle Requiring Additional Steps to Restabilize and Proceed Developmentally in Divorced Families

Phase	Emotional Process of Transition: Prerequisite Attitude	Developmental Issues
Divorce		
1. The decision to divorce	Accept inability to resolve marital tensions	Accept one's own part in the failure of the marriage
2. Planning the breakup of the family system	Support viable arrangements for all parts of the family system	Work cooperatively on problems such as custody, visitation, and finances Deal with extended family members about the divorce
3. Separation	Develop cooperative coparental relationship and joint financial support of children Work on resolution of attachment to spouse	Mourn loss of intact family Restructure marital and parent-child relationships and finances; adapt to living apart Realign relationships with extended family; stay connected with spouse's extended family
4. The divorce	Work on emotional divorce: Overcome hurt, anger, guilt, etc.	Mourn loss of intact family: give up fantasies of reunion Retrieve hopes, dreams, expectations from the marriage Stay connected with extended families
Postdivorce families		
1. Single-parent (custodial household or primary residence)	Maintain financial responsibilities, continue parental contact with ex-spouse, and support contact of children with ex-spouse and his or her family	Make flexible visitation arrangements with ex-spouse and spouse's family Rebuild own financial resources Rebuild own social network
2. Single-parent (noncustodial)	Maintain parental contact with ex-spouse and support custodial parent's relationship with children	Find ways to continue effective parenting relationship with children Maintain financial responsibilities to ex-spouse and children Rebuild own social network

Adapted from: Carter and McGoldrick 1988.

remaining connected with extended families, in order to restabilize and developmentally proceed. More than intact families, divorced and postdivorce families are likely to experience a roller-coaster pattern, with peaks of emotional tension at transition points through the life course of the family.

According to Carter and McGoldrick (1988), if divorced persons do not successfully accomplish the transitions and accompanying tasks in the life course of the divorced family and then remarry, they may take a residue of anger with them. Such residue can interfere with stepfamily integration and consequently a successful remar-

riage. Historically, remarried families have been expected to behave like intact nuclear families, and thus little attention has been given to additional tasks confronting these families. For example, remarried families have been expected to act as if a prior family system or systems never existed. Therefore, one of the major tasks of the remarried family is to restructure the family boundaries to allow for inclusion of a new spouse/stepparent and to make room for relationships of all children with biological (including noncustodial parents), grandparents, and other extended families (Carter and McGoldrick 1988). The goal of this model is to invent a new form of family structure by (a) giving up the old model and accepting the complexity of the remarried family, (b) maintaining permeable boundaries that permit the shifting of household memberships, and (c) working for open communication between all parents, grandparents, children, and grandchildren (see Table 1.3).

It is also recognized that families who live in poverty are characterized by an alternative developmental model (Fulmer 1989; Hines 1989). For example (and not to imply that all poor families are black), there is less calendar time in poor black families for de-

velopmental stages; consequently, there may be inadequate time to accomplish accompanying developmental tasks (Hines 1989). This shortened calendar may be loosely divided into three stages (Hines 1989):

Adolescence/unattached young adulthood. During this time, poor black adolescents often find themselves with adult responsibilities, and instead of "growing away" from their families they are often "torn away," leaving them ill-equipped to deal with later stages of development. In addition, although a few are able to establish themselves in the world of work, many are

Table 1.3

Remarried Family Formation: A Developmental Outline

Steps	Tasks	Developmental Issues
Phase I Recover from loss and enter new relationship.	Mourn the loss of the predivorce family and foster recovery from this loss.	Recognize unique history of reconstituted family; accept normality of establishing a new relationship.
Phase II Conceptualize and plan new marriage.	Come to terms with lack of self confidence about ability to sustain relationships and fear about repeating mistakes. Refocus investment in new family members as sources of gratification. Resolve loss of the first partner and former family system.	Work on openness in new relationships. Plan for maintenance of cooperative financial and co-parental relationships with former spouses. Help children deal with fears, loyalty conflicts, and membership in two-family systems. Realignment of relationships with extended family to include new spouse and children. Maintain biological/adoptive parent-child connections.
Phase III Reconstitution of family.	Accept new spouse in parental discipline and nurturing roles. Establish and sustain generational boundaries. Recognize and deal with impact of absent parent/former spouses.	Recognize new family as a unique family form in its own right. Restructure new family boundaries to allow inclusion of new spouse/ stepparent. Realign relationships, including financial arrangements to permit interweaving of several systems. Foster relationships of children with biological/adoptive parents, grandparents, and other extended family. Share memories and develop new family's history to foster family integration.

Adapted from: Ransom, Schlesinger, Derdeyn 1979 and Carter and McGoldrick 1988.

only able to find menial work or are enticed to the underground economy as a quick end to poverty.

Low-income, young black persons have little time, if any, to develop skills needed to successfully negotiate intimate relationships. Consequently, young women may think that their only chance for positive identity is to become a mother. In contrast, because of limited job options and few chances of fulfilling the societal functions of adult males, young men often become transient figures in heterosexual relationships.

The family with children. This stage for poor black women, as with other low-income populations, often begins when they are teenagers and unmarried. If married, they may find themselves in conflicted relationships as a result of not having had the opportunity to complete the tasks of childhood and adolescence. Also, this may be a period when the grandmother becomes a primary source of assistance, if not the actual head of the family. The integration of additional persons into the family system may not be experienced as a major stress, however, because boundaries are often more flexible to accept newcomers.

The family in later life. In contrast to the middle-class model, this period does not imply a lessening of daily responsibilities or a focus on retirement issues for low-income blacks. Older adults often continue working, even if in poor health. In addition, they may never experience an empty nest stage in their family or household. For example, a grandmother may be responsible for the care of her grandchildren and great-grandchildren.

Proposed Model for Todays Committed Relationships

For the purposes of this book, an adaptation of a model proposed by Scanzoni, Polonko, Teachman, and Thompson (1989) will be utilized. This "sexually bonded or based primary relationships" (SBPR) model focuses on processes and change in contrast to traditional notions about family development (assumed to be linear and moving through "stages").

The SBPR model is applicable to individuals in a variety of committed close relationships, including traditional marriages, gay and lesbian relationships, divorced families, and cohabiting couples, as well as other relationships that might emerge throughout the life course of individuals. It is based on the premise that no one structure is best for meeting the needs of families or individuals because the concept "family" has different meanings for different individuals (Ahrons and Rodgers l987). Viewing committed relationships through the lens of the SBPR model eliminates the assumption that relationships, including marriage, endure into old age and produce at least one child.

This model describes the development of committed relationships in terms of four phases: Formation, maintenance, change, and dissolution. For the purposes of this text, we are defining these phases as:

Formation. Early stages of a relationship when persons become acquainted and move into more serious and committed stages. This phase could also take place as couples renew their relationships as a result of change in the individuals or their relationships.

Maintenance. This phase can occur many times throughout the history of committed relationships. For example, it could be described as those times when the relationship plateaus but still requires attention and maintenance for continuance. It is important to remember that even during this time, change is occurring both within the individual and in the committed relationship, but these changes are minor and do not imply major transitions.

Change. This phase occurs anytime a committed relationship or the individuals in a relationship change to the degree that the parties involved must make adjustments in the relationship and in their individual lives. This period of time could parallel the "transitions" referred to later in this chapter.

Dissolution. This phase occurs when the ties of a committed relationship are weakening and individuals are "growing apart." During this phase a relationship may end if either individual so desires; however, ending a relationship is not inevitable. Rather, individuals involved in a committed relationship could recognize that dissolution is occurring and could make the decision to enter into a phase of change or (re)formation, thereby rebuilding the relationship.

A major assumption of this model is that these phases do not necessarily take place in a linear fashion. Rather, persons may move from one phase to another in sequence, may skip phases, or may return to a previous phase. Thus, committed relationships are assumed to be ongoing and continuously in processes of change.

In addition to the phases, the SBPR takes into account three patterns or structural elements: legal, residential, and economic partnership status. Historically, in traditional families these three patterns have been predictable and, in general, merged together in one set of characteristics. For example, a couple would marry (legal), live together (residential), and merge their economic resources or become dependent on the sole source of income, usually earned by the husband as the major breadwinner for the marriage/family. In contrast, committed couples in today's society often live together (residential) without being legally married (legal), but may merge their economic resources (economic resources). Other couples may be in a "commuting relationship" and not share a common residence (residence) or economic resources (economic partnership) but be legally married (legal). Therefore, it is easy to see how the three patterns—legal, residential, and economic partnership—can no longer be assumed to simultaneously exist.

In summary, many models help explain how families change over the life course. Historically, the majority of approaches have been based on the assumption that a family's interaction patterns are driven by age, developmental needs, and procreation of children. However, multiple changes have influenced this image of the family, and today a wide variety of committed relationships can be defined as "family" by the participating persons. Therefore, it is necessary to view families over the life course through a different lens—that is, models must allow for the flexibility in a variety of family forms.

Transitions

A key concept for understanding families over the life course is the transitions that families experience as they move from one stage of development to another. These periods may be as important as, if not more important than, the stages. Transitions signify the need for families to change. It is during times of transition that families change in structure and develop new routines. In addition, transitions are often associated with changes or shifts in family composition (births, marriages, leaving home, death, or other significant rites of passage) and are often marked by ceremonies, celebrations, and other rituals. A transition has been described as a period of time between stages in which families "flounder, search for, and try out new ways before developing their roles and 'settling' into new behavior patterns" (Aldous 1996, 13). Periods of transition vary in length of time and are characterized by discontinuities to the degree that families must alter their structure and routines.

It is during transitions that families are likely to experience higher levels of stress as they shift from familiar rules, roles, patterns of behavior, expectations, and interaction patterns to new ones. Although these familiar patterns are not appropriate for the next stage of development and must be adapted, they serve as a foundation for successful family change. For example, families who have accomplished the tasks appropriate for families with adolescent children will have this foundation to build on as they approach the stage of family life when children are expected to leave their family of origin. In addition, transitions may be smoother if families experiment with new patterns (e.g., adolescent children hold summer jobs away from home) while still holding onto the comfort and familiarity of old patterns (Hansen and Johnson 1979).

The stress associated with transitions is also affected by whether the next stage of development is "on time" or "off time" as well as expected or unexpected. In general, on- and off-time transitions are determined by social norms and are age- and stage-graded (Rodgers and White 1993). Even though societal attitudes regarding what is appropriate for on-time and off-time family events have become more flexible, a woman such as Mrs. Middleton's daughter, who gave birth when her youngest child was in college, would be viewed by many as "off-time." In contrast, a couple getting married before the birth of their first child is generally viewed as being "on-time." Similarly, those transitions necessitated by unexpected family events (death of a family member) create periods of greater stress than events that were expected (birth of a much wanted baby).

All families experience transitions; however, not all families experience the same path after the transition. Over time, transitions can be described as

> paths taken and not taken. . . at any one time a married couple may stay married or get divorced, one of the spouses may die, or they might have a child. . . (any decision) would move a family to new series of possible alternative transitions. . . The process chart over time would look like a tree with many branches. (Klein and White 1996, 128–129)

In addition, some families skip stages and the accompanying transitions (Winton 1995). For example, many remarried families skip the stage of a "married couple without children," and as "instant families" (Roberts and Price 1987), they will never experience any stage of family life that does not involve children, even if the children are adults. Rather, they may bring families together who are at various stages of development. These families must deal with a multitude of transitions and tasks that result from combining families.

Transitions may also involve shifting from a "family affair" with fewer individual choices to an increased focus on "individual" transitions (Hagestad and Neugarten 1985). In the past, the timing of transitions depended largely on the family's economic resources (Rowntree 1901), whereas today spouses and sometimes adolescent children are no longer as tightly bound together by economic necessity. Therefore, transitions may be more of an individual than a family event (Hareven 1977).

This is not to say that transitions, however individually oriented, are not influenced by the larger family system. In most cases, while there are no formal rules or laws that apply to transitions, there are very strong (spoken and unspoken) life course expectations for all family members. For example, in Mrs. Middleton's family, her children were aware from an early age that their parents expected them to go to college. In addition, numerous studies indicate that when children do not leave home when they are "supposed to," parents experience a sense of strain and personal failure (Hagestad and Neugarten 1985).

Personal and family transitions not only affect the nuclear family, they affect the extended family network. For example, counterpoint transitions or countertransitions (Hagestad and Neugarten 1985; Klein and White 1996) are transitions by one person that result in transitions for others. For example, when a person gets married, his or her parents assume the role of "in-law." Furthermore, when couples become parents, their parents become grandparents, and their grandparents become great-grandparents.

Theories of Human Development

The changes experienced by families over the life course can be understood only within the context of human development. Most theories of families across time have stemmed from theories of individual development when individual development was seen as highly related to family change. The most common way scholars have studied development through the life course has been to focus on stages, and most stage theories have evolved from theories related to child development. Many of the early stage theories of human development were strongly influenced by Sigmund Freud (1963).

Freud's Stage Theory

Freud based his writing and the development of his psychoanalytic theory on the knowledge he gleaned from the patients he saw in therapy. His basic premise was that early childhood experiences and unconscious motivations influence a child's behavior, which in turn influences the development of the child's personality. The basic structure of personality, according to Freud (1963), includes (a) the *id* (basic instincts and urges that are present from birth), (b) the *ego* (powers of reasoning that help the id find expression and that begin to develop during the first year of life), and (c) the *superego* (the conscience or sense of right and wrong that develops from parents and societal teaching).

Freud largely focused his psychosexual theory of development on children. The basic premise of his age-based schema of development was that the centers of sensual sensitivity, or erogenous zones, shift from one body zone to another as children get older. These stages are:

Oral stage. In the first year of life, the source of pleasure centers on the child's mouth (sucking, chewing, biting)

Anal stage. From 18 to 36 months of age. The child's pleasure focuses on anal activity (elimination, toileting activities, and toilet training).

Phallic stage. From ages 3 to 6. The focus is on the genitals; boys develop an Oedipal complex (in love with mother, jealous of father), and girls develop the Electra complex (in love in father, jealous of mother).

Latency stage. From age 6 to puberty, children repress their interest in sexuality and develop intellectual, physical, and social skills; they shift from self to others as they become interested in developing friendships.

Genital stage. Beginning in puberty, individuals seek sexual stimulation and satisfaction from a member of the opposite sex outside of family.

Freud believed that the child wishes to take the place of the opposite-sex parent. Any disruption in the parent-child relationship derives from the child's perception of the parental relationship. One of the tasks of childhood is to resolve inner conflicts; therefore, the child gives up any claim on the opposite-sex parent and thus begins to identify with the same-sex parent. It is through this identification process that the child acquires the previous generation's moral values, gen-

der roles, and cultural norms (Bengtson and Allen 1993).

Freud emphasized the interaction between human development and tasks at various stages of family life. He viewed the mother as having a direct influence on the development of the child's personality. For example, in the oral stage, the mother's task is to supply the child with an appropriate amount of oral stimulation. He felt that the child's id is in danger of becoming too powerful if the mother feeds the child whenever he or she cries. In contrast, the child's superego may be too controlling if the mother withholds food. Freud believed it is the mother's responsibility to maintain an appropriate balance between under- and over-stimulation during the oral stage of development.

Freud's ideas and theories had a tremendous impact on the field of psychology. He was a pioneer in articulating a relationship between parent and child, noting that parents have a strong influence on their children's personality. Yet, because Freud believed that personality is firmly established at a young age, he did not examine parental or other influences beyond the teen years.

Erikson's Stage Theory

Extending Freud's contributions, Erikson (1980) contended that people develop in psychosocial stages throughout the life course. According to Erikson (See Table 1.4), there are eight stages of development throughout life, and individuals must master psychosocial tasks at each stage if they are to successfully move to the next one. If the task is successfully mastered at a stage, a positive quality is built into the personality and further development takes place. If the task is not mastered, a negative quality is incorporated, resulting in increased vulnerability and a lack of further development (Erikson 1950, 1980). For example, if during the first year of life, children's needs are not met and they do not learn to trust, successful development will be impaired throughout the remaining stages.

In contrast to Freud, Erikson saw children as developing through psychosocial, rather than psychosexual stages; he also contended that development continues over the

Table 1.4

Erikson's Stages of Development

Erikson's Stages	Approximate Age	Tasks
Trust vs. mistrust	Infancy (first year)	Infants learn they can trust that others will care for their basic needs (sustenance, protection, comfort, affection), or they develop a distrust if needs are not met.
Autonomy vs. shame and doubt	1–3 years	Children assert sense of autonomy and independence; learn to feed themselves, play alone, explore the world (with supervision). If too restricted by caregivers, children develop a sense of shame and doubt about their abilities.
Initiative vs. guilt	Preschool years (3–5)	Motor and intellectual skills continue to develop; children explore their environment, experience new things, assume more responsibility. If they are made to feel too anxious because caregivers cannot accept developing initiative, will develop a feeling of guilt over perceived misbehaviors.
Industry vs. inferiority	Middle and late childhood (6 to puberty)	Period of enthusiasm; children develop a feeling of self-worth through mastering knowledge and intellectual skills and interaction with others. Alternative is that the child feels inferior in relation to others.
Identity vs. identity confusion	Adolescence (12–20 years)	Adolescents develop a strong sense of self, who they are, what they are about, where they are going; explore careers. It is important for them to explore alternative solutions to roles.
Intimacy vs. isolation	Early adulthood (20s, 30s)	Develop close relationships with others, find oneself yet losing oneself in another person. The alternative is remaining isolated from meaningful relationships.
Generativity vs. stagnation	Middle adulthood (40s, 50s)	Assume roles of responsibility in community, work, teaching and caring for next generation. Alternative is that they become self-centered and stagnant.
Integrity vs. despair	Late adulthood (60 and over)	Older adults evaluate their lives, accept them for what they are. The alternative is despair because they cannot find meaning in their lives.

Adapted from: Erikson 1950.

life course into old age. Erikson also understood the mutuality of individual and family development. He recognized both the influence of family on the child's development and the influence of the child on the family: "Babies control and bring up their families, as much as they are controlled by them" (Erikson 1950, 69).

Despite his recognition of the reciprocity between parents and children, Erikson focused on the influence of parents on the child. He believed that parents influenced their children's personality through limit setting and the development of trust. Through the parent-child relationship, children develop a sense of self and the capacity for re-

latedness to others. As children learn the rules of society through their parents' limit setting, they internalize patterns of transactions with others, leading to the development of a conscience.

Erikson also believed that culture plays an important role in the development of children and families. Cultural values are passed down from generation to generation as children internalize transactions with their parents. He proposed that children respond differently to a similar situation because of differences in culture, age, and socioeconomic background. For example, parents in different cultures have different guidelines for limit setting. The outcome for a child may be viewed as "good" in one culture and "bad" in another because cultures have differing values that inevitably affect children.

Children are also part of their parents' development. One of Erikson's tasks for adults is the development of generativity, and he saw the need to nurture as a central task in adult development; having or caring for children is a way for adults to guard against becoming stagnant in their lives.

Newman and Newman (1999) expanded Erikson's stages of development from eight to eleven (see Table 1.5) in their psychosocial theory of human development. Newman and Newman contend that new stages of human development can be expected as culture evolves, with theories of human development expanding accordingly. Similar to Erikson, Newman and Newman also emphasize that certain tasks must be accomplished at each stage of life and that doing so is critical to the psychological and social growth of individuals in a modern, technological society. Their model lists 42 developmental tasks, with the assumption that each task builds on previously accomplished tasks. For example, they assume that a 15-year-old has mastered the tasks of children at younger ages.

It is evident that Eriksonian theory provides a broad context in which human development may be studied. It links the processes of child development to the later stages of adult life, to the needs of society, and to the ability of societies to interact with one another. This theory also accounts for the interaction between parents and children, as it emphasizes the effect of each on the other's development. During childhood, adolescence, and early adulthood, the individual's relationships expand and take on greater variety, depth, and intensity. In later adulthood, however, a person may return to a smaller number of primary relationships that provide depth and intimacy. However, relationships between the individual and those around him or her continue to have a reciprocal influence.

Adult Development

Daniel Levinson (1978, 1986, 1996) developed two of the few paradigms of adult development—one for men and another for women. His first model was based on intensive interviews with 40 middle-age men as well as on biographies; the second was based on interviews with 45 women. Levinson concluded that the sequences of stages and structure in his theory of adult development is similar for both women and men—that is, the stages and tasks are about the same across gender, class, and culture. He argued, however, that differences exist in the ways women and men move through the stages, and variation also occurs as a result of life circumstances. The stages of development in Levinson's models are:

Early adult transition. This stage takes place during ages 17 to 22 and is a period when individuals are between childhood and adulthood. Persons at this stage are beginning to take on responsibilities associated with the adult world in a mature fashion.

Entry life structure for early adulthood. This stage is marked by decision making: Decisions need to be made about career, marriage, separation from the family of origin, and general lifestyle. Individuals define themselves in the adult world through these decisions.

Age 30 transition. During this period, individuals evaluate the previous stage in terms of decision making. They make major or minor adjustments according to how they feel about their lives. For example, many single women and men who wish to have children often feel pressure to get married, as having children may have been a goal that is not yet attained.

Culminating life structure for early adulthood. At ages 33 to 40, most men and women attempt to establish a stable and secure place for themselves in the world. During this stage, individuals are in the process of working toward dreams or goals for adulthood.

Midlife transition. This stage, ages 40 to 45, is marked as a bridge between youthful adulthood and middle adulthood. The major task at this time is to evaluate the ending of the early-adult years and look forward to the beginning of the middle-adult years. This stage is a time of facing new challenges and

Table 1.5	
Developmental Tasks Associated With Life Stages	
Lifestages	**Developmental Tasks**
Prenatal	No developmental tasks
Infancy (Birth to 2 years)	Develop social attachment Sensory, perceptual, and motor functions mature Foster sensorimotor intelligence and primitive causality Understand the nature of objects and the creation of categories Emotional development
Toddlerhood (Ages 2–4)	Enhance locomotion skills Participate in fantasy play Develop language skills Learn self-control
Early school age (Ages 4–6)	Identify with one's sex-role Develop morally Self-theory Learn to play in groups
Middle school age (Ages 6–12)	Foster friendship Concrete operations Learn skills Self-evaluation Participate in team play
Early adolescence (ages 12–18)	Physical maturation Develop formal operations Emotional development Foster membership in the peer group Sexual relationships
Later adolescence (Ages 18–22)	Autonomy from parents Develop gender identity Internalize morality Choose careers
Early adulthood (Ages 22–34)	Exploring intimate relationships Childbearing and rearing Work Lifestyle
Middle adulthood (Ages 34–60)	Manage career Nurture marital relationship Expanding caring relationships Manage household
Later adulthood (Ages 60–75)	Promote intellectual vigor Redirect energy toward new roles and activities Accept one's life Development a new point of view about death
Very old age (75 until death)	Cope with physical changes of aging Develop a psychohistorical perspective Travel through uncharted terrain

Adapted from: Newman and Newman 1999.

seeking the rewards that accompany middle adulthood, as well as developing a new sense of self that is dependent on the merging of prior stages with ones to come.

Entry life structure for middle adulthood. The major task in this stage which occurs from ages 45 to 50, is to create a structure for the next decade or so. This stage is similar to the stage of early adulthood in that the individual may have the same job and family. However, it is different because of the changing nature of relationships in one's job and family as one gets older. Therefore, this is a period of establishing oneself in middle adulthood and enjoying the benefits that accompany this age.

Age 50 transition. This stage, which occurs from age 50 to 55, is characterized by an evaluation and exploration of the self in terms of what has been accomplished and where one would like to be. Developmental crises are common at this stage, especially if the individual is not content with previous decisions and life changes made over the past 10 or 15 years.

Culminating life structure for middle adulthood. This stage generally occurs from 55 to 60 years of age and provides individuals with an opportunity to work on their goals and aspirations for this time in their lives.

Late adult transition. This stage is the conclusion of middle adulthood and the beginning of late adulthood and occurs when people are approximately 60 to 65 years old. This period is one of reflection on the past stages and preparation for the shift into late adulthood.

Conclusions

All individuals and families change over the life course, and the ordering and arrangement of these changes are similar across cultures and historical periods. However, the stagewise progression may vary widely for several reasons, including family structure. According to the life course perspective, families change over time in terms of members and roles that members perform inside and outside the family. In addition, as families and individuals change, or as each enters or exits stages or phases of development, the transitions are marked by significant interpersonal and structural changes. Individual and family progression across time is modified by changing societal forces, such as economic depression. At each phase, however, individual and family tasks must be accomplished in order to proceed developmentally.

The development of individuals and families is a parallel process. For example, most stages of family development are based, to a significant degree, on the age of the individuals in the family. This is particularly true for several models that have based the stage of family development, to a large degree, on the age of the children. It is generally assumed that families with young children must deal with tasks related to that stage of family life as well as with the developmental needs of preschool age children. In general, families in which parents are experiencing individual developmental tasks associated with middle age must also deal with those tasks associated with adolescent development and perhaps with the family tasks of launching children at the appropriate time. In the later stages of the life course, families are confronted with individual issues that focus on aging parents, retirement, young adults, and, for some families, the issues surrounding the developmental issues of young children. Nuclear families must also deal with developmental tasks associated with the multiple stages represented in their extended families.

Many scholars have addressed the development of families over time. This conceptualization has been influenced by a diversity of approaches and has salient implications for researchers, family life educators, therapists, and other practitioners. Looking at families over the life course provides a wealth of knowledge regarding issues confronting families, how families interact internally, and how families respond to both external and internal influences. It must be remembered, however, that there are exceptions to the traditional models that focus on intact nuclear families—often to the neglect of the diversity reflected in families today. Nevertheless, all families, must deal with issues related to expansion and contraction and to the realignment of relationships that accompanies the entry, exit, and development of family members. In addition, all families, regardless of type, are confronted with a variety of tasks in order to adequately function. Therefore, a life course perspective is instrumental to an understanding of families as dynamic structures in the context of wider society.

Discussion Questions

1. Develop a family tree or genogram of at least three generations for your family. Describe the characteristics of each generation based on a life course perspective.

2. What are the basic developmental tasks for each generation of your family as depicted in question 1?

3. Trace the history of the life course perspective for viewing families. What are the advantages and disadvantages of each approach?

4. Why are family transitions so important? What are some important transitions your family has experienced, and what were the key challenges during these transitions?

5. How are individual and family development related? Use your family to explain this connection.

Glossary

Cohort time Age categories in which people are grouped, based on when they were born.

Developmental tasks Normative expectations of families at different stages over the life course.

Generational time Rank order of positions that individuals hold in families, as well as roles, expectations, and identities associated with these positions.

Historical time Societal changes over time; emphasis on events that occur with passage of time.

Individual time Roughly refers to chronological age; periods of an individual's life based largely on age (childhood, adolescence, young adulthood, middle age, old age.)

Life course Changes in individuals, families, and other social units over time.

Stages Stable periods of family life; divisions from those stages that precede and follow.

Transitions Times when families are shifting from one stage to another.

Suggested Readings

Aldous, J. (1996). *Family Careers: Rethinking the Developmental Perspective*. Thousand Oaks, CA: Sage.

Bengtson, V. I., and Allen, K. R. (1993). The life course perspective applied to families over time. In P. G. Boss, W. J. Doherty, W. J. LaRossa, R. Schumm, and S. K. Steinmetz (Eds.), *Sourcebook of Family Theories and Methods: A Contextual Approach* (469–499). New York: Plenum.

Duvall, E. M. (1957). *Family Development*. New York: Lippincott.

Klein, D. M., and White, J. M. (1996). *Family Theories: An Introduction*. Thousand Oaks, CA: Sage.

Newman, B. M., and Newman, P. R. (1999). *Development Through Life: A Psychosocial Approach*. Pacific Grove, CA: Brooks/Cole.

Bibliography

Ahrons, C. R., and Rodgers, R. H. (1987). *Divorced Families: A Multidisciplinary Developmental View*. New York: W. W. Norton.

Aldous, J. (1978). *Family Careers: Developmental Change in Families*. New York: Wiley.

Aldous, J. (1996). *Family Careers: Rethinking the Developmental Perspective*. Thousand Oaks, CA: Sage.

Atkinson, A. B., Maynard, A. K., and Trinder, C. G. (1983). *Parents and Children: Income in Two Generations*. London: Heineman.

Bengtson, V. I., and Allen, K. R. (1993). The life course perspective applied to families over time. In P. G. Boss, W. J. Doherty, W. J. LaRossa, R. Schumm, and S. K. Steinmetz (Eds.), *Sourcebook of Family Theories and Methods: A Contextual Approach* (469–499). New York: Plenum.

Burgess, E. W. (1926). The family as a unity of interacting personalities. *The Family, 7,* 3–9.

Burton, I. M., and Bengtson, V. I. (1985). Black grandmothers: Issues of timing and continuity in roles. In V. I. Bengtson and J. Robertson (Eds.), *Grandparenthood* (304–338). Beverly Hills, CA: Sage.

Carter, E., and McGoldrick, M. (Eds.). (1988). *The Changing Family Cycle: A Framework for Family Therapy* (2nd ed.). New York: Gardner.

Duvall, E. M. (1957). *Family Development.* New York: Lippincott.

Duvall, E. M. (1977). *Marriage and Family Development* (5th ed.). Philadelphia: Lippincott.

Elder, G., Jr. (1974). *Children of the Great Depression: Social Change in Life Experience.* Chicago: University of Chicago Press.

Elder, G., Jr. (1975). Age differentiation and the life course. In A. Inkeles (Ed.), *Annual Review of Sociology* (Vol. 1, 165–190). Palo Alto, CA: Palo Alto Annual Reviews.

Erikson, E. H. (1950). *Childhood and Society.* New York: Norton.

Erikson, E. H. (1980). *Identity and the Life Cycle.* New York: Norton.

Freud, S. (1963). *Three Essays on the Theory of Sexuality.* New York: Basic.

Fulmer, R. (1989). Lower-income and professional families: A comparison of structure and life cycle processes. In B. Carter and M. McGoldrick (Eds.), *The Changing Family Life Cycle* (545–584). Boston: Allyn and Bacon.

Glick, P. C. (1947). The family cycle. *American Sociological Review, 12,* 164–174.

Hagestad, G. O., and Neugarten, B. L. (1985). Age and the life course. In R. H. Binstock and E. Shanas (Eds.), *Handbook of Aging and the Social Sciences* (35–61). New York: Van Nostrand Reinhold.

Hansen, D. A., and Johnson, V. A. (1979). Rethinking family stress theory: Definitional aspects. In W. R. Burr, R. Hill, F. I. Nye, and I. L. Reiss (Eds.), *Contemporary Theories about the Family, Vol I: Research-based Theories* (582–603). New York: Free Press.

Hareven, T. K. (1977). Family time and historical time. *Daedalus, 106,* 57–70.

Hareven, T. K. (Ed.). (1978). *Transitions: The Family and the Life Course in Historical Perspective.* New York: Academic.

Havighurst, R. J. (1948). *Developmental Tasks and Education.* Chicago: University of Chicago Press.

Hill, R., and Rodgers, R. H. (1964). The developmental approach. In H. T. Christensen (Ed.), *Handbook of Marriage and the Family* (171–211). Chicago: Rand McNally.

Hines, P. M. (1989). The family life cycle of poor black families. In B. Carter and M. McGoldrick (Eds.), *The Changing Family Life Cycle* (515–544). Boston: Allyn and Bacon.

Holman, T. B., and Burr, W. R. (1980). Beyond the beyond: The growth of family theories in the 1970s. *Journal of Marriage and the Family, 42,* 729–742.

Klein, D. M., and White, J. M. (1996). *Family Theories: An Introduction.* Thousand Oaks, CA: Sage.

Levinson, D. J. (1978). *Seasons of a Man's Life.* New York: Knopf.

Levinson, D. J. (1986). A conception of adult development. *American Psychologist, 41,* 3–14.

Levinson, D. J. (1996). *The Seasons of a Woman's Life.* New York: Knopf.

Mattessich, P., and Hill, R. (1987). Life cycle and family development. In M. B. Sussman and S. K. Steinmetz (Eds.), *Handbook of Marriage and the Family* (437–469). New York: Plenum.

Newman, B. M., and Newman, P. R. (1999). *Development Through Life: A Psychosocial Approach.* Pacific Grove, CA: Brooks/Cole.

Ransom, J. W., Schlesinger, S., and Derdeyn, A. (1979). A stepfamily in formation. *American Journal of Orthopsychiatry, 49,* 36–44.

Roberts, T. W., and Price, S. J. (1987). Instant families: Divorced mothers who marry never-married men. *Journal of Divorce, 11,* 71–92.

Rodgers, R. H. (1973). *Family Interaction and Transaction: The Developmental Approach.* Englewood Cliffs, NJ: Prentice-Hall.

Rodgers, R. H., and White, J. M. (1993). Family developmental theory. In P. G. Boss, W. J. Doherty, R. LaRossa, W. R. Schumm, and S. K. Steinmetz (Eds.), *Sourcebook of Family Theories and Methods: A Contextual Approach* (225–254). New York: Plenum.

Rowntree, E. S. (1901). *Poverty: A Study of Town Life.* London: Longmans Green.

Scanzoni, J., Polonko, K., Teachman, J., and Thompson, L. (1989). *The Sexual Bond: Rethinking Families and Close Relationships.* Newbury Park, CA: Sage.

White, J. M. (1991). *Dynamics of Family Development: The Theory of Family Development.* New York: Guilford.

Winton, C. A. (1995). *Frameworks for Studying Families.* CT: Dushkin. ✦

Section II

Structural Variations Across the Life Course

Several family forms that have often been neglected by life course analysis are addressed in this section. They include divorced families, remarried families, gay and lesbian families, African-American families, cohabitators, and never-married families. These chapters lend credence to the assumption that the developmental perspective can be used to look at a wide variety of family forms. ✦

Chapter 2
Divorced Families Over the Life Course

Kimberly J. M. Downs
University of Missouri-Columbia

Marilyn Coleman
University of Missouri

Larry Ganong
University of Missouri

Although divorce may be thought of strictly as a legal event, individuals experience divorce as a multifaceted process that begins months or even years prior to the legal declaration that the marriage has ended. The process of divorce may begin early in the relationship, even before marriage in some cases, and continues long after the legal dissolution (Duck 1982; Hopper 1993). This process is not a uniform one; the dynamics of divorce are complex, and the experience of divorce is likely to be quite distinct for different family members.

Although statistically divorces are fairly common, the divorce process is unscheduled, unpredictable, and lacking the rituals or rites of passage that accompany most life transitions. Unfortunately, many scholars have treated divorces as if they were events with universal dynamics and uniform consequences. This mindset has interfered with our understanding of the divorce process and has hampered the development of appropriate intervention techniques. The key to understanding the changes brought about by divorce lies in deciphering how, through words and actions, individuals give developmental shape and meaning to their experiences.

The life course approach to the study of divorce provides a framework by which scholars may examine divorce as a process involving individual and interpersonal transitions. That is, the life course perspective recognizes that the effects of experiences that occur at one point in the life course often depend on earlier experiences. According to Hagestad and Neugarten (1985), transitions are key concepts in a life course approach to the study of families. Transitions are "long-term processes that result in a qualitative reorganization of inner life and external behavior" (Cowan 1991, 5). The transition of divorce is self-initiated for some individuals, but for others divorce constitutes a countertransition—that is, a transition produced by the life changes of others. For example, in many cases only one member of the couple wants a divorce. For them, divorce is a transition, but for their unwilling partner it is a countertransition. Additionally, just as marriage and parenthood are countertransitions that create new roles (i.e., in-laws, grandparents), divorce is a countertransition that removes roles (i.e., in-laws). Divorce creates a countertransition for two generations: the parents and the children of the divorcing couple.

Countertransitions mean that some family members (parents of the divorcing couple, children, maybe even one of the divorcing partners) involuntarily begin the divorce process. Therefore, they may be reactive, defensive, angry, and confused. It is likely that family members who experience divorce as a countertransition will begin the divorce process feeling out of control—of themselves, their relationships, and their family life (Hagestad and Smyer 1982). For these individuals, divorce is likely to be more stressful and the adjustment to new tasks less successful than for family members who have sought the divorce or who have at least welcomed the initiation of divorce by someone else.

In addition to focusing our attention on transitions as long-term processes, a life course perspective on the phenomenon of divorce emphasizes the social ecology in which the divorce occurs and is experienced (Bengtson and Allen 1993). Divorce-related experiences are affected by the age-graded nature of society as well as by history, gender, race, and social class. Contributing to the social ecology are three dimensions of time: (a) ontogenetic time, or the developmental levels of individual family members; (b) generational time, or the generational position of family members, and the roles and expectations associated with each position; and (c) historical time, which includes the geopolitical or economic events that influence each cohort (Bengtson and Allen 1993). The examination of these three time dimensions is important in developing a complete understanding of the experiences of divorced and divorcing families.

The meanings given to individuals' life transitions, whether at the ontogenetic or generational level, are derived from the cultural context and values surrounding the transition (Bengtson and Allen, 1993). The historical context in which an individual was raised (i.e., his or her cohort) has implications for the manner in which the individual interprets the significance of the transition (Hagestad and Smyer 1982). In the case of divorce, longitudinal data indicate that divorce has increasingly become a common transition for American families (Thornton 1985), although it remains somewhat stigmatized because it represents the failure to maintain the socially desirable status of marriage (Hagestad and Smyer 1982). In addition, families construct their own meanings surrounding life transitions through interactions with one another and through their social structural location (Bengtson and Allen 1993). Together, these factors impart a great diversity to the experiences of divorced and divorcing families.

The Social Ecology of Divorce in the United States

The majority of individuals who divorce their spouses are younger than age 45 (Clarke 1995), thus making divorce a more normative experience for those who are middle-aged or younger. Divorces obtained by persons age 45 and older account for less than 20 percent of all divorces in the United States: less than 2 percent of divorces are obtained by those over age 65 (Clarke 1995). While the percentages of mid- to late-life divorces have been increasing in recent years (Clarke 1995), some of these reported divorces reflect the dissolution of a second or subsequent marriage. Cohort changes may also become apparent in the coming years as the trend for individuals to enter their first marriages at increasingly later ages may result in more middle- to later-life divorces (U.S. Bureau of the Census 1995). Therefore, examining the phenomenon of divorce within a life course framework should prove fruitful.

Little information is available regarding divorce processes in racial and ethnic minority family groups, although demographic data document the prevalence of divorce within these families. African-American families are more likely to divorce than Americans of European descent, yet both Hispanics and African Americans are less likely to seek a legal divorce after an informal separation than are European Americans (Hetherington, Bridges, and Insabella 1998). Such data provide clues that divorce processes are different among various racial and ethnic groups. These differences may be attributed to minority families often occupying different social structural locations and possibly having different cultural values regarding divorce than the white, middle-class samples reported in most divorce research. Therefore, it is likely that minority family groups experience divorce differently than is described in most current research. Enlarging this body of research to include more minority families may result in new ways to help all divorcing families by examining the ways in which different groups cope with and manage stressors associated with divorce.

Women tend to divorce at a slightly earlier age than men because women tend to marry older men. For example, in 1990 (the most recent year for which data were available),

7.8 percent of men aged 20–24 obtained a divorce or annulment, as compared to 13 percent of women in this age category (Clarke 1995). This trend continued until the 30 to 34 year-old cohort, in which equal percentages of divorces were reported for both sexes. In older cohorts, however, men reported more divorces than women (Clarke 1995).

Overall, a dramatic increase has occurred in the number of divorced individuals in recent years. The proportion of *currently* divorced individuals, not including those who have subsequently remarried, increased from 3.2 percent in 1970 to 9.2 percent in 1994 (U.S. Bureau of the Census 1995). This increase has been reflected in legal reforms, which are part of the social context of divorce. For example, legal institutions largely focus on divorcing families with minor children (Fine and Fine 1994). Court jurisdictions in which divorcing parties are required to participate in mediation or divorce education often only require that families with minor children participate in these programs. Although families with children have more complex issues to resolve, such policies preclude childless couples and couples with adult offspring from receiving institutional support in coping with their divorce. Although such disparities in institutional support are important to examine, in this chapter we limit our remarks to divorcing families with children.

The following sections illustrate how the combination of ontological, generational, and historical issues contribute to the cultural context and social construction of divorce. These issues are explored in three types of families: those with young children, those with adolescent children, and those for whom divorce occurred in midlife.

Divorce in Families With Young Children

After six years of marriage, Steve and Lisa separated shortly before the oldest of their three children entered the first grade. They felt as if they were constantly quarreling and that none of their issues were being resolved. Lisa and the children initially stayed in the family home in order to maintain some stability in the children's lives. Steve rented a small one-bedroom apartment about two miles away so that he would still be close enough to stay involved with his children. Lisa was awarded the state minimum amount of child support, which was not enough for her to remain at home with her children. Her search for paid employment led her to find steady full-time work at the local plastics factory. Despite having two sources of income, she eventually had to sell the house, as the mortgage payments were too high. Luckily, she was able to find a smaller two-bedroom house in the same town, although the neighborhood was not as nice as the old one, the children were in a different school district, and they were not as close to Steve's apartment. Now Lisa shares a bedroom with her daughter; her two sons share the other bedroom. Because she works outside of the home during the day, Lisa had to enroll the two younger children in day care and her oldest in an afterschool program for "latchkey kids."

In families with young children, the initial separation entails numerous transitions for family members. For example, a divorcing family, such as Steve and Lisa's, may consist of a father who has just recently established his occupational career, and a mother who is several years his junior who will likely be awarded custody of their children (Buehler and Gerard 1995). In this situation, family members are faced with several tasks, including (a) redefining family roles, (b) accommodating to changes in daily routines, (c) adapting to restrictions in the amount of personal contact with one another, (d) resolving occupational and financial issues, and (e) reorganizing parent-child relationships.

Redefinition of Roles

One of the tasks of divorcing families is to establish clear boundaries between the parenting relationship and the relationship the parents formerly had as spouses (Ahrons and Rodgers 1987). Thus, the two parents must shift their attention from their spousal relationship to the relationship they now have as co-parents to their biological children. Parents accomplish this transition in a number of ways. Ahrons and Rodgers (1987) created a typology of co-parental relationships based on their degree of cooperation, ranging from Perfect Pals (i.e., parenting does not change, with parents attending their child's events together, spending holidays together as a family, etc.) to Fiery Foes (i.e., the ex-spouses refuse to recognize each other as having any parental rights). Another extreme is the Dissolved Duos, in which one parent gradually withdraws from the child's life completely. Some of these styles of relating become more difficult to maintain as former spouses remarry or the activities of children constrain parental involvement. For example, when a Perfect Pal remarries, the new spouse may object to the amount of time the parents spend together with the child.

Changes in Routines

It is unavoidable that the transition from a two-parent household to two single-parent households results in changes in the family's daily routines. Any tasks that were formerly completed by a nonresidential parent must be performed by the remaining parent, performed by the child, or not done at all. Children react to these changes in routines in different ways. Young children are constrained by egocentric preoperational thought (Kurdek 1986); their concerns about divorce may therefore include worries about rituals pertaining to them. "Who will read to me at bedtime now that Daddy is gone?" "Who will make chicken soup for me if I'm sick and Mommy isn't here?" Whereas young children are primarily concerned about how the divorce will affect their daily routines, older, less egocentric children are more capable of considering their parents' perspectives on the divorce process.

Parents may also have difficulty in maintaining their daily parenting routines in the face of their divorce. A parent who is struggling with the emotional ramifications of divorce may not be able to discipline and supervise the child as well as before the divorce. There also is some evidence that these effects may accumulate as parents and their children negotiate additional transitions and countertransitions, such as new romantic partners for parents (Brody and Forehand 1988).

Changes in Personal Contact

A change in a parent's residential status also results in a change in the amount of contact between family members. Regardless of the physical custody arrangement, the child will likely see less of each parent. One exception is when ties to the nonresidential parent are completely severed, leaving the residential parent with full-time care of the child. Another exception is when a parent who previously took a minor role in raising the child becomes more involved postdivorce. For example, fathers who had delegated most of the parenting tasks to their wives may now find that they enjoy nurturing their children. Typically, parents who are divorced spend less time as a couple with their children than they did when they were married; many postdivorce parent-child activities do not include the other biological parent. The exceptions is the Perfect Pals relationship (Ahrons and Rodgers 1987).

Occupational and Financial Issues

Overall, the financial picture for custodial mothers is more bleak than for noncustodial fathers. Perhaps because of the marriage gradient and less participation in the workforce, divorced mothers typically experience a 30 percent decline in their standard of living, compared to a 15 percent increase realized by divorced men (Furstenberg and Cherlin 1991). Therefore, it is not unusual for a former stay-at-home parent to enter the workforce in order to pay the bills. Some parents who were already employed outside the home have to either start a second job or work more hours to make ends meet. New or increased participation in the paid workforce consequently decreases parents' availability to their children. Ontogenetically, young children are at a stage of development in which a great deal of adult care and supervision are needed, and it is more difficult to find time to care for children in families where both parents are employed. Therefore, the separating parents must negotiate a way in which the children are appropriately cared for while the overall economic solvency of the family is maintained.

Even though increased family earning becomes essential to the survival of the family, the adults may be less prepared to fulfill such economic demands. Often adults with young children have had a relatively short time to become established in their careers—the typical male reaches his highest earning potential in midlife (U.S. Bureau of the Census 1995). Similarly, many young women have had even less of an opportunity to advance their careers, because they had not anticipated the need to have a career or have had to take leave from their jobs because of child-rearing responsibilities. Therefore, younger adults will not have the same financial resources available to them as adults separating later in life.

Continuing Parent-Child Relationships

Many of the tasks of the divorcing family with young children center on parenting issues, and the completion of such tasks is often a source of contention between divorcing spouses. One task for Lisa and Steve to consider is the involvement that they will each have in raising their children. It is normative for both parents to participate in their children's upbringing, but this issue becomes more complicated when one of the parents lives in a different household and does not have the opportunity to interact frequently with the children. Each parent may complain about the perceived lack of rules at the other parent's house, and the different parenting ideologies that existed during the marriage may now become major sources of contention between the two divorcing spouses.

As a result of changes in the amount of contact between family members and the degree of parental involvement, former partners are faced with the task of renegotiating their parenting roles (Ahrons and Rodgers 1987). During this renegotiating, power issues arise that may not be easily resolved as the divorce process continues. For example, a common power issue is child custody. Although shared physical custody is becoming more common, the majority of wives still receive physical custody of their children (Fox

and Kelly 1995; Furstenberg and Cherlin 1991). Nineteen of the fifty states have statutes indicating the presumption or the preference that both parents retain legal custody of their children—i.e., joint legal custody (Buehler and Gerard 1995). Therefore, the children often become pawns in the parental struggle for autonomy over their children. Even though it may not be legal to do so, mothers may control their children's access to their fathers, and fathers may withhold child support or refuse to grant the requisite legal permission for activities such as travel. Unfortunately, children are often the unintended targets of conflicts between their divorced parents; it is the children who suffer when their parents' conflicts preclude them from seeing each other or taking a trip together.

Continuing the Transition for Families With Young Children

Three years after their divorce was finalized, Steve and Lisa still see each other fairly often. Steve has remarried and has a new baby with his second wife, while Lisa remains a single parent. After a lengthy court dispute, Lisa and Steve were awarded joint physical custody of their three children, all of whom are now in elementary school. The kids stay with their mother during the week and with their father during the weekends, one weeknight, and for six weeks during the summer. Steve and Lisa have difficulty in maintaining consistent rules for the children in their two households, and the children are often exposed to derogatory remarks made by one parent about the other. Lisa still shares a bedroom with her daughter, a situation that neither of them is comfortable with because of the lack of privacy. As for the boys, although they have occasional conflicts over their shared bedroom, these conflicts are soon resolved; many of their friends also share a bedroom with a sibling.

The Diversity in Experience

Although Steve and Lisa's family illustrates many common situations that face divorced couples with young children, it is impossible to represent the full range of experiences that such couples encounter. For example, Steve's ability to spend time with his older nonresidential children may be hampered by his responsibilities toward his new wife and child. Additionally, his new wife may resent the time he spends away from her and their new baby as well as the time she and Steve must devote to Steve's children when they are living with the couple. Alternately, if Lisa had remarried instead of Steve, he may have been pressured to relinquish some of his involvement with his children. A third possibility would be for Steve and Lisa to have a highly cooperative co-parenting relationship in which child-rearing responsibilities are performed freely and equally between the two households, rather than the ex-spouses constantly undermining each other's parenting abilities. Another possible situation would be for either of the divorced parents to move out of state, thus limiting the accessibility between a parent and the children. Of course, many more possible scenarios exist that contribute not only to the heterogeneity of the divorce experience but to a wide range of positive and negative influences on children.

Divorce in Families With Adolescent Children

Lisa's oldest sister, Karen, has recently divorced her husband of 18 years, Jack. Karen and Jack have two children together, Jacob (age 15) and Michelle (age 17). Karen was awarded physical custody of the children, but she has had many arguments with Jacob because he wants to move in with his father, who lives about 45 miles away. Karen often confides in her daughter, and Michelle resents that her mom discloses so many details about the relationship between Karen and Jack. Karen's parents are quite upset about the divorce and miss their previous close relationship with Jack.

Adolescence is a time when children begin to assert their individuality and independence (e.g., Erikson 1959; Hetherington and Clingempeel 1992; Kurdek 1986). However, many of the transitions that occur with a parental divorce make these efforts more difficult and potentially pose more problems for the family with adolescent children. Such

families must still face the tasks of redefining their roles, and the major component of such redefinition is the identity development of adolescents and their parents. The continuing parent-child relationship has the additional risk of potential parentification of the adolescent child, as the adolescent is called on by the residential parent to assume non-normative adult responsibilities within the household. A final task for divorcing families with adolescent children is to coordinate the beginnings of new relationships with those outside the household.

Identity Formation

Identity establishment is not only one of the tasks of adolescence, it is also a major issue for adults who have divorced. In postdivorce relationships, adults must establish identities as divorced individuals as well as identities as single parents. Although divorced adults who have children maintain their identity as a parent, they are no longer a spouse and need to learn to separate these two roles. Unfortunately, rather than establish new, independent identities, many divorced people remarry quite rapidly; nearly 30 percent of divorced adults are remarried within 12 months (Wilson and Clarke 1992), and the median interval between divorce and remarriage is only three years (Glick 1980). Perhaps because of these mutual strivings for identity on the part of divorcing parents and their adolescent children, adults and children may not be as emotionally available to one another to help in coping with the divorce transition.

Parentification of Adolescent Children

Several developmentally inappropriate actions may occur as a result of a parent's search for postdivorce identity, and these actions can vary depending on the adolescent's gender. For example, as illustrated by the relationship between Karen and Michelle, an adolescent daughter may take on a type of therapeutic relationship with her mother, resulting in the parentification of the daughter (e.g., Boszormenyi-Nagy and Spark 1973; Goldman and Coane 1977). Parentification, a term found in the clinical literature, refers to the phenomenon in which a child is called on to assume a parental role within the family.

Longitudinal data support the assertion that the mother-daughter dyad becomes a key conflictual relationship for both individuals. Mother-daughter relationships in divorced families are characterized by sustained conflict as the daughter negotiates adolescence, as compared to decreasing levels of mother-daughter conflicts in nondivorcing and remarried families (Hetherington and Clingempeel 1992). This finding may be confounded by the fact that divorced mothers were also found to be more consistently involved in their daughters' lives, as compared to the decreased mother-daughter involvement in non-divorced and remarried families (Hetherington and Clingempeel 1992). These findings indicate that mothers and daughters in divorcing families may have more difficulty separating and individuating from each other because mothers become emotionally dependent on adolescent daughters. In turn, conflicts between the mother and daughter may be sustained because the daughter is not given the freedom to develop a sense of identity.

The relationship between adolescent sons and their mothers is also characterized by sustained levels of conflict during adolescence, although divorced mothers do not maintain the high levels of involvement found in the mother-daughter dyads (Hetherington and Clingempeel 1992). Adolescent boys who find themselves in their mother's custody often take on the role of "man of the house," the male version of parentification. Alternately, mother-son conflicts may lead some sons to express a desire to live with their fathers; in these cases, sons elect to avoid daily conflicts with their mothers or to gain more freedom. As a result of her son's elective relocation, the mother may feel abandoned by him, and determine that she has been an unsuccessful parent. As a result, her self-esteem and identity as a mother may suffer.

The Beginning of New Relationships

Another unique characteristic of divorcing when one has adolescent children is the possibility of entering dating relationships at the same time as one's child is beginning to date. Although dating is a normative activity for adolescents, historically it has not been a normative activity for middle-aged adults. Friday-night negotiations for the family car take on new dimensions as both parent and child require transportation for themselves and their dates. Similarly, a parent who is dating and contemplating a sexual relationship with the dating partner may worry whether this is appropriate behavior to model for the adolescent child.

Overall, an adolescent has a lot of power regarding the potential success of a parent's future relationships. For example, the adolescent may intentionally sabotage the relationship out of dislike for the parent's potential partner. Similarly, the privileged position that the adolescent assumes as a result of parentification may be eliminated because the parent is dating. In this case, the adolescent may rebel at the loss of status within the family. The seeds of destruction of many postdivorce romantic relationships are sown during the divorce period. Conversely, adolescents may be supportive of parents' efforts to find new partners if they see that their parents are happier.

The Diversity in Experience

According to life course theory, a cohort becomes more heterogeneous as it moves through time because individuals will have had more opportunities to experience and give definition to unique phenomena (e.g., Bengtson and Allen 1993; O'Rand 1996). Divorce is one of these phenomena that contribute to a cohort's heterogeneity. For example, the children of both Lisa and Karen may belong to the same cohort, but the divorce-related experiences of Karen's adolescent children will be different from those of Lisa's children once they reach adolescence. If Lisa remains single and does not cohabit with a partner, her children will have spent several years living mostly in a single-parent household before they reach adolescence; interpersonal relationships will have been reorganized into new patterns of interaction by this time. In Karen's situation, the more recent divorce transition is coupled with the volatile adolescent period, thus making divorce potentially more difficult to deal with.

Divorcing at Midlife

Not long after Steve's divorce was finalized, his parents, Paul and Barbara, also divorced after nearly 30 years of marriage. Paul said that he had waited until the children were grown before divorcing—he initiated the divorce proceedings soon after his sons were stabilized in their careers. Barbara was disappointed that her marriage was no longer as exciting and romantic as it had originally been, but she assumed this is what happens over time. She felt they should stay together because of the shared experiences and memories.

Overall, Barbara had a relatively easy time adjusting to the divorce. She had been a part-time employee at the local library since her two sons entered high school, and she was able to start working full-time after the separation. She had many friends to whom she could turn for support, and her two sons lived close enough to help her with the yardwork on the weekends. Paul, on the other hand, had recently taken an early retirement from his job as a mechanical engineer and at age 56 did not have many social contacts outside of work. He was reluctant to ask his family members for assistance, although he had never done many household tasks and had few domestic skills. After a period of depression, he is now actively seeking a new partner and enjoying dating.

The issues facing those divorcing at midlife are distinct from those divorcing at other periods in the life cycle. In terms of ontogenetic development, children are becoming self-sufficient adults, and aging parents may begin to contemplate their own mortality (Neugarten 1967). These issues may result in a divorce experience that is highly liberating to middle-aged adults, who are now free to pursue individual interests rather than being constrained by obligations to their family of procreation. Alternately, divorce in midlife has the potential to increase an individual's sense of vulnerability (Hagestad and Smyer 1982). Because of these issues, couples who divorce in midlife must face the tasks of (a) redefining their roles, (b) maintaining or renegotiating relationships with adult children, and (c) resolving financial crises precipitated by divorce.

Redefinition of Roles

Marriages that are dissolved in midlife frequently require individuals to perform household tasks they have not done in years, if ever (Ahrons and Rodgers 1987; Hagestad and Smyer 1982). If a couple performed household work according to gender-stereotyped norms, the man may need to learn how to cook and clean, whereas the woman may need to contend with yardwork and financial management. However, the adult children of the couple may be instrumental in providing their divorcing parents with assistance in performing chores that were formerly the responsibility of the ex-spouse (Ahrons and Rodgers 1987). This may be a particularly important issue for those cohorts or subgroups in which traditional gender roles were particularly strong.

Women who divorce in midlife are experiencing the loss of a number of roles in a relatively short period of time, and only some of these transitions are normative. For example, the experience of launching one's children in midlife is normative and accompanied by support from society (Hagestad and Smyer 1982). However, divorce during this same age period is defined as a non-normative transition that entails a loss of status (Hagestad and Smyer 1982). A divorced woman is no longer able to maintain roles that she may have held for decades, such as homemaker or wife.

Relationships With Adult Children

Unlike other families, divorcing parents may not have adequate resources to assist their young adult children; money that was previously available to lend for a down payment on a house becomes tied up in divorce proceedings or must be divided between the divorcing couple. In addition, adult children are quite capable of voicing their opinions regarding their parents' divorce and potential repartnering, and such convictions may be a source of conflict within the family, or a point of support. In essence, an adult child who disapproves of parental divorce may serve as the gatekeeper in controlling the parent's access to their grandchildren. Similarly, a disapproving adult child may withhold care or support (emotional and/or financial) from divorcing parents later in life.

The generational roles are reversed when an adult child is able to provide a divorcing parent with social support stemming from the child's *own* divorce experiences (Ahrons and Rodgers 1987). Although adult children are possible sources of support, often fathers in particular do not realize this potential. Divorced men have significantly less contact with their adult children and report their adult children as being potential sources of support significantly fewer times than men still in their first marriages, regardless of the child's age at the time of divorce or whether the man has remarried (Cooney and Uhlenberg 1990). One implication of this finding is that middle-age divorced men are more likely to remain isolated and not seek assistance from their adult children. The adult children may not develop a strong relationship with their father, and grandchildren may have fewer chances to get to know their grandfather. This situation has implications for the future identity of the family because a link to the past has become weakened or is perhaps missing altogether. It is also possible that divorced fathers will find themselves at greater risk when they become elderly because support from children may be less forthcoming (Cooney and Uhlenberg 1990).

Financial Issues

Women who divorce in midlife also experience a unique set of circumstances. Economically, they are similar to women who divorce earlier in the life course, although a woman who divorces after 20 years as a homemaker may have fewer resources in terms of job skills and occupational status than is likely to be found in younger women. Subsequently, many women take low-paying jobs. Career women may be somewhat insulated from the financial effects of divorce, but overall, women are not able to maintain the same standard of living that they had when they were married (Furstenberg and Cherlin 1991).

Midlife divorce also has implications for a woman's future financial security. It has been shown that women who have divorced in middle age are less financially secure than their cohorts who have recently been widowed or have remained married (Uhlenberg, Cooney, and Boyd 1990). Compared to married or recently widowed women, those who divorce in midlife have greater participation in the labor force, are less likely to own their own homes, and are more likely to share expenses with a roommate rather than live alone (Uhlenberg et al. 1990). The overall financial picture of many women who divorce in midlife includes the prospect of entering the workforce in order to be able to afford to share a rental property. The alternative is moving in with one's adult children.

The Diversity in Experience

The situation portrayed in our case example is useful for illustrating the different timetables that divorcing spouses may experience in regard to their marital dissolution. Paul, as initiator of the divorce, is voluntarily severing his roles and responsibilities as Barbara's husband, whereas Barbara does not voluntarily experience the loss of her roles assumed in her marriage to Paul (Hagestad and Smyer 1982). Paul will also had more time to build divorce-related supports and coping mechanisms, although he does not appear to have maximized these opportunities.

In terms of the multiple trajectories of the life course, midlife divorce may reflect a first divorce or subsequent marital dissolution. Similarly, the divorce may be a dissolution of a 30-year marriage or a 3-year marriage. Those who divorce in midlife may or may not have children. The children of people divorcing at midlife are likely to represent a wide range of ages, particularly as the trend for delayed childbearing continues (U.S. Bureau of the Census 1995). The number of children per divorcing family is likely to vary widely as well. The numbers and ages of children have a direct impact on the amount and type of support that divorcing midlife parents may receive from them. For example, young adult children may be more capable of contributing to their parents' financial well-being than children who are still in childhood or adolescence. Although children of any age may express support for a parent, a child's perceptions and consequent understanding of parental divorce is largely dependent on the child's cognitive maturity (Kurdek 1986). Therefore, not all children will be capable of providing the same type of emotional support to their parents; only children who have gone through their own marital dissolution will be able to give experience-related support and advice.

Conclusions

On one hand, divorce has become so common that some would say it should be considered a normative event in the life course. However, unlike becoming a parent or retiring, there is no culturally shared view of "on time" for divorce. Despite the prevalence of divorce and the existing legal guidelines for divorcing individuals, few informal social norms are available for guiding appropriate divorce timing and behaviors (Hagestad and Smyer 1982). Similarly, there are no established rituals through which individuals may either celebrate or mourn their divorce. The timing of divorce is important to consider, because while average marital durations may be calculated, there are no cultural values dictating the "right" time to divorce (Hagestad and Smyer 1982). This lack of social norms imparts an uncertainty to divorcing individuals.

The advantages of on-time transitions are that people can prepare for them. For example, one can prepare for parenthood by reading child-rearing manuals, baby sitting for friends, and observing children and parents together. One can prepare for retirement by developing hobbies, attending to investments, and psychologically rehearsing a different role in life. Scheduled or "on time" transitions are widely shared by the many cohorts who are experiencing the same transitions; therefore, these people can be a source of social support and knowledge acquired from experience.

However, because divorce typically is neither scheduled nor expected, one can do little to prepare for it. Additionally, the size of the cohort and availability of social support will vary depending on when during the life course the process occurs. For example, there is probably more cohort support when divorce occurs early in the life course, when the transition is more common, "on time," or normative. The duration of the marital relationship is another important consideration in examining divorce from a life course perspective. It is clear that longer relationships offer more time for members to develop as individuals, solidify roles and interaction patterns within the family, and establish family meanings associated with the events they experience together. Nonetheless, because divorce carries a stigma even when many are experiencing this transition, divorcing people may be reluctant to seek support or share gained wisdom.

The legal institutions that one encounters during divorce also influence the divorce experience. Although *some* federal law may guide divorce legislation (i.e., the Uniform Child Support Enforcement Act), the majority of divorce legislation is conducted and implemented at the state level (Buehler and Gerard 1995). Consequently, uniformity in legislation is difficult to achieve across states, and changes in divorce legislation may occur at different rates in different states. One example of the disparity in divorce law is the "tender years doctrine," in which the best interests of the child dictate that he or she should be in the mother's custody. However, parents' and men's rights groups challenged this assumption in the 1970s, and the tender years doctrine is no longer the legal standard in 45 states (Buehler and Gerard 1995). More recently we are seeing legal changes in the role of grandparents and stepparents in child visitation and custody (see Buehler 1995, Buehler and Gerard 1995 for reviews of divorce laws). Legal changes are often not accompanied by research examining the impact of the legislation; laws are passed before their implications can be assessed or documented. Such legal changes also contribute to the heterogeneity of divorce over time and make the legal experience of divorce different for those divorcing at different times and in different locations.

Overall, we see the overarching task of any divorcing family to be the establishment of stability within that family. The term "stability" in family science literature often refers to one's marital status, but our meaning here is different. Postdivorce stability within the family entails individual family members coming to terms emotionally with the divorce transition; they feel in control of their lives and are able to make predictions about what to expect in the future. In addition, the co-parenting relationship is well defined, with both parents being involved in raising their children and providing the best environment possible in which their children will grow and develop.

Clinicians, researchers, and other family professionals have the potential to influence the ways in which individuals, families, and the larger society view the divorce phenomenon. The ontogenetic, generational, and historical contexts in which the individuals and families are embedded influences the way that the divorce (counter)transition is defined and experienced. It is neither appropriate nor accurate to assume that the divorce experience is monolithic for all families or all individuals within a particular family.

Discussion Questions

1. Discuss whether or not divorce is considered an "on-time" transition, using examples to support your conclusion.

2. From a life course perspective, what are the key similarities and differences between newly divorcing families with young children and divorcing families with adolescent children?

3. Explain how the concepts of ontogenetic time, generational time, and historical time affect the experience of divorce in midlife.

4. What are some of the ways in which factors such as gender, race, and social class can influence the divorce experience of individuals and families?

Glossary

Countertransition Involuntary life transition due to the life changes of others.

Divorce Legal dissolution of a marriage.

Generational time The roles and expectations associated with one's generational placement in the family.

Historical Time The geopolitical and/or economic events that influence a particular cohort.

Legal custody The court-awarded prerogative to make legal decisions regarding the health, education, and welfare of a child. Joint or shared legal custody refers to situations in which both parents have this responsibility; often parents are required to come to a mutual agreement on legal custody issues regarding their child.

Ontogenetic time An individual's developmental level.

Parentification Process by which a child assumes roles within the family that are typically performed by a parent.

Physical custody The legal arrangement dictating with whom a child resides and who supervises the child. Joint or shared physical custody is an arrangement in which the child spends periods of time living with each parent.

Separation Informal dissolution of a marriage; it may occur in the process of obtaining a legal divorce.

Tender years doctrine Legal assumption that placing a child in the mother's custody would be in the child's best interests.

Suggested Readings

Ahrons, C. R., and Rodgers, R. H. (1987). *Divorced Families: A Multidisciplinary Developmental View*. New York: W. W. Norton.

Duck, S. (1982). *Personal Relationships 4: Dissolving Personal Relationships*. New York: Academic.

Kurdek, L. A. (1986). Children's reasoning about parental divorce. In R. D. Ashmore and D. M. Brodzinsky (Eds.), *Thinking About the Family: Views of Parents and Children* (233–276). Hillsdale, NJ: Erlbaum.

Rice, J. K. (1994). Reconsidering research on divorce, family life cycle, and the meaning of family. *Psychology of Women Quarterly, 18,* 559–584.

Bibliography

Ahrons, C. R., and Rodgers, R. H. (1987). *Divorced Families: A Multidisciplinary Developmental View.* New York: W. W. Norton.

Bengtson, V. L., and Allen, K. R. (1993). The life course perspective applied to families over time. In P. G. Boss, W. J. Doherty, R. LaRossa, R. Schumm and S.K. Steinmetz (eds.) *Sourcebook of Family Theories and Methods: A Contextual Approach.* New York: Plenum.

Boszormenyi-Nagy, I., and Spark, G. M. (1973). *Invisible Loyalties: Reciprocity in Intergenerational Family Therapy.* Hagerstown, MD: Harper and Row.

Brody, G. H., and Forehand, R. (1988). Multiple determinants of parenting: Research findings and implications for the divorce process. In E. M. Hetherington, and J. D. Arasteh (eds.) *Impact of Divorce, Single Parenting and Stepparenting on Children* (117–133). Hillsdale, NJ: Erlbaum.

Buehler, C. (1995). Divorce law in the United States. *Marriage and Family Review, 21,* 99–120.

Buehler, C., and Gerard, J. M. (1995). Divorce law in the United States: A focus on child custody. *Family Relations, 44,* 439–458.

Clarke, S. C. (1995). Advance report of final divorce statistics, 1989 and 1990. *Monthly Vital Statistics Report* (National Center for Health Statistics, Vol. 43., No. 9, Supplement). Hyattsville, MD: National Center for Health Statistics.

Cooney, T. M., and Uhlenberg, P. (1990). The role of divorce in men's relations with their adult children after midlife. *Journal of Marriage and the Family, 52,* 677–688.

Cowan, P. A. (1991). Individual and family life transitions: A proposal for a new definition. In P. A. Cowan and M. Hetherington (Eds.), *Family Transitions* (3–30). Hillsdale, NJ: Erlbaum.

Duck, S. (1982). A topography of relationship disengagement and dissolution. In S. Duck (Ed.), *Personal Relationships 4: Dissolving Personal Relationships* (1–30). New York: Academic.

Erikson, E. H. (1959). Identity and the life cycle: Selected papers (Monograph). *Psychological Issues, 1,* 1–171.

Fine, M., and Fine, D. (1994). An examination and evaluation of recent changes in divorce laws in five Western countries: The critical role of values. *Journal of Marriage and the Family, 56,* 249–263.

Fox, G. L., and Kelly, R. (1995). Determinants of child custody arrangements at divorce. *Journal of Marriage and the Family, 57,* 693–708.

Furstenberg, F. F., and Cherlin, A. J. (1991). *Divided Families: What Happens When Parents Part.* Cambridge, MA: Harvard University.

Glick, P. C. (1980). Remarriage: Some recent changes and variations. *Journal of Family Issues, 1,* 455–478.

Goldman, J., and Coane, J. (1977). Family therapy after the divorce: Developing a strategy. *Family Process, 16,* 357–362.

Hagestad, G. O., and Neugarten, B. L. (1985). Age and the life course. In E. Shanas and R. Binstock (Eds.), *Handbook of Aging and the Social Sciences* (2nd ed., 36–61). New York: Van Nostrend and Reinhold.

Hagestad, G. O., and Smyer, M. A. (1982). Dissolving long-term relationships: Patterns of divorcing in middle age. In S. Duck (Ed.), *Personal Relationships 4: Dissolving Personal Relationships* (155–188). New York: Academic.

Hetherington M. and J. D. Arasteh (Eds.), *Impact of Divorce, Single Parenting and Step-Parenting on Children* (117–133). Hillsdale, NJ: Erlbaum.

Hetherington, E. M., Bridges, M., and Insabella, G. (1998). What matters? What does not? Five perspectives on the association between marital transitions and children's adjustment. *American Psychologist, 53,* 167–184.

Hetherington, E. M., and Clingempeel, W. G. (1992). Coping with marital transitions: A family systems perspective. *Monographs of the Society for Research in Child Development, 57,* (2–3, Serial No. 227).

Hopper, J. (1993). The rhetoric of motives in divorce. *Journal of Marriage and the Family, 55,* 801–814.

Kurdek, L. A. (1986). Children's reasoning about parental divorce. In R. D. Ashmore and D. M. Brodzinsky (Eds.), *Thinking About the Family: Views of Parents and Children* (233–276). Hillsdale, NJ: Erlbaum.

Neugarten, B. (1967). Continuities and discontinuities of psychological issues into adult life. *Human Development, 12,* 121–130.

O'Rand, A. M. (1996). The cumulative stratification of the life course. In R. H. Binstock, L. K. George, V. W. Marshall, G. C. Myers, and J. H. Schulz (eds.), *Handbook of aging and the social sciences* (4th ed.,188–207). San Diego, CA: Academic.

Schumm, R. and S. K. Steinmetz (Eds.), *Sourcebook of Family Theories and Methods: A Contextual Approach* (469–499). New York: Plenum.

Thornton, A. (1985). Changing attitudes toward separation and divorce: Causes and consequences. *American Journal of Sociology, 90,* 856–872.

Uhlenberg, P., Cooney, T., and Boyd, R. (1990). Divorce for women after midlife. *Journal of Gerontology, 45,* S3–S11.

U.S. Bureau of the Census. (1995). *Statistical Abstract of the United States* (115th ed.). Washington, DC.

Wilson, B. F., and Clarke, S. C. (1992). Remarriages: A demographic profile. *Journal of Family Issues, 13,* 123–141. ✦

Chapter 3
Remarried Families Over the Life Course

Margaret Crosbie-Burnett

Katrina McClintic
University of Miami

Hope for a better conjugal relationship than one has experienced in the past must be a pervasive characteristic of humans. The proliferation of millions of stepfamilies is an embodiment of this hope. Stepfamilies are defined by the presence of a parent-child relationship that predates the couple relationship. Beyond this core defining structure, there are many types of stepfamilies, including divorced parents who remarry or cohabit, widows and widowers who are parents and who remarry or cohabit, and never-married parents who marry or cohabit. In each of these situations the new partner could be someone of the same or opposite sex, and one or both partners could bring children into the family. Also, in each of these situations, some or all of the children could be residents of, or visitors to, the home. Adding to the complexity, stepfamilies can be of mixed race, can be of mixed culture, or can include an adopted or foster child and grandparents or other kin. The term *stepfamily* can be used to denote only one household or, as with the term *divorced families*, to denote households linked together biologically, emotionally, finan-

cially, and perhaps legally by children in common.

Working within the paradigm of family development, this chapter is organized by the transitions stepfamilies experience in various stages of their development throughout the life course and by the tasks required to successfully move from one developmental stage to the next. In addition, we address the natural tensions between family members' individual development and the family's development that can exist in these "recycled" families. We will follow stepfamilies through the transitions with three themes: family role transitions and the concomitant realignment of boundaries, individual psycho-emotional adjustment of family members, and changes in financial and legal aspects of families. In addition, we will point out aspects of stepfamilies on which empirical research has been conducted or clinical observations have been made, and aspects on which our understanding is based on only anecdotal evidence or on what we expect based on our theories.

Developmental Tasks for Successful Transitions

Meet the Smith-Hernandez family. Susan Smith is divorced and has a son, David, who is 12, and a daughter, Jane, who is 14. The children live with Susan and visit their father fairly regularly. Susan advanced her career after she divorced, had a sufficient income, and enjoyed the freedom of being single. When she met Carlos, she fell in love with "this handsome and intriguing man." Carlos Hernandez is a Nicaraguan immigrant whose first wife and child were killed in 1985 during the Nicaraguan rebellion. Carlos and Susan are newlyweds who did not seek guidance about stepfamily living because they believe that "our love is so strong, it will carry us through any difficulty." Susan's former husband, John Smith, who is the children's father, lives in the next town and is cohabiting with Mary; they have a baby son, Nick.

Transition #1: Initial Integration

Nearly all of the research and clinical writings on stepfamilies have focused on the initial integration of the new family, describing samples of dominant-culture, middle-class, post-divorce, and remarried family households in which the minor children reside rather than visit. More is known about this initial transition (Crosbie-Burnett 1994) than any later transition. Although little is known about other demographic populations, studies have found no differences in stepfamily adjustment between dominant-culture and African-American families within the same social class (Carr 1994; Fine, McKenry, Donnelly, and Voydanoff 1992). There is virtually no literature on other ethnic minority stepfamilies. Preliminary findings with gay and lesbian stepfamilies suggest that, like heterosexual stepfamilies, they experience the stresses that are a function of stepfamily structure (Crosbie-Burnett and Helmbrecht 1993; Wright 1998).

Role transitions and realignment of boundaries within a stepfamily household. Prerequisite tasks for healthy stepfamily development include successful grieving over prior family losses and an openness to a new type of family that is not a reconstitution of a prior family. For example, previously coupled adults and their children need to grieve and let go of the prior family, either for what it was or what they wished it might have been, in order to embrace the new family with the energy and flexibility that stepfamilies require. Another important task is learning about successful stepfamilies, either by reading books or attending some type of group for stepfamilies.

A major task for new stepfamilies is to integrate two or more family cultures into one new culture (Jacobson 1995). This means including a stepparent in a single-parent household or, if both adults have children, uniting two single-parent households. A realignment of boundaries around the family's subsystems is necessary in order to find an appropriate place for the stepparent(s) in the leadership subsystem of the new family (Hobart 1988). In addition to the usual leadership subsystem focused in any family, stepfamily subsystems include the biologically related subsystem(s), the conjugal subsystems, and possibly one or two biological

sibling subsystems. The major realignment task is to include the new stepparent(s) in the family group in general, and the leadership subsystem in particular, and to relieve an older child from leadership responsibilities and privileges, excluding that child from the leadership subsystem.

In many single-parent households, an older child has become part of the leadership subsystem of the family, playing much of the role of the parent's partner both emotionally and functionally (i.e., managing the household and parenting younger children). One of the most difficult tasks for new stepfamilies is displacing of a child from the leadership subsystem. The longer a child has functioned in this position of power, as the biological parent's confidante or helpmate, the more difficult the displacement is likely to be. For families with older adolescents who are preparing to leave home, displacement may even be inappropriate, in which case the stepparent becomes an addition to the leadership subsystem. There is growing evidence, however, that if the child is secure in the biological parent-child relationship, he or she can tolerate the presence of and even displacement by a stepparent (Anderson and White 1986; Garmezy 1991; Marsiglio 1992). This means that the stepparent should not try to "come between" the biological parent and child by, for example, demanding that the biological parent side with the new spouse during disputes, or trying to assert authority over the child. The directive that stepparents should not try to discipline a stepchild until a trusting relationship has been built is by far the most validated "fact" about stepfamilies (Bray 1988; Hetherington, Cox, and Cox 1985; Visher and Visher 1982). Keep in mind however, that not allowing the man of the house the authority to discipline children is contradictory to the traditional male-dominant families of some ethnic minorities and religions.

Carlos longed to "reconstitute" the family he had lost. He had never allowed himself to grieve his deep loss. He tried to "be strong." Even though he believed that he was ready to "move on" with his life, it became evident that he was not. Because his family had been killed when he was not home, he frequently called his wife throughout her work day to assure himself that she was safe; he became very upset if she was a few minutes late arriving at work or home. Furthermore, this stepfamily needed to blend two cultures into one. As a Nicaraguan, Carlos believed in traditional sex roles. Susan had become a career woman who expected Carlos to share household duties with her, the same way she had shared them with Jane during her time as a single parent. As the "man of the house," Carlos believed it was his duty to discipline the children, but when he struck David for disobeying him, Jane stood between David and Carlos and began screaming at him about American child abuse laws.

In the "visiting" households, the same task of realignment of boundaries and role transitions found in residential stepfamilies must occur if the children have established themselves in that household when the non-residential parent recouples. When the recoupling occurs before the children have spent time in the nonresidential household, it is the couple who must expand their family boundary in order to make a place for the children. Inherent in this change is a role transition for the nonresidential parent's partner, from lover or spouse to stepparent. Stepparents who have no experience rearing children have the additional task of acquiring parenting skills and learning about normal child development (Palisi, Orleans, Caddell, and Korn 1991).

Perhaps the most difficult challenge regarding family role transitions is the ambiguity of the stepparent role. Particularly when both biological parents are active in a child's life, it is not clear what role a stepparent should play (Crosbie-Burnett 1989; Whitsett and Land 1992). Conversely, it is not clear what role a stepchild with two active parents should take in relation to stepparents. The task is to negotiate roles and a steprelationship that is mutually suitable for all relevant family members, whether the stepparent role be similar to that of a biological parent, an aunt/uncle, an adult friend, or a housemate (Crosbie-Burnett 1984).

The importance of negotiating the stepparent role and the steprelationship is supported by a variety of studies: Longitudinal studies have shown, for early adolescents, that stepfather-stepchild relationships become more negative over time (Bray 1992) and that stepfathers become increasingly disengaged from the children in response to the children's ignoring or resisting stepfathers' attempts to be emotionally closer (Hetherington and Clingempeel 1992). The stepchild's receptivity to the stepparent's attempts to initiate a relationship appears to be more important than the stepparent's behavior (Brown, Green, and Druckman 1990). Of grave concern are findings that a disengaged parenting style for stepparents has been associated with poor psychosocial adjustment for adolescents (Crosbie-Burnett and Giles-Sims 1994).

One well-supported and broad factor in the adjustment of stepfamilies is the necessity of flexibility, as opposed to rigidity, of family roles (including gender roles) and household boundaries (Bray and Berger 1993; Henry and Lovelace 1995; Pill 1990; Waldren, Bell, Peek, and Sorrell 1990). The flexibility characteristic of African-American families offers some examples on how to handle these role and relationship transitions more easily (Crosbie-Burnett and Lewis 1993). For instance, it is quite common for persons who are not related by blood or marriage to be considered "family" because they contribute emotionally, practically, or financially to the family. Alternatively, the rigidity of boundaries and family roles in Hispanic families may create problems for Hispanic stepfather families. Traditionally Hispanic families abide by traditional sex roles and are hierarchical, with older family members and males having more status and authority than younger members and females.

Because the Smith-Hernandez family did not educate themselves about stepfamilies, they began to blame each other for their problems. Susan and Carlos were considering divorce, but they went to a family therapist for one last try. The therapist educated them about typical stepfamily dynamics and recommended popular books for the adults and the children. The therapist helped Carlos grieve for his late wife and child. This helped him to stop being so anxious and to stop trying to replace his lost child with his stepchildren, who had resisted his attempts to be a traditional father to them. They often reminded him that they already had a father. In therapy Carlos and the children were able to talk about types of steprelationships that would be mutually suitable for Carlos, Susan, and each child. As part of Carlos' letting go of a traditional father role, he allowed the household boundary to be flexible enough to include John in decisions that he and Susan had made about his stepchildren's behavior at home.

Another major task in the initial integration of a stepfamily is the development of a strong conjugal relationship; this means building a protective boundary around the couple. In addition to developing emotional intimacy in the conjugal subsystem, the couple must negotiate a division of labor with respect to household tasks, child care, and decision making power. Even though remarried couples tend to report that their decision-making is egalitarian (Coleman and Ganong 1989; Crosbie-Burnett and Giles-Sims 1991), research shows that the division of labor is consistent with traditional sex roles (Demo and Acock 1993; Guisinger, Cowan, and Schuldberg 1989)—although less so than for first-marrieds (Ishii-Kuntz and Coltrane 1992). This traditional division of labor is problematic for many father-stepmother households; stepmothers have reported resentment that the father is not doing enough parenting of his own children (Guisinger et al. 1989) and that he is not supporting the stepmother in her parenting role (Morrison and Thompson-Guppy 1985). In addition, there is evidence that remarrying mothers and stepmothers who quit working to spend more time being wives and mothers are less happy in their marriages than women who do not (Crosbie-Burnett 1988). Regardless of spouses' actual behavior, both research and clinical observations suggest that marital satisfaction is related more to the *perception* that tasks are shared equitably than it is to the *actual* division of labor between the spouses (Guisinger et al. 1989). Given these findings, the task for the couple is to learn to negotiate a division of labor that each of them *believes* is equitable.

Another area of concern in stepfamilies is sibling relationships. Although little is known about this area, there is evidence that parental remarriage negatively affects relationships between biological siblings (Anderson and Rice 1992; White and Reidmann 1992). The task here would be to strengthen relations between siblings because they can function as social support for each other during the stressful times of stepfamily development. Although stepsiblings are not usually as emotionally close as siblings, they have been reported to have positive relationships in general (Ganong and Coleman 1993). Clinicians have identified sources of potential difficulty in stepsibling relations: sibling rivalry; sexual attraction; competition for parental attention, space, and material goods; and changes in family size, sex ratio, and birth order (Rosenberg and Hajal 1985; Walsh 1992).

Inherent in the role transitions and changes of subsystem boundaries in a new stepfamily household is the task of creating new norms and rules that will maintain the changes. Perhaps the most enjoyable aspect of this task is overtly creating new family traditions and rituals for holidays, birthdays, anniversaries, and other special events. This can be conducive to building family integration and cohesion. Also, one seemingly paradoxical method for strengthening family integration and promoting new norms is for each dyad to spend one-on-one time together engaging in activities that are enjoyable for both. These new rituals are reassuring to old relationships (e.g., parent-child) (Cooney, Hutchinson, and Leather 1995) and strengthen new relationships (e.g., conjugal and stepparent-child).

A caveat about family research must be kept in mind: Various studies have claimed to show the "impact" of the marital relationship (Skopin, Newman, and McKenry 1993), the biological parent-child relationship (Marsiglio 1992), or the steprelationship (Clingempeel and Segal 1986; Crosbie-Burnett and Giles-Sims 1994; Fine 1995) on an individual's happiness or on another relationship. However, because these studies are all correlational, we cannot know the direction of the effects. We do know, however, that relationships do not function independently; the various relationships and individuals do systemically influence other parts of the stepfamily.

On an intrapersonal level, research with stepfamilies has suggested that the personality characteristics of tolerance for ambiguity, cognitive complexity, and personal flexibility facilitate adjustment to stepfamily living (Clingempeel, Brand, and Segal 1987). This means that a task for individuals in new stepfamilies might be to try to increase their flexibility and tolerance for ambiguous roles and relationships. One way to do so is by attending to one's cognitions (e.g., beliefs, attributions, schemas) about families and about behaviors of other family members (Crosbie-Burnett and Lewis 1993), discussing them as a family, and practicing more flexible approaches to family life. In addition to individual members' working on relationships within the family, each member should maintain social support outside the family.

If the new stepfamily household fails to complete necessary tasks and integration is unsuccessful, the new family will break apart in one of two ways, both of which involve the extrusion, or forcing out, of a family member. If the stepparent is not successfully integrated into the family, the conjugal unit will separate or divorce, extruding the stepparent, and the family will revert back to the single-parent family (Hermansen 1993). Alternatively, a "problematic" child may be excluded from the household in order to preserve the conjugal relationship.

Role transitions and realignment of boundaries between the households of separated or divorced co-parents. Recoupling or remarriage of a parent usually forces change in the co-parental relationship if contact between the co-parents exists. For example, in situations in which the co-parents have had a close relationship, distancing may be necessary in order not to threaten a new conjugal relationship. Alternatively, it is not uncommon for a nonresidential father who has been relatively uninvolved with his children and former partner to become very involved when a stepfather becomes part of his children's household. In either case, the boundaries between the households and the family roles are likely to change. For example, a nonresidential father may now have to share the father role with his child's stepfather.

Research findings clearly direct the task for families on this issue. When the nonresidential parent is active in a child's life in positive ways and conflict between households is minimal, children function better (Crosbie-Burnett 1991; Hanson and McLanahan 1996; Strother and Jacobs 1984), and stepfamily integration does not suffer (Furstenberg and Nord 1985; Pink and Wampler 1985). When the nonresidential parent and the residential stepparent are not competitive (Crosbie-Burnett 1989), and boundaries are clearly defined (Weston and Macklin 1990), marital satisfaction in the stepfamily is higher. The task is for the adults to negotiate flexible interhousehold boundaries and roles that promote healthy, nonresidential parent-child relationships. Inherent in this task is acceptance of the constant changes in household composition as children move between households.

John and Susan had a friendly divorce. For a few years after the divorce they each had a key to the other's home because doing so supported their successful co-parenting. Carlos could not tolerate another man having such access to his home, so Susan had to ask John for the key, thus making the boundary higher around the new stepfamily, and John more peripheral in Susan's stepfamily household. Fortunately, Carlos, John, Susan, and later Mary, were able to talk about the boundary between the households (i.e., making telephone calls, arriving with and without notice, interrupting family time) and to create rules that allowed John and his children access to each other while still respecting the integrity of the new stepfamilies.

Role transitions and realignment of boundaries between stepfamily household and the older generation. Stepgrandparents' acceptance of stepgrandchildren varies widely, but most stepgrandchildren are open to having positive relations with stepgrandparents. However, if either generation was opposed to the remarriage, the quality of the stepgrandparentchild relationship is likely to be diminished (Ganong and Coleman 1994). The task for stepgrandparents is to accept and grieve their child's first marriage in preparation for accepting the new marriage and the children that have accompanied it (Henry, Ceglian, and Ostrander 1993).

Individuals' development versus family development. There are a variety of ways in which the usual confluence of individual development and family development become out of sync in stepfamilies. First, parents and their adolescent children may be dating at the same time. Not only can this be embarrassing for the adolescents, but parental involvement in a romantic relationship can mean less supervision of adolescents. Furthermore, while adolescent stepchildren are individuating from the family and desiring to spend more time with peers, the new family needs to build cohesion by engaging in activities involving the whole stepfamily. Finally, although nearly all child developmentalists would agree that losing a parental figure to whom a child is bonded, whether through death, separation, or divorce, interferes with normal child development. In contrast, few would agree on whether adjusting to a new parental figure or new stepsiblings interferes with normal child development.

For childless stepparents, "instant parenting" of children is inconsistent with the usual way that adults psychologically develop into parents (Roberts and Price 1987); parenting usually begins with pregnancy. Also, it is not uncommon for childless stepmothers and biological fathers to be out of sync in their desires regarding parenting. A stepmother may decide that she would like to have a baby, whereas a biological father may be enjoying the freedom of not being responsible for minor children. When these conflicts between developmental needs occur, the family members' task is to listen to and respect the needs of all concerned and negotiate a compromise.

When John met Mary, she was happy as a successful executive with a corporation. Mary had claimed that she did not ever want children. She was John's dream second life-partner; she was intelligent and independent, did *not want a legal marriage, and loved to travel. He enjoyed his children and was a good father, but he was counting the years until Jane and David would be independent and he and Mary could "do their thing." As Mary approached 40 years of age, she became disenchanted with the corporate world and, having become rather fond of her stepchildren, decided that all she really wanted was to have her own baby. This threw Mary and John's relationship into crisis; John even considered leaving Mary. Meanwhile, Mary became pregnant, and John grieved for his lost plans while also anticipating with joy his new baby.*

Changes in financial and legal aspects within a stepfamily household. The ambiguity of the stepparent role is reflected in our legal system (Buser 1991; Mason and Simon 1995; Ramsey 1994), as well as in the everyday lives of families. Although stepparents who have not legally adopted stepchildren have *no* legal parental rights or responsibilities (Fine and Fine 1992), some government programs, such as Aid to Families with Dependent Children and government-sponsored student loan programs, demand consideration of a stepparent's income in the calculation of benefits. Furthermore, the income of a stepparent (nonresidential stepmother) who is legally married to a parent is deemed available for child support. Also, some states are now allowing postdivorce visitation rights for stepparents who can prove that they functioned in a parental role during the marriage (Duran-Aydintug and Ihinger-Tallman 1995; Mason and Simon 1995). There is a national movement toward legally acknowledging the contribution of stepparents who do support and care for children (Fine and Fine 1992).

Although a remarriage is no different legally from a first marriage, a remarriage or recoupling is financially very different. Both residential and visiting stepfamily households can be financially complex, and adults and children alike are hypervigilant to the distribution of money and goods, which become symbols of love. Because the children are not the biological children of both adults, there is always the question of who is financially responsible for which children. How much should a stepparent contribute, if any? Should a nonresidential couple share the responsibility for making child support payments? There are no social norms for guidance, so each couple must decide what is right for them.

With respect to the process of handling money in the stepfamily home, the question regarding how many "pots of money" to keep is at issue. Should a couple pool incomes and child support monies, keep separate accounts, or do a combination of both? Research suggests that pooling money versus keeping separate accounts is not related to the couple's happiness with stepfamily life (Pasley, Sandras, and Edmondson 1994). Delicate questions arise with respect to property and other assets as well. Should a childless stepparent be responsible for paying a lower proportion of rent or mortgage? If one partner brought many more assets to the relationship than the other, should assets be pooled, since they would be considered marital property if a legal divorce ensued? The task for the couple is to reach an agreement, at least tentatively, on the answers to these and related financial questions but to be open to renegotiations as the family and its members develop. Ideally, this is done before marrying or cohabiting.

Changes in financial and legal aspects between households of co-parents. Most households of co-parents are financially as well as biologically and emotionally linked, even if the issue is child support payments. In complex situations, child support monies can flow into a stepfamily household from a nonresidential parent, only to flow out to the household of the stepparent's biological children. Remarriage of either parent is often a cue for an ex-spouse to initiate court proceedings to request a reduction (if the payer) or an increase (if the recipient) of child support payments. At the very least, recoupling of a parent causes a change in the network of households and causes financial concern, especially for family members in the other household. It is not uncommon for a new stepparent to want more monies to stay within his or her household. The task is to assure that financial obligations between households continue to be met.

When Carlos and Susan began cohabiting, Carlos was unemployed. John was angry because he perceived that "my money is supporting my ex's boyfriend, and I cannot do a thing about it." Susan claimed that John's money was supporting his children, and her earnings were supporting Carlos. Susan and Carlos pooled money, creating a system that worked for them within their household but that created problems between co-parenting households.

Transition #2: Addition of a New Baby Born into a Stepfamily Household

Role transitions and realignment of boundaries. The addition of a baby born to the couple creates a new subsystem within the household and can also force role changes. First, it creates a new traditional nuclear family subsystem (mother, father, child) within the stepfamily. This can make an only stepchild feel like an outsider. Second, the birth legitimizes and validates a previously childless stepparent as a "real" parent in the household and gives an only stepchild the new role of sibling. If the new baby is born into the residential household of a stepchild, the new half-sibling appears to be experienced as a new full sibling (Bernstein 1989; Ganong and Coleman 1988).

The effect of the birth of a baby on stepfamily relationships has shown mixed results, probably because there are many factors (e.g., age differences and amount of contact between all family members) that moderate these relationships (Ganong and Coleman 1994). It does not necessarily solidify the new conjugal relationship, as some couples hope. If the baby is born into a child's visiting household, the child and residential parent may feel threatened that the baby will draw attention and resources from the existing children.

Individuals' development versus family development. The arrival of a baby into a family of older children creates numerous possibilities of individual developmental stages and family development being out of sync. Parents having their first mutual baby are by definition at a "new nuclear family" stage. The same family may also be rearing adolescents; thus, the stepfamily is simultaneously at two different family stages. On individual levels, a midlife parent who is anticipating the freedom of an empty nest could feel resentful about starting over again. Adolescents, who are trying to become comfortable with their own sexuality issues, may be embarrassed by a pregnant or lactating mother or stepmother.

Changes in financial and legal aspects. While there are no relevant legal implications of a baby born into a stepfamily, there are financial implications. A baby requires resources for its care, disrupting the delicate status quo of stepfamily finances. If the child is placed in day care, the cost may compete with college costs for older children. If the baby is born into the nonresidential household, pressure can come from the nonresidential stepparent to decrease support for "those" children in order to support "our" baby.

The task in this transition is to encourage family members of both households to express their thoughts and feelings so that compromises and plans for handling delicate situations can be made. Specifically, children residing in the household or a linked household need to be assured that they are still important and loved, and the level of financial support they need must be maintained.

When baby Nick arrived, David was beginning puberty and feeling very awkward and insecure about himself. He was demanding of John's attention, and seemed chronically angry at home. In a fit of tears and rage one evening, he blurted out, "Why does Dad need another son? Aren't I enough? How can I be as cute as a baby?" Because Susan and John had a healthy co-parental relationship, they talked about David's feelings, and took action to reassure him. The following spring, however, John told Jane and David that he could no longer afford to send them to summer camp for a week.

Transition #3: Home Leaving of Stepchildren

Role transitions and realignment of boundaries. When children leave home for college, the military, or independent living, it

is a time of shifts in boundaries for any family. The unique aspects of home leaving for stepchildren are a function of the stepfamily's dynamics. Sometimes the home leaving is premature because the family has failed to integrate the subsystems and the adolescent is extruded from the family (Aquilino 1991; White and Booth 1985). Alternatively, sometimes it is difficult for adolescents who had functioned in the role of Mom or Dad's confidante and protector to leave a parent who is in an unhappy or abusive marriage or partnership. Also, after all of the stepchildren— "the reminders of the old marriage"—have left both homes and the parents are living their "new lives," stepchildren who have left home can feel a sense of loss of a family base. Alternatively, parents may be in competition for grown children's time and try to buy their presence during holidays and the like by contributing to college costs or rent, placing the grown children in difficult, anxiety-provoking situations in which they have to choose one parent over the other.

Individuals' development versus family development. If the stepfamily is simultaneously at the two stages of rearing young children and launching older children, home leaving of older children can be more difficult than it is in traditional families. Older children who were parental figures to younger half-siblings may have a difficult time being away from "my baby." Similarly, young children at concrete stages of cognitive functioning do not understand why big brother or sister "doesn't love me anymore" because he or she has left home.

Changes in financial and legal aspects. The only legal implication of home leaving is the liability of legal parents for the behaviors of minor children, but this liability is not unique to stepchildren. Financially, the home leaving can cause friction among the parents and stepparents if the grown child is not financially independent. Most child support agreements expire when the child reaches 18 years of age. Therefore, questions like "Who will pay for Susie's car repairs or college texts?" have no clear answer. Stepparents can believe that they have already "done enough" for the stepchildren and urge parents to invest in their own household, and possibly their young children, rather than in the grown children. This can place the biological parent in an excruciating loyalty dilemma. Furthermore, some stepparents are already supporting their own biological children's college education.

In order to successfully handle this transition, family members need to support the continuation of half-sibling and stepsibling relationships as children leave home. For example, frequent telephone calls and cards to younger children and drawings by younger children mailed to older children can facilitate feelings of closeness. Parents and stepparents should not abandon these grown children, financially or emotionally; they should continue to make grown children feel valued in their families.

Transition #4: Adult Stepchildren and Elderly Stepparents

Role transitions and realignment of boundaries. The last stage of family development begins with the transition from being an independent couple with grown children to becoming more dependent on others for care and possibly financial support, and eventually losing one's partner to death. It is well established that female family members (wives, sisters, daughters, and daughters-in-law) perform elder care more than male family members do. Is this process disrupted if the adult daughter is remarried? Research suggests that although never-married daughters are the most common elder-care givers (Litvin, Albert, Brody, and Hoffman 1995), there is little difference in the elder care provided by daughters who are divorced, separated, or remarried; however, these daughters provide less elder care than daughters in first marriages (Brody, Litvin, Albert, and Hoffman 1994). This difference appears to be related to higher levels of labor force participation by daughters from disrupted marriages (Cicirelli 1983). Virtually nothing is known about the elder care given by stepdaughters who were reared by a stepparent or by those who became a stepdaughter due to the recoupling of an elderly parent.

Individuals' development versus family development. Stepfamilies into which a second generation of children was born are more likely to experience caring for both minor children and elderly parents simultaneously. The middle-aged adults are said to be "the sandwich generation." They are at the developmental stage of caring for parents, but because they have begun a "new" family, they have the added stress of caring for two generations of dependent family members. The task for these families is to solicit help from any source—social services, friends, family, paid caregivers. In some situations the children and the elders can enrich each others' lives.

Mary was the youngest and only daughter in her family of origin. When her mother, a widow, became ill with cancer and needed daily care, Mary took her into her home. By then Nick was 10 years old. As an only child in the household, he was jealous of his mother giving an inordinate amount of attention to another family member and got into trouble at school in order to gain back some of his mother's attention. Mary was struggling with "sandwich generation" stress. At holiday time John hoped that Jane and David could spend a week with them, but Mary told John that she could not handle any more. Because Jane and David had another home as an option, they were not invited to spend time with their father.

Changes in financial and legal aspects. Related to elder care is the financial responsibility for elderly family members. As parents and stepparents become unable to care for themselves, the task for the group of adult children, stepchildren, and children-in-law is to assess the human and financial resources available in the relevant households and make plans for their parental figures' final years. In stepfamilies, this may be all the more difficult because adult stepsiblings are not as close emotionally as siblings (White and Riedmann 1992), yet it is all the more necessary because norms regarding obligations between steprelations are nonexistent.

If financial resources are plentiful, the transition to the elderly stage of family life includes decisions about inheritance. How most parents and stepparents divide resources among children, stepchilden, grandchildren, and stepgrandchildren in their wills is not known, although preliminary studies suggest the presence of a social norm that obligations toward step(grand)children are much weaker than obligations toward (grand)children, and the elderly favor biological (grand)children over step(grand) children when naming beneficiaries in a will (Burgoyne and Morrison 1997; Coleman, Ganong, and Cable 1997). However, if a step(grand)parent wants to leave assets to step(grand)children, the elder must name them in a will because in no state are stepchildren included in the category of "children" as beneficiaries under intestate statutes regarding inheritance when no will exists (Fine and Fine 1992). The task, of course, is for the couple to create wills that designate how their resources will be distributed, ideally before they become elderly.

Remarriage in the Grandparent Generation

With the graying of America, increasing numbers of grandparents will recouple and remarry; the current rate of remarriage for persons over 65 years is 3 per 1000 for women and 17 per 1000 for men (Bulcroft, Bulcroft, Hatch, and Borgatta 1989). The research on this generation of remarrieds has focused on the antecedents and consequences of remarriage. For both men and women, the likelihood of remarriage is associated with more recent divorce or widowhood, smaller households, more education, and better health; for men it is also associated with being older and being employed (Bulcroft et al. 1989). Divorced women remarry more often than widowed women, while the opposite is true for men (Wu and Balakrishnan 1994).

Role transitions and realignment of boundaries. There is some evidence that remarrying grandparents tend to shift boundaries and family roles to focus less on progeny. Two studies suggested that it is the disruption of the grandparents' first marriage that causes them to change focus and that remarriage has virtually no subsequent effect. Divorce of this generation was found to be associated with decreased social, instrumental, and financial support of adult children, and remarriage did not change the

amount of any of these types of support (White 1992). Similarly Marks (1995) found that both divorced and remarried parents reported feeling less obligated to their adult children; however, giving support to adult children was associated with more well-being, for women only.

Many successful elder remarriers report that the psychological boundary around their marriage includes acceptance of each other's deceased spouses (Vinick 1983). Acceptance of one's prior spouse is similar to a stepparent's acceptance of a stepchild's biological parent of the same sex. This acceptance of pre-existing primary relationships is a similar task for stepfamily members at different stages of life.

Individuals' development versus family development. The task for older parents who recouple or remarry is to strike a balance between the role of helpful, mature parent and grandparent, consistent with traditional family development, and the role of new spouse, an impetus for individual development. Once elders have created this new developmental stage for themselves by remarrying, it appears to have a positive effect on them as individuals. (There appears to be no research on cohabiting elderly couples.) Compared to the elderly who do not remarry, remarriage after widowhood and divorce was found to be associated with improved economic conditions, better health, and reports of being happy with life in general (Bulcroft et al. 1989; Wu and Balakrishnan 1994). Men reported being motivated to remarry to avoid loneliness and to be cared for; they reported finding social benefits while women reported more psychological benefits (Vinick 1978). In one study, wives' closeness, commitment, and satisfaction were associated with consensus between the spouses, less negative means of resolving conflicts, and belief that their husband share problems with others: however, no such relationships were found for the husbands (Pasley and Ihinger-Tallman 1990).

Changes in financial and legal aspects. Important legal and financial implications occur when elders remarry. Spouses are responsible for each others' financial obligations, but they are also the beneficiary of assets at a spouse's death. This means that if an elder remarries, some or all assets that would have been inherited by children will now flow to the new spouse if no will exists. In the case of remarriage of elders, prenuptial agreements regarding assets are not uncommon, and creating a will is an important task for remarriers who have progeny.

Conclusion

Basic research with diverse populations is needed in order to understand how the unique aspects of stepfamily structure and dynamics manifest themselves in the contexts of various subcultures of the United States and other cultures of the world. Some of these populations include visiting stepfamily households, multiple generation stepfamilies, ethnic minority stepfamilies, gay and lesbian stepfamilies, stepfamilies formed from first coupling or marriage of single parents, affluent and lower-class stepfamilies, stepfamilies formed after widowhood or divorce of elderly individuals, and cohabiting stepfamilies. Within a life span perspective, cross-sectional and longitudinal research is needed to understand how stepfamilies maneuver through the stages of family development. Given the proliferation of stepfamilies, we need to know how to encourage healthy steprelations, not only for the welfare of dependent children but for the benefit of creating stable adult relationships and care for elders.

Applied research is needed to design the best ways to educate couples who are intending to form stepfamilies. Prevention programs abound, but they are grossly underutilized. There is virtually no research comparing various interventions with troubled stepfamilies, whereas there are excellent guidelines for clinicians working with stepfamilies (Sager et al. 1983; Visher and Visher 1988); thus, empirically validated interventions need to be developed.

Our social institutions must become more amenable to stepfamilies and stepfamily members. Our legal system, insurance companies, schools, and colleges assume traditional family relationships (Crosbie-Burnett 1994). Even as the number of stepfamilies increases, they are too often invisible in the policies and procedures of our institutions and are, therefore, too often benignly mistreated. Heightened awareness of the implications of policy at all levels would support the successful adaptation of stepfamilies as they maneuver through the stages of family development and make our society truly more family friendly.

Discussion Questions

1. Describe some important individual or family characteristics or behaviors that can help make the initial integration of the stepfamily more successful.

2. Discuss the role of the stepparent. What makes this role so difficult to define?

3. Explain how individual and stepfamily development can be "out of sync." Give examples.

4. Discuss financial difficulties that may arise during different transitions of stepfamily life.

5. How can helping professionals assist the stepfamily in negotiating transitional tasks successfully?

6. Develop a research question for an area of the stepfamily literature that merits further investigation.

Glossary

Stepfamily May denote only one household or, in cases of divorce, multiple households linked together biologically, emotionally, financially, and perhaps legally, by children in common.

Family boundaries Define who is considered to be a member of a family; best if flexible in remarried families.

Role ambiguity Lack of clarity regarding appropriate roles of family members; characteristic of many stepparents in relation to their stepchildren.

Recoupling Term used for remarriage.

Suggested Readings

Booth, A., and Dunn, J. (1994). *Stepfamilies: Who Benefits? Who Does Not?* Hillsdale, NJ: Erlbaum.

Ganong, L. H., and Coleman, M. (1994). *Remarried Family Relationships*. Thousand Oaks, CA: Sage.

Hetherington, E. M., and Clingempeel, W. G. (1992). Coping with marital transitions: A family systems perspective. *Monographs of the Society for Research in Child Development*, 57(2–3, Serial No. 227), 1–242.

Ihinger-Tallman, M., and Pasley, K. (1987). *Remarriage*. Newbury Park, CA: Sage.

Maglin, N. B., and Schniedewind, N. (1989). *Women in Stepfamilies: Voices of Anger and Love*. Philadelphia: Temple University Press.

Pasley, K., and Ihinger-Tallman, M. (Eds.). (1987). *Remarriage and Stepparenting: Current Research and Theory*. New York: Guilford.

Pasley, K., and Ihinger-Tallman, M. (Eds.). (1994). *Stepparenting: Issues in Theory, Research, and Practice*. Westport, CT: Greenwood.

Sager, C. J., Brown, H. S., Crohn, H., Engel, T., Rodstein, E., and Walker, E. (1983). *Treating the Remarried Family*. New York: Brunner/Mazel.

Visher, E. B., and Visher, J. S. (1988). *Old Loyalties, New Ties: Therapeutic Strategies With Stepfamilies*. New York: Brunner/Mazel.

Bibliography

Anderson, E. R., and Rice, A. M. (1992). Sibling relationships during remarriage. *Monographs of the Society for Research in Child Development*, 57(2–3, Serial No. 227), 149–177.

Anderson, J.Z., and White, C.D. (1986). An empirical investigation of interactive and relationship patterns in functional and dysfunctional nuclear families and stepfamilies. *Family Process*, 25. 407–422.

Aquilino, W. S. (1991). Family structure and home-leaving: A further specification of the relationship. *Journal of Marriage and the Family*, 53, 999–1010.

Bernstein, A. C. (1989). Gender and stepfamily life: A review. *Journal of Feminist Family Therapy*, 1(4), 1–27.

Bray, J. H. (1988). Children's development in early remarriage. In E. M. Hetherington and J. D. Arasteh (Eds.), *The Impact of Divorce, Single Parenting and Stepparenting on Children* (279–298). Hillsdale, NJ: Erlbaum.

Bray, J. H. (1992). Family relationships and children's adjustment in clinical and nonclinical stepfather families. *Journal of Family Psychology*, 6, 60–68.

Bray, J. H., and Berger, S. H. (1993). Developmental issues in stepfamilies research project: Family relationships and parent-child interactions. *Journal of Family Psychology*, 7, 76–90.

Brody, E. M., Litvin, S. J., Albert, S. M., and Hoffman, C. J. (1994). Marital status of daughters and patterns of parent care. *Journal of Gerontology*, 49, S59–S103.

Brown, A. C., Green, R. J., and Druckman, J. (1990). A comparison of stepfamilies with and without child-focused problems. *American Journal of Orthopsychiatry*, 60, 556–566.

Bulcroft, K., Bulcroft, R., Hatch, L., and Borgatta, E. F. (1989). Antecedents and consequences of remarriage in later life. *Research on Aging*, 11, 82–106.

Burgoyne, C. B., and Morrison, V. (1997). Money in remarriage: Keeping things simple and separate. *Sociological Review*, 45, 363–394.

Buser, P. J. (1991). Introduction: The first generation of stepchildren. *Family Law Quarterly*, 25, 1–18.

Carr, C. J. (1994). *African–American and European–American Stepfamilies*. Unpublished doctoral dissertation, University of Miami.

Cicerelli, V. G. (1983). A comparison of helping behavior to elderly parents of adult children with intact and disrupted marriages. *Gerontologist*, 23, 619–625.

Clingempeel, W. G., and Segal, S. (1986). Stepparent-stepchild relationships and the psychological adjustment of children in stepmother and stepfather families. *Child Development*, 57, 474–484.

Clingempeel, W. G., Brand, E., and Segal, S. (1987). A multilevel-multivariable-multidevelopmental perspective for future research on stepfamilies. In K. Pasley and M. Ihinger-Tallman (Eds.), *Remarriage and Stepparenting: Current Research and Theory* (65–93). New York: Guilford.

Coleman, M., and Ganong, L. H. (1989). Financial management in stepfamilies. *Lifestyles: Family and Economic Issues*, 10, 217–232.

Coleman, M., Ganong, L. H., and Cable, S. M. (1997). Beliefs about women's intergenerational family obligations to provide support before and after divorce and remarriage. *Journal of Marriage and the Family*, 59, 165–176.

Cooney, T. M., Hutchinson, M. K., and Leather, D. M. (1995). Surviving the breakup? Predictors of parent–adult child relations after divorce. *Family Relations*, 44, 153–161.

Crosbie-Burnett, M. (1984). The centrality of the step relationship: A challenge to family theory and practice. *Family Relations, 33,* 459–464.

Crosbie-Burnett, M. (1988). Relationship between marital satisfaction and labor force participation in remarrying couples. *Family Perspective, 22,* 347–358.

Crosbie-Burnett, M. (1989). Impact of custody arrangement and family structure on remarriage. *Journal of Divorce, 13*(1), 1–16.

Crosbie-Burnett, M. (1991). Impact of joint versus sole custody and quality of the coparental relationship on adjustment of adolescents in remarried families. *Behavioral Sciences and the Law, 9,* 439–449.

Crosbie-Burnett, M. (1994). The interface between stepparent families and schools: Research, theory, policy, and practice. In K. Pasley and M. Ihinger–Tallman (Eds.), *Remarriage and Stepparenting: Current Research and Theory* (199–216). New York: Guilford.

Crosbie-Burnett, M., and Giles–Sims, J. (1991). Marital power in stepfather families: A test of normative–resource theory. *Journal of Family Psychology, 4,* 484–496.

Crosbie-Burnett, M., and Giles–Sims, J. (1994). Adolescent adjustment and stepparenting styles. *Family Relations, 43,* 394–399.

Crosbie-Burnett, M., and Helmbrecht, L. (1993). A descriptive empirical study of gay male stepfamilies. *Family Relations, 42,* 256–262.

Crosbie-Burnett, M., and Lewis, E. A. (1993). Use of African–American family structures and functioning to address the challenges of European–American postdivorce families. *Family Relations, 42,* 243–248.

Demo, D. H., and Acock, A. C. (1993). Family diversity and the division of domestic labor: How much have things really changed? *Family Relations, 42,* 323–331.

Duran-Aydintug, C., and Ihinger–Tallman, M. (1995). Law and stepfamilies. *Journal of Divorce and Remarriage, 21*(3–4), 169–192.

Fine, M. A. (1995). The clarity and content of the stepparent role: A review of the literature. *Journal of Divorce and Remarriage, 24,* 19–34.

Fine, M. A., and Fine, D. R. (1992). Recent changes in laws affecting stepfamilies: Suggestions for legal reform. *Family Relations, 41,* 334–340.

Fine, M. A., McKenry, P. C., Donnelly, B. W., and Voydanoff, P. (1992). Perceived adjustments of parents and children: Variations by family structure, race, and gender. *Journal of Marriage and the Family, 54,* 118–127.

Furstenberg, F. F., Jr., and Nord, C. W. (1985). Parenting apart: Patterns of childrearing after marital disruption. *Journal of Marriage and the Family, 47,* 893–904.

Ganong, L. H., and Coleman, M. (1988). Do mutual children cement bonds in stepfamilies? *Journal of Marriage and the Family, 50,* 687–698.

Ganong, L. H., and Coleman, M. (1993). An exploratory study of stepsibling relationships. *Journal of Divorce and Remarriage, 19,* 125–141.

Ganong, L. H., and Coleman, M. (1994). *Remarried Family Relationships.* Thousand Oaks, CA: Sage.

Garmezy, N. (1991). Resilience in children: Adaptation to negative life events and stressed environments. *Pediatric Annals, 20,* 459–466.

Guisinger, S., Cowan, P. A., and Schuldberg, D. (1989). Changing parent and spouse relations in the first years of remarriage of divorced fathers. *Journal of Marriage and the Family, 51,* 445–456.

Hanson, T. L., and McLanahan, S. S. (1996). Double jeopardy: Parental conflict and stepfamily outcomes for children. *Journal of Marriage and the Family, 58,* 141–154.

Henry, C. S., Ceglian, C. P., and Ostrander, D. L. (1993). The transition to step-grandparenthood. *Journal of Divorce and Remarriage, 19,* 25–44.

Henry, C. S., and Lovelace, S. G. (1995). Family resources and adolescent family life satisfaction in remarried family households. *Journal of Family Issues, 16,* 765–786.

Hermansen, D. (1993). *Predictors of Remarital Stability and Satisfaction.* Unpublished doctoral dissertation, University of Miami.

Hetherington, E. M., and Clingempeel, W. G. (1992). Coping with marital transitions: A family systems perspective. *Monographs of the Society for Research in Child Development, 57*(2–3, Serial No. 227), 1–242.

Hetherington, E. M., Cox, M., and Cox, R. (1985). Long–term effects of divorce and remarriage on the adjustment of children. *Journal of the American Academy of Child Psychiatry, 24,* 518–530.

Hobart, C. W. (1988). The family system in remarriage: An exploratory study. *Journal of Marriage and the Family, 50,* 649–661.

Ishii–Kuntz, M., and Coltrane, S. (1992). Remarriage, stepparenting, and household labor. *Journal of Family Issues, 13,* 215–233.

Jacobson, D. S. (1995). Critical interactive events and child adjustment in the stepfamily: A linked family system. In D. K. Huntley (Ed.), *Understanding Stepfamilies: Implications for*

Assessment and Treatment (73–86). Alexandria, VA: American Counseling Association.

Litvin, S. J., Albert, S. M., Brody, E. M., and Hoffman, C. (1995). Marital status, competing demands, and role priorities of parent–caring daughters. *Journal of Applied Gerontology, 14,* 372–390.

Marsiglio, W. (1992). Stepfathers with minor children living at home: Parenting perceptions and relationship quality *Journal of Family Issues,* 13, 195–214.

Marks, N. F. (1995). Midlife marital status differences in social support relationships with adult children and psychological well–being. *Journal of Family Issues, 16,* 5–28.

Mason, M. A., and Simon, D. W. (1995). The ambiguous stepparent: Federal legislation in search of a model. *Family Law Quarterly, 29,* 445–482.

Morrison, K., and Thompson–Guppy, A. (1985). Cinderella's stepmother syndrome. *Canadian Journal of Psychiatry, 30,* 521–529.

Palisi, B. J., Orleans, M., Caddell, D., and Korn, B. (1991). Adjustment to stepfatherhood: The effects of marital history and relations with children. *Journal of Divorce and Remarriage, 14,* 89–106.

Pasley, K., and Ihinger–Tallman, M. (1990). Remarriage in later adulthood: Correlates of perceptions of family adjustment. *Family Perspective, 24,* 263–274.

Pasley, K., Sandras, E., and Edmondson, M. E. (1994). The effects of financial management strategies on quality of family life in remarriage. *Journal of Family Economic Issues, 15,* 53–70.

Pill, C. J. (1990). Stepfamilies: Redefining the family. *Family Relations, 39,* 186–193.

Pink, J. E., and Wampler, K. S. (1985). Problem areas in stepfamilies: Cohesion, adaptability, and the stepfather–adolescent relationship. *Family Relations, 34,* 327–335.

Ramsey, S. H. (1994). Stepparents and the law: A nebulous status and a need for reform. In K. Pasley and M. Ihinger–Tallman (Eds.), *Stepfamilies: Issues in Theory, Research, and Practice* (217–238). Westport, CT: Greenwood.

Roberts, T. W., and Price, S. J. (1987). Instant families: Divorced mothers marry never–married men. *Journal of Divorce, 11*(1), 71–92.

Rosenberg, E. B., and Hajal, F. (1985). Stepsibling relationships in remarried families. *Social Casework, 66,* 287–292.

Sager, C. J., Brown, H. S., Crohn, H., Engel, T., Rodstein, E., and Walker, E. (1983). *Treating the Remarried Family.* New York: Brunner/Mazel.

Skopin, A. R., Newman, B. M. and McKenry, P. C. (1993). Influences on the quality of the stepfather-adolescent relationship. *Journal of Divorce and Remarriage, 17,* 181–196.

Strother, J., and Jacobs, E. (1984). Adolescent stress as it relates to stepfamily living: Implications for school counselors. *The School Counselor, 32,* 97–103.

Vinick, B. H. (1978). Remarriage in old age. *Journal of Geriatric Psychiatry, 11,* 75–77.

Vinick, B. H. (1983). Remarriage by the elderly. *Medical Aspects of Human Sexuality, 17,* 111–116.

Visher, E. B., and Visher, J. S. (1982). Children in stepfamilies. *Psychiatric Annals, 12,* 832–841.

Visher, E. B., and Visher, J. S. (1988). Treating families and problems associated with remarriage and step relationships. In C. S. Chilman, E. W. Nunnally, and F. M. Cox (Eds.), *Families in Trouble: Vol. 5. Variant Family Forms* (222–244). Beverly Hills, CA: Sage.

Waldren, T. E., Bell, N. J., Peek, C. W., and Sorrell, G. (1990). Cohesion and adaptability in postdivorce remarried and first married families: Relationships with family stress and coping styles. *Journal of Divorce and Remarriage, 14,* 13–28.

Walsh, W. (1992). Twenty major issues in remarriage families. *Journal of Counseling and Development, 70,* 709–715.

Weston, C. A., and Macklin, E. D. (1990). The relationship between former–spousal contact and remarital satisfaction in stepfather families. *Journal of Divorce and Remarriage, 14*(2), 25–47.

White, L. K. (1992). The effect of parental divorce and remarriage on parental support for adult children. *Journal of Family Issues, 13,* 234–250.

White, L. K., and Booth, A. (1985). The quality and stability of remarriages: The role of stepchildren. *American Sociological Review, 50,* 689–698.

White, L. K., and Riedmann, A. (1992). When the Brady Bunch grows up: Step/half- and full-sibling relationships in adulthood. *Journal of Marriage and the Family, 54,* 197–208.

Whitsett, D. P., and Land, H. M. (1992). Role strain, coping, and marital satisfaction of stepparents. *Families in Society: The Journal of Contemporary Human Services, 73*(2), 79–92.

Wright, J. M. (1998). *Lesbian Step Families: An Ethnography of Love.* New York: Haworth.

Wu, Z., and Balakrishnan, T. R. (1994). Cohabitation after marital disruption in Canada. *Journal of Marriage and the Family, 56,* 723–734. ✦

Chapter 4
Gay/Lesbian Families Over the Life Course

Katherine R. Allen
Virginia Polytechnic Institute
and State University

Karen L. Wilcox
Ohio University

Where to begin discussing family variations by sexual orientation diversity is somewhat arbitrary, since families can have biological, marital, adoptive, and chosen ties. Potentially, any family can be considered a gay or lesbian family because any family is likely to have at least one member who is gay, lesbian, or bisexual whether now or at some time in the future (Allen and Demo 1995).

The life course perspective provides a useful framework for understanding the influence of normative and non-normative transitions on individuals and families (Demo and Allen 1996). It also offers a more dynamic approach to the earlier concept of static stages based on marital and parental transitions and allows us to analyze variability and complexity in families. It was not until recently that family scholars began to seriously consider sexual orientation. To introduce the influence of sexual orientation on the life course of individuals and families, we begin with vignettes of families and relationships in which sexual orientation matters.

Timmy is 8 years old and lives with his two moms. He has just found out that one of his moms' best friends, to whom he is very close, is also a lesbian, but he's never seen Annie with a partner. He asks his moms, "How can you be gay if you don't have a partner?"

A woman greets a colleague at a professional meeting. She blurts out, "Mary, I just have to tell you that I'm getting a divorce from my husband because I've fallen in love with another woman." Instead of the shock or rejection Mary anticipates, her friend smiles broadly and says, "Oh, how wonderful! My daughter is a lesbian, too!"

Charlie is a retired minister living in a small southern town. Although deeply satisfied with his relationships with his children and grandchildren, he has watched his friends cope with their children's divorces, drug abuse, and deaths. He is thankful he has not had to deal with anything like that. On his 85th birthday, the newspaper writes a story about Charlie and his family. A few days later, Charlie's grandson, Chet, a promising lawyer in town, comes out as a gay man. Chet's parents seek Charlie's advice. How can they deal with a gay son in the context of their religion? How can they come to grips with loving their son while keeping faith with what they have been taught? Charlie is deeply perplexed by this news, although he has to admit that he always thought his grandson might be gay. He had just pushed it out of his mind. Now he faces a choice of whether to uphold the tenets he has always preached, which would ultimately lead to rejecting his grandson and his grandson's "lifestyle," or take an uncertain road toward trying to understand his grandson in a different light.

These vignettes and those that follow are true stories based on the research we have conducted or the experiences of people we know. These stories indicate the vast diversity among families in which there are gay, lesbian, and bisexual members. These vignettes provide examples of the complexity involved in a discussion of sexual orientation from a family life span perspective. It is important to study sexual orientation because increasingly, our society is bringing this issue into the public arena. Each year, more and more young adults "come out" to their parents (Savin-Williams and Esterberg in press), and gay and lesbian issues are more visible in the media.

In this chapter, we begin by discussing life course issues affecting individuals and families as a way to locate the discussion of sexual orientation diversity across time. Next, we examine families in which a young adult comes out to parents and family members, followed by a discussion of partnership and parenting as central issues in the young- to middle-adult years. Fourth, we discuss families in which gay or lesbian experiences are relevant to older adults. Finally, we present future directions for research and interventions relevant to gay and lesbian families.

Life Course Issues Across Time

Regardless of age, several issues surface as individuals attempt to deal with their same-sex attraction and sexual orientation. First, heterocentrism and homophobia are ever-present. *Heterocentrism* is the belief in and practice of valuing heterosexuality as the norm (Herek, Kimmel, Amaro, and Melton 1991). Therefore, anything that differs from heterosexuality is treated as subordinate to or deviant from the norm, and heterosexuality is taken as the assumed standard against which all sexual orientations and gender identities are compared. It holds that men and women can and should be attracted and sexually connected only to each other. The implications of heterocentrism are that legal marriage is reserved only for opposite-sex partners and that partners who are gay and lesbian are, in the legal sense, strangers to each other. *Homophobia* is the irrational fear and hatred of gay, lesbian, and bisexual people and is based on stereotype and myth (Blumenfeld 1992; Pharr 1988). Homophobia is a prejudice that is internalized by individuals through child-rearing practices and passed down intergenerationally. It is publicly supported by laws and de facto discrimination that lead to unequal treatment for lesbian, gay, and bisexual individuals and their families.

Second, identity formation is a component of the self that necessitates continual exploration for individuals of all ages. As individuals encounter realizations about self-identification as gay, lesbian, bisexual, or heterosexual, they make choices about how to act, or not act, on their discoveries. Sexual orientation is a complex mix of many dimensions, including sexual attraction, sexual behavior, sexual fantasies, emotional preference, social preference, self-identification, lifestyle choice, and changes over time (Klein 1990).

Third, the coming out process is a vital component for adolescents, young adults, middle-aged adults, and older adults. Age cohort has been found to influence the expectations and acceptability of coming out, as the gay and lesbian rights movement has increasingly made this process less difficult (Allen 1997; Herdt and Boxer 1993; Quam and Whitford 1992; Savin-Williams 1998). Motives and fears considered in the coming-out process at any age include a desire for honesty with self and others, fear of rejection, presence or lack of support, acceptance of self, and fear of stigmatization and prejudice (Ben-Ari 1995; Quam and Whitford 1992; Savin-Williams 1998). Regardless of the strategy, coming out is not an event but rather a life-long process (Allen 1995). In Rhoads' (1995) two-year ethnographic study of the coming-out experiences of gay and bisexual college men, one student described coming out as "something that has a beginning but never really ends" (69). Another participant commented that there are "different levels of 'outness' that people reach over time" (69).

Fourth, many studies show that the most feared challenge for lesbians and gay men is telling their families (Ben-Ari 1995; Boxer, Cook, and Herdt 1991; D'Augelli 1991; Savin-Williams 1998). The reaction of family members, especially parents, plays a significant role in the person's present and future relationships with his or her family (Ben-Ari 1995; Savin-Williams 1998; Savin-Williams and Dube 1998; Strommen 1989). Social support systems play an important part in the development of gay and lesbian identities (D'Augelli 1991; Herdt and Boxer 1993;

Weston 1991). Quam and Whitford (1992), for example, demonstrate that integration into a social environment offering support through service and political organizations helps older adults adjust to the aging process.

Fifth, the methodological issue of sampling cuts across research at all stages of the life course. In order to gather empirical evidence on the lives of lesbians, gay men, and bisexuals, researchers need access to diverse populations and their families (Harry 1983). Therefore, information about sexual orientation and family relations needs to be integrated into general family research (Allen and Demo 1995; Quam and Whitford 1992; Savin-Williams 1998). Sexual orientation is a feature of all human experience, not simply a concern for gays and lesbians; everyone has a sexual orientation.

Adolescents and Young Adults: Identity and Coming Out

Sarah is a sophomore in college. She has always dated men. Now she finds herself in a friendship with Kate and realizes she is attracted to her. She is confused by her feelings and anxiously confides to another friend that she is questioning her sexual orientation.

Identity Formation

During adolescence and young adulthood, a developmental focus is identity exploration (D'Augelli 1991). This can be a difficult period, as questions and challenges regarding becoming independent often conflict with parental expectations (Herdt 1989). Individuals may hereto deal with the recognition of feelings of attraction toward same-sex individuals, decisions about ways to deal with sexual orientation among family and friends, and the potential consequences of sharing this information.

Social stigmas and prejudice make it difficult to resolve the conflict between what a young person feels and what he or she has been taught regarding sexual orientation. Allport (1958) describes prejudice as a negative attitude based on overgeneralization or error. As youths struggle with issues of identity formation, they explore and consider

how claiming an identity as gay, lesbian, or bisexual may affect their relationships with family, friends, and the larger community.

Coming Out to Family and Friends

Joe has decided to come out to his parents. He writes them a letter, saying he needs to reveal to them who he really is and tells them about his relationship with another man. He asks his parents to try to understand that he cannot hide his sexual orientation from them any longer. After a few days, his mother calls him and tells him that he is her son and she will always love him, no matter what. He anxiously awaits what his father has to say.

Although more adolescents and young adults are coming out to their parents, the process is still difficult. Coming out of the closet to parents can be troublesome because young people often fear their parents will reject them. This fear may result in a delay of disclosure until the person feels a sense of detachment from the family of origin. Many young adults report that their recognition of feelings of same-sex attraction and self-identification as gay, lesbian, or bisexual occurred during early to late adolescence, yet they did not act on their feelings or disclose their identity to their family until they had left home (Ben-Ari 1995; Martin 1982; Savin-Williams 1998).

The initial disclosure of gay or lesbian sexual identity is usually to a close friend who is trusted to offer support (D'Augelli and Hershberger 1993). It can be a relief to realize that someone is available to talk to about this issue; the individual experiences a new sense of comfort about the ability to be himself or herself.

The process of coming out can take many forms. Young adults may disclose their sexual orientation through face-to-face conversations with one or both parents, by writing a letter, or by dropping hints through the language used in discussing relationships with friends. Disclosure to mothers usually occurs prior to disclosure to fathers (Savin-Williams 1998). There is a sense that mothers are more understanding and accepting than fathers. Initial reactions of parents to their child's disclosure often include feelings of responsibility, blame, and guilt, as well as a mixture of shock, disappointment, and anger.

Savin-Williams and Dube (1998) compare parental reactions to a son or daughter disclosing their gay, lesbian, or bisexual orientation to Kübler-Ross' (1969) stages of accepting one's own death. In a way, parents may feel they have experienced a death through the loss of their hopes and dreams for their child to follow a normative life course, which means heterosexual marriage and parenthood. The developmental model of parental reactions that Savin-Williams and Dube present includes shock, denial and isolation, anger, bargaining, depression, and acceptance. Not all parents will experience all of these stages, and they may experience them in a different order and to differing degrees, yet components of each stage are likely to occur. Empirical evidence is needed to test the mourning/loss stages as well as the differences between parents' initial reaction to a son or daughter coming out to them and ways the parent-child relationship changes or remains the same.

Vulnerabilities of Coming Out or Being Out

A prevalent fear about coming out is the potential exclusion from family and friendship networks. Ben-Ari (1995) found that the perception of being rejected was the greatest fear in coming out to parents, while the most frequent motive to do so was a need not to hide or live a lie. In addition, during adolescence, when acceptance by peers is a major concern, the anticipation of being stigmatized and excluded from peer groups is a frightening reality and deterrent.

Risks that lesbian and gay youth face after disclosure include verbal and physical abuse, poor school performance, running away from home, substance abuse, criminal activity, and suicide attempts (Savin-Williams 1994). The death of Matthew Shepherd in the fall of 1998 exemplified the threat of victimization for gay and lesbian individuals. In fact, victimization of lesbians and gays has been consistently found to be the most common form of bias-related violence, whether the victim was known or merely suspected of being lesbian or gay (Berrill

1990; Comstock 1991; Herek 1989). In other words, people can be beaten up just for looking gay. When Pilkington and D'Augelli (1995) surveyed 194 lesbian, gay, and bisexual youths between the ages of 15 and 21, they found that most had experienced some form of victimization because of their sexual orientation. The researchers examined the social contexts in which anti-lesbian/gay victimization occurred and found that no social environment (family, school, work, community) was free from risk of harm.

Another risk for adolescents is suicide. The National Center for Health Statistics (1993) reports that suicide is the third leading cause of mortality for adolescents in the United States. Lesbian, gay, and bisexual youths have been identified as being at an elevated risk (Remafedi 1994); approximately one-third have attempted suicide (Herdt and Boxer 1993). Feelings of isolation and a struggle with the socialization that "homosexuality is wrong" leads to considering desperate measures to escape dealing with same-sex desires. The number of gay and lesbian youth who commit suicide may be underestimated, because many suicides have not disclosed their sexual orientation (Hershberger, Pilkington, and D'Augelli 1997).

Support Networks

Teresa, a heterosexual single woman, is teaching a course on family relationships. During class, she asks students to break into groups to discuss the strengths and challenges of different family types. In the group assigned to discuss gay families, two students say that they can't think of any strengths because they do not think being gay or lesbian is right. Teresa reminds the students of the readings on children's experience of living with diversity and the positive impact of understanding how oppression and opportunity structure life experience for others. She confronts the students' prejudice with empirical evidence about gay families.

Social support is needed from family and friends as youth continue to search for accurate information and ways to create understanding about themselves and others. Availability of accurate information about lesbians and gay men is critical to breaking down stereotypes that lead to discrimination against gays and lesbians. The values held by family members play a vital role in their reactions to, and support of, the disclosure that a son, daughter, sister, or brother is gay or lesbian (Strommen 1989). Youths report many benefits in disclosing their sexual orientation, including a greater sense of freedom and liberation, a sense of pride in being honest with oneself, and genuine acceptance from family members (Savin-Williams 1998).

Adult role models provide a more safe and comfortable environment for lesbian and gay youth (Martin 1982). Therefore, it is important for adolescents and young adults to be familiar with gay and lesbian adults. Doing so will encourage identity formation by modeling a variety of successful, happy, and fulfilled gay men and lesbians.

Understanding the attitudes of peers and school personnel toward gay men, lesbians, and bisexuals can play a significant role in creating a comfortable space that enables members of a community to thrive. In a study of college students, Simoni (1996) found that being younger, having less education, being male, and having less-educated parents were associated with negative attitudes toward lesbians and gay men. When Engstrom and Sedlacek (1997) studied a sample of university students, they found that male students, more than female students, expressed more intensive prejudicial attitudes toward gay men than toward lesbians.

Telljohann and Price (1993) conducted a qualitative study of 120 gay and lesbian youths (ages 14 to 21) from eight youths centers across the United States. The results of this study indicated that support within the school community was weak or nonexistent. The researcher's suggestions included developing support groups for gay and lesbian students, developing a referral network within the community, and taking a stronger stand against discrimination and abuse through education and policy.

Gay Men and Lesbians as Partners and Parents

Same-Sex Relationship Development

McWhirter and Mattison (1984) proposed a six-stage model to describe relationship development among gay male couples; Clunis and Green (1988) applied this model to lesbian partnerships. In the McWhirter and Mattison (1984) model, stage 1, *blending*, occurs in the first year. At this stage couples are coming together, and are intensely engaged in preoccupation with and longing for the partner. Sexual activity is high. The second stage, *nesting*, occurs over the next few years, characterized by building a home together, compatibility, and increasing ambivalence about the relationship. The *maintaining* stage comes next, in the fourth and fifth years of the relationship, in which the individual partners begin to express dissatisfactions with their union and must deal with their conflicts. The fourth stage, *building*, occurs from 6 to 10 years, with couples establishing independent habits and individual productivity. The *releasing* stage corresponds with midlife developmental issues, and occurs from years 11 to 20. It is characterized by a renewed sense of trust on the one hand yet taking each other for granted on the other. The final stage, *renewing*, comes after 20 or more years of living together and is characterized by financial and emotional security, the restoration of romance, health and loss issues, and reminiscence about the history of the relationship. Kurdek and associates (1994) found this model to be applicable to lesbian, gay, and heterosexual couples.

Partnerships Among Gay Men and Lesbians

Susan and Jane are raising Susan's son, Nick, by a previous marriage. After several years, Jane decides to use donor insemination to conceive a child. When their daughter, Tina, is born, Susan, as the primary breadwinner, attempts to add Tina to her health insurance policy at work, but her request is denied.

There are no definitive data on the number of gay and lesbian couples, but past surveys indicate that between 45 percent and 80 percent of lesbians and between 40 percent and 60 percent of gay men are involved in a committed romantic relationship (Kurdek 1994). In his review of 236 heterosexually married, 66 gay cohabiting, and 51 heterosexual cohabiting couples, Kurdek (1998) concluded that gay and lesbian unions have a great deal in common with heterosexual marriages. He found that the strength of five dimensions of relationship quality (intimacy, autonomy, equality, constructive problem solving, and barriers to leaving), linked to two relationship outcomes (relationship satisfaction and relationship dissolution), was equivalent among the three types of couples. Gay and lesbian couples reported more autonomy, fewer barriers to leaving, and more frequent relationship dissolution. Lesbian couples also reported more intimacy and equality in their relationships. As Schwartz (1994) found in her research on heterosexual and gay and lesbian couples, same-sex couples tend to follow a model of best friendship, rather than the role complementation that is common in heterosexual partnerships (Schwartz 1994).

One issue connected to relationship stability for gay and lesbian partners is lack of legal protection. Although many gay and lesbian couples have made long-term commitments to each other, and many celebrate their union in a *commitment ceremony* in the presence of family and friends (Sherman 1992), no state as yet legally recognizes same-sex marriage. The National Defense of Marriage Act (DOMA), signed into law in 1995, defines marriage as a union only between one man and one woman and bans federal acknowledgment of marriages between a man and a man or a woman and a woman (Gallagher 1996). Now 38 states have a DOMA law.

The fundamental right to marry, regardless of gender, is central to the case for same-sex marriage (Editors of the *Harvard Law Review* 1990). Gays and lesbians are denied equality and civility when they are denied this basic right (Eskridge 1996). Zicklin (1995) summarized the legal and financial advantages of state-sanctioned marriage denied to same-sex partners: the right of inheritance if a spouse dies without a will, Social Security survivor benefits, inclusion of mar-

ried spouse on a partner's health insurance, immunity from having to testify against a spouse in a criminal proceedings, residency for a foreign spouse of a U.S. citizen, and the right to visit one's spouse in government-run institutions, such as prisons and hospitals.

Gay and Lesbian Parenting

George, a junior in high school, has been raised by his biological mother and her partner since he was 3 years old. During civics class, his teacher comments that allowing lesbians and gay men to legally marry would destroy the institution of marriage. A student in the class states that children should be raised by a mother and a father because they need the opportunity to have both a male and female role model. Otherwise, they may turn out to be gay or lesbian themselves. George is angry about these uninformed views and decides to share his experience as a child of lesbian parents.

Rohrbaugh (1992) identified three types of family structures: blended families, single-parent families, and couples having children together. Because gay fathers and lesbian mothers often became parents in the context of a heterosexual marriage, blended families are probably the most common type of family structure. Given the difficulty gay men face in obtaining custody of children, most gay male stepfamilies are typically noncustodial households; children are not as likely to live with their fathers as with their mothers (Crosbie-Burnett and Helmbrecht 1993). During the 1970s it became apparent that many gay men and lesbians were intent on having children in the context of gay partnerships (Pies 1988). Donor insemination is one solution for lesbians who desire to get pregnant.

Lesbian and gay families are increasing. In their 1990 publication, the Editors of the *Harvard Law Review* concluded that "approximately three million gay men and lesbians in the United States are parents, and between eight and ten million children are raised in gay or lesbian households" (119). There is every reason to believe that a "lesbian baby boom" is occurring, given the unprecedented number of lesbians having children in the context of their partnerships

(Patterson 1995). These families are changing the definition of family from one based on law to one based on emotional bonds and family ties (Stacey 1996; Weston 1991).

In her review of 12 studies comparing children of lesbian or gay parents to children of heterosexual parents on gender identity, gender role behavior, and sexual orientation, Patterson (1992) demonstrated that children's development in gay or lesbian families does not differ from children's development in families headed by heterosexual parents. She also concluded that children of lesbian and gay parents have normal and satisfactory relationships with peers and adults of both sexes. Instead of the pursuit of differences, with the heterosexist assumption that children automatically fare worse in gay or lesbian households, the empirical evidence is that attention, love, and support are far more important ingredients in successful child rearing than sexual orientation is. As with other studies of family diversity, what really matters for children is "somebody has got to be crazy about that kid" (Bronfenbrenner and Weiss, 1983, 398).

Gay and lesbian families offer many strengths for children and parents. Various researchers have pointed to four major opportunities for creating a positive environment for child rearing. First, by growing up in a multicultural environment, children learn to respect, empathize with, and tolerate the multicultural environments in which others live (Laird 1993). Second, children can benefit from observing adults who practice more androgynous gender roles and socialization practices (Blumstein and Schwartz 1983; Schwartz and Rutter 1998). Third, by living in an intentional family, children come to understand that families are based not only on biological or genetic relationships but also on love, self-definition, and choice (Laird 1993; Weston 1991). Finally, as gay cultural centers emerge and become increasingly visible, children of gay and lesbian parents experience strong ties in the gay community that can deepen and support their family relationships (Allen 1997; Herdt 1992).

Gay and Lesbian Issues for Older Adults

Steven had been married for 40 years. Despite the success of his marriage, he always felt something was missing. One day, he met another man at a business dinner. Afterward, whenever he listened to the radio, his thoughts went immediately to this man. He realized he had never thought about his wife in such a romantic way. He found the feelings so intense that he could no longer deny them. Steven realized he desired this other man, and he and his wife agreed to divorce. Now in a committed relationship with another man, he feels fulfilled for the first time in his life.

Older Gay Men and Lesbians

It is difficult to estimate the number of older gay men and lesbians because there is a lack of a clear definition of who is gay or lesbian (Berger 1984), and not all older lesbians and gay men are willing to reveal their sexual identity (Poor 1982). In addition, the terms that older lesbians and gay men use to describe themselves are not always the same terms used today. When Kehoe (1988) asked a participant in her study of 100 lesbians over age 65, "What word do you prefer to use to describe your emotional and/or sexual preference?" (46). The response was "Anything but lesbian" (46).

The differences for older gays and lesbians are more closely related to generational issues (Adelman 1991; Cruikshank 1991; Kochman 1993). Choices that may seem adaptive for one generation may be maladaptive for another generation (Adelman 1991). Younger members of the gay and lesbian community who are activists should not look down on the choice of invisibility made by older members. They should understand that fewer options were available for older generations, and in the past the choice of coming out carried a greater risk than it does today (Faderman 1991). Indeed, until the mid-1970s, homosexuality was classified as a mental disorder by the American Psychiatric Association and the American Psychological Association (Herek et al. 1991).

In studies of older men and women, little attention was paid to gays and lesbians until the 1970s, and research has focused almost exclusively on gay men. The exclusion of older lesbians may be because of what Kehoe (1986) terms the "triply invisible minority" as a result of gender, age, and sexual orientation.

The popular stereotype of older lesbians and gay men is very negative. Older gay men are portrayed as depressed, lonely, oversexed, and living without the support of family and friends (Kelly 1977), while older lesbians are portrayed as lonely, unattractive, and unemotional (Berger 1982). To the contrary, studies conducted with older gay men have shown them to be well adjusted, self-accepting, and adapting well to the aging process (Berger 1982; Francher and Henkin 1973; Friend 1980; Kelly 1977; Kimmel 1978; Weinberg 1970). In addition, studies of older lesbians have shown them to be happy and well adjusted to their lives and the aging process (Martin and Lyon 1979; Raphael and Robinson 1980).

Friend (1991) developed a model of identity formation for older gays and lesbians based on opposite ends of a continuum of potential responses to heterosexism. At one end of the continuum are those individuals whose identities conform to the stereotypes and exhibit internalized homophobia—i.e., "stereotypic older lesbian and gay people." He describes those who respond to heterosexism by reconstructing a positive and affirmative sense of self as "affirmative older lesbian and gay people." The group identified as "passing older lesbian and gay people" are characterized by having a strong investment in either passing as nongay or nonlesbian, or not appearing to be stereotypically gay or lesbian.

Difficulties faced by older gays and lesbians are highly related to the stigma associated with being gay or lesbian. In his study of older gay men, Vacha (1985) found that "the discrimination that comes with aging is compounded by the discrimination that comes with being a homosexual" (78). Respondents in Adelman's (1991) study who had not disclosed their sexual orientation to co-workers felt the need to work harder and achieve more because they were gay. This is a common method of adapting to being a member of a stigmatized group (Goffman 1963). Some authors also suggest that strategies developed in order to deal with being a member of a stigmatized group transfer to coping with the stigma due to aging (Francher and Henkin 1973; Friend 1980).

The general concerns of older gays and lesbians are the same as those of all seniors: health care, transportation, satisfactory housing, availability of jobs and job training, retirement, opportunity to make meaningful use of leisure time, body changes, loss of friends, lack of consistent mobility, and being old in a youth-oriented society (Kochman 1993; Quam and Whitford 1992; Raphael and Meyer 1993). Quam and Whitford (1992) asked a question in their study about whether or not being gay or lesbian helped one adjust to the process of aging. Of the 80 individuals surveyed, 68 percent believed that being gay or lesbian was helpful because (a) having a gay or lesbian identity allowed them to accept themselves as they are, (b) they had a supportive community, (c) the stress of being in a sexual and social minority helped strengthen their beliefs and mental health, and (d) their status forced them to plan more carefully for their future.

An older lesbian participant in Adelman's (1991) study stated that "I don't think anybody, if they cannot accept with good grace whatever they are, can be happy" (22). The compilation of stories in *Long Time Passing: Lives of Older Lesbians* (Adelman 1986) substantiate her findings that the most important factor for determining psychological well-being for older lesbians is the level of homophobia in society and in oneself.

Older Parents of Adult Gay Children

Older parents of adult gay and lesbian children confront unexpected challenges when a child is gay. Socialization for parenting in adulthood does not prepare individuals to understand or accept homosexuality (Allen, Demo, Walker, and Acock 1996). Having a gay, lesbian, or bisexual child is a non-normative experience (Filler and Suitor 1991), and is certainly not how most parents expect their children to "turn out" (Ryff, Schmutte, and Lee 1996).

Research on older parents of gay children is practically nonexistent. Allen and Wilcox (1996) attended monthly meetings of support groups for parents, families, and friends of lesbians and gay men and conducted in-depth interviews with 15 participants. They found that the process of coming to terms with having a gay child involved several transitions. A major transition was moving away from denial or complacency and toward political involvement and advocacy. Parents defined their current activism as linked to earlier involvement in civil rights for other minority groups. Following the initial experience of discomfort and struggle, parents eventually became mobilized because of the discrimination and social prejudice their children faced, and they were motivated by love for their children. Parents in this study also recognized they had dealt with stigma in the past, as in the case of a father with a gay brother, a mother raised by her father since infancy, and a man whose father was disabled in a farming accident. Parents learned what was really important in their families, such as "supporting my child" and facing unresolved issues in their own lives.

Conclusions

Researchers agree that there is no way to precisely identify the number of people who are gay and lesbian because of difficulties in conducting surveys and the ways in which respondents distort private information. Yet most researchers begin with the assumption, originally proposed by Kinsey and his colleagues (1948, 1953), that approximately 10 percent of the population at any one time is gay or lesbian (McWhirter, Sanders, and Reinisch 1990). In addition, the estimated 6 to 8 million gay or lesbian adults who are parents of dependent children (Editors of the *Harvard Law Review* 1990) is expected to increase (Benkov 1994).

A great deal of research about sexual orientation is needed for all aspects of the life course. Only three areas comprise our knowledge base to date about gay and lesbian families: same-sex partnerships and ro-

mantic relationships; lesbian mothers (and to a lesser degree) gay fathers; and the psychological development and social adjustment of children of lesbian and gay parents (Laird 1993). We know very little about the multiple life course contexts of families in which sexual orientation is relevant (Allen and Demo 1995; Demo and Allen 1996). Although research is accumulating on gay and lesbian partnerships, we need to know much more about the developmental course of these relationships (Peplau and Cochran 1990).

More attention must be given to the special concerns of older gays and lesbians. We need longitudinal studies of gay aging, as well as studies that include people of different racial and economic backgrounds. Future research should include people who differ in gender role behavior and appearance to learn about whether or not masculine-appearing women and effeminate-appearing men experience stigma differently than those who can pass for heterosexual (Cruikshank 1991). Comparisons are also needed with parents of adult children in other stigmatized groups. For example, how does having a gay adult child compare to other non-normative life course events and transitions, such as having an adult child in a racially mixed marriage (Allen et al. 1996)?

Honoring the uniqueness and diversity of gay and lesbian families must be a priority for people of all ages. It is crucial to gain a more complete understanding of the struggles and triumphs of all families, including those with gay and lesbian members. Creating a welcoming dialogue to highlight the contributions of gay and lesbian families gives voice to a population that has much to give to, and receive from, a just society.

Discussion Questions

1. What challenges do gay and lesbian families face?

2. What are heterocentrism, heterosexism, and homophobia? How are they related? Why are they so prevalent? How can they be counteracted?

3. What obligation does society have to address proactively the violence against gays, lesbians, and bisexuals, including the high suicide rate among teens dealing with being or feeling gay?

4. What are some of the strengths of gay and lesbian families?

5. How would the world be different if gay, lesbian, and bisexual families had the same rights and privileges as heterosexual families?

Glossary

Coming Out Publicly declaring one's sexual orientation.

DOMA (Defense of Marriage Act) Federal law passed in 1995 that defines marriage as a union between one man and one woman and bans federal acknowledgment of marriages between a man and a man and a woman and a woman.

Heterocentrism The belief and the practice of valuing heterosexuality as the norm.

Homophobia Irrational fear and hatred of gay, lesbian, and bisexual people based on stereotype and myth.

PFLAG Organization of Parents, Families, and Friends of Lesbians and Gays. Largest support group of its kind.

Suggested Readings

Bernstein, R. A. (1995). *Straight Parents/Gay Children: Keeping Families Together*. New York: Thunder's Mouth Press.

Eskridge, W. N., Jr. (1996). *The Case for Same-Sex Marriage: From Sexual Liberty to Civilized Commitment*. New York: Free Press.

Rafkin, L. (Ed.). (1996). *Different Daughters: A Book by Mothers of Lesbians* (2nd ed.). Pittsburgh, PA: Cleis Press.

Savin-Williams, R. C., and Cohen, K. M. (Eds.). (1996). *The Lives of Lesbians, Gays, and Bisexuals: Children to Adults*. Fort Worth, TX: Harcourt Brace.

Bibliography

Adelman, M. (Ed.). (1986). *Long Time Passing: Lives of Older Lesbians*. Boston: Alyson.

Adelman, M. (1991). Stigma, gay lifestyles, and adjustment to aging: A study of later-life gay men and lesbians. In J. A. Lee (Ed.), *Gay Midlife and Maturity* (7–32). New York: Harrington Park.

Allen, K. R. (1995). Opening the classroom closet: Sexual orientation and self–disclosure. *Family Relations, 44,* 136–141.

Allen, K. R. (1997). Lesbian and gay families. In T. Arendell (Ed.), *Contemporary Parenting: Challenges and Issues* (196–218). Thousand Oaks, CA: Sage.

Allen, K. R., and Demo, D. H. (1995). The families of lesbians and gay men: A new frontier in family research. *Journal of Marriage and the Family, 57,* 111–127.

Allen, K. R., Demo, D. H., Walker, A. J., and Acock, A. C. (1996, November). *Older Parents of Gay and Lesbian Adult Children*. Paper presented at the annual meeting of the National Council on Family Relations, Kansas City, MO.

Allen, K. R., and Wilcox, K. W. (1996, November). *Becoming an Activist: Older Parents of Adult Gay Children*. Paper presented at the annual meeting of the Gerontological Society of America, Washington, DC.

Allport, G. (1958). *The Nature of Prejudice*. Garden City, NY: Doubleday.

Ben-Ari, A. (1995). The discovery that an offspring is gay: Parents', gay men's, and lesbians' perspectives. *Journal of Homosexuality, 30,* 89–112.

Benkov, L. (1994). *Reinventing the Family: The Emerging Story of Lesbian and Gay Parents*. New York: Crown.

Berger, R. M. (1982). The unseen minority: Older gays and lesbians. *Social Work, 27,* 236–242.

Berger, R. M. (1984). Realities of gay and lesbian aging. *Social Work, 29,* 57–62.

Berrill, K. (1990). Anti–gay violence and victimization in the United States: An overview. *Journal of Interpersonal Violence, 5,* 274–294.

Blumenfeld, W. J. (Ed.). (1992). *Homophobia: How We All Pay the Price*. Boston: Beacon.

Blumstein, P., and Schwartz, P. (1983). *American Couples*. New York: William Morrow.

Boxer, A. M., Cook, J. A., and Herdt, G. (1991). Double jeopardy: Identity transitions and parent–child relations among gay and lesbian youth. In K. Pillemer and K. McCartney (Eds.), *Parent–child Relations Throughout Life* (59–92). Hillsdale, NJ: Erlbaum.

Bronfenbrenner, U., and Weiss, H. B. (1983). Beyond policies without people: An ecological perspective on child and family policy. In E. F. Zigler, S. L. Kagan, and E. Klugman (Eds.),

Children, Families and Government (393–414). London: Cambridge University Press.

Casper, V., Schultz, S., and Wickens, E. (1994). Breaking the silences: Lesbian and gay parents and the schools. *Teachers College Record, 94,* 109–135.

Chasnoff, D., and Cohen, H. (1997). *It's Elementary: Talking About Gay Issues in School.* Women's Educational Media, 2180 Bryant Street Suite 203, San Francisco, CA 94110.

Clunis, D. M., and Green, G. D. (1988). *Lesbian Couples.* Seattle, WA: Seal.

Comstock, G. D. (1991). *Violence Against Lesbians and Gay Men.* New York: Columbia University Press.

Crosbie-Burnett, M., and Helmbrecht, L. (1993). A descriptive empirical study of gay male stepfamilies. *Family Relations, 42,* 256–262.

Cruikshank, M. (1991). Lavender and gray: A brief survey of lesbian and gay aging studies. In J. A. Lee (Ed.), *Gay Midlife and Maturity* (77–87). New York: Harrington Park.

D'Augelli, A. R. (1991). Gay men in college: Identity processes and adaptations. *Journal of College Student Development, 32,* 140–146.

D'Augelli, A. R., and Hershberger, S. L. (1993). Lesbian, gay, and bisexual youth in community settings: Personal challenges and mental health problems. *American Journal of Community Psychology, 21,* 421–448.

Demo, D. H., and Allen, K. R. (1996). Diversity within lesbian and gay families: Challenges and implications for family theory and research. *Journal of Social and Personal Relationships, 13,* 417–436.

Editors of the *Harvard Law Review.* (1990). *Sexual Orientation and the Law.* Cambridge: Harvard University Press.

Engstrom, C. M., and Sedlacek, W. (1997). Attitudes of heterosexual students toward their gay male and lesbian peers. *Journal of College Student Development, 38,* 565–576.

Eskridge, W. N., Jr. (1996). *The Case for Same-sex Marriage: From Sexual Liberty to Civilized Commitment.* New York: Free Press.

Faderman, L. (1991). *Odd Girls and Twilight Lovers: A History of Lesbian Life in Twentieth-Century America.* New York: Penguin.

Francher, S. J., and Henkin, J. (1973). The menopausal queen. *American Journal of Orthopsychiatry, 43,* 670–674.

Friend, R. A. (1980). GAYging: Adjustment and the older gay male. *Alternative Lifestyles, 3,* 231–248.

Friend, R. A. (1991). Older lesbian and gay people: A theory of successful aging. *Journal of Homosexuality, 20,* 99–118.

Gallagher, J. (1996, July 23). Love and war. *The Advocate: The National Gay and Lesbian Newsmagazine,* pp. 22–28.

Goffman, E. (1963). *Stigma: Notes on the Management of Spoiled Identity.* New York: Simon & Schuster.

Harry, J. (1983). Gay male and lesbian relationships. In E. D. Macklin and R. H. Rubin (Eds.), *Contemporary Families and Alternative Lifestyles: Handbook on Research and Theory* (216–234). Beverly Hills, CA: Sage.

Herdt, G. (1989). Gay and lesbian youth: Emergent identities and cultural scenes at home and abroad. *Journal of Homosexuality, 17,* 1–42.

Herdt, G. (Ed.). (1992). *Gay Culture in America.* Boston: Beacon.

Herdt, G., and Boxer, A. (1993). *Children of Horizons: How Gay and Lesbian Teens Are Leading a New Way Out of the Closet.* Boston: Beacon.

Herek, G. M. (1989). Hate crimes against lesbians and gay men: Issues for research and policy. *American Psychologist, 44,* 948–955.

Herek, G. M., Kimmel, D. C., Amaro, H., and Melton, G. B. (1991). Avoiding heterosexist bias in psychological research. *American Psychologist, 46,* 957–963.

Hershberger, S. L., Pilkington, N. W., and D'Augelli, A. R. (1997). Predictors of suicide attempts among gay, lesbian, and bisexual youth. *Journal of Adolescent Research, 12,* 477–497.

Kehoe, M. (1986). Lesbians over 65: A triply invisible minority. *Journal of Homosexuality, 12,* 139–152.

Kehoe, M. (1988). Lesbians over 60 speak for themselves. *Journal of Homosexuality, 16,* 1–11.

Kelly, J. (1977). The aging male homosexual: Myth and reality. *The Gerontologist, 17,* 328–332.

Kimmel, D. C. (1978). Adult development and aging: A gay perspective. *Journal of Social Issues, 34,* 113–130.

Kinsey, A. C., Pomeroy, W. B., and Martin, C. E. (1948). *Sexual Behavior in the Human Male.* Philadelphia: W. B. Saunders.

Kinsey, A. C., Pomeroy, W. B., Martin, C. E., and Gebhard, P. H. (1953). *Sexual Behavior in the Human Female.* Philadelphia: W. B. Saunders.

Klein, F. (1990). The need to view sexual orientation as a multivariable dynamic process: A theoretical perspective. In D. P. McWhirter, S. A. Saunders, and J. M. Reinisch (Eds.), *Homosexuality/heterosexuality: Concepts of Sexual Orientation* (277–282). New York: Oxford University Press.

Kochman, A. (1993). Old and gray. In J. Adleman, R. Berger, M. Boyd, V. Doublex, M. Freedman, W. S. Hubbard, M. Kight, A. Kochman, M. K. R. Meyer, and S. M. Raphael (Eds.), *Lambda Gray* (93–99). North Hollywood, CA: Newcastle.

Kübler-Ross, E. (1969). *On Death and Dying.* New York: Macmillan.

Kurdek, L. A. (1994). In A. R. D'Augelli and C. J. Patterson (Eds.), *Lesbian and Gay Identities Over the Lifespan: Psychological Perspectives on Personal, Relational, and Community Processes* (243–261). New York: Oxford University Press.

Kurdek, L. A. (1998). Relationship outcomes and their predictors: Longitudinal evidence from heterosexual married, gay cohabiting, and lesbian cohabiting couples. *Journal of Marriage and the Family, 60,* 553–568.

Laird, J. (1993). Lesbian and gay families. In F. Walsh (Ed.), *Normal Family Processes* (2nd ed., 282–328). New York: Guilford.

Martin, A. D. (1982). Learning to hide: The socialization of the gay adolescent. *Adolescent Psychiatry, 10,* 52–65.

Martin, D., and Lyon, P. (1992). The older lesbian. In B. Berzon (Ed.), *Positively Gay* (2nd ed., 111–120). Berkeley, CA: Celestial Arts.

McWhirter, D. P., Sanders, S. A. and Reinisch, J. M. (Eds.) (1990). *Homosexuality/Heterosexuality: Concepts of Sexual Orientation.* New York: Oxford University Press.

McWhirter, D. P., and Mattison, A. M. (1984). *The Male Couple: How Relationships Develop.* Englewood Cliffs, NJ: Prentice–Hall.

National Center for Health Statistics (1993, January 7). Advance report of final mortality statistics, 1990. *Monthly Vital Statistics Report, 41*(7). Hyattsville, MD: U.S. Public Health Service.

Patterson, C. J. (1992). Children of lesbian and gay parents. *Child Development, 63,* 1025–1042.

Patterson, C. J. (1995). Families of the lesbian baby boom: Parents' division of labor and children's adjustment. *Developmental Psychology, 31,* 115–123.

Peplau, L. A., and Cochran, S. D. (1990). A relationship perspective on homosexuality. In D. P. McWhirter, S. A. Saunders, and J. M. Reinisch (Eds.), *Homosexuality/Heterosexuality: Concepts of Sexual Orientation* (321–349). New York: Oxford University Press.

Pharr, S. (1988). *Homophobia: A Weapon of Sexism.* Little Rock, AR: Chardon Press.

Pies, C. (1988). *Considering Parenthood* (2nd ed., updated). San Francisco: Spinsters/Aunt Lute.

Pilkington, N. W., and D'Augelli, A. R. (1995). Victimization of lesbian, gay, and bisexual youth in community settings. *Journal of Community Psychology, 23,* 34–56.

Pillemer, K., and Suitor, J. J. (1991). "Will I ever escape my child's problems?" Effects of adult children's problems on elderly parents. *Journal of Marriage and the Family, 53,* 585–594.

Poor, M. (1982). The older lesbian. In M. Cruikshank (Ed.), *Lesbian Studies* (165–173). Old Westbury, NY: Feminist Press.

Quam, J. K., and Whitford, G. S. (1992). Adaptation and age–related expectations of older gay and lesbian adults. *The Gerontologist, 32,* 367–374.

Raphael, S. M., and Meyer, M. K. R. (1993). Old lesbians seizing the moment, changing their world. In J. Adleman, R. Berger, M. Boyd, V. Doublex, M. Freedman, W. S. Hubbard, M. Kight, A. Kochman, M. K. R. Meyer, and S. M. Raphael (Eds.), *Lambda gray* (101–113). North Hollywood, CA: Newcastle.

Raphael, S. M., and Robinson, M. K. (1980). The older lesbian. *Alternative Lifestyles, 3,* 207–229.

Remafedi, G. (Ed.). (1994). *Death by Denial: Studies of Suicide in Gay and Lesbian Teenagers.* Boston: Alyson.

Rhoads, R. A. (1995). Learning from the coming out experiences of college males. *Journal of College Student Development, 36,* 67–74.

Rohrbaugh, J. B. (1992). Lesbian families: Clinical issues and theoretical implications. *Professional Psychology: Research and Practice, 23,* 467–473.

Ryff, C. D., Schmutte, P. S., and Lee, Y. H. (1996). How children turn out: Implications for parental self-evaluation. In C. D. Ryff and M. M. Seltzer (Eds.), *The Parental Experience in Midlife* (383–422). Chicago: University of Chicago Press.

Savin-Williams, R. (1994). Verbal and physical abuse as stressors in the lives of lesbian, gay male, and bisexual youths: Associations with school problems, running away, substance abuse, prostitution, and suicide. *Journal of Consulting and Clinical Psychology, 62,* 261–269.

Savin-Williams, R. C. (1998). The disclosure to families of same–sex attractions by lesbian, gay, and bisexual youths. *Journal of Research on Adolescence, 81,* 49–68.

Savin-Williams, R. C., and Dube, E. M. (1998). Parental reactions to their child's disclosure

Chapter 4 ✦ *Gay/Lesbian Families Over the Life Course* 63

of a gay/lesbian identity. *Family Relations, 47,* 7–13.

Savin-Williams, R. C., and Esterberg, K. G. (in press). Lesbian, gay, and bisexual families. In D. H. Demo, K. R. Allen, and M. A. Fine (Eds.), *Handbook of Family Diversity.* New York: Oxford University Press.

Schwartz, P. (1994). *Peer Marriage: How Love Between Equals Really Works.* New York: Free Press.

Schwartz, P., and Rutter, V. (1998). *The Gender of Sexuality.* Thousand Oaks, CA: Pine Forge.

Sherman, S. (Ed.). (1992). *Lesbian and Gay Marriage: Private Commitments, Public Ceremonies.* Philadelphia: Temple University Press.

Simoni, J. M. (1996). Pathways to prejudice: Predicting students' heterosexist attitudes with demographics, self–esteem, and contact with lesbians and gay men. *Journal of College Student Development, 37,* 68–76.

Stacey, J. (1996). *In the Name of the Family: Rethinking Family Values in the Postmodern Age.* Boston: Beacon.

Strommen, E. F. (1989). "You're a what?": Family member reactions to the disclosure of homosexuality. *Journal of Homosexuality, 18,* 37–58.

Telljohann, S. K., and Price, J. H. (1993). A qualitative examination of adolescent homosexuals' life experiences: Ramifications for secondary school personnel. *Journal of Homosexuality, 26,* 41–56.

Tierney, W. G. (1992, March/April). Building academic communities of difference: Gays, lesbians, and bisexuals on campus. *Change, 24,* 41–46.

Vacha, K. (1985). *Quiet Fire: Memoirs of Older Gay Men.* Trumansburg, NY: Crossing Press.

Weinberg, M. S. (1970). The male homosexual: Age–related variations in social and psychological characteristics. *Social Problems, 17,* 527–537.

Weston, K. (1991). *Families We Choose: Lesbians, Gays, Kinship.* New York: Columbia University Press.

Zicklin, G. (1995). Deconstructing legal rationality: The case of lesbian and gay family relationships. *Marriage and Family Review, 21,* 55–76. ✦

Chapter 5

African-American Families

Trends and Issues Over the Life Course

Karen Weddle-West
University of Memphis

The task of describing a group as diverse as African-American families is challenging and is constrained by numerous factors in addition to life course variations. A discussion of African-American families within the contexts of region, ethnicity, socioeconomic status, and age differences reveals much diversity. Additionally, there is variation within each of these contexts because no cultural group is monolithic. With these caveats in mind, the purpose of this chapter is to discuss African-American families in regard to family interaction and development over time.

The Challenge of Theoretical Frameworks

Family life cycle and family development theories historically have been used to explain and predict patterned changes in individuals or family units over time. This scholarship on family formations has tended to focus on life cycles, normative stages, and transitions among families from the majority culture. However, theoretical frameworks of family development are constantly evolving as scholarship and research be-

comes more inclusive and responsive to cultural variations (Klein and White 1996).

Dilworth-Anderson and Burton (1996) call for a reframing of family development theory in the study of ethnic minority families. These authors pose the question, "How can the historical, social, and political experiences of ethnic minority families be reflected in creating stages of family development?" (326). Dilworth-Anderson, Burton, and Johnson (1993) have noted that the life course perspective, family stress theory, and feminist theory are more inclusive of cultural issues than other frameworks.

Klein and White (1996) remind us that theories are not finite; they are constantly being refined and reconstructed. Good theories, they suggest, not only explain and predict behavior, but are empirically sound, and practical, and "give serious attention to the social and historical contexts affecting or affected by its key ideas" (259). It is this *contextualization* that is lacking in the applicability of traditional family development theory to African-American families. Stack and Burton (1993) assert that traditional family development theory is constrained by linearity and is not accommodating of the powerful forces of change brought about by chronic, unyielding racism and poverty. Families experiencing chronic racism and poverty may have distinct "nonlinear" paths of development. Limited life options (actual or perceived) significantly constrict the timing of major life events and transitions.

For example, adolescent parenting is typically viewed as a nonlinear path of adolescent development with significant negative consequences for impoverished adolescent parents, their families, and the children. However, many African-American adolescent parents view child bearing and child rearing as symbols of hope, adult status, and productivity in an environment that is often lacking in other productive roles. Thus, traditional family development theories might explain adolescent parenthood for teenagers in poverty as a deviant path of development because these theories give limited consideration to the cultural and social forces that affect this life choice. Indeed, many adolescent mothers and fathers proudly proclaim that their babies are the best thing that ever happened in their lives. The baby may be viewed as a sign of self-worth and affirmation/validation of the human potential. In environments where options are limited and opportunities for success are few, this line of reasoning is logical in many ways. Time is a precious resource. The question "Why waste time struggling for things not guaranteed, like a good education, a good career, and a good income before becoming a parent?" might best represent the decision-making process among adolescent parents living in impoverished environments within a racist environment.

Hines (1989) has suggested that the family life cycle can be a useful framework for intervention with impoverished African-American families, providing that professionals are cognizant of specific factors associated with poverty: (a) a truncated life cycle with ill-defined transitions, (b) female-headed or extended family households, (c) numerous, unpredictable life crises (i.e., unemployment, death, incarceration, addictions), and (d) limited resources that force a reliance on government institutions. Hines contends that traditionally defined developmental tasks are often impeded by poverty and racism, to the extent that different, not necessarily deviant, paths are sought and taken.

The ecological framework appears to be an appropriate tool for the study of ethnic and minority families across time. Bronfenbrenner's theory of human ecology explains and predicts "human behavior as a consequence of the interaction between the environment and the person" (Klein and White 1996, 227). This theory recognizes the social forces that influence family units. A significant addition to Bronfenbrenner's ecology of human development is the "chronosystem," which incorporates time as the developmental history of the individual and its effect on development. Thus, the powerful influences of culture, race, ethnicity, temporal contexts, and socioeconomic status become both major tenets of the theory and critical independent variables (not covariants) in the study of culturally diverse families.

Cohort/Time Effects

An accurate understanding of African-American families must incorporate the influences of the political, social, and cultural forces of specific time periods. Clearly, the functioning of African-American families and other minority groups is affected by governmental laws, policies, and rights. For example, a discussion of African-American families during the pre–Civil Rights era in terms of marriage patterns, fertility, and socioeconomic status yields a very different picture of black families when compared to those of today. This is clearly illustrated by examining research conducted on black children's self-esteem. Based on the seminal research of the Clark and Clark doll studies during the 1950s, the self-esteem of black children was found to be low and negative (Clark 1963). This classic body of research was conducted during a period of widely accepted institutional racism. A major implication from the Clark study is that children internalized their devalued status in American society. These research findings were later used as evidence in the *Brown vs. Board of Education* decision favoring desegregation in the schools. In contrast, research on African-American children's self-esteem during the Civil Rights movement and thereafter has primarily reflected high and positive levels of self-esteem. Essentially, the social and political climate of the particular time period must be considered in order to understand African-American families, as time and cohort effects often serve as major determinants of family functioning and family development for minority groups.

Historical Background

The historical origins of African-American families is a fundamental prerequisite to understanding the family life of contemporary black families. Coming from different regions of Africa, many blacks initially came to America as free men or indentured servants and worked alongside other pioneers of various races. With varying degrees of success, some of these early immigrant families were able to acquire land, access educational institutions, and live the remainder of their lives in relatively stable environments (McAdoo 1998; Staples 1988).

However, most African-American families are products of the institution of slavery. Therefore, the history of African-American families is unique because their immigration was largely involuntary. Accounts of slave families in historical archives serve as testimony to family members' relentless will to maintain some semblance of family organization and stability. In the classic work *Slavery in America: Theodore Weld's American Slavery as It Is* (Curry and Cowden 1972), personal narratives, eyewitness accounts, and newspaper articles document tortured, maimed, beaten, and yoked slaves who literally risked their lives to be reunited with wives, husbands, and children. The following account is illustrative of the slave families' struggle of unity and the high levels of attachment that existed in slave families:

> A slave who had been separated from his wife, because it best suited the convenience of his owner, ran away. He was taken up on the plantation where his wife, to whom he was tenderly attached, then lived. His only object in running away was to return to her—no other fault was attributed to him. For this offence he was confined in the stocks six weeks, in a miserable hovel, not weather-tight. He received fifty lashes weekly during that time, was allowed food barely sufficient to sustain him, and when released from confinement, was not permitted return to his wife. His master, although himself a husband and a father, was unmoved by the touching appeals of the slave, who entreated that he might only remain with his wife, promising to discharge his duties faithfully; his master continued inexorable, and he was torn from his wife and family. The owner of this slave was a professing Christian, in full membership with the church, and this circumstance occurred when he was confined to his chamber during his last illness. (narrative and testimony of Sarah M. Grimke)

Even though many slave holders kept slave families together in order to increase labor productivity, many were separated. There are hundreds of accounts of slave families' attempts at reunification following forced separation. These accounts exemplify slave families' resiliency and the strong value placed on family despite that most "peculiar institution" known as slavery (Blassingame 1972).

The variation in family structure and organization among slave families has been documented by numerous scholars (e.g., Blassingame 1972; Gutman 1976). Gutman's definitive scholarship on African-American families during and after slavery, when slave families married in record numbers, revealed that although some harsh and extremely punitive slave holders separated slave families, African-American families were primarily made up of two parents regardless of income (Taylor 1994). Gutman acknowledged that the father's role was diminished by slavery, but the adaptability and resiliency of slaves led to many stable, two-parent family units. Therefore, the prevailing paradigm of the dysfunctional, pathological, female-headed African-American family historically was not the norm, nor does it appear to be as directly linked to slavery or Africa as reported by some investigators (e.g., Frazier 1939; Moynihan 1965). On the contrary, the family was conjugal in structure and served as a crucial psychological and emotional buffer during and after slavery.

Family Formation Among Contemporary African-American Families

One of the more recent trends among younger cohorts of African Americans is a decline in the rate and timing of marriage. Analyzing census data, Tucker and Mitchell-Kernan (1995) reported a decrease in the percentage of black women ever married from 74 percent in 1940 to 63 percent in 1990. Marriage rates among black men changed from 64.5 percent in 1940 to 57 percent in 1990. This decline has been accompanied by a more recent delay in the timing of marriage. For example, African Americans married earlier than most other groups in 1940 but now clearly marry later. "Today, one quarter of black women and less than one of eight black men have married by their early twenties" (Tucker and Mitchell-Kernan 1995, xvii).

Reasons for the Delay and Timing of Marriage

Although demographers and scholars have documented declining marriage rates for the total population in America, most researchers acknowledge a more dramatic decline for African Americans (Schoen 1995). One of the prevailing explanations for this decline is the sex ratio imbalance (Keicolt and Fossett 1995; Staples 1988). Staples and Johnson (1993) report that "according to the U.S. Bureau of the Census, there are almost 1,500,000 more black women than men over the age of 15" (103).

In addition, educational levels of African-American women are higher than those of African-American men. Family scholars note that marital choice has traditionally been based on the social norm of hypergamy—that is, women choosing to marry men of equal or higher social status. However, the measures of social status that are most desired by women (i.e., higher incomes and educational levels, good careers, and stable employment) are often difficult for many African-American men to attain. Thus, the number of desirable African-American men is further reduced (Staples and Johnson 1993).

Unemployment is a critical reason for a decline in marriage rates. Unemployment rates among African-American young men have reached alarming proportions, which clearly limits the ability of men to support families (Testa and Krough 1995). High unemployment rates are related to drug use and crime, as unemployed youth often resort to unorthodox and illegal means of generating income; the result is a large proportion of African-American men being incarcerated. These poverty-related problems are so disproportionately high that Gibbs (1988) has referred to young African-American men as an "endangered species," and Darity and Myers (1995) describe the cumulative effects of these indicators as the "marginalization" of African-American men. Therefore, analyzing census and other data sources from 1976 to 1985, economists Darity and Myers concluded that high rates of institutionalization, mortality, and unemployment among African-American men, as well as imbalances in sex ratios, combine to explain the decline in marriage rates among African Americans.

Attitudes Toward Marriage

Despite the decline and delay of marriage among African-Americans, Tucker and Mitchell-Kernan (1995) found in their California survey of marriage attitudes among whites, blacks, and Latinos that most African Americans want to marry at some point in their lives. African American women and men reported a greater awareness of the sex ratio imbalance or more simply stated a realization that there are "not enough men." Although the study revealed that economic factors were predictive of individuals' expectations to marry, all unmarried respondents indicated that the primary reason they had not married was because they had not yet met the "right person" (158). This research by Tucker and Mitchell-Kernan supports previous research (Staples and Johnson 1993), suggesting that African-American women and men have not rejected marriage as an institution but rather are experiencing the effects of unbalanced sex ratios and the marginalization of African-American men.

Because of societal and structural constraints, Staples and Johnson (1993) explain that African-American men and women have often violated the conventional age, educational, and income norms that characterize many marriages in America. Historically, African-American parents have worked hard to send their female children to college so that they will not have to be relegated to the limited job options available to uneducated African-American women (i.e., custodians, cooks, domestic workers). Male children have been expected to enter the workforce after high school because their job options, although limited, have been greater than those available to women. Thus, the educational levels of African-American women traditionally have been higher than those of African-American men. For example, marriages between female schoolteachers and male postal workers have not been uncommon in the African-American community. Indeed, heterogamous marriages like these were considered ideal because of the higher income typically paid to male employees in various blue-collar occupations and the government sector.

Family Functioning

Research on well-functioning African-American families has increased over the last ten years but remains relatively limited. Much of the previous research on African-American families was based on multi-problem poverty households, with a focus on male absence. Consequently, research on marriage patterns and marital roles among African-American middle-class and upper-class families is underrepresented in the literature in spite of the increasing number of African Americans moving into the middle class.

Middle-Class Families

The overwhelming majority (87 percent) of middle-class African-American families are nuclear in structure, with both spouses employed (Hill et al. 1993). Indeed, educational level and employment of the wife is often cited as a primary indicator of middle-class status within African-American families (Malveaux 1988). Most middle-class heads of households in African-American families are employed in the public sector, the government, or other professional occupations (Hill et al. 1993); however, there is tremendous diversity in employment patterns among middle-class African-American families (Coner-Edwards and Spurlock 1988). Family functioning within black middle-class families tends to adhere to traditional values (Hill 1972), including kinship bonds, achievement orientation, religious conviction, work orientation, and flexible roles within the family. Coner-Edwards and Spurlock also included delay of gratification, high self-reliance and self-empowerment, and a strong ethnic orientation as common values among middle-class African-American families.

What appears to be a departure from the norm is the growing number of middle-class African-American families who establish a residence outside the inner city (DeGenova 1997). Historically, African-American families in the middle and lower classes resided in the same community because of segregation in housing practices. Consequently, African-American communities traditionally were diverse in terms of social class. Increasingly, however, lower-class African-American families are living in neighborhoods segregated by race and class, with the absence of upwardly mobile adult role models living in close proximity to inner-city youth.

Female-Headed Households

Parenthood for many African-American women is often unaccompanied by marriage. At present, about half of all African-American children are born to single mothers. This represents a significant increase in female-headed family structures within the African-American community. In contrast, in 1940 only about one-fourth of African-American families were single parent in structure (Tucker and Mitchell-Kernan 1995). Many demographers and economists have cited adolescent pregnancies among African Americans as the major reason for the recent increase in female-headed households. However, critical analyses of census data conducted by Hill et al. (1993) indicate that African-American adolescent mothers, who are disproportionately poor and single, are not financially able to establish separate residences, and thus account for "less than 5 percent of all black families headed by women" (31). There has actually been a decrease in the number of births to African-American adolescents since 1960. Thus, the recent increase in the number of female headed households primarily is related to the increasing numbers of children born to African-American women in the 20–29 age cohort. As previously discussed in this chapter, this cohort of African-American women has also experienced the greatest "shortage" of available, marriageable African-American men. Therefore, the increase in the birth rate for this cohort of women may be indicative of lifestyle options.

Another common misconception is the relationship between female-headed families and family dysfunction. Historical accounts (Blassingame 1972) and ethnographic studies (Stack 1974) have long demonstrated that female family headship is not inherently dysfunctional. Since slavery, African-American families have used a variety of coping and survival strategies to overcome the financial and emotional stressors often incurred when rearing children in single-parent homes. These strategies have included mutual reliance on extended kin, church, and other religious institutions; androgynous socialization of children; exposure of boys to adult male role models such as uncles, brothers, companions, and community leaders in the absence of husbands; and the provision of child care for younger children by older male and female siblings. Many scholars refer to the strategy of androgynous socialization of children as adaptive, while others refer to the strategy of reciprocity of services among extended kin as a distinctive coping mechanism dating back to African origins (Sudarkasa 1988). Thus, there is ample evidence to suggest that African-American female heads of households are not inherently dysfunctional, and they have adapted well to societal oppression and structural constraints. For example, numerous successful African-American adults are the products of female-headed households and are quick to express their admiration and dedication to hard-working, strong mothers who had confidence in their children's abilities and paved their way to success.

Extended Family

As noted previously, extended family households are not uncommon among African-American families. The extended family structure typically is made up of grandparents (particularly grandmothers), their adult children, and their grandchildren but may also contain other relatives, including fictive kin. Qualitative and ethnographic research on the importance of the extended family within the African-American community (McAdoo 1997; Stack 1974) reveals that much of the resilience found in African-American families can be attributed to the support provided by extended kin. African-American families in high-risk situations and environments have often relied on extended kin to assist in times of emotional, financial, and familial crises. Patterns of African-American cultural transmission often reflect a reciprocity of services between generations throughout the life cycle. The older generation provides services to younger generations during the child rearing years, and the younger generation is then expected to assist older family members in their times of need.

Research has suggested that extended kin has a strong impact on the upward mobility of African-American families (McAdoo 1988). Using a primarily nuclear family sample of middle-class African Americans, McAdoo interviewed 178 family units and found that patterns of upward mobility "were often impossible without the support of extended family" (166). Proximity to extended kin, not co-residence, appears to be the most common pattern in African-American families. Indeed, many scholars assert that the extended kin support is an "Africanism" that has persisted over time (Sudarkasa 1988).

Children and Child Rearing

The Status of African-American Children

Literature and research in family studies have often neglected the study of children beyond childbearing and family structure, as if family development involved only adult members. However, life span and family development theories suggest that the study of children is fundamental to the study of adult family development. Unfortunately, much of the discussion of African Americans centers around the "at-risk" status of children and their parents as a result of pervasive poverty and related problems in the black community. However, a focus on poor families alone belies the well-functioning parenting strategies of African-American culture. For too long, sensationalized reports have depicted African-American parents as dysfunctional or absent, harsh and punitive, or incompetent and abusive (e.g., Moynihan 1965). However, culturally sensitive research on parenting practices among African-American families presents a profile of adaptive, resilient, and functional parenting (Hale-Benson 1986).

The Children's Defense Fund in *The State of America's Children Yearbook* (1995) revealed that "the number of poor children in the United States in 1993, 15.7 million, was the highest in 30 years" (17). Almost half (46 percent) of African-American children were living below the poverty line in 1993. Rexroat's (1994) comprehensive analysis of the economic status of African-American children shows that the period from 1959 to 1979 represented a decline in poverty from 64.8 percent to 37.9 percent. However, in 1984, "over half of all black children under three were poor," which reflected a 10 percent increase over a five-year period (8). The youngest African-American children are the poorest, and poverty rates continue to increase for this population. Consequently, more than half of all African-American children enter society in poverty. This fact alone helps explain the disproportionate rates of infant mortality, accidental deaths, and death from diseases among African-American children (Children's Defense Fund, 1995). The sequelae of problems stemming from poverty carry enormous costs at the macro level and certainly negatively impact children's development at the micro level. Research conducted 40 years ago and confirmed today has revealed that poor nutrition among the impoverished is a significant contributor to and predictor of academic delays because children who are inadequately nourished are less attentive. These and other poverty-related problems prompted some of the most effective, holistic governmental interventions, such as Head Start, designed to mitigate the negative effects of poverty on children's development. However, such programs only serve one-third of the needy population.

A cursory review of the disproportionately high poverty rates among African-American children has led many policymakers to target female-headed households as the primary culprit. However, Rexroat's (1994) analysis reveals that family structure is not the most significant predictor of poverty among African-American children, as it does not explain "why black children who live in intact two-parent families throughout their childhood are as likely to be poor as white children who spend their entire childhoods in single-parent families" (2). Yet, the disproportionate number of female-headed households in the African-American community is related to poverty rates and children's status. Today, most African-American children (54 percent) live in single-parent families (Tucker and Mitchell-Kernan 1995). Moreover, because African-American women heading households continue to be disproportionately underemployed or unemployed, the children in these households are disproportionately poor. Hill et al. (1993) report that "despite their higher educational and occupational levels, black women heading families were three times more likely to be unemployed in 1985 (16.4 percent) than they were in 1970 (5.6 percent)" (27). Economic conditions like recessions, downsizing, and unemployment rates affect minorities differentially, especially minority women (Malveaux 1988). Therefore, unemployment and underemployment of African-American women, not family structure, are most directly linked to the increasing rates of poverty among African-American children (Hill et al. 1993; Rexroat 1994). African-American women employed in stable occupations significantly contribute to the decrease in the number of children in poverty in both single-parent and nuclear families.

African-American Child Rearing

One of the strengths consistently documented in the African-American community is the resiliency of its children (Hale-Benson 1986). Robert Coles (1964), in his book *Children in Crisis: A Study of Courage and Fear,* provided extensive qualitative data on the coping mechanisms and resilience displayed by African-American children during the forced desegregation of Southern schools. *The Ruby Bridges' Story* (Marshall 1997) was recently televised and illuminated the courage and fortitude of this little girl at the center of the racial and political firestorm of desegregation efforts in a Southern school. Her parents had equipped her with the requisite coping skills for dealing with rejection, threats, racial slurs, harassment, and isolation. She was taught both to expect racial hostility and the skills required to overcome it while maintaining a positive self-concept. These coping skills included spirituality, knowledge about racial issues, compassion for those intolerant of diversity, and academic readiness. This tenuous balance between maintaining high self-esteem while preparing children for racism is characteristic of the *racial socialization* process that many African-American parents have successfully inculcated.

Another strength of African-American child rearing is bicultural socialization (Hale-Benson 1986; Peters 1988). African-American children learn behavioral and language systems that are differentially appropriate, situation specific, and contingent on environmental settings. Many African-American children are reared in homes and communities in which language, level of activity, and environmental stimuli are culturally distinct and richly different. For example, research has revealed a physical/motor precocity among African infants, with the onset of developmental motor milestones occurring at ages above the developmental norms for Caucasian infants (Bril and Sabatier 1986). Researchers have attributed this advanced motor development to culturally distinct ways of handling infants (Fogel 1997). Advanced mobility leads to early independence and exploration of the environment, which clearly foster optimal development. Consequently, this precocity provides an excellent opportunity to capitalize on active learning (Hale-Benson 1986).

Bicultural socialization is also evidenced in African-American children's language. Most African-American children are fluent in African-American vernacular English, sometimes referred to as Ebonics. Because residential segregation has increased across the country, Ebonics is often the language of the community. Facility in Ebonics is viewed by some as critical to children's overall functioning and serves as a bridge between formal institutions like the school and less formal home and community environments. Code switching—the ability to transition from Ebonics to mainstream American English—is also important for children's academic achievement, because mainstream American English is standard in schools and wider society. Even though schools often devalue the strengths found in culturally specific patterns of language and activity differences (Irvine 1991), these strengths have contributed to the resilience and survival of the African-American family.

The concept of gender role convergence is often discussed in relationship to sex role socialization among African-American children and is typically perceived as a strength. African-American boys are often expected to provide nurturing and caretaking roles for younger siblings, and African-American girls are often reared to acquire the competencies and skills needed for independent living as a adult. Both boys and girls are socialized to be assertive, independent, and nurturing (Lewis 1975). This androgynous socialization process among African-American children has been documented extensively over time and extends into adult gender role literature. Hossain and Roopnarine (1993) examined parenting roles among intact African-American families with infants. These researchers found that although African-American mothers spent significantly more time than fathers in caregiving and household tasks, African-American fathers appeared to spend a considerable amount of time in child-care tasks, particularly when compared to the time spent by other ethnic group fathers.

Parenting Strengths and Transmission of Values

When Hurd, Moore, and Rogers (1995) assessed strengths and competencies of African-American parents, their findings confirmed previous strengths identified earlier (Hill 1972) and demonstrated that African-American parents receive support from other adults, provide instruction on coping with pains in life, instill racial pride, and expose children to positive African-American male role models. When Phinney and

Chavira (1995) conducted interviews to investigate patterns of ethnic socialization across three minority groups of parents of adolescents (Japanese Americans, African Americans, and Mexican Americans), they found significant ethnic differences, with African-American parents reporting more discussions of prejudice and coping styles. Proactive coping styles in response to prejudice were related to higher self-esteem among the adolescents in this study. Geismer (1973) conducted a longitudinal study of low-income African-American families and found that despite hardship caused by poverty, many families evidenced high-quality functioning in child rearing.

The value of education among African-American families has been discussed by numerous scholars (Hill 1972; Staples and Johnson 1993). The realization that education is the "way out" is imprinted on the minds of African-American parents and children despite the knowledge that because of racism that education may not have the same utility for them as it does for other groups. That is, the income levels for college-educated African Americans have historically been lower than the income levels for white Americans with similar levels of education (Staples 1988). However, the value of education is evidenced by African Americans' higher preference for educational settings even during their children's early years. Fuller, Holloway, and Liang (1996) find that African-American families preferred (in comparison to white and Latino families) center-based child care for preschoolers even after controlling for family income and structure.

Older Members in African-American Families

The elderly are expected to make up about 15.3 percent of the African-American population by the year 2030 (Williams 1990). This increase is a result of a real increase in longevity, along with a phenomenon referred to as the "racial crossover in mortality." African-Americans experience a higher mortality and morbidity rate in all age groups in comparison to whites with the exception of the very old—those 70–80 years or older (Kart 1990; Watson 1990) Within this age group, African-American men and women have lower death rates than whites. Essentially, there is change in the death rates by race (racial crossover), in this older cohort.

Research investigating family functioning and the quality of life among elderly African-American families has increased over the past decade. Contributing to the increase in our understanding of the African-American elderly are reports based on the National Survey of Black Americans (NSBA). The NSBA was conducted in 1979–1980 and included national data on 2,100 African Americans 18 years and older, with 581 respondents in the 55 years and older age group (Coke and Twaite 1995). The most consistently cited factors related to higher quality of life from this and numerous other studies include church affiliation, extended kin networks, health, and income (Coke and Twaite 1995; Harel, McKinney, and Williams 1990; Hill 1972; McAdoo 1988).

Grandparents

Watson and Koblinsky (1997) report a 40 percent increase in the number of grandparents rearing children, representing about 4 million children, and note that more African-American children live with grandparents than white children do, approximately 13 percent and 3 percent respectively. Research on African-American grandparents, though limited, has increased and supports the centrality of grandparents in African-American child rearing. However, much of the research has focused on the significance of grandparents as "rescuers" during times of their children's family crises (unemployment, illness, divorce, eviction). It is important not to minimize the critical roles that African-American grandparents have played in the maintenance of families during crises, but it is equally important to extend our knowledge of grandparenting processes during normative times. Most research confirms that grandparents in African-American families play key roles in the socialization of grandchildren.

The stereotype of the domineering, invincible, indefatigable black grandmother is yielding to a more accurate depiction of women of strength, courage, resiliency, and needs. It is indeed a difficult balancing act to discuss the incredible contributions of African-American grandmothering while simultaneously considering issues of role strain, role ambivalence, failing health, and depressed economic environments that many experience. Using the Grandparents Strengths and Needs Inventory, Watson and Koblinsky (1997) examined the relative strengths and needs of working-class African-American and Anglo-American grandparents. They found that African-American grandmothers reported more involvement and value in teaching and socializing their grandchildren than Anglo-American grandparents did. However, black grandmothers also reported greater needs for information to support their grandparenting roles and greater frustration with the social ills that threaten the well-being of their grandchildren. Essentially, the roles and function of African-American grandparents remain salient and serve as critical emotional buffers to their children and grandchildren. African-American grandparents are often viewed as mentors and sages possessing wisdom about surviving and thriving as minority citizens. Yet the enormity of the contributions that African-American grandparents have made and continue to make to their families and to the community often mask their needs and frailties.

Poverty rates continue to negatively affect older African Americans (Hill et al. 1993; Watson 1990). Watson reported a 36.3 percent poverty rate for the older African-American population in 1983, and Hill et al. (1993) predicted that this rate will increase because of reductions in government programs. Because longevity for women is higher than for men, elderly African-American female heads of households tend to experience higher rates of poverty.

Significance of the Church

The church has served vital functions within the African-American community, particularly for seniors. Since slavery, the church has functioned as an educational and business institution, a counseling center, a center for social and civil rights reform and enlightenment, a financial aid and social support center, and a place of worship. Many African Americans who were relegated to jobs at the lowest end of the socioeconomic ladder could find dignity within the church. It is within this institution that sanitation engineers can serve as heads of the trustees or deacon boards, and female custodians can serve as presidents of the "mothers'" board or the church "circle" group and be accorded all of the admiration and respect that accompany these roles (Hale-Benson 1986; McAdoo 1988; Staples and Johnson 1993). The church has also served as a training ground for numerous successful orators, civil rights leaders, musicians, singers, and educators. Indeed, historians assert that all successful self-help movements targeting the improvement of the status of African Americans have been either initiated or facilitated by the church (Billingsley 1992). For these reasons, and because of their faith, the elderly find much comfort in the church.

Research on the role of the church in the lives of older African Americans has consistently shown a positive relationship between religiosity and self-report measures of quality of life. When Coke (1991) surveyed 166 older African-Americans she found that more than half of her sample reported regular church attendance, and three-fourths of these respondents defined themselves as religious individuals. Moreover, Coke found a positive significant relationship between reported church attendance and life satisfaction. Similarly, Taylor (1988) used data from the NSBA on a subsample of African Americans 55 years and older and found high levels of church attendance and membership (about two-thirds of the respondents reported church membership); he also found that levels of church participation increased with age.

Older persons in the African-American community tend to live in inner-city areas where there has been a massive depletion of large businesses and other thriving institutions. As a result, the church is one of the few institutions surviving in neighborhoods where many older African Americans reside. Consequently, networks of social support, health-care screenings, and assistance to the elderly are often established in churches (Taylor 1988). Examinations for hypertension and glaucoma, as well as equipment for mammograms, are common in black churches throughout the country.

Conclusions

African-American families are confronted with challenges over the life course. These challenges are related to their historical origins, continued societal racism, and sex ratio imbalance. In spite of these adversities, however, African-American families have survived by utilizing culturally distinct strengths and resources. This is evident in such factors as socialization of children, family structural variations, emphasis on education, the incorporation of extended family, the androgynous roles of men and women, and the role of church as a source of community organization and support. It is necessary, therefore, when looking at the life course of African-American families to consider the influences of phenomena such as culture, class, and diversity.

Discussion Questions

1. How does the historical background of African-American families affect families of today?

2. How does the life cycle differ for African-American families?

3. How would you account for the declining rate of marriage and the increase in female-headed households in the black community?

4. What is the role of grandparents in African-American families compared to that in Caucasian families?

5. What are the strengths in child rearing in African-American families?

Glossary

Bicultural socialization Learning to live in two cultures; in this case the African-American culture and the larger, primarily white, culture.

Ebonics A term used by some scholars to describe African-American vernacular English.

Gender role conversion Androgynous socialization of children; boys and girls are reared to take on responsibilities of both genders as needed.

Marginalization The economically disadvantaged status and related problems of young African-American men.

Racial crossover in mortality The fact that mortality and morbidity rates are higher for African Americans in all age groups with the exception of those 70–80 years of age.

Suggested Readings

Billingsley, A. (1992). *Climbing Jacob's Ladder: The Enduring Legacy of African-American Families.* New York: Simon & Schuster.

Coles, R. (1964). *Children in Crisis: A Study of Courage and Fear.* New York: Dell.

Gibbs, J. T. (Ed.). (1988). *Young, Black, and Male in America: An Endangered Species.* Westport, CT: Auburn House.

McAdoo, H. P. (Ed.). (1997). *Black Families.* Newbury Park, CA: Sage.

Wakschlag, L. S., Chase–Lansdale, P. L., and Brooks–Gunn, J. (1996). Not just "ghosts in the nursery." Contemporaneous intergenerational relationships and parenting in young African-American families. *Child Development, 67,* 2131–2147.

Bibliography

Billingsley, A. (1992). *Climbing Jacob's Ladder: The Enduring Legacy of African-American Families.* New York: Simon & Schuster.

Blassingame, J. (1972). *The Slave Community.* New York: Oxford.

Bril, B., and Sabatier, C. (1986). The cultural context of motor development: Postural manipulations in the daily life of Bambara babies (Mali). *International Journal of Behavioral Development, 9,* 439–453.

Children's Defense Fund. (1995). *The State of America's Children Yearbook.* Washington, DC.

Clark, K. B. (1963). *Prejudice and Your Child.* Boston: Beacon.

Coke, M. M. (1991). *Correlates of Life Satisfaction Among the African-American Elderly.* New York: Garland.

Coke, M. M., and Twaite, J. A. (1995). *The Black Elderly: Satisfaction and Quality of Later Life.* New York: Haworth.

Coles, R. (1964). *Children in Crisis: A Study of Courage and Fear.* New York: Dell.

Coner-Edwards, A. F., and Spurlock, J. (1988). *Black Families in Crises: The Middle Class.* New York: Brunner/Mazel.

Curry, R. O., and Cowden, J. D. (1972). *Slavery in America: Theodore Weld's American Slavery as It Is.* Itasca, IL: Peacock.

Darity, W. A., and Myers, S. L. (1995). Family structure and the marginalization of black men: Policy implications. In M. B. Tucker and C. Mitchell-Kernan (Eds.), *The Decline in Marriage Among African Americans* (263–308). New York: Russell Sage Foundation.

DeGenova, M. K. (1997). *Families in Cultural Context: Strengths and Challenges in Diversity.* Mountain View, CA: Mayfield Publishing.

Dilworth-Anderson, P., and Burton, L. M. (1996). Rethinking family development: Critical conceptual issues in the study of diverse groups. *Journal of Social and Personal Relationships, 13*(3), 325–334.

Dilworth-Anderson, P., Burton, L. M., and Johnson, L. B. (1993). Reframing theories for understanding race, ethnicity, and families. In P. G. Boss, W. J. Doherty, R. LaRossa, W. R. Schumm, and S. K. Steinmetz (Eds.), *Sourcebook of Family Theories and Methods: A Contextual Approach* (627–646). New York: Plenum.

Fogel, A. (1997). *Infancy: Infant, Family, and Society.* St. Paul, MN: West.

Frazier, E. F. (1939). *The Negro Family in the United States.* Chicago, IL: University of Chicago.

Fuller, B., Holloway, S. D., and Liang, X. (1996). Family selection of child-care centers: The influence of household support, ethnicity, and parental practices. *Child Development, 67,* 3320–3337.

Geismer, L. L. (1973). *555 Families: A Social-Psychological Study of Young Families in Transition.* New Brunswick, NJ: Transaction.

Gibbs, J. T. (Ed.). (1988). *Young, Black, and Male in America: An Endangered Species.* Westport, CT: Auburn House.

Gutman, H. (1976). *The Black Family in Slavery and Freedom, 1750–1925.* New York: Pantheon.

Hale-Benson, J. (1986). *Black Children: Their Roots, Culture, and Learning Styles.* Baltimore, MD: Johns Hopkins University.

Harel, Z., McKinney, E. A., and Williams, M. (Eds.). (1990). *Black Aged: Understanding Diversity and Service Needs.* Newbury Park, CA: Sage.

Hill, R. (1972). *The Strengths of Black Families.* New York: Emerson Hall.

Hill, R., Billingsley, A., Engram, E., Malson, M., Rubin, R. H., Stack, C., Stewart, J., and Teele, J. E. (1993). *Research on the African-American Family: A Holistic Perspective.* Westport, CT: Auburn House.

Hines, P. M. (1989). The family life cycle of poor black families. In B. Carter and M. McGoldrick (Eds.), *The Changing Family Life Cycle* (513–554). Needham Heights, MA: Allyn and Bacon.

Hossain, Z., and Roopnarine, J. L. (1993). Division of labor and child care in dual-earner African-American families with infants. *Sex Roles, 29,* 571–583.

Hurd, E. P., Moore, C., and Rogers, R. (1995). Quiet success: Parenting strengths among African Americans. *Families in Society, 76*(7), 434–443.

Irvine, J. J. (1991). *Black Students and School Failure: Policies, Practices, and Prescriptions.* New York: Praeger.

Kart, C. S. (1990). Diversity among black males. In Z. Harel, E. McKinney, and M. Williams (Eds.), *Black Aged: Understanding Diversity and Service Needs* (100–113). Newbury Park, CA: Sage.

Keicolt, K. J. and Fossett, M. A. (1995). Mate availability and marriage among African Americans: Aggregate– and individual–level analyses. In M. B. Tucker and C. Mitchell-Kernan (Eds.), *The Decline in Marriage Among African-Americans* (121–135). New York: Russell Sage Foundation.

Klein, D. M., and White, J. M. (1996) *Family Theories: An Introduction.* Thousand Oaks, CA: Sage.

Lewis, D. (1975). The black family: Socialization and sex roles. *Phylon, 36,* 221–237.

Malveaux, J. (1988). The economic statuses of black families. In H. P. McAdoo (Ed.), *Black Families* (133–147). Newbury Park, CA: Sage.

Marshall, H. (1997). *The Ruby Bridges Story.* New York: Disney Press.

McAdoo, H. P. (1988). Transgenerational patterns of upward mobility in African-American families. In H. P. McAdoo (Ed.), *Black Families* (148–168). Newbury Park, CA: Sage.

McAdoo, H. P. (Ed.). (1997). *Black Families.* Newbury Park, CA: Sage.

McAdoo, H. P. (1998). African-American families. In C. Mindel, R. Habenstein, and R. Wright (Eds.), *Ethnic Families in America:*

Patterns and variations (361–381). Upper Saddle River, NJ: Prentice-Hall.

Moynihan, D. (1965). *The Negro Family: The Case for National Action*. Washington, DC: U.S. Government Printing Office.

Peters, M. F. (1988). Parenting in black families with young children: A historical perspective. In H. P. McAdoo (Ed.), *Black Families* (228–241). Newbury Park, CA: Sage.

Phinney, J. S., and Chavira, V. (1995). Parental ethnic socialization and adolescent coping with problems related to ethnicity. *Journal of Adolescence, 5*, 31–53.

Rexroat, C. (1994). *The Declining Economic Status of Black Children: Examining the Change*. Washington, DC: Joint Center for Political and Economic Studies Press.

Schoen, R. (1995). The widening gap between black and white marriage rates: Context and implications. In M. B. Tucker and C. Mitchell-Kernan (Eds.), *The Decline in Marriage Among African Americans* (103–116). New York: Russell Sage Foundation.

Stack, C. (1974). *All Our Kin*. New York: Harper.

Stack, C. B., and Burton, L. M. (1993). Kinscripts. *Journal of Comparative Family Studies, 24*, 157–170.

Staples, R. (1988). The Black American family. In C. Mindel, R. Habenstein, and R. Wright (Eds.), *Ethnic Families in America* (303–324). New York: Elsevier.

Staples, R., and Johnson, L. (1993). *Black Families at the Crossroads*. San Francisco, CA: Jossey-Bass.

Sudarkasa, N. (1988). Interpreting the African heritage in Afro-American family organization. In H. P. McAdoo (Ed.), *Black Families* (27–43). Newbury Park, CA: Sage.

Taylor, R. J. (1988). Correlates of religious noninvolvement among black Americans. *Review of Religious Research, 30*, 126–139.

Taylor, R. L. (Ed.). (1994). *Minority Families in the United States: A Multicultural Perspective*. Engelwood Cliffs, NJ: Prentice-Hall.

Testa, M., and Krough, M. (1995). The effect of employment on marriage and black males in inner-city Chicago. In M. B. Tucker and C. Mitchell-Kernan (Eds.), *The Decline in Marriage Among African-Americans* (59–95). New York: Russell Sage Foundation.

Tucker, M. B., and Mitchell–Kernan (Eds.). (1995). *The Decline in Marriage Among African-Americans*. New York: Russell Sage Foundation.

Wakschlag, L. S., Chase-Lansdale, P. L., and Brooks-Gunn, (1996). Not just "ghosts in the nursery." Contemporaneous intergenerational relationships and parenting in young African-American families. *Child Development, 67*, 2131–2147.

Watson, J. A., and Koblinsky, S. A. (1997). Strengths and needs of working-class African-American and Anglo-American grandparents. *International Journal of Aging and Human Development, 44*, 149–165.

Watson, W. H. (1990). Family care, economics, and health. In Z. Harel, E. McKinney, and M. Williams (Eds.), *Black Aged: Understanding Diversity and Service Needs* (50–68). Newbury Park, CA: Sage.

Williams, M. (1990). African-American elderly experiences with Title II: Program assumptions and economic well-being. In Z. Harel, E. McKinney, and M. Williams (Eds.), *Black Aged* (146–164). Newbury Park, CA: Sage. ✦

Chapter 6

Cohabiting and Never-Married Families Across the Life Course

Geoffrey K. Leigh
University of Nevada

During the 1960s and 1970s, considerable debate occurred among scholars about the "decline of the family" and whether the institution of "the family" was in danger of collapsing (Blumstein and Schwartz 1983). While much of the debate was as ideological as it was empirical, it has become clear that there is not just one type of family but rather a variation in family forms, with many types on the increase (Macklin 1987). Although images of the past have narrowly defined the term "family," recent trends acknowledge greater options (Prinz 1995) as well as acceptance of and participation in other living arrangements (Axinn and Barber 1997; Bumpass, Sweet, and Cherlin 1991; London 1998).

Two increasingly common variations from the traditional family are cohabiting and never-married families. Generally, cohabiting families consist of two adults living together in the same household who are also involved in a primary relationship that usually includes a sexual relationship without a legal marriage. In some cases, the couple may have a "commitment" ceremony, but it would not include a marriage license or someone performing the ceremony with the intent of performing a legally recognized ceremony. Never-married families encompass those people who are not cohabiting and have never had a legally binding marriage.

This chapter addresses developmental approaches to studying families, demographic changes in family formation, and variations in cohabiting and never-married families. In addition, it offers implications for needed research and interventions with cohabiting and never-married families.

Developmental Perspectives

When scholars are interested in studying changes over time, they have typically used some type of developmental perspective to frame and interpret their research or the social issue to be addressed. For example, identifying changes in attachment with infants or with adults over time has relied upon the developmental approach of psychoanalytic theory (Bretherton 1993). Scholars have also been interested in how problems or experiences in childhood affect outcomes during adolescence or adulthood, which represents a life span perspective (Rutter 1980). From a life span perspective, scholars are interested in the description and explanation of changes and processes in the life course of *individuals* over time—anywhere from conception to death (Leigh and Loewen 1987). From this point of view, development is seen as long-term change sequences in a historical context (Labouvie 1982). Attention primarily is focused on the identification of key transition points from one life stage or event to another and the important characteristics or tasks that are associated with each life stage or event. In this way, researchers are able to identify significant qualitative changes or important sequences that are common across individual development. Examples include outcomes with at-risk youth or characteristics of people in particular contexts, such as increasing intimacy in dating couples.

Developmental approaches have also been used to study changes in *groups* such as couples and families (Leigh and Loewen 1987). In this case, the interest is in how couples or families systematically change—again attempting to identify patterns and processes that are important and consistent over time (Bengtson and Allen 1993). In contrast to an individual perspective, the usual focus of family development is on structural changes over the existence of a family (Rodgers and White 1993) or on the initial development of a relationship, focusing on the time prior to some type of commitment or living arrangement (Berscheid and Reis 1998). As with individual developmental perspectives, changes often occur at significant transition points, or at times when families experience systematic types of change, such as the entry or departure of a family member within a system.

Most family development work has focused on structural changes in family systems (Rodgers and White 1993), as those are the easiest aspects to identify and measure for family scholars. The other major work, which has focused on relationship development, has been the investigation of dating relationships and the development of commitment in couples (Berscheid and Reis 1998). Although considerable research has been done on family dynamics and interactions in a variety of relationships, little work has focused on systematic changes in couples' relationship dynamics or interactions over time (Chung 1990). The research closest to analyzing relationship development in heterosexual couples is Papernow's (1984) description of changes for stepfamilies. Even with this proposed model of development, there remains little in the literature describing systematic changes in couples' relationship dynamics or interaction patterns.

There are three other exceptions to this paucity of scholarship on relationship dynamics as they change over time, although most of this work has been done with gay and lesbian unions. McWhirter and Mattison (1984) describe six stages that long-term gay male couples tend to experience as their relationship progresses from early commitment to 20 years and later. The six stages are blending (limerence, equalizing the partnership); nesting (homemaking, finding compatibility); maintaining (reappearing of the individual, establishing tradi-

tions, dealing with conflict); building (collaborating, establishing independence, dependability of partners); releasing (trusting, merging of resources, taking each other for granted); and renewing (achieving security, shifting perspectives, restoring partnership). The stages are not set for every couple, with only rough estimates of time for each stage, acknowledging that variation occurs with different couples.

In a similar approach, Slater (1995) outlines five stages of a lesbian family life cycle, from formation to ongoing couplehood, the middle years, generativity, and couples over sixty-five. In contrast to heterosexual couples, the focus on gay and lesbian couples is primarily on the relationship itself, although children are often involved in these families (Blumstein and Schwartz 1983). Still, researchers have attempted to identify transition points of the relationship dynamics or patterns rather than structural aspects common to most models of heterosexual couples. Such a difference in approach may have occurred because gay and lesbian relationships may be less concerned about reconstructing gender roles with same-sex partners and are, therefore, different from most heterosexual couples (Scanzoni, Polonko, Teachman, and Thompson 1989; Schwartz 1994).

Berscheid and Lopes (1997) have outlined one approach to understanding relationship satisfaction and stability over time. In contrast to the individual or family development perspectives, Berscheid and Lopes focus on the more general and interdisciplinary studies of close relationships (Berscheid and Reis 1998; Duck 1993; Perlman and Duck 1987). The model Berscheid and Lopes describe is based on social exchange theory and was developed in an attempt to better understand "the interplay over time between the internal dynamics of the relationship and its external context" (135). Central to the model is the dynamic interactions of the interpersonal relationship and the probability of changes from personal and environmental forces interfacing with the relationship. Although the model does not attempt to describe normative or typical changes in close relationships, it does outline important influences that may affect a relationship over time and determine its fate. In addition, consistent with much of the literature on close relationships, the model goes beyond simply describing marital relationships by including all types of close and personal relationships. Yet, more needs to be done to test the model further (Berscheid and Lopes 1997); although the model identifies general personal and environmental parameters and interconnections, many of the specifics about change or normative aspects of inter-individual changes have not yet been developed.

Demographic Trends of Cohabiting and Never-Married Families

Since the political and social changes of the 1960s, the general public and scholars alike have focused on variations in family types and structures. This focus often has been on the baby boom cohort (1946–1962), who have tended to delay marriage, contributing to the increasing prevalence of cohabiting and never-married families. Since the mid-1960s, people have been getting married in fewer numbers, getting married at a later age, divorcing at higher rates, remaining single longer, and cohabiting in greater numbers (Bumpass and Sweet 1989; Bumpass et al. 1991; Grossbard-Schechtman 1993). The considerable attention to the baby boom cohort has been, in part, because they have been so accessible for scholarly research. Although scholars have only rather recently focused on these nontraditional family types, such lifestyle choices have been occurring for decades in the United States and other countries, especially among those with fewer resources and among older people who already have achieved some independence (Bumpass et al. 1991; Oppenheimer, Blossfeld, and Wackerow 1995).

Interestingly, the decline in marriage rates has been offset by the increase in cohabitation, and this trend may have prevented the divorce rate from continuing its pre-1980 increase. It is estimated that about 20–24 percent of unmarried American adults between ages 25 and 34 are cohabiting (Waite 1995), and by their early 30s approximately half of the population has participated in cohabita-

tion at some point in their life, while nearly two-thirds of those separated or divorced under age 35 have cohabited (Bumpass and Sweet 1989).

Cohabitants are more likely to be older and to have had less than a high school education, and they are more likely to have been raised in families who received welfare, who were headed by a single parent, or whose father had a higher education and income (Bumpass and Sweet 1989; Willis and Michael 1994). In addition, some argue that men have been more likely to cohabit when they had lower job market prospects, whereas women have been more likely to cohabit when they had better job market prospects (Manning and Smock 1995; Willis and Michael 1994), although other scholars have found the exact opposite for men (Bumpass et al. 1991) and for women (Oppenheimer et al. 1995). More important, cohabiting single mothers have benefited more economically from the living arrangement than have cohabiting single fathers, who tend to be financially better off raising a family alone (Hilton and Hill 1999). Still, uncertainties surrounding men's ability to be gainfully employed does seem to play an important role in the timing of cohabitation or marriage (Oppenheimer et al. 1995).

In addition to the increasing numbers of cohabiting adults, the percentage of never-married adults has increased slightly for white men and women (27 percent and 21 percent) and dramatically for black men and women (46 percent and 39 percent). Whereas white men and women continue to enter marriage and then leave it in larger numbers than in the past (Waite 1995), black men and women appear to be *avoiding* marriage. This decision is believed to be influenced by blacks' socioeconomic disadvantage during childhood, higher levels of mother's schooling, greater female independence (Manning and Smock 1995), lower benefits of marriage, and fewer available marital partners with the ability to contribute economically (Oppenheimer 1994; Waite 1995).

The decline in marriage and increase in cohabitation in the United States is similar to what has occurred in Western European countries during the same period; yet the rates are not as high in the United States as in some countries in Europe and Latin America. Sweden and Guatemala, for example, both have cohabitation rates much higher than those in the United States, and these rates continue to increase (Grossbard-Shechtman 1993). Given the diversity of cohabitation rates in different countries, Prinz (1995) has proposed a typology of developmental social changes regarding cohabitation and the role it plays in the course of partnership transition. Similar to individual and family developmental perspectives, he suggests that cohabitation begins as a deviant phenomenon with only a small percentage of the population participating in such a union, as is the case currently in Italy. Next, cohabitation is seen primarily as a prelude to marriage, as occurs in Germany, the Netherlands, and Austria. Cohabitation then becomes more of an alternative to marriage as attitudes towards marriage change, as has been occurring in France, Finland, Great Britain, and Norway. Finally, cohabitation is seen as an acceptable type of union, with greater proportions of the population viewing it as an acceptable end relationship—a situation slowly being approached in Sweden and possibly some Latin American countries (Grossbard-Schechtman 1993; Prinz 1995).

In addition to the changes in family formation, other demographic changes are occurring that relate to modifications in relationships. Currently, because of reductions in infant mortality, life-threatening disease, and improvements in nutrition and health care, people in many industrialized countries are living much longer (Goldman 1993; Hatch 1995; Kramarow 1995). An increasing number of these older individuals are choosing to never marry throughout the life course (Waite 1995), and a growing number of people choose to cohabit, and thus technically are not married but are not living alone. Finally, with relatively high rates of both divorce and remarriage and initiating and ending of cohabiting relationships, individuals are increasingly living in serial close relationships, which means that they will live alone and in marital and/or cohabiting rela-

tionships at different times of their lives (Scanzoni et al. 1989). Such changes have a great impact on the way we think about marriage, families, and relationships over the life course of individuals (Waite 1995).

Although theories have been applied to diverse aspects of individual and family development, including relationship development, no one has yet attempted to apply developmental aspects to relationships of cohabiting couples. Therefore, using a developmental perspective and the available literature, I will provide an overview of developmental changes in relation to different types of cohabitation and changing issues facing people choosing to cohabit or never marry.

Variations in Cohabitation

As previously mentioned, cohabitation is used in the United States primarily as a period to test the relationship or as a trial marriage without the formal ceremony or legal ramifications (Bumpass and Sweet 1989; Bumpass et al. 1991; Willis and Michael 1994). However, cohabitation has several variations. Cohabitors enter unions with various reasons and interests for relationships over the life course (Prinz 1995; Rindfuss and VandenHeuvel 1992). The following sections describe different types of cohabitation in relation to the purpose and the developmental aspects of the relationship. These types are not summaries of previous work but rather a conceptualization of the literature as it is integrated with a developmental approach.

Trial Marriage

Marci and Paul have just finished college, where they met and became involved in a relationship. Both want to get married eventually, but they are not yet sure about their relationship lasting. Neither has been married, and they would eventually like to have children. Both, however, are just starting their careers; he is in business and she is a dental hygienist. Marci and Paul want to save money, buy a house, and make sure their relationship works before making a public ceremony of their commitment.

Marci and Paul's relationship represents the most common form of cohabitation: trial marriage, which many young people enter prior to formal marriage (Bumpass and Sweet 1989; Smock and Manning 1997). Increasing proportions of first marriages begin as cohabitation (Bumpass and Sweet 1989), operating as a proxy for the engagement period (Oppenheimer et al. 1995). A marriage ceremony may be the best time to publicly cement bonds rather then when the commitment actually took place (Oppenheimer et al. 1995). In these cohabiting relationships, there is typically an expectation, at least by one partner, that they will eventually marry, but for many there is no date specified for marriage (Bumpass et al. 1991). A person who does not plan to marry his or her partner typically does not plan to marry at all (Sweet and Bumpass 1992). For this group, cohabitation is not a major rejection of marriage but a delay of marriage (Oppenheimer et al. 1995). And although such unions occur at all ages, younger adults tend to make up the largest proportion in this type of cohabitation.

Those cohabiting as a trial marriage typically form unions when they are employed and have been in a dating relationship for some time (Liefbroer, Gerritsen, and Gierveld 1994). For this group, particularly white females, pregnancy can often be a catalyst for marriage. However, pregnancy does not appear to be a motivation to marry for whites with fewer resources or for blacks, who generally are more accepting of the informal union (Manning and Smock 1995; Waite 1995). The desire to begin bearing children also does not seem to influence the timing of the transition to formal marriage (Manning 1995); when Cohabitors do marry, the timing of their first birth appears to be similar to that for women who never cohabited (Manning 1995). Cohabiting partners tend to marry when the man has higher earnings, higher education, and full-time employment; conversely, the female's socioeconomic and employment status appears to have little impact on the decision to marry (Smock and Manning 1997).

Those cohabiting as a trial marriage also move into formal unions when other major lifestyle changes occur, such as getting a job or graduating (Oppenheimer et al. 1995). These trial marriages, however, are more often terminated by separation than by marriage (Bumpass et al. 1989), and when they become legal through ceremonies, they tend to be more unstable (DeMaris and Rao 1992; Hall and Zhao 1995; Rindfuss and VandenHeuvel 1992) as couples report lower-quality relationships, lower commitment, and greater likelihood of divorce (Thomson and Colella 1992). However, such instability may be more a reflection of the individual characteristics of those who progress through many relationships, or serial cohabitation (DeMaris and MacDonald 1993), rather than a result of the transition to marriage itself. The presence of children, however, seems to have a stabilizing effect on cohabiting relationships (Wu 1995).

Alternative to Singlehood

A second group of young people sees cohabitation more as an alternative to marriage. It is estimated that 20 percent of young people do not expect to marry at all or to remarry if they have divorced (Bumpass et al. 1991). For this group, cohabitation seems to be more of an ideological choice, reflecting their experience with parents who cohabited or divorced. These Cohabitors are characterized by a looser bond (Schoen and Weinick 1993), more negative attitudes toward marriage as compared to married or other cohabiting individuals (Axinn and Barber 1997), more nontraditional values, more positive attitudes toward separation and divorce, and less positive attitudes toward childbearing (Axinn and Thornton 1996). Yet the ideology of these Cohabitors does not imply a rejection of permanence or traditional family values, especially for whites (Axinn and Barber 1997; Rindfuss and VandenHeuvel 1992). In fact, some have suggested that for these individuals, cohabitation is more of an alternative to being single than a rejection of marriage (Rindfuss and VandenHeuvel 1992; Sweet and Bumpass 1992).

This alternative-to-singlehood group includes many blacks and Puerto Ricans; their informal unions are similar to marriage in terms of the commitment, but they are much less likely to move toward marriage (Landale and Fennelly 1992), even with a pregnancy (Manning and Landale 1996). Cohabitors in these cultural groups tend to approve of a committed sexual relationship that includes children outside of a legally sanctioned union (Oropesa 1996).

Functional Cohabitation

Margarite and Juan have been living together for about two years now and have been able to work through some difficulties. They are both very busy with careers in academia, and they carve out time for each other besides the professional work they do together. Both are happy they have decided not to have children, especially with the mixed support they feel from both families because of the mixing of ethnic backgrounds. Still, they have been doing well, are committed to the relationship, and are opposed philosophically to giving power to a church or society to approve their relationship and union.

Margarite and Juan represent yet another group who cohabit: those who view the relationship as similar to marriage but as an alternative to the formal institution. In contrast to the group who make the choice as a trial marriage or the group who make this choice as an alternative to singlehood, this third group emphasizes the functional aspect of the alternative (Bumpass et al. 1991; Oppenheimer et al. 1995). In this case, the economic reasons are more important than ideology in determining the decision to cohabit. These individuals see the cohabiting relationship as yielding greater benefits than marriage. Such a decision most commonly occurs among those individuals with fewer resources and with poor prospects for change of their economic situation. This type may occur at any time in the life course, but it predominantly seems to occur in the middle years.

Peer Cohabitation

Jason and Mindi have just moved in together. It's the first time either has lived with someone other than a spouse. Jason has been married twice before and Mindi has been married once. They both have grown children from previous marriages who are pretty much on their own, although they visit regularly and still have financial dependence. Neither Jason nor Mindi is interested in having more children. Both have established careers, he as a teacher and she as a physician, and both maintained separate households long into the relationship, as they valued their own independence and routine. Yet when they moved to a new city, they decided to buy a large enough house for them to have space while also spending more time together. At this point, they both agree that there isn't much need to formalize their relationship through marriage. For them, the choice is to either live separately or cohabit.

Jason and Mindi represent a fourth group of cohabitors: middle-aged adults who see cohabitation as an alternative to marriage. Because at least one partner has been married and divorced, in many cases they are disillusioned with marriage. Nearly two-thirds of second partnerships begin as cohabitants (Willis and Michael 1994). These individuals have a positive view of remaining single and independent while at the same time they desire an intimate relationship (Rindfuss and VandenHeuvel 1992). This group also may fall into what Schwartz (1994) refers to as "peer marriage," which is much more egalitarian in terms of both sex roles and power. Peer Cohabitors tend to focus on the relationship itself, having fewer distractions with children and at times even careers. This is the type of relationship that may evolve into what Welwood (1996) describes as "the path of intimate relationship," placing an emphasis on learning and discovery of self and other through relationships—somewhat similar to Hopson and Hopson's (1994) model of black couples. Although both of these approaches deal with marriage, the issues and dynamics are applicable to middle-aged peer Cohabitors.

Cohabitation Among Older Adults

Theresa and Ahmad both lost their longtime companions in the past five years. They have many friends, engage in many activities, and enjoy retirement. They are healthy, busy, and having more fun in life now than ever before. They both like to travel and are grateful to have the time and financial support to get away at times. They also really enjoy the companionship and sexual interaction, which is easier now that they are living in the same house. Their children stay in contact but live in other cities, which gives them even fewer responsibilities and things to tie them down. They also are grateful for the learning about themselves and relationships that comes with this union.

Theresa and Ahmad represent a fifth group: older cohabiting adults who may have had a previous marriage that ended by divorce or death or who were never previously married. These older individuals want a close relationship but may not see marriage as a necessary requirement for the union. Cohabitation still does not occur among a large segment of the older population (Bumpass and Sweet 1989), although its prevalence may be underestimated as a result of too restrictive definitions of cohabitation or because Cohabitors report that they are married (Hatch 1995). However, projections call for a significant increase in cohabitation among the elderly in the near future (Hatch 1995). In this age group there is greater loneliness for those without a partner compared to those who have intimate relationships, and many (but not all) desire an intimate relationship when possible.

Gay and Lesbian Cohabitation

Mary and Linda moved in together not long after Mary's divorce. They have been together for seven years now, and they have continued to grow and learn from their relationship. They have also worked out some of the difficulties experienced by Linda, who has not had children, when Mary's son and daughter moved in with them. As with many stepfamilies, there was an adjustment for all of them, but things have worked out well. The children are adolescents now and thinking of careers and relationships, and all are happy about the honesty and caring that has been shared in this committed family.

Mary and Linda represent an increasingly visible group of cohabitants: those who, because of sexual orientation, are unable to marry legally. Often the expectation for these couples is that their relationship will not last, yet a large number of gay and lesbians enjoy long-term, committed relationships that are not publicly documented (Blumstein and Schwartz 1983; McWhirter and Mattison 1984; Slater 1995). These relationships seem to be similar in many ways to heterosexual ones in terms of life course issues, including the challenges and threats common to any close relationship (Berscheid and Reis 1998; Blumstein and Schwartz 1983). In some cases, the relationships parallel legal marriages, with the same commitments, challenges, and satisfactions (Blumstein and Schwartz 1983). In other cases, the relationships are alternatives to being single, again similar to the situation with heterosexual Cohabitors.

Cohabitation Types Over the Life Course

As indicated earlier, this typing of cohabiting relationships is a conceptual means for distinguishing the reason for the relationship and the tendency for it to occur at particular times over the life course. Although any type may occur at any time—and in the case of gay and lesbian relationships, they typically do occur over the entire life course—some types are seen more frequently at certain times than others. The trial marriage and alternatives-to-singlehood types tend to occur with younger couples. The functional type also occurs with young people, although the greatest numbers probably occur at slightly older ages. The peer relationship type seems to occur more with middle age. Such a typology, of course, only represents a "best estimate" until scholars begin to empirically distinguish different types among cohabiting couples and provide more accurate numbers and timing of types across the life course.

As cohabitation becomes more acceptable as a general type of union formation, we may also see a change in types over the life span. For example, couples may begin as a trial relationship early in their lives, then move to more of a peer relationship and then the cohabitation style of older couples. In this way, we may begin to focus more on the changes in relationships and interaction patterns that occur over the life course, as shown in the work by McWhirter and

Mattison (1984), Slater (1995), and Berscheid and Lopes (1997), rather than to emphasize structural factors or changes in family membership.

Cohabitation and Children

Approximately 40 percent of cohabiting households include children (Bumpass et al. 1991). This involves some 2.2 million children overall. Although these children are less likely to live in poverty than children in single-parent families, they also are not as economically well off as children who live in married-couple families (Manning and Lichter 1996). Children of cohabiting unions are more likely to cohabit themselves, and there is general approval of cohabitation among young adults today (Axinn and Barber 1997; Sweet and Bumpass 1992).

From this literature review of cohabiting families, five main points emerge that are important in terms of understanding cohabitation across the life course. First, it is clear that many people live in cohabiting families, but the cohabitation may well occur at different points across the life course and even at multiple times in people's lives. While the greatest incidence of cohabiting occurs among young adults, it is increasingly occurring in older age groupings across the life course. It also is clear that there are intergenerational influences and connections; children of parents who cohabit are more likely to do so themselves in one form or another. Third, some styles of cohabitation are more similar to marital relationships, whereas others are more similar to non-union relationships. Again, it is impossible to classify cohabitation into a single style or motivation. Fourth, because of the variety of cohabiting types, various terms have been developed to label cohabiting relationships, such as "unions," "close relationships" (Berscheid and Lopes 1997) or even "sexually based primary relationships" (Scanzoni et al. 1989). Given the greater acceptance, prevalence, and even normative nature of cohabitation today compared to the past, new terms that accurately reflect this diversity become increasingly important. Finally, no matter how couples are classified or relationships defined, the emo-

tional experience of dissolving a union such as cohabitation is similar to dissolving a marriage or similar close relationships (Axinn and Barber 1997; Berscheid and Reis 1998).

Never-Married Families

The greatest number and proportion of never-married individuals and families naturally occurs among young adults because of the early pregnancy and the delay in marriage that occur for this group. Young people also have had less opportunity to make the choice to marry or cohabit as they are moving into the period when such choices are being made. With increasing age, we find fewer never-marrieds, although because of divorce there are still a large number of single adults (Waite 1995).

The most dramatic increase in never-married adults is among black men and women: approximately 40 percent of black women and almost half of black men have never been married (Waite 1995). Manning (1993) reports that approximately one-fourth of first children born to never-married women were born to Cohabitors, which leaves a large proportion of the nation's children with never-married single mothers. While many women who are pregnant form a union either through marriage or cohabitation (Manning 1993), others remain single and find it a preferable option. For some of these women, it is not just about choice, but also about priorities. For example, school enrollment and age at completing school, rather than educational attainment per se, tend to delay marriage (Oppenheimer et al. 1995). Such delays begin to influence lifestyle choices because options for marriage tend to decline across the life span, especially for women, as men die at younger ages and younger men are not normatively appropriate for relationships with older women (Hatch 1995).

Yet, as outlined in the section on cohabitation, intimate relationships of all kinds are being more closely compared to being single, especially as values change and people increasingly see remaining single as a viable or preferable option (Sweet and Bumpass

1992). For example, among never-married families, fertility expectations, nonfamilial activities, and home ownership rates more closely resemble single than married individuals (Rindfuss and VandenHeuvel 1992). In addition, never-married persons who desire to and expect to cohabit in the future are much more accepting of divorce, are less likely to think that it is better to be married, and are more likely to have egalitarian sex-role attitudes than those who do not (Sweet and Bumpass 1992).

Never-Married Relationships and Health

One of the main areas of research and debate, beyond demographic information related to the never-married population, has to do with the benefits of intimate relationships for physical and mental health. A number of researchers extol the benefits of marriage, yet it remains difficult to demonstrate whether relationships are responsible for better physical and mental health or whether this finding is due to selectivity (Waite 1995). Kurdek (1991) found that married persons reported greater happiness and less depression than those in cohabiting relationships, who themselves reported greater happiness and less depression than those who lived without an intimate relationship. However, physical health was not found to be related to marital status, and age and education were as strong or stronger predictors than marital status in predicting depression. In another study, Hilton and Hill (1999) found that for fathers, cohabitation was related to higher role satisfaction than for fathers living without an adult partner, and role satisfaction was related to lower levels of depression.

This correlation between relationship status and health has also been established in other cultural contexts. In Great Britain, for individuals below age 70, long-term illness is least prevalent among the married and most prevalent among the never-married (Murphy, Glaser, and Grundy 1997). In Japan, never-married individuals have the highest mortality rate and presumably much poorer health, possibly because of the strong norm for marriage within Japanese society (Goldman 1993).

Lillard and Panis (1996) argue that persons who may benefit most in terms of health and lower mortality risks are more likely to marry and remain married, thus selectively moving into the group that facilitates a better outcome for them. In addition, there may be other factors that both promote good health and encourage marriage, and those factors may differ for never-married persons and may hinder healthy lifestyles for this latter group. It appears that for some at least, the presence of another adult in a relationship may have a positive impact on both physical and mental health (Lillard and Panis 1996; Waite 1995). What appears to be most critical for good physical and mental health are lifestyle choices, information about nutrition and exercise, and the closeness or intimacy that comes from many different types of relationships, including secure peer relationships (Koski and Shaver 1997). An interesting finding by Woodward (1988), in light of other studies, is that those who scored highest on a loneliness scale were not the elderly, those living in homes for the elderly, or even the widowed, but rather young people who were single mothers without resources, alcoholic individuals, college students, low-income single parents, and rural high school students.

Most people would agree that close relationships are important for people, whether in an intimate, sexually based close relationship or another type of intimate relationship (Perlman and Fehr 1987). Yet it appears that as people get older, they learn how to develop and maintain such close relationships, even when they are not living with someone in the same household. It is this type of security, which some argue comes from secure attachment regardless of when it is applied to relationships over the life course (Koski and Shaver 1997), that is important to the better health, greater happiness, lower depression, and other general indicators of well-being associated with being in a committed relationship. Experience in developing such relationships, and an appreciation of their importance to one's well-being, appears to develop as people mature. At the same time, as individuals develop throughout the life course, with a focus on many types of relationship possibilities, they may be more likely to maintain and cherish the importance of such relationships. Understanding both the importance and diverse possibilities of relationships allows individuals to make other choices besides moving into a cohabiting or marital arrangement in order to experience the benefits of close relationships (Berscheid and Lopes 1997).

Summarizing this work in relation to the life course is challenging because so little is really understood about never-married adults, their reasons for never marrying, and the changes in their relationships that may take place over time. What appears to happen, however, is that many young people focus on tasks (education, employment, etc.) or preferences to remain single while young. Although large proportions marry during their 20s and 30s, some remain focused on other priorities or maintain the preference of being single. With age, options for marriage decline, and for those who have had other priorities, their values may also change. The change may not be so much toward marriage or cohabitation as in the value placed on friendships and the role they play. As one learns to develop or work out close friendships, such relationships enhance one's life without the challenges of cohabitation or marriage. For those wanting greater solitude and space, such arrangements are not only acceptable but ideal. Thus, the focus from priority to changing values to enhanced relationships may describe the changes over the life course for a majority of individuals who never marry.

Conclusions

Additional scholarship is needed to further develop this area of study. The development of a model that outlines changes in relationship dynamics or interaction patterns over time is needed. Such a model may be an elaboration of Berscheid and Reis's (1998) early relationship development model or of stage descriptions of gay and lesbian relationships (McWhirter and Mattison 1984; Slater 1995). However, a more specific approach would be a critical contribution to the field, such as expanding Scanzoni et al.'s

(1989) work on sexually based primary relationships to include a description of change over the life span.

A second area for future work is further delineation of the types of cohabitation. Given that cohabiting has been acquiring some degree of legitimate family status by an increasing proportion of the population (Bumpass et al. 1991), it is important that such relationships be understood in their complexity rather than trying to study and characterize all cohabiting couples as a simple, unified group. Further, it is important to understand variations in cohabitation as it occurs over the life span, incorporating dynamic aspects and changes that occur with different types of cohabiting couples.

Another area of investigation that would seem productive is the application of what Welwood (1996) describes as "the relationship as path," which focuses on the complex development of individuals through relationships. Closely connected to this idea is the work on electrodynamic field theory and human energy fields (Burr 1972; Collinge 1998; Hunt 1996; Leigh and Metzker 1997; Reed 1996), which focuses on the electromagnetic energy in people's bodies and how it behaves when they interact with others. This work holds promise for shedding light on aspects of development and relationships that heretofore have been difficult to explain (Leigh and Metzker 1997).

Finally, understanding cohabiting and never-married relationships is important for those interested in prevention and intervention. Rather than maintaining a focus on the structure of close relationships, preventive work can help individuals learn about individual choices and the advantages and disadvantages inherent in each. For example, people may learn to develop close intimate relationships while also choosing not to maintain a household with someone just to share intimacy. Others may choose a marital relationship without feeling like they must forgo other close relationships in order for the marriage to be successful. It will be important for professionals working with cohabiting and never-married individuals to see beyond the basic categories of relationship structures and functions, investigating the complexity of each choice and family lifestyle.

Discussion Questions

1. Compare the developmental approaches of individual and family theorists in terms of cohabiting and never-married families.

2. Identify some of the major changes in demographic trends for the United States with regard to family formation and other types of unions.

3. Describe the essential aspects of each of the six groups of cohabitors outlined in this chapter.

4. Explain the major issues being faced by never-married individuals and families.

5. What are some of the major challenges being faced by scholars in terms of future theory, research, and application related to cohabitation and never-married family structures?

Glossary

Secure attachment Based on Bowl by's theory of human attachment, describes close relationships characterized by intimacy, respect, and trust, as compared to avoidant or anxious relationships characterized by partners' fears of abandonment. May also be used to describe an individual's predisposition toward close relationships—secure, avoidant, or anxious.

Sexually bonded or based primary relationship (SBPR) model A model by Scanzoni et al. (1989) that addresses a variety of committed close relationships, including traditional marriages, gay and lesbian relationships, divorced families, cohabiting couples, and other relationships that might emerge throughout an individual's life course. It is based on the premise that no one structure is best for meeting the needs of families or individuals because the concept *family* has different meanings for different individuals.

Union Relationship that can take various forms, usually including some type of his-

tory, expected future, and commitment on the part of participants.

Suggested Readings

Berscheid, E., and Lopes, J. (1997). A temporal model of relationship satisfaction and stability. In R. J. Sternberg and M. Hojjat (129–159), *Satisfaction in Close Relationships*. New York: Guilford.

Bumpass, L. L, and Sweet, J. A. (1989). National estimates of cohabitation. *Demography, 26,* 615–625.

Macklin, E. D. (1987). Nontraditional family forms. In M. B. Sussman and S. K. Steinmetz (Eds.), *Handbook of Marriage and the Family* (317–353). New York: Plenum.

Scanzoni, J., Polonko, K., Teachman, J., and Thompson, L. (1989). *The Sexual Bond: Rethinking Families and Close Relationships*. Newbury Park: Sage.

Welwood, J. (1997). *Love and Awakening*. New York: HarperPerennial.

Bibliography

Axinn, W. G., and Barber, J. S. (1997). Living arrangements and family formation attitudes in early adulthood. *Journal of Marriage and the Family, 59* 595–611.

Axinn, W. G., and Thornton, A. (1996). The influence of parents' marital dissolutions on children's attitudes toward family formation. *Demography,33,* 66–81.

Bengtson, V. I., and Allen, K. R. (1993). A life course perspective applied to families over time. In P. G. Boss, W. J. Doherty, R. LaRossa, W. R. Schumm, and S. K. Steinmetz (Eds.), *Sourcebook of Family Theories and Methods: A Contextual Approach* (469–499). New York: Plenum.

Berscheid, E., and Lopes, J. (1997). A temporal model of relationship satisfaction and stability. In R. J. Sternberg and M. Hojjat, *Satisfaction in Close Relationships* (129–59). New York: Guilford.

Berscheid, E., and Reis, H. T. (1998). Attraction and close relationships. In D. T. Gilbert, S. T. Fiske, and G. Lindzey (Eds.), *The Handbook of Social Psychology* (4th ed.) (193–281). Boston: McGraw-Hill.

Blumstein, P., and Schwartz, P. (1983). *American Couples*. New York: William Morrow.

Bretherton, I. (1993). Theoretical contributions from developmental psychology. In P. G. Boss, W. J. Doherty, R. LaRossa, W. R. Schumm, and S. K. Steinmetz (Eds.), *Sourcebook of*

Family Theories and Methods: A Contextual Approach (275–297). New York: Plenum.

Bumpass, L. L, and Sweet, J. A. (1989). National estimates of cohabitation. *Demography, 26,* 615–625.

Bumpass, L. L., Sweet, J. A., and Cherlin, A. (1991). The role of cohabitation in declining rates of marriage. *Journal of Marriage and the Family,* 53, 913–927.

Burr, H. S. (1972). *Blueprint for Immortality: The Electric Patterns of Life.* Essex, England: C.W. Daniel.

Chung, H. (1990). Research on the marital relationship: A critical review. *Family Science Review, 3,* 41–65.

Collinge, W. (1998). *Subtle Energy.* Warner Books: New York.

DeMaris, A., and MacDonald, W. (1993). Premarital cohabitation and marital instability: A test of the unconventionality hypothesis. *Journal of Marriage and the Family,* 55 399–407.

DeMaris, A., and Rao, K. V. (1992). Premarital cohabitation and subsequent marital stability in the United States: A reassessment. *Journal of Marriage and the Family,* 54, 178–190.

Duck, S. (1993). *Social Concept and Relationships.* Newbury Park, CA: Sage.

Duck, S. (1993). *Learning about Relationships.* Newbury Park, CA: Sage.

Goldman, N. (1993). The perils of single life in contemporary Japan. *Journal of Marriage and the Family,* 55, 191–204.

Grossbard-Schechtman, S. (1993). *On the Economics of Marriage: A Theory of Marriage, Labor, and Divorce.* Boulder: Westview Press.

Hall, D. R., and Zhao, J. Z. (1995). Cohabitation and divorce in Canada: Testing the selectivity hypothesis. *Journal of Marriage and the Family,* 57, 421–427.

Hatch, R. G. (1995). *Aging and Cohabitation.* NY: Garland.

Hilton, J. M., and Hill, L. C. (1999). A comparison of factors contributing to depression in cohabiting and noncohabiting custodial single parents. Manuscript under review.

Hopson, D. S., and Hopson, D. P. (1994). *Friends, Lovers, and Soul Mates: A Guide to Better Relationships Between Black Men and Women.* New York: Fireside.

Hunt, V. V. (1996). *Infinite Mind: Science of the Human Vibrations of Consciousness.* Malibu, CA: Malibu Publishing Co.

Koski, L. R., and Shaver, P. R. (1997). Attachment and relationship satisfaction across the life span. In R. J. Sternberg and M. Hojjat,

Satisfaction in Close Relationships (26–55), New York: Guilford.

Kramarow, E. A. (1995). The elderly who live alone in the United States: Historical perspectives on household change. *Demography, 32* 335–352.

Kurdek, L. A. (1991). The relations between reported well–being and divorce history, availability of a proximate adult, and gender. *Journal of Marriage and the Family,* 53, 71–78.

Labouvie, E. W. (1982). Issues in life-span development. In B.B. Wolman (Ed)., *Handbook of Developmental Psychology* (54–62). Englewood Cliffs, NJ: Prentice-Hall.

Landale, N. S., and Fennelly, K. (1992). Informal unions among mainland Puerto Ricans: Cohabitation or an alternative to legal marriage? *Journal of Marriage and the Family,* 54 269–280.

Leigh, G. K., and Loewen, I. R. (1987). Utilizing developmental perspectives in the study of adolescence. *Journal of Adolescent Research, 2,* 303–320.

Leigh, G. K., and Metzker, J. A. (1997). Reconceptualizing our view of children and the role of parents: A theoretical model for change. Paper presented at the annual meetings of the National Council on Family Relations, Arlington, VA, November.

Liefbroer, A. C., Gerritsen, L., and Gierveld, J. D. (1994). The influence of intentions and life course factors on union formation behavior of young adults. *Journal of Marriage and the Family, 56,* 193–203.

Lillard, L. A., and Panis, C. W. A. (1996). Marital status and mortality: The role of health. *Demography, 33,* 313–327.

London, R. A. (1998). Trends in single mothers' living arrangements from 1970 to 1995: Correcting the Current Population Survey. *Demography, 35* 125–131.

Macklin, E. D. (1987). Nontraditional family forms. In M. B. Sussman and S. K. Steinmetz (Eds.), *Handbook of Marriage and the Family* (317–353). New York: Plenum.

Manning, W. D. (1993). Marriage and cohabitation following premarital conception. *Journal of Marriage and the Family,* 55, 839–850.

Manning, W. D. (1995). Cohabitation, marriage, and entry into motherhood. *Journal of Marriage and the Family,* 57 191–200.

Manning, W. D., and Landale, N. S. (1996). Racial and ethnic differences in the role of cohabitation and premarital childbearing. *Journal of Marriage and the Family,* 58 63–77.

Manning, W. D., and Lichter, D. T. (1996). Parental cohabitation and children's economic well-being. *Journal of Marriage and the Family, 58,* 998–1010.

Manning, W. D., and Smock, P. J. (1995). Why marry? Race and the transition to marriage among Cohabitors. *Demography, 32,* 509–520.

McWhirter, D. P., and Mattison, A. M. (1984). *The Male Couple: How Relationships Develop.* Englewood Cliffs, NJ: Prentice-Hall.

Murphy, M., Glaser, K., and Grundy, E. (1997). Marital status and long-term illness in Great Britain. *Journal of Marriage and the Family, 59,* 156–164.

Oppenheimer, V. K. (1994). Women's rising employment and the future of the family in industrial societies. *Population and Development Review, 20* 293–342.

Oppenheimer, V. K., Blossfeld, H. P., and Wackerow, A. (1995). United States of America. In Blossfeld, H. P. (Ed.), *The New Role of Women: Family Formation in Modern Societies* (150–173). Boulder, CO: Westview Press.

Oropesa, R. S. (1996). Normative beliefs about marriage and cohabitation: A comparison of non-Latino whites, Mexican Americans, and Puerto Ricans. *Journal of Marriage and the Family, 58,* 49–62.

Papernow, P. (1984). The stepfamily cycle: An experimental model of stepfamily development. *Family Relations, 33,* 355–364.

Perlman, D., and Duck, S. (1987). *Intimate Relationships: Development, Dynamics, and Deterioration.* Newbury Park: Sage.

Perlman, D., and Fehr, B. (1987). The development of intimate relationships. In D. Perlman and S. Duck (Eds.), *Intimate Relationships: Development, Dynamics, and Deterioration* (13–42). Newbury Park: Sage.

Prinz, C. (1995). *Cohabiting, Married, or Single.* Brookfield, VT: Avebury.

Reed, H. (1996). Close encounters in the liminal zone: experiments in imaginal communication. Part I. *Journal of Analytical Psychology, 41,* 81–114.

Rindfuss, R. R., and VandenHeuvel, A. (1992). Cohabitation: A precursor to marriage or an alternative to being single? In S. J. South and S. E. Tolnay (Eds.), *The Changing American Family: Sociological and Demographic Perspectives* (118–142). Boulder, CO: Westview Press.

Rodgers, R. H., and White, J. M. (1993). Family development theory. In P. G. Boss, W. J. Doherty, R. LaRossa, W. R. Schumm, and S. K. Steinmetz (Eds.), *Sourcebook of Family Theories and Methods: A Contextual Approach* (225–254). New York: Plenum.

Rutter, M. (1980). *Changing Youth in a Changing World.* Cambridge, MA: Harvard University Press.

Scanzoni, J., Polonko, K., Teachman, J., and Thompson, L. (1989). *The Sexual Bond: Rethinking Families and Close Relationships.* Newbury Park: Sage.

Schoen, R., and Weinick, R. M. (1993). Partner choice in marriages and cohabitations. *Journal of Marriage and the Family, 55* 408–414.

Schwartz, P. (1994). *Love Between Equals.* New York: Free Press.

Slater, S. (1995). *The Lesbian Family Life Cycle.* New York: Free Press.

Smock, P. J., and Manning, W. D. (1997). Cohabiting partners' economic circumstances and marriage. *Demography, 34,* 331–341.

Sweet, J. A., and Bumpass, L. L. (1992). Young adults' views of marriage, cohabitation, and family. In S. J. South and S. E. Tolnay (Eds.), *The Changing American Family: Sociological and Demographic Perspectives* (143–170). Boulder, CO: Westview Press.

Thomson, E., and Colella, U. (1992). Cohabitation and marital stability: Quality or commitment? *Journal of Marriage and the Family, 54,* 259–267.

Waite, L. J. (1995). Does marriage matter? *Demography, 32,* 483–505.

Welwood, J. (1996). *Love and Awakening.* New York: HarperPerennial.

Willis, R. J., and Michael, R. T. (1994). Innovation in family formation: Evidence on cohabitation in the United State. In Ermischi, J. and Naohiro, O. (Eds.), *The Family, Market, and the State in Ageing Societies* (9–42). Oxford: Clarendon Press.

Woodward, J. C. (1988). *The Solitude of Loneliness.* Lexington, MA: Lexington Books.

Wu, Z. (1995). The stability of cohabitation relationships: The role of children. *Journal of Marriage and the Family, 57,* 231–236. ✦

Section III

Processes Through the Life Course of Families

Several topics which continue over the life span of families are addressed in this section. These include marital relationships, violence, the relationship between communities and families, health issues, caregiving, economics, religion, parent-child relationships, family life education, interventions, and policies issues. It is evident, from the content of these chapters that even though issues change, they persist over the life course of families. ✦

Chapter 7
Marital Relationships

A Life Course Perspective

Jacki A. Fitzpatrick

Karen S. Wampler
Texas Tech University

The diversity of family lifestyles has received increasing attention in the last few years; marriage (legally sanctified union among heterosexual adults), however, remains the most popular choice. According to the United States Bureau of the Census (1994), 60 percent of Americans adults (18+ years of age) are currently married and an additional 17 percent have been married in the past. The median age for first marriage in 1994 was 24.5 years for females and 26.7 years for males, the highest levels since 1890 (U.S. Bureau of the Census 1994).

The purpose of this chapter is to review the developmental tasks faced by couples across the lifespan of marriage. Based on a qualitative study of healthy marriages, Wallerstein (1994) identified these main psychological tasks that must be accomplished to promote enduring and satisfying relationships: (a) building a marital identity, (b) defining relationships with the social network, and (c) establishing the marriage as a zone of nurturance and safety. However, when and how these tasks are confronted and carried out may vary by racial/ethnic group and socioeconomic class. This chapter examines how each of these tasks is played out in the early, middle, and later phases of marriage.

The Early Years

Herbert and Leslie met in college and dated for three years before getting married. Herbert knew that he wanted to marry Leslie early in their relationship, but she wanted to delay this decision until after graduation. Leslie is very close to her family and expected to live in the same neighborhood, but Herbert is a very private person and wanted clear limits on contact with the in-laws. Normally Herbert and Leslie got along with each other very well, but they had been under a lot of strain while trying to make wedding arrangements. Herbert had to deal with conflicts between his single friends and Leslie's demands for his time. Leslie felt that Herbert would "zone out" when she tried to include him in discussions of wedding plans with her mother and sisters. Secretly, each of them considered elopement as a way out.

The entry to marriage, particularly a wedding, can be a time of great excitement and stress. During this time, the couple may be distracted by the details of the ceremony and honeymoon and pay less attention to their relationship. Indeed, although many couples may plan a wedding, few may actually plan a marriage. For those willing to engage in premarital counseling/education, "the good news is that there is more information available now than ever before to help couples take meaningful steps to prevent divorce and preserve meaningful relationships" (Stanley, Markman, St. Peters, and Leber 1995, 392).

The first few years of marriage, typically referred to as the honeymoon phase, are critical because the pattern of dynamics established at this phase will serve as a foundation for the future of the marital relationship. The marriage is likely to undergo many transformations across the life cycle, but this early phase serves as a template by which the later phases are judged. Tasks left undone in the early years will be problematic later. For example, developing a pattern of conflict avoidance is likely to lead to the accumulation of unresolved issues and distancing between the couple.

Building a Marital Identity

A marital identity represents the extent to which partners perceive that they are connected and integrated into each other's lives. It reflects a sense of "we-ness" or couplehood. This identity is reflected in the partners' beliefs about each other as well as their patterns of interaction (Wallerstein, 1994).

One important element of creating an identity is to understand and address the expectations that partners bring to marriage. For example, Ruvolo and Veroff (1997) examined how the discrepancy between ideal and real visions of the spouse affected marital well-being during the first year of marriage. They found that greater discrepancies were associated with less marital satisfaction as newlyweds and one year later. Similarly, Kurdek (1991) reported that marital distress at the third year of marriage was positively associated with increases in unrealistic relationship beliefs and decreases in expressiveness and emotional investment over time. Beliefs affect not only marital quality but ongoing interactions as well. This has been supported by research on attributions, or the explanations spouses generate to explain marital events. A series of studies have shown that spouses who blame marital problems on the partner's character are associated with both negative affective (e.g., whining) and behavioral (e.g., ineffective problem-solving) responses (Baucom, Epstein, Rankin, and Burnett 1996). Indeed, Ruvolo and Veroff (1997) argued that to the extent that couples begin their marriages with optimism and have ideals which they expect their partners to fulfill, the lower the satisfaction when these ideals are violated.

Alternatively, those partners who create or accept realistic standards for their marriage will likely be more satisfied and behave in ways that create a positive marital identity. This is consistent with Oggins, Veroff, and Leber's (1993) argument that "marital well-being is particularly closely tied to spouses' feeling that their partners value them and show this in behavior and words" (506). For example, self-disclosure has long been recognized as an important contributor to marital satisfaction and the primary means by which intimacy is achieved (i.e.,

Hendrick 1981). As Leslie and Herbert shared more of their life stories, goals, dreams, and stresses with each other, they felt their lives becoming increasingly entwined. Indeed, Bruess and Pearson (1993) argue that married partners use idiosyncratic communication (e.g., pet names) to create a couple culture. In their cross-sectional study of marriages, they found that satisfied spouses used more idioms than dissatisfied spouses over the life span of the marriage. They also reported that childless couples married less than five years had the highest rates of idiom use, suggesting that idioms might serve an important function in this stage of relationship development. So when Leslie and Herbert share babytalk or call each other "Sweetykins" and "Stinker," they are promoting the intimacy and uniqueness of their relationship.

In a study of African-American and Caucasian-American newlyweds, Oggins et al. (1993) highlighted other marital interactions that may promote identity. They found that African-American spouses reported more self-disclosure, more positive sexual interactions, and fewer areas of disagreement than Caucasian spouses, but affective affirmation was a significant predictor of happiness for all subsamples. Similarly, husband newlywed satisfaction was positively related to affectional behaviors by both husband and wife two years later (Huston and Vangelisti 1991). And in a study of nonverbal behaviors among Australian couples, Noller and Feeney (1994) reported that husbands' early marital satisfaction was associated with greater accuracy in decoding wives' nonverbal messages. Such decoding is essential because it may reduce misunderstandings that contribute to conflict (Noller and Feeney 1994) and promote sensitivity to partner moods (Wallerstein 1994).

Another important means of creating a marital identity is shared time with one's partner. Although shared time is often defined by dating activities in premarital relationships, it is structured in different ways after the wedding. For example, Huston, McHale, and Crouter (1986) conducted a longitudinal study that examined changes in the pattern of activities during the first year of marriage. Although they found no decrease in the frequency of shared activities, the nature of the activities changed substantially. Spouses reported that they spent less time together in leisure activities and conversation and more time completing instrumental tasks (e.g., shopping, yardwork, housework). Additionally, the rate of enjoyable activities (e.g., expressing approval) declined approximately 40 percent during the year. Interestingly, the rate of negative activities did not increase over the year; however, they may have become more salient in the absence of some pleasurable activities. In this context, it is not surprising that most couples find it difficult to maintain the emotional intensity of the honeymoon phase. However, such patterns also highlight the value of maintaining leisure in marriage and continuing to "date" one's spouse. In other words, continuing to engage in pleasurable activities and taking time to be together other than during the completion of instrumental tasks may contribute to positive affective changes in the first year. For Herbert and Leslie, they have an understanding that Friday nights are to be reserved for them, and they typically spend this time watching movies, just as when they were dating.

Defining Relationships With the Social Network

Marital identity and patterns of interaction are not created in isolation. Rather, they are created in the context of the broader social relationships that each partner brings to the marriage, as well as the newer "couple friends" in their lives. This complex of social relationships represents the couple's social network. One task of early marriage is to determine the ways in which the network members will be part of the marital life.

It might be expected that the transition to marriage would signal an automatic reduction in the involvement with the social network so that the couple can dedicate more time to their romantic relationship. Given the changes found in couple time, this shift might seem highly advisable (Huston et al. 1986). However, this is not always the case. Network members are often part of the couple's life long before marriage and may even

affect the development of the courtship process. Based on retrospective interviews with newlywed spouses, Surra (1987) identified four types of relationship pathways to marriage and the reasons for changes in commitment across the pathways. Those in the *accelerated* pathway moved quickly toward marriage and withdrew from activities with network members as the romantic relationship progressed. Commitment turning points were most frequently linked to interpersonal/normative reasons, such as expectations for marriage. Couples in the *prolonged* type had the longest pathways and remained involved with the social network throughout courtship. For this type, commitment changes were most often tied to uncontrollable life circumstances.

The *intermediate* type of pathway was characterized by moderate length and active involvement with the social network. Intermediates most frequently identified dyadic reasons (nature of relationship) for commitment changes. Couples in the *accelerated-arrested* pathway moved quickly toward marriage but then slowed momentum. This type was characterized by a more severe withdrawal from both the network and romantic partner during engagement and into the marriage. Those in the accelerated-arrested type also most frequently identified reasons related to the social network for commitment turning points. Interestingly, couples in the accelerated-arrested pathway may also have the lowest level of involvement with the social network but are most strongly influenced by third parties (e.g., friends, family) in determining the future of the relationship.

Similarly, Johnson, Huston, Gaines, and Levinger (1992) generated a marital typology that reflected, among other factors, the degree of network involvement after the wedding. Based on interviews with couples who had been married for approximately two years, the researchers identified (a) a *parallel* marriage type in which husbands spend more time with friends and wives spend more time with extended family, (b) a *symmetrical* type characterized by husbands and wives who spend equal time with family and friends, (c) a *differentiated* companionate type, indicative of couples who spend little time with network members, and (d) a *reversed* type in which husbands are more involved with both family and friends than wives are. The researchers argued these marital types reflected the partners' views about leisure, gender, and interdependence as a marital unit. Given Leslie's greater involvement and connectedness with her family, her marriage would be consistent with the parallel type.

According to Timmer, Veroff, and Hatchett (1996), the definition of social network involvement also reflects cultural views of family. The authors argued that compared to Caucasian Americans, African Americans value extended family to a greater degree. Based on interviews with couples in their first and third years of marriage, they found that family plays an important role in marital adjustment. More specifically, as African-American husbands and wives became closer to the husband's family, marital happiness increased; this was particularly helpful to high-stress marriages. A similar pattern did not emerge for Caucasian couples.

Involvement with the social network can also facilitate the development of a marital identity. According to Timmer et al. (1996), African-American women's family ties can be strong to the point that they may interfere with the formation of new relationships. However, women's integration into the in-law family network may "disrupt the potentially negative consequences of being over-embedded in one's family of origin" (355) and provide further socialization into the marital role.

Establishing a Zone of Safety and Nurturance

Clearly, new couples face many challenges in their relationships with each other and their extended family. Under these conditions, it is critical that spouses have a sense that their marriage is a safe environment in which they will be protected from harm (physical or psychological) and supported. Two major ways to establish this zone of safety are to provide social support and to engage in prosocial conflict resolution.

These factors have long been associated with satisfying relationships and are two key dimensions of interpersonal competence.

Much of the literature on social support focuses on support from outsiders (family and friends) given to one or both spouses rather than support spouses give to each other. Yet the husband or wife may be the most common source of support, particularly if the marriage is an important relationship and spouses share much time together. And given that many spouses also see their partners as best friends, they take much of the responsibility for social support that would be expected from this friendship. According to Cutrona, Hessling, and Suhr (1997), there is a certain degree of reciprocity in spousal support. In their study of spouses married approximately four years, they found that although personality influenced the provision of support, the best predictor of support a spouse received was the amount they had given the partner in their last interaction. Such support is critical during the early years of marriage as couples also face the tasks of establishing their marital relationship and negotiating the degree of parental involvement in their lives. So when Herbert told Leslie's parents that they needed some private time as a couple and that the parents were not free to visit them without calling first, he expected Leslie to back him up in this discussion. In exchange for this concession, Leslie needed Herbert to spend more time listening to and supporting her as she dealt with the demands of her promotion.

Another important factor in creating a zone of safety is learning ways to successfully resolve conflicts. Similar to other marital tasks, conflict resolution doesn't simply "kick in" after the wedding. Rather, it is influenced by the pattern of premarital interactions, partner characteristics, and the social context of the relationship.

For example, Acitelli, Douvan, and Veroff (1993) focused on marital attitudes when they studied the similarity of spousal attitudes toward conflict among black and white newlyweds. They found that perceived similarity was (a) greater than actual similarity and (b) a stronger predictor of marital well-being than actual similarity. The researchers argued that perceived similarity is powerful because spouses are creating a shared reality during the first year of marriage, which in part reflects couple norms about conflict resolution. Interestingly, although no cultural differences were reported in the first year, they were evident in a follow-up study (Acitelli, Douvan, and Veroff 1997). By the third year of marriage, wives' understanding of husbands' conflict tactics was related to higher satisfaction for black couples and lower satisfaction for white couples. The authors speculated that the social norms of the honeymoon period in early marriage may be so strong that they overcome cultural differences which only become apparent after the first year.

Noller, Feeney, Bonnell, and Callan (1994) also found a relationship between conflict and marital quality in early marriage. In a study of Australian couples, they assessed conflict tactics and satisfaction prior to the wedding and twice again during the first two years of marriage. The authors found a reciprocal pattern between these factors: early satisfaction predicted later conflict tactics, and early tactics predicted later satisfaction. More specifically, they stated, "There were no changes over time in the use of conflict patterns, suggesting that destructive communication patterns which cause problems later in marriage are present before marriage" (245). In contrast, highly satisfied spouses over time used more positive strategies, such as reasoning or compromise.

Overall, such research suggests that the early years of marriage are an important time in which spouses begin creating an identity, defining their social relationships, and establishing a safe relationship. Their premarital relationship in part shapes the nature of the marital relationship, but many other factors can influence how the marital relationship develops over time. Similarly, the early years of marriage create a context for middle marriage, but this middle phase also represents some changes in marital tasks.

The Middle Years: Maintaining Relationships in the Face of Competing Demands

Although Leslie and Herbert expected marriage to be easier over time, that did not turn out to be true. As Leslie became more established at work, they finally had a sense of financial security. This was a critical time in her career, but her job required more time away from home, and she was caught in a tug-of-war between her family and her work. Leslie's sister told her that their parents would not be able to live alone in the house much longer and that somebody was going to have to take them in. Herbert wanted to be supportive and admired her ambition, but he also wanted to have children and felt that wouldn't happen if they didn't make it a priority in the next few years.

Less is known about the middle years of marriage than the early years. Most of our images of marriage in movies and books focus on the beginning of relationships, or, less often, on the traumatic end of relationships, through either divorce or death. Rarely do we see what happens after "they fall in love and get married." Perhaps the day-in, day-out maintenance of relationships is not viewed as very interesting. The middle years of marriage are harder to define because there is little agreement about the time frame covered (particularly in the absence of children) and because of cultural differences in the context of marriage. For example, because of shorter life expectancy and higher divorce rates, the middle years of marriage may be less salient for many African Americans. In Hispanic cultures, the marital relationship may be less central than the ties between parents and their adult children (Wilkinson 1987). Clearly, this stage is becoming more distinct and important as life expectancy increases and couples spend more years together after the children leave home. Even though middle marriage has not long been recognized as a stage in the family life cycle, married couples continue to face key developmental tasks.

Building a Marital Identity: Balancing Marriage and Individual Growth

Long-term trajectories of relationships are, in part, determined by the characteristics that each individual brings to the relationship. Although these individual attributes are often more emphasized in the dating and mate selection literature, they continue to be important in the middle years of marriage. For example, Kelly and Conley (1987), in a longitudinal study of 300 couples over a period of 45 years, found that low neuroticism of the husband and wife and high impulse control of the husband were better predictors of long-term positive outcomes (marital satisfaction, stability) than early socialization or marital attitudes. This does not mean that the outcome of the marriage is *determined* by the personality characteristics; rather, these traits continue to play an important role in relationship quality over time.

Another trait proven to be predictive of marital satisfaction is adult attachment style. Many readers will be familiar with the concept of attachment style from research on the interaction of young children with their parents. Some literature has suggested that attachment styles developed with a primary caregiver in early childhood can serve as a template for adult romantic relationships (Simpson 1990). In romantic relationships, *secure* adults are defined as comfortable in depending on others and as wanting to be close to their partners. In contrast, *avoidant* individuals are defined by their difficulty in trusting others and discomfort in close relationships. *Ambivalent* adults are identified by a simultaneous desire to be very close to their partners and a reluctance and worry about the relationship. Adult attachment style has been found to be highly related to individual psychological and dyadic adjustment (Shaver and Brennan 1992). Herbert and Leslie both have secure attachment styles. Although they are experiencing some challenges in this marital phase, they are comfortable in openly expressing their viewpoints, offering support, and addressing conflicts, and they have confidence that their relationship will survive.

Given that these characteristics are defined as relatively unchanging and enduring, how does this become a task for middle marriage? Essentially, it means that an important task for each spouse is to continue to work on self-growth and maturity to overcome deficits from the past. Often, it means working through issues such as family-of-origin problems, addictions, and unrealistic relational expectations. To resolve such issues, opportunities for self-growth such as 12-step meetings, therapy, and enhanced spirituality are important to middle marriage

Defining Relationships With the Social Network: Maintaining Boundaries

One of the most stable research findings about marriage over time is that marital satisfaction declines during the early years, reaches its lowest point during the middle years, and increases again in the later years (e.g., Feeney 1994). Generally, these changes are the result of a decline in positives during the middle years accompanied by an increase in the number of stresses. Stresses include increased work demands, parenting of adolescents, financial responsibilities for young adult children and aging parents and for older kin.

One of the inevitable tasks of the middle years of marriage is to realign family boundaries to allow for the expansion of family networks (in-laws as children marry, grandchildren) simultaneously with the contraction of these networks (loss of parents, children leaving home). Less is known about changes in the social network for couples without children. It is assumed that couples without children would also experience changes in their social network as a result of loss of parents and changes in friends' lives, for example, through marriage and divorce. Although they have no children of their own, these couples would also experience expansion through births of nieces and nephews. The issue of whether to have children came to a head for Herbert and Leslie when her mother died of cancer. As Herbert had a more flexible work schedule, he spent more time with Leslie's parents. Although he was never close to his own father, Herbert and his father-in-law became close as they shared the trials and tribulations of a lengthy illness together. Leslie felt somewhat displaced by Herbert's greater closeness to her family, so she took a leave of absence from her job prior to her mother's death and reconnected with her family in a way that had been missing for several years. Leslie and Herbert also had two children in the next three years.

In many middle-class families, the period of launching children has been extended because of difficulties some young adults experience in becoming independent (such as economic pressures and divorce). The family in the middle years of marriage has sometimes been described as an "accordion" to emphasize these alternating periods of children moving in and out of the home. More frequently than in the past, couples in the middle years of marriage end up raising their grandchildren. Simultaneously, couples in the middle years of marriage have continuing responsibility for aging parents and, with increasing life expectancy, may keep these responsibilities well into retirement.

Maintaining a Zone of Safety and Nurturance

Each individual must take primary responsibility for his or her growth and level of psychological adjustment, but the emotional support offered by one's marriage partner is a crucial factor in psychological adjustment. Beach, Fincham, Katz, and Bradbury (1996), in a major review, found that perceptions of social support from one's partner were "uniquely beneficial" to psychological and physical health. This sense of support is closely related to attachment style, and it is assumed that those with a secure attachment style will be better able to offer and benefit from such support. Emotional support is closely related to the sense of safety and nurturance and of being "at home" with the other (Wallerstein 1994). Although providing emotional support to one's life partner may be part of a satisfying marriage, the relative importance of providing this support varies by culture. For example, in many African-American families a large network of extended family and close friends considered equivalent to family are important sources of support and may render the support function of marriage somewhat less important.

The importance of social support varies by gender as well. In a study of long-term marriage, Acitelli and Antonucci (1994) found that emotional support in marriage was closely linked to marital satisfaction, especially for wives. In turn, evidence has accumulated that wives often carry the bulk of the responsibility for providing emotional support in marriage (Acitelli and Antonucci 1994; Gottman 1994). Recently, marital therapists have begun to emphasize the importance of emotional support by both partners. This emphasis has been described as helping both provide acceptance of the partner through high levels of validation, compassion, and sympathy, and the avoidance of attempts to change the partner (Jacobson and Christensen 1996). Thus, the middle years of marriage offer couples new opportunities for refocusing on the marriage (Walsh 1988).

Another way to think about the exchange of support and other resources is the "bank account" (Gottman 1979). More specifically, a useful metaphor for marriage is a bank account containing a large amount of money. At any one time, one spouse may be putting in or taking out a lot more than the other, but in the long run there is plenty for both. Thus, a crucial aspect of maintaining a positive relationship in the middle years is keeping a high balance of positives. It is only when the bank balance comes close to zero or is overdrawn that each partner begins to watch each transaction and to demand equity: "I'm not doing this until you do that!" Indeed, when the account is overdrawn, it is difficult to deposit positives because negative attributions are often given to behavior that was previously viewed as positive. For example, bringing flowers two weeks after a forgotten birthday has less ability to restore a positive balance to the account than remembering the birthday on time. Such relational omissions (e.g., forgetting important events or ignoring partner preferences) can add to a sense of mistrust or disappointment, which can promote a tone of negativity in the relationship. This tone then primes partners to behave in more adverse ways, which can come to permeate the relationship over time. So it is important that partners work to resolve such relational issues as they occur and seek opportunities to engage in positive behaviors. Perhaps the most important way of encouraging positives is to offer high levels of emotional support, spend time together in mutually satisfying activities, and maintain a positive sexual relationship (Wallerstein 1994).

Unresolved conflict dramatically interferes with accumulating positives in the relationship. A high level of conflict is closely tied to a lower level of emotional support (Beach et al. 1996) and is one of the strongest predictors of lower marital satisfaction across the life cycle (Feeney 1994). Conflict management is also closely tied to personality and individual characteristics. For example, there are strong links between poor psychological adjustment and negative behaviors in resolving conflict.

Because of the development of observational methods, including videotaped couple interactions, we know a good deal about spousal conflict resolution. One of the most common negative ways of handling conflict has been called the *demand-withdraw pattern* (Noller 1993). The most typical version of this pattern is that the wife demands change from her husband in a negative way, and the husband withdraws from interaction (Carstensen, Gottman, and Levenson 1995). Many explanations have been offered for this pattern, including gender differences in the ability to tolerate emotional arousal (Gottman 1994) and power differences in the relationship, with husband withdrawal representing a way for him to maintain or take back power (Noller 1993).

In addition to husband withdrawal (or "stonewalling"), Gottman (1994) identified other couple-interaction behaviors predictive of marital distress and eventual separation/divorce. In a summary discussion of ways to balance these negative behaviors, Gottman, Katz, and Hooven (1997) state:

> The best single predictor of dissolution across studies tends to be contempt, particularly the wife's contempt. Contempt is the single clearest index of the disintegration of affectionate and empathetic emotional connection in the marriage, and there is ample evidence that the antidote of contempt is admiration. The behavior of defensiveness is an essential element in this process cascade, and it fuels the process of emotionally distancing the couple. There is ample evidence across several laboratories that the antidote for defensiveness is validation. (196)

It is important to note that the research does not indicate that negatively valanced emotions, such as anger or frustration, should be suppressed. Such emotions should be shared with the partner, but this should be done in a nonpunitive manner. Indeed, attachment theory and much research suggest that expression of these emotions in a caring relationship is a key aspect of marital success.

Conflict management also contributes to the nature of the marital identity. For example, a basic aspect of marriage is a balance of autonomy and relatedness. In the middle years of marriage, a renegotiation of this balance may be crucial to continuing marital success (Wallerstein 1994). Research has shown that many types and styles of marriages are successful. For example, Fitzpatrick (1988) identified three types of satisfying couple relationships based on the preferred style of (a) conflict resolution and (b) balance of autonomy and interdependence. *Traditionals* value interdependence and engage in conflict only on key issues. *Separates* value autonomy and avoid conflict. *Independents* value both interdependence and autonomy and engage in direct confrontation over a wide range of issues. Interestingly, Gottman (1994) identified three very similar types of satisfied couples. In addition, he identified two types of dissatisfied couples—one characterized by a high level of hostility and the other by a combination of hostility and withdrawal. With the changes in their careers and families, Leslie and Herbert realized that their lives were becoming increasingly intertwined. So they were moving from being Separates early in their marriage to being Independents during the middle years.

In sum, relatively less is known about the middle phase of marriage than the earlier years. However, research indicates that important tasks remain that couples must address, and diverse marital pathways reflect how these tasks are accomplished. The results of these marital tasks at this phase have important implications for the later years of marriage.

Older Years: Keeping a Meaningful Relationship in the Face of Loss

Leslie and Herbert were working hard to make the new house a home. Now that both of their children had families of their own, it seemed unnecessary to stay in the old house. Herbert was now retired and liked the friends in their new community. Leslie could never completely abandon her work, so they agreed that she would do consulting on a part-time basis as long as it didn't interfere with their family time. Although they still had occasional quarrels and problems, Herbert and Leslie had never felt closer than during their recent years together.

Much has been written about the elderly. Unfortunately, most of this literature focuses on retirement, relationships with children, aging, and death. Even though the population of elderly women who are divorced is the most rapidly growing group (Uhlenberg, Cooney, and Boyd 1990), this phase of marriage is also lasting longer than at any other time in history, with more emphasis on couple activities and leisure (Dickson 1995). The extended contact, particularly after retirement, creates new challenges for couples. This stage also depends on culture, with some groups continuing to focus on parent-child ties. Many European-American couples live in age-segregated communities, whereas many minority families, particularly Hispanic and African American, continue to remain close to children and grandchildren, with less focus on the marital relationship (McGoldrick 1988).

What is known about this phase of marriage suggests continuity between the middle and late years of the marriage, with generally high levels of marital satisfaction (e.g., Dickson 1995). For example, Carstensen et al. (1995) compared a group of couples in their 40s and 50s with a group in their 60s and 70s. The characteristics of the marriages reflected the same pattern for both groups. The only difference was a finding of somewhat less negativity and more affection in the older group. Johnson (1985), in her research of long-term marriages, found some unique characteristics emerging that pulled couples closer together, including a sense of survivorship and pride in the length of marriage. Other researchers (e.g., Troll, Miller, and Atchley 1979) identified an evolution in marital feelings over time, with longer marriages characterized by attachment more than affection and loyalty more than ardor. Although there appears to be generally high marital satisfaction in late life, there are unique challenges in the later phase.

Holding on to a Marital Identity

A task in late marriage is to continue to find meaning in the relationship in the face of physical decline and death. One of the most difficult aspects of life that some couples must face has been labeled "ambiguous loss" (Boss 1991). For example, with Alzheimer's disease, the spouse may still be physically present, but the person who was known and loved is gone. Similarly, changes in physical health may interfere drastically with the ability to function as a couple in terms of time spent together, shared activities, and sexuality. Additionally, older spouses must face their own mortality (Walsh 1988). However, the literature on widowhood suggests that it is often more difficult to accept the loss of a spouse than to accept the inevitability of one's own death.

According to Wallerstein (1994), a key aspect of identity in later marriage "involves the capacity and willingness of each partner to maintain a vision of the other that combines early idealizations with a firm grasp of the present reality" (649). One way to address these visions is the "life review" (Walsh 1988). A life review entails re-evaluating of life goals and achievements and coming to terms with these experiences. This examination includes a review of the marital relationship and shared history between the spouses. Often such a life review is prompted by questions from adult children or grandchildren about the early years of the marriage and changes over time. Other times, it might be that the couple reminisces with each other, friends, or siblings about important moments in their life together. Sometimes, a life review is triggered by a family crisis. After Herbert's first heart attack, he and Leslie spent many hours reliving the most important moments of their marriage and how she would continue if he died.

Defining Relationships With the Social Network: Developing Additional Social Supports

Couples who have been independent and self-sufficient may be forced to rely increasingly on outside supports as physical health declines and the partners are less able to care for each other. In European-American families, this may mean more involvement of social service agencies and adult children in their lives. Mancini and Blieszner (1992) found that relationships with adult children become even more important for those over 65, whether the parent is married, divorced, or widowed. For Mexican-American and African-American couples, this may mean less of a change, given the pattern of more integration of adult children into their lives as a couple all along (Falicov 1996; Hines and Boyd-Franklin 1996). Just as Leslie made career sacrifices when her mother was dying, she expected her children to help deal with family changes precipitated by Herbert's illness.

Marriage as a Zone of Safety: Continuing to Nurture Each Other

Even with the generally positive outlook of this period, conflicts may increase, especially over health and dependency issues. To deal with these issues, couples often used a joking, bantering style as a way of coping (Johnson 1985). Like Fitzpatrick (1988), Dickson (1995) conducted interviews with couples who had been married over 50 years and identified three types of marriage. *Connected* couples were characterized by high intimacy and interdependence. *Functional separate* couples were characterized by positive feelings but many separate activities. *Dysfunctional separate* couples were characterized by negative feelings, conflict, and

separate activities. In her interviews, Dickson (1995) found that the two satisfied types (connected and functional separates) identified mutual respect, agreement on degree of closeness, and a mutual vision/life plan as key to their marital happiness. In sharp contrast, those in dysfunctional marriages based their long-term relationship on the unacceptability of divorce and used distance as a means of conflict suppression. In the face of his health problems, Herbert came to depend on Leslie more and more over the passing years. When she stopped consulting altogether, Herbert found himself the recipient of her undivided attention. Although this situation was initially appealing, he soon found that her constant care was more than he needed. Fortunately, he felt comfortable joking with her about this, and Leslie was able to pull back and give him the room to enjoy the independence he had left. So they moved from being an Independent couple in their middle years to being a Connected couple now.

Even given the physical and social changes that may surround older adulthood, the spouse usually remains an important source of social support, providing opportunities for affection, reassurance of worth, and intimacy (Mancini and Blieszner 1992). The bond of marriage can be critical to a continued sense of security and emotional stability. This fact is illustrated very well in the comic strip "For Better or For Worse," when the grandfather talks about putting his wife in the hospital for what is probably a terminal illness and says to his daughter that he is "losing his best friend." It is clear that the ability of spouses to provide a "secure base" and "safe haven" continues to be a crucial aspect of marriage in the later years (Dorfman, Homes, and Berlin 1996).

Conclusions

This chapter highlighted the ways in which identity, network, and safety tasks are accomplished across the life span of marriage. Although there are other tasks that may be important for some couples (e.g., balancing the spouse's and children's psychological needs), we focused on tasks we felt were relevant to all marriages. In examining these tasks, we noted that although there are some similarities across time, there are also unique aspects of each task as the marriage (and partners) mature.

As this chapter suggests, a good deal of study has been dedicated to understanding marriage. Across stages, researchers have focused extensively on conflict resolution, social support, and relational cognitions. Our knowledge of these relational phenomenon has been enhanced by multimethod studies (e.g., Gottman 1994) that included both insider and outsider perspectives on marital interactions. Additionally, cross-cultural studies have begun to identify both common and idiosyncratic patterns of marital interactions.

However, some significant limitations to marital research should be considered. First, although cross-cultural studies have become more prominent, researchers still focus predominantly on white, European-American, middle-class couples, and studies of early marriage frequently focus on college students, ignoring social class, cultural, and age variations. Therefore, it is important to refrain from using these middle-class marriages as a template by which to evaluate all marriages. In addition, because many cohabiting and gay and lesbian unions clearly resemble legal marriage, future work should investigate relationship dynamics in these couples across the life course. Second, much of the research has examined only one phase of marriage. There are only a few cross-sectional studies that assess similarities/differences across marital phases, and rarer still is longitudinal research that tracks changes in marriages across time. Additionally, much of the research focuses on the adjustment to early marriage, with less attention being given to the marital processes of middle or later marriage. Research on these later phases has primarily focused on marital outcomes from other events (e.g., parenthood, launching children, retirement), rather than on the marriage itself. Further, couples without children have been relatively ignored in the family life cycle literature. Given these gaps, conclusions about marital relationships should be made with caution.

Our knowledge about marital development can be enhanced in several ways. First, more research should be conducted on daily interactions between marital partners. Such research would inform us about the small but important ways that spouses support and interfere, share and disagree with each other. Given the increasing life span of individuals (and thus their relationships), research that focuses on middle and later marital phases would help us understand how couple behavior promotes relationship longevity. Additionally, more ethnographic research that examines spouses' views of their own relationships is warranted. Retrospective interviews have been used successfully with newlyweds (e.g., Surra 1987) and helped us to understand the multiple pathways leading to marriage. The next logical step is to examine the multiple pathways through marriage over the years.

Another important advancement would be the integration of clinical and nonclinical perspectives. Much of the nonclinical empirical work takes a developmental approach and focuses on specific periods or transitions in marriage (e.g., transition to parenthood). This approach is limited by its focus on events rather than processes. In contrast, the clinical literature tends to focus on relational processes with little consideration of the developmental context in which marriages exist. From this perspective, the phases of marriage are treated as interchangeable or irrelevant. Given the popularity of premarital and postmarital intensive couple workshops, it seems prudent to combine the best elements of both approaches and tailor such relational workshops more specifically to the needs of couples at various stages of the marital life span. Finally, the marital literature would be enhanced by more cross-cultural research. Given the strength of the social context across the marital life span, it is important to identify the dimensions of marriage that are truly "universal" and those that are unique to particular cultures or subcultures.

Discussion Questions

1. What are three key developmental tasks of marriage?

2. What processes are continuous across the early, middle, and later phases of marriage?

3. What processes are unique to each phase?

4. How does culture affect fulfillment of these tasks?

5. How does personality affect fulfillment of these tasks?

Glossary

Connected couples Couples characterized by high intimacy and interdependence.

Dysfunctional separate couples Couples characterized by negative feelings, conflict, and separate activities.

Functional separate couples Couples characterized by positive feelings but many separate activities.

Marital identity The extent to which partners perceive that they are connected and integrated into each other's lives.

Suggested Readings

Beavers, W. R. (1985). *Successful Marriage: A Family Systems Approach to Couples Therapy.* New York: Norton.

Carter, B., and McGoldrick, M. (1988). *The Family Life Cycle: A Framework for Family Therapy,*, 2nd ed. New York: Gardner.

Cate, R. M., and Lloyd, S. A. (1992). *Courtship.* Newbury Park, CA: Sage.

Gottman, J. M. (1994) *What Predicts Divorce: The Relationship Between Marital Processes and Marital Outcomes.* Hillsdale, NJ: Erlbaum.

Pierce, G. R., Sarason, B. R., and Sarason, I. G. (Eds.). (1996). *Handbook of Social Support and the Family.* New York: Plenum.

Bibliography

Acitelli, L., and Antonucci, T. C. (1994). Gender differences in the link between marital support and satisfaction in older couples. *Journal of Personality and Social Psychology, 67,* 688–698.

Acitelli, L., Douvan, E., and Veroff, J. (1993). Perceptions of conflict in the first year of marriage: How important are similarity and understanding? *Journal of Social and Personal Relationships, 10,* 5–19.

Acitelli, L., Douvan, E., and Veroff, J. (1997). The changing influence of interpersonal perceptions on marital well-being among black and white couples. *Journal of Social and Personal Relationships, 14,* 291–304.

Baucom, D. H., Epstein, N., Rankin, L. A., and Burnett, C. K. (1996). Assessing relationship standards: The Inventory of Specific Relationship Standards. *Journal of Family Psychology, 10,* 72–88.

Beach, S. R. H., Fincham, F. D., Katz, J., and Bradbury, T. N. (1996). Social support in marriage: A cognitive perspective. In G. R. Pierce, B. R. Sarason, and I. G. Sarason (Eds.), *Handbook of Social Support and the Family* (43–65). New York: Plenum.

Boss, P. (1991). Ambiguous loss. In F. Walsh and M. McGoldrick (Eds.), *Living Beyond Loss: Death and the Family* (164–175). New York: Norton.

Bruess, C., and Pearson, J. (1993). "Sweet pea" and "pussy cat": An examination of idiom use and marital satisfaction over the life cycle. *Journal of Social and Personal Relationships, 10,* 609–615.

Carstensen, L. L., Gottman, J. M., and Levenson, R. W. (1995). Emotional behavior in long-term marriage. *Psychology and Aging, 10,* 140–149.

Cutrona, C., Hessling, R., and Suhr, J. (1997). The influence of husband and wife personality on marital support interactions. *Personal Relationships, 4,* 379–394.

Dickson, F. C. (1995). The best is yet to be: Research on long lasting marriages. In J. T. Wood and S. Duck (Eds.), *Under-studied Relationships: Off the Beaten Track* (22–50). Thousand Oaks, CA: Sage.

Dorfman, L., Homes, C., and Berlin, K. (1996). Wife caregivers of frail elderly veterans: Correlates of caregiver satisfaction. *Family Relations, 45,* 46–55.

Falicov, C. J. (1996). Mexican families. In M. McGoldrick, J. Giordano, and J. K. Pearce (Eds.), *Ethnicity and Family Therapy* (2nd ed., 169–182). New York: Guilford.

Feeney, J. A. (1994). Attachment style, communication patterns, and satisfaction across the life cycle of marriage. *Personal Relationships, 1* 333–348.

Fitzpatrick, M. A. (Ed.). (1988). *Between Husbands and Wives: Communication in Marriage.* Beverly Hills, CA: Sage.

Gottman, J. (1979). *Marital Interaction: Experimental Investigations.* New York: Academic.

Gottman, J. M. (1994). *What Predicts Divorce: The Relationship Between Marital Processes and Marital Outcomes.* Hillsdale, NJ: Erlbaum.

Gottman, J. M., Katz, L. F., and Hooven, C. (1997). *Meta-emotion: How Families Communicate Emotionally.* Mahwah, NJ: Erlbaum.

Hendrick, S. (1981). Self-disclosure and marital satisfaction. *Journal of Personality and Social Psychology, 40,* 599–606.

Hines, P. M., and Boyd-Franklin, N. (1996). African-American families. In M. McGoldrick, J. Giordano, and J. K. Pearce (Eds.), *Ethnicity and Family Therapy* (2nd ed., 66–84). New York: Guilford.

Huston, T., McHale, S., and Crouter, A. (1986). When the honeymoon's over: Changes in the marital relationship over the first year. In R. Gilmour and S. Duck (Eds.), *The Emerging Field of Personal Relationships* (109–132). Hillsdale, NJ: Erlbaum.

Huston, T., and Vangelisti, A. (1991). Socioemotional behavior and satisfaction in marital relationships: A longitudinal study. *Journal of Personality and Social Psychology, 61,* 721–733.

Jacobson, N. S., and Christensen, A. (1996). *Integrative Couple Therapy: Promoting Acceptance and Change.* New York: Norton.

Johnson, C. L. (1985). The impact of illness on late-life marriages. *Journal of Marriage and the Family, 47,* 165–172.

Johnson, M., Huston, T., Gaines, S., and Levinger, G. (1992). Patterns of married life among young couples. *Journal of Social and Personal Relationships, 9,* 343–364.

Kelly, E. L., and Conley, J. J. (1987). Personality and compatibility: A prospective analysis of marital stability and marital satisfaction. *Journal of Personality and Social Psychology, 52,* 27–40.

Kurdek, L. (1991). Predictors of increases in marital distress in newlywed couples: A 3–year prospective longitudinal study. *Developmental Psychology, 27,* 627–636.

McGoldrick, M. (1988). Ethnicity and the family life cycle. In B. Carter and M. McGoldrick (Eds.), *The Family Life Cycle: A Framework for Family Therapy* (2nd ed., 69–90). New York: Gardner.

Mancini, J. A., and Blieszner, R. (1992). Social provisions in adulthood: Concept and measurement in close relationships. *Journal of Gerontology, 47,* 14–20.

Noller, P. (1993). Gender and emotional communication in marriage: Different cultures or differential social power? *Journal of Language and Social Psychology, 12,* 132–152.

Noller, P., and Feeney, J. (1994). Relationship satisfaction, attachment, and nonverbal accuracy in early marriage. *Journal of Nonverbal Behavior, 18,* 199–221.

Noller, P., Feeney, J., Bonnell, D., and Callan, V. (1994). A longitudinal study of conflict in early marriage. *Journal of Social and Personal Relationships, 11,* 233–252.

Oggins, J., Veroff, J., and Leber, D. (1993). Perceptions of marital interaction: Among black and white newlyweds. *Journal of Personality and Social Psychology, 65,* 494–511.

Ruvolo, A., and Veroff, J. (1997). For better or for worse: Real-ideal discrepancies and the marital well-being of newlyweds. *Journal of Social and Personal Relationships, 14,* 223–242.

Shaver, P. R., and Brennan, K. A. (1992). Attachment styles and the "Big Five" personality traits: Their connections with each other and with romantic relationship outcomes. *Personality and Social Psychology Bulletin, 18,* 536–545.

Simpson, J. (1990). Influence of attachment styles on romantic relationships. *Journal of Personality and Social Psychology, 59,* 971–980.

Stanley, S. M., Markman, H. J., St. Peters, M., and Leber, B. D. (1995). Strengthening marriages and preventing divorce. *Family Relations, 44,* 392–401.

Surra, C. (1987). Reasons for changes in commitment: Variations by courtship type. *Journal of Social and Personal Relationships, 4,* 17–33.

Timmer, S., Veroff, J., and Hatchett S. (1996). Family ties and marital happiness: The different marital experiences of black and white newlywed couples. *Journal of Social and Personal Relationships, 13,* 335–359.

Troll, L., Miller, S., and Atchley, R. (1979). *Families in Later Life.* Belmond, CA: Wadsworth.

Uhlenberg, P., Cooney, T., and Boyd, R. (1990). Divorce for women after mid-life. *Journal of Gerontology, 45,* S3–S11.

U.S. Bureau of the Census. (1994). *Marital Status and Living Arrangements: March 1994* (20–484). Washington, DC: U.S. Government Printing Office.

Wallerstein, J. S. (1994). The early psychological tasks of marriage: Part I. *American Journal of Orthopsychiatry, 64,* 640–650.

Walsh, F. (1988). The family in later life. In B. Carter and McGoldrick (eds.), *The Changing Family Life Cycle: A Framework for Family Therapy* (2nd ed., 311–332). New York: Gardner.

Wilkinson, D. (1987). Ethnicity. In M. B. Sussman and S. K. Steinmetz (Eds.), *Handbook of Marriage and the Family* (183–210). New York: Plenum. ✦

Chapter 8
A Life Course Approach to Family Violence

Richard Gelles
University of Pennsylvania

In New York City, a police officer kills his wife and two children and then commits suicide. In New Jersey, a rabbi hires a hit man to kill his wife. In Philadelphia, a foster mother beats her child to death and throws the body into a river. In South Carolina, Susan Smith first claims that a black man kidnapped her two sons, then days later admits she pushed her car into a lake, drowning her two boys, strapped into seatbelts in the car. A substantial portion of the nation watched transfixed for years as former football star/broadcaster/movie actor O.J. Simpson was tried twice—once in criminal court, once in a civil suit—for the murder of his ex-wife, Nicole Brown Simpson, and Ron Goldman.

Off the front page and later in the broadcast news shows are shorter, less dramatic stories. Shootings, stabbings, and beatings of family members and intimates with nonfatal outcomes make news only if the story is unusual—newlyweds exchanging gunfire in a parking lot after the wedding reception—or if the protagonists are well-known: Pamela Anderson Lee is attacked by her ex-husband, drummer Tommy Lee, or septuagenarian actor Harry Morgan strikes his wife.

Beyond the news stories and talk shows are the daily and often regular pushings, shovings, punchings, and other acts of physical violence that make up the majority of instances of violence between intimates.

Over the last three decades, family and intimate violence has been transformed from an issue obscured by selective inattention to a problem that receives increasing professional, public, and policy attention. The explosive growth in our knowledge and understanding of the various aspects and facets of family violence has produced a wealth of empirical data along with deep and intensive controversies about those data and their meaning (Gelles and Loseke 1993). While this chapter is titled "Family Violence," there really is no unified field of study or practice that falls neatly under that term. Family violence is only rarely viewed as a holistic problem. The "balkanization" of the field of family violence, which includes research, practice, and social policy, has significantly limited the application of a life course perspective to violence between intimates. None of the major reviews of family violence (National Research Council 1993b, 1996, 1998) nor the major edited volumes (Ohlin and Tonry 1989; Van Hasselt, Morrison, Bellack, and Hersen 1988) even mention the concept "life course" in the index, let alone devote significant attention to the life course as a theoretical construct that could illuminate the problem of family violence. Barnett and her colleagues' (1997) family violence text, while titled *Family Violence Across the Life Span*, uses the life span as a chapter organizing device but does not use or mention life course as a conceptual framework. One article that does examine violence from a life course perspective is Suiter and her colleagues' analysis of marital violence (1990).

This chapter examines family violence as a unified field. As I have stated elsewhere (Gelles 1997), although it is important to understand the nature and causes of child maltreatment or violence against women, concentrating on just one form of violence or abuse may obscure the entire picture and hinder a more complete understanding of the causes and consequences of violence and abuse between intimates. The forms of family violence often overlap—researchers have found that child abuse is more likely to occur in homes where there is domestic violence—

and in some instances violence toward women and children is carried out by the same individual (Davis 1988; Edleson 1996; Gelles 1998; Hughes, Parkinson, and Vargo 1989; Straus, Gelles, and Steinmetz 1980). Second, some of the proximate factors associated with one form of intimate violence (age, socioeconomic status, stress, social isolation) are also associated with other forms of family violence. Lastly, a holistic approach to family violence may allow for the use of theoretical perspectives, such as the life course perspective, that may be less applicable or appropriate when considering individual forms of violence, abuse, and maltreatment.

Although a life course perspective has been applied to marital violence and to sexual victimization (Gelles and Wolfner 1994; Suiter, Pillemer, and Straus 1990), as noted above the life course perspective has not been applied to the diverse aspects of intimate violence. Thus, there are few papers, studies, or data that specifically use the life course perspective that can be summarized in this chapter.

Families, Intimate Relationships, and Violence

Before I begin to examine family violence through the lens of a life course perspective, it is important to explicitly define the key terms. While at first glance it may seem obvious what "family violence" means, a closer look reveals that defining the key terms is often complex and controversial.

Defining Violence

The question of what is meant by *violence* has been debated for more than three decades. One definition is that violence is *any* act that is harmful to the victim. This broad definition of violence includes physical attacks, threatened physical attacks, psychological or emotional aggression and abuse, sexual assaults or threatened sexual assaults, and neglectful behavior. The narrower definition confines the term to only acts of physical violence.

There is no consensus as to how broad or narrow the definition of violence should be

or as to how to define the specific components of any definition (e.g., violence, neglect, rape, psychological abuse). The discussions about the appropriate definition of violence are influenced by a variety of perspectives. First, there is the scientific or research perspective, which seeks a clear nominal definition that is grounded in theory and that can be reliably and validly operationalized. This perspective tends toward a narrow definition of violence, because violence is, at least theoretically, conceived to be conceptually distinct behavior from other methods of inflicting harm or pain on another person (Etzioni 1971). The humanistic perspective takes a broader approach and offers a definition that captures the full range of harm that can be inflicted on individuals—*harm* being defined as acts of commission or omission that interfere with a human being achieving her or his developmental potential. Finally, political approaches define violence in terms of advocacy or political goals. Thus, feminists define the problem as one of "violence against women" rather than spouse abuse, domestic violence, or family violence.

One widely used definition of violence is that violence is "any act carried out with the intention, or perceived intention, of causing physical pain or injury to another person. The physical pain could range from the slight pain of a slap to a murder" (Gelles and Straus 1979). The National Research Council's panel on "Assessing Family Violence Interventions" used the following definition of "violence":

> Family violence includes child and adult abuse that occurs between family members or adult intimate partners. For children, this includes acts by others that are physically and emotionally harmful or that carry the potential to cause physical harm. Abuse of children may include sexual exploitation or molestation, threats to kill or abandon, or lack of emotional or physical support necessary for normal development. For adults, family or intimate violence may include acts that are physically or emotionally harmful or carry the potential to cause harm. Abuse of adult partners may include sexual coercion or assaults, physical intimidation, threats to kill or to harm, restraint of nor-

mal activities or freedom, and denial of access to resources. (National Research Council 1998, 19)

Defining Family

Lost in the controversy over the definition of violence has been the term *family*. It is often taken for granted that the term *family violence* refers to violence that occurs between family members. *Family* is conventionally defined as a "group of two or more persons related by birth, marriage, or adoption and residing together in a household" (U.S. Bureau of the Census 1992). Although scholars have vigorously debated this definition and developed alternative definitions (see Gelles 1995 for a summary), the conventional definition is most widely used.

Were we to use the conventional definition of family in the study of family violence, most, but not all, forms of violent acts would be covered. However, violence between dating partners does not fit within the conventional definition of family, as dating partners are not related by birth, marriage, or adoption. Similarly, violence in gay or lesbian relationships does not fit within the conventional definition of family, although it would fit under some scholars' definitions. Conforming to the traditional definition would result in overlooking the substantial level of violence that occurs in gay and lesbian relationships. Estimations of the extent of violence in such relationships range from 11 to 45 percent (Brand and Kidd 1986; Renzetti 1992). Finally, the violence that occurs between divorced partners would not fit within the conventional definition. Thus, some students of family violence (Gelles 1997) have argued that the term *family* should be replaced by *intimate* and that the resulting focus should be on violence in intimate relationships.

The Extent and Patterns of Violence Over the Life Course

Because little research has applied a life course perspective to family or intimate violence, few studies have examined the extent of violence in terms of specific stages in the individual or family life course. This section presents findings of existing research on the relationship between age of offender and age of victim, and the occurrence of family and intimate violence and abuse.

Criminal Violence

An 8-year-old girl disappeared in Jacksonville, Florida. After a two-day search, her body was found stuffed in a waterbed in the home of a neighbor. The girl had been stabbed to death before her body was hidden in the bed. The killer was a 10-year-old boy. In Chicago, a 10-year-old and an 8-year-old boy threw a 5-year-old to his death from the roof of a building. When young assailants commit homicide or acts of criminal violence, the stories make national headlines because they are so unusual.

Violence, whether inside or outside family and intimate relationships, is an age-graded phenomenon. Research on criminally violent behavior finds that the rates for murder and nonnegligent manslaughter are highest for those aged 15 to 24, with the 20–24 group having the highest rate, as measured by arrests (National Research Council 1993a).[1] The rates of homicide and nonnegligent manslaughter decrease for each age group over 24, with the rate for those 65 years of age and older about the same as for those 14 years of age or younger. The same general trend occurs for aggravated assault, with the highest rate for those 20 to 24. However, the rate for those 65 years and older is much lower than that for 14 and younger (National Research Council 1993a).

These statistics, which are arrest rates for a specific year—in this case 1990—do not tell the complete story about the relationship between age and violence because they are cross-sectional. Longitudinal research adds further evidence about the age-graded nature of violent behavior.

Delbert Elliott (1994) has reported on the data from his National Youth Survey, a longitudinal study of a national probability sample of 1,725 youths aged 11–17 that began in 1976. Nine waves of data were analyzed for the youth panel, who were aged 27 to 33 when interviewed for the ninth wave in 1993. Elliott examined how the behavioral repertoires of serious violent offenders develop over time and what proportion of those who initiate serious violent offending continue serious violent offending into adulthood.

As with most other studies of youth violence, Elliott (1994) found that serious violent behavior is primarily a male adolescent/ early adulthood phenomenon. For males older than 24, the rate of serious violent offending was half that at peak ages and less than that for 12 years of age. The onset of serious violent behavior tends to occur at about age 12 and increases rapidly between the ages of 13 and 14, peaks between the ages of 14 and 15, and then declines thereafter. Elliott's data, unlike the arrest data reported earlier in this section, are based on self-reports. Elliott notes that first arrests for serious violent behavior tend to occur several years after the initiation of this type of offense. Also, as with other studies of youth violence, Elliott found that serious violent offenders constituted less than 5 percent of the National Youth Survey sample but accounted for 83 percent of the index offenses.

Family and Intimate Violence: Offenders

Not surprisingly, research on family and intimate violence also finds that intimate violence is an age-graded phenomenon. Age is one of the most consistent risk factors for the perpetration of family and intimate violence (National Research Council 1998). However, the peak ages for family and intimate violence are slightly older than the peak ages for criminal violence. Analyses of violence toward children and violence toward partners find that family and intimate violence are most likely to be carried out by those between the ages of 18 and 30.

Child maltreatment. In December 1995, Elisa Izquierdo was killed by her biological mother, Awilda Lopez. Mrs. Lopez was apparently convinced that Elisa was under a spell and that the spell had to be beaten out of her. Mrs. Lopez tortured her daughter repeatedly. She slapped, punched, and burned Elisa. She raped and sodomized Elisa with toothbrushes and hairbrushes. Finally, she killed Elisa by throwing her against a wall. Elisa is one of about 1,200 children killed by their parents or caretakers each year.

Official reports of child abuse and neglect, including The Third National Incidence Study of Child Abuse and Neglect (NIS-3) (U.S. Department of Health and Human Services 1996) and the National Child Abuse and Neglect Data System (NCANDS) (National Center on Child Abuse and Neglect 1997) do not provide data on the age of the reported or suspected perpetrator. Data on age of offender and violence toward children are available from the National Family Violence Surveys (Wolfner and Gelles 1993). These surveys here found an inverse relationship between age and violence toward children.

Violence toward women. One of the atypical aspects of the O.J. Simpson case is that Simpson was 49 years old at the time that he was alleged to have killed his ex-wife. An analysis of the data from the same 1985 National Family Violence Survey found that young men are significantly more likely to abuse their spouses and partners (Fagan and Browne 1994). For male offenders, the highest rate is for men age 18 to 19 and the lowest rate is for men 50 and older (Gelles, Lackner, and Wolfner 1994; Suiter et al. 1990). Over 20 percent of men between the ages of 26 and 35 had committed at least one act of intimate violence in the previous year. Violence was reported by 7.2 percent of men age 36 to 50 and by 4.2 percent of men age 50 and older.

Family and Intimate Violence: Victims

Because a great deal of the data on family and intimate violence is based on official reports focusing on victims or on self-reports from victims, more data are available on the age of the victims of intimate and family violence.

Child maltreatment. The risk of homicidal violence is greatest among children less than one year of age. Forty-one percent of the victims of fatal child abuse are less than a year old, most of the victims are younger than 2 years old, and only 10 percent are older than 4 (Levine, Compaan, and Freeman 1994; McClain, Sacks, and Frohlke 1993).

The NIS-3 survey of recognized and reported child abuse found an "inverted U-shaped" relationship between all forms of maltreatment and the child's age (U.S. Department of Health and Human Services 1996). The peak age group for maltreatment victimization was 6 to 8 years old; the lowest rate of reported and recognized maltreatment was birth to 2 years old. The pattern for specific forms of maltreatment varied. The rate of recognized and reported physical abuse was lowest for birth to 2 years old and peaked at ages 6 to 8 and again at 12 to 14. The rate of sexual abuse was near zero for birth to 2 years of age, peaked at ages 6 to 8, and remained at the same level until age 14, with a small decrease in the rate for ages 15 to 17. Because neglect makes up nearly 50 percent of all reports of child maltreatment, the age pattern for neglect was essentially the same as the pattern for all forms of maltreatment. The peak rate of injury for children was for those ages 6 to 8.

Data from the National Family Violence Survey (Wauchope and Straus 1990) also reveal an "inverted U-shaped" relationship between age and physical punishment and age and more severe violence toward children. The lowest rates of physical punishment and severe violence were for the youngest children, under age 1, and the oldest children, 16 or older. The peak age for both physical punishment and severe violence was between ages 2 and 3. This is somewhat younger than the peak age for maltreatment in the studies of recognized and reported child maltreatment. This apparent inconsistency can be resolved if we assume that the onset of physical violence begins some time before instances of physical punishment and violence are recognized and officially reported (similar to the inconsistency between self-reports and arrest data on criminal violence). Wauchope and Straus (1990) also report on the chronicity of violence toward children. Chronicity, or mean number of assaults on a child per year, is highest for 2- to-4 year-olds and then generally declines, with the exception of an increase around 12 to 14 years of age.

Violence toward women. As would be expected as a result of marital age homogamy, women age 18 to 19 have the highest rates of victimization, whereas the lowest rate is for women age 50 years and older.

Data from the National Crime Victimization Survey are consistent with data from the National Family Violence Surveys. Here again, there is an inverse relationship between age and violent victimization of women (Bachman 1994; Bachman and Saltzman 1995). However, for all forms of victimization, the highest rates of violence are reported by women 12 to 18 years old. This is primarily because of the high rate of women being victims of violence at the hands of friends or acquaintances. For violence in intimate relations, women age 19 to 29 years old report the highest rates of victimization.

Domestic homicide has a different age distribution, with the victims being older than the victims of nonfatal violence. The modal age of a domestic homicide victim (male or female) is 30 to 59. Sixty-five percent of all spousal homicide victims are 30 to 59 years of age (Dawson and Langan 1994). An analysis of intimate partner and family homicides in New York City between 1990 and 1994 found that the majority of intimate-partner homicide victims were women between the ages of 20 and 39 (Wilt, Illman, and Brody Field 1997).

A Life Course Perspective

The fact that the collective data on child maltreatment and domestic violence indicate that family violence is an age-graded phenomenon does not, in and of itself, support a life course explanation for this relationship. The negative or curvilinear relationship between age and family violence could be evidence of life course variations and transitions influencing the risk of family violence. On the other hand, the data could be evidence of a cohort effect—that is, variations in the rate of offending or victimization could be the result of differences in the experiences of individuals raised in a particular historical period.

Suiter and her colleagues (1990) examined data from the two National Family Violence Surveys to assess whether the negative relationship between age and marital violence was a cohort effect or a life course phenomenon. They found no evidence of a cohort effect. Young men (age 18 to 29) had the highest rates of violence in 1975. This same cohort, who would have been 28 to 39 at the time of the 1985 survey, had a lower rate of marital violence than the men 18 to 29 in 1985. The same pattern was found for female offenders, thus ruling out a cohort effect.

Suiter and her colleagues were unable however, to identify life course transitions or developmental tasks that explained the changing rate of marital violence. The variables available for analysis were inadequate to do more than observe that as the rates of marital violence declined with age, so did the rates of marital conflict, husband's drinking, and verbal aggression.

Transitions

Research on family violence does offer some tentative insights into the relationship between life course stages and transitions and the risk of family violence. Thus, this section identifies some of the key stages in the life course that have been identified as having higher rates of family violence.

Courtship and cohabitation. The earliest students of family violence, having uncovered much higher rates of violence in marriage than had been expected, coined the phrase "the marriage license as a hitting license" (Gelles 1974; Straus 1975). This phrase suggested that rates of violence in marriage were higher than the rate of violence among nonmarried couples. However, subsequent research on dating couples and couples who cohabited found that violence in dating and cohabiting relationships was actually more common than among married couples (Lane and Gwartney-Gibbs 1985; Stets and Straus 1990; Yllo and Straus 1981). Studies that examined the possibility of violence in dating and courtship found that between 10 and 67 percent of dating relationships involve violence (Sugarman and Hotaling 1989).

Here again, the question is whether these high rates are a consequence of age or life course factors. Without controlling for age, dating couples do indeed have higher rates of assault than married couples. When age is controlled, dating couples have the lowest rate of violence and cohabiting couples have

the highest rates of violence (Suiter et al. 1990).

What is it about cohabiting couples, or cohabitation as a life course stage, that produces the highest rate of intimate violence? While both married and cohabiting couples share the conflicts and problems that are inherent in any primary group, cohabiters may lack the stake in the relationship and stake in conformity that keeps conflict from escalating to violence. Cohabitation may involve less psychological, social, and material investment and commitment to the partner and the relationship.

Pregnancy. Pregnancy is one stage in the family life course that has received considerable attention in terms of an increased risk of battering. Not only does it appear that women are more likely to be hit and abused when they are pregnant, but the nature of the attacks seems to change. One woman reported to us, "It was weird. Usually he hit me in the face with his fist, but when I was pregnant he used to hit me in the belly. It was weird."

It may not have been "weird." A number of studies have found an increased risk of violence toward women who are pregnant (Campbell, Pugh, Campbell, and Visscher 1995; Carlson 1977; Flitcraft 1977; Gayford 1975; Gelles 1975; Giles-Sims 1985; Walker 1979, 1984). Gazmararian and her colleagues (1996) report that the prevalence of violence during pregnancy ranges from 0.9 percent to 20.1 percent. It is presumed by many researchers that the onset of pregnancy or the developmental transitions associated with pregnancy create stresses and other problems that increase men's use of force and violence toward their partners. However, when I examined the relationship between violence and pregnancy, controlling for age, I found that the relationship between violence and pregnancy disappeared when age is controlled (Gelles 1988). Thus, the apparent relationship occurred because young women were more likely to be victims of domestic violence *and* were more likely to be pregnant.

Children. The previously reviewed data on age of child and child maltreatment indicates that newborn children and infants have the highest risk of being victims of fatal child abuse. There are a number of plausible explanations for this finding—some of which are related to a life course perspective. First, newborns and infants may be more fragile, and thus more susceptible to a fatal injury. On the other hand, the stresses associated with childbirth and a new child may increase the risk of parental violence or maltreatment. Newborns can create financial and economic stress, not to mention the demands of caring for a dependent child.

Unfortunately, there have been no studies that examine whether first-born children run the greatest risk of fatal abuse compared to later-born children, so it is not possible to determine whether the key aspect is the developmental task of the onset of children into a family or the task of childbirth in and of itself, irrespective of whether the child is first or later born.

The early years of marriage and family. Scholars who apply a life course perspective to the family note that a complex relationship exists among work, life course, and the economy (Nock 1992). In the early years of marriage, the income in families where wage earners hold either blue-or white-collar jobs typically exceeds family needs. However, the birth of a child tends to bring the balance of income and needs close together for white-collar workers and brings needs above resources for blue-collar workers (See Nock 1992, 282). In blue-collar families, needs exceed income until the last child leaves home, while needs are about equal to income in white-collar families until the last child leaves home. An economic model or theory of family violence (see Gelles and Straus 1979) would explain the higher rates of all forms of family violence during the early years of marriage as a function of the "life cycle squeeze" caused by needs exceeding resources.

The life cycle squeeze is particularly problematic for families in which the husband or wife is unable to find work. Unemployment and underemployment are important risk factors for both child maltreatment and domestic violence (Straus et al. 1980).

Divorce and separation. One life stage that has received some attention from do-

mestic violence researchers is the increased risk of severe and fatal violence during separations or divorce. The most severe violence tends to occur immediately after the breakup of an intimate relationship. Women are more likely to be victims of a homicide when they are estranged from their husbands. The risk of a homicide is greatest in the first two months after a separation (Wilson and Daly 1993).

Feminist theory (Dobash and Dobash 1979; Pagelow 1984; Smith 1991a, 1991b; Yllo 1983, 1988, 1993), which views violence as a pattern of coercive control exercised by men to maintain power in a patriarchal society, offers a partial explanation for the increased risk of violence when an intimate relationship ends. Other researchers (see for example Jacobson and Gottman 1998) explain the danger created by a separation as a function of the personality of the batterer. Some batterers, whom Jacobson and Gottman call "pitbulls," fear being abandoned by their partners and use severe or fatal violence to control the partner when the relationship is ending. Other batterers, whom Jacobson and Gottman call "cobras," do not generally respond to the end of the relationship in such a volatile or dangerous fashion.

Remarriage. Some researchers (see Kalmuss and Seltzer 1986) have found the rate of marital violence to be higher in remarriages than first marriages. However, when age is controlled, there is no difference in the rate of violence in first marriages when compared to remarriages (Stets and Straus 1990).

Later-Life Families. The data on age and violence presented so far clearly show that the risk of all forms of family violence decreases with age. Obviously, when children leave home they significantly reduce the likelihood of being victims of any form of child maltreatment. During the earlier life course stages, the less time children are at home, the less time they are vulnerable to violence and abuse. Marital violence also decreases with age. This may be a function of the offenders "aging out" of their violent behavior (for any number of reasons, including biological changes or an increase in stake in conformity). Another explanation is that women may be leaving violent men and thus do not continue to be involved with violent offenders later in the life course.

One form of family violence that does increase in later life is maltreatment of the elderly. Abuse of the elderly has generated a significant amount of professional and public concern, yet it remains a poorly understood facet of intimate violence. In part, this is because the study of elder abuse is a recent development.

Abusive treatment toward the elderly can take many forms. Caretakers may tie an aged relative to a bed or chair in order to go shopping or finish the housework. Caretakers may overmedicate their parents to "ease" the older person's discomfort and to make him or her more manageable. Other caretakers resort to physical attacks to "make elderly relatives mind" or to coerce them into changing a will or signing the house or social security checks over to them. Some caretakers have used such excessive physical violence or have neglected the needs of the older person to such an extent that the person has died.

The varied forms of the mistreatment of the elderly are typically grouped into four categories: *physical abuse,* the infliction of physical pain or injury, including punching, bruising, restraining, or sexually molesting; *psychological abuse,* the infliction of mental anguish, such as humiliating or intimidating, and threatening harm; *financial abuse,* the illegal or improper exploitation of the elder's property or assets; and *neglect,* including refusal or deliberate failure to fulfill a caretaking obligation, such as abandoning the elder or denying food or health care. Some definitions of elder abuse include a fifth category, "self abuse," where the harm is inflicted by the elder himself or herself.

Estimates of the proportion of those 65 years of age or older who are abused or neglected range from 4 to 10 percent (Pagelow 1989). Wolf (1995) estimates that 5 percent of those 65 or older were victims of physical abuse, psychological abuse, financial exploitation, or neglect in the previous year. A rate of 5 percent would mean that 2 million elders are abused each year.

It is not clear whether abuse of the elderly is caused by the increased dependency of the elder victim or the dependency of the elder's caregiver. Some researchers argue that resentment over having to care for a dependent parent or relative is a key causal factor (see, for example, Steinmetz 1993), whereas other researchers have found that it is the dependency of the abuser and not the elder that is a risk factor (Hwalek, Senstock, and Lawrence 1984; Pillemer 1985, 1993; Wolf, Strugnell, and Godkin 1982). Especially in cases of physical abuse, the perpetrators tend to be financially and emotionally dependent on those they abuse. The explanation for this contradiction to the common-sense explanation for the occurrence of elder abuse is that abuse is an act carried out as a response to perceived powerlessness (Finkelhor 1983). The adult child who is still dependent on the elderly parent may strike out or maltreat as a compensation for the lack, or loss, of power.

It is noteworthy that while abuse of the elderly by their children or caregivers receives the most public and professional attention, the most common abuser of someone over the age of 55 years of age is the individual's spouse or partner (Pillemer and Finkelhor 1988).

Cultural Issues

The main focus of this chapter has been an examination of family violence across the life course. Thus, the major concern has been the age-and life stage-related aspects of intimate and family violence. There are other important social, cultural, and demographic factors that also influence the onset, duration, and impact of violence between intimates. Social class, unemployment, and social stress are important factors that either increase the risk of conflict and violence or insulate families from the occurrence of violence and maltreatment. Low income, unemployment, and stressful events increase the risk of violence, while social support decreases the risk of violence (Gelles 1997; National Research Council 1998).

The relationship between race and ethnicity and intimate violence is more complicated. Both official report data and self-report survey data often report that child abuse and violence toward women are over-represented among racial and ethnic minorities. These differences are not just a function of racial and ethnic minority families having lower incomes than white households. For some minority groups, violence has become a cultural adaptation to economic stress and discrimination. On the other hand, the social support provided by families, friends, and neighbors in minority communities insulates many households from the impact of stress and results in a lower than expected occurrence of intimate violence (Gelles 1997).

Conclusions

The findings presented in this chapter make it clear that age is related to the likelihood of engaging in family or intimate violence and being the victim of such violence. Suiter and her colleagues (1990) have ruled out that the age association is a cohort effect. Thus, the high rate of violence among those in their late teens and early twenties is somehow related to age or life course stage. Unfortunately, while research on the life course and family violence can suggest which stages may have the highest rates of intimate violence, we as yet do not know whether developmental tasks related to these stages play any causal role in the higher rate of intimate violence.

Learning more about the relationship between the life course, life course stages, and developmental tasks can provide important theoretical insights into the etiology of family and intimate violence and would provide important information that can be used to develop interventions, prevention programs, and policies that can ameliorate intimate violence and its consequences.

Discussion Questions

1. What is the relationship between age and violent behavior? Which age groups have the highest risk of engaging in family or intimate violence? Which age groups have the highest risks of becom-

ing victims of family and intimate violence?

2. Is the association between age and violence a cohort effect? What evidence is there to support your answer?

3. Is the risk of domestic violence greater during pregnancy?

4. What is the most dangerous life course stage in terms of violence toward women?

5. What are the developmental task issues related to the occurrence of violence toward the elderly?

Glossary

Family Traditionally, a group of two or more persons related by birth, marriage, or adoption and residing together in a household. In the study of family violence, a better term would be *intimate relationships* (includes dating, cohabitation, and gay and lesbian relationships).

Inverted U-shaped relationship of violence against children The phenomenon that the lowest rate of violence is birth to 2 years old, the peak age for maltreatment is 6 to 8 years old, and then the rate decreases at about age 15.

Life cycle squeeze The situation that occurs when economic needs exceed resources; it occurs for many blue-collar families when children are born and continues until the last child leaves home.

Violence Any act carried out with the intention, or perceived intention, of causing physical pain or injury to another person.

Suggested Readings

Barnett, O. W., Miller–Perrin, L., and Perrin, R. D. (1997). *Family Violence Across the Life Span: An Introduction.* Thousand Oaks, CA: Sage.

Gelles, Richard. (1997). *Intimate Violence in Families* (3rd ed.). Thousand Oaks, CA: Sage.

National Research Council. (1998). *Violence in Families: Assessing Prevention and Treatment Programs.* Washington, DC: National Academy Press.

Suiter, J., Pillemer, K., and Straus, M. (1990). Marital violence in a life course perspective. In M. A. Straus and R. J. Gelles (Eds.), *Physical Violence in American Families* (305–317). New Brunswick, NJ: Transaction.

Bibliography

Bachman, R. (1994). *Violence Against Women: A National Crime Victimization Survey Report.* Washington, DC: U.S. Department of Justice, Bureau of Justice Statistics.

Bachman, R., and Saltzman, L. (1995). *Violence Against Women: Estimates from the Redesigned Survey.* Washington, DC: U.S. Department of Justice, Bureau of Justice Statistics.

Barnett, O. W., Miller-Perrin, L., and Perrin, R. D. (1997). *Family Violence Across the Life Span: An Introduction.* Thousand Oaks, CA: Sage.

Brand, P. A., and Kidd, A. H. (1986). Frequency of physical aggression in heterosexual and female homosexual dyads. *Psychological Reports, 59,* 1307–1313.

Campbell, J. C., Pugh, L. C., Campbell, D., and Visscher, M. (1995). The influence of abuse on pregnancy intentions. *Women's Health Issues, 5,* 214–223.

Carlson, B. (1977). Battered women and their assailants. *Social Work, 22,* 455–460.

Davis, K. A. (1988). Interpersonal violence: The children as victims. *Issues in Comprehensive Nursing, 11,* 291–302.

Dawson, J. M., and Langan, P. A. (1994). *Murder in Families.* Washington, DC: U.S. Department of Justice, Bureau of Justice Statistics.

Dobash, R. E., and Dobash, R. (1979). *Violence Against Wives.* New York: Free Press.

Edleson, J. L. (1996). The overlap between woman abuse and child abuse. *Domestic Violence Abuse Project: Training and Research Update, 8,* 1.

Elliott, D. S. (1994). Serious violent offenders: Onset, developmental course, and termination—The American Society of Criminology Presidential Address. *Criminology, 32,* 1–21.

Etzioni, A. (1971). Violence. In R. K. Merton and R. Nisbet (Eds.), *Contemporary Social Problems* (709–741). New York: Harcourt Brace Jovanovich.

Fagan, J. A., and Browne, A. (1994). Violence between spouses and intimates: Physical aggression between women and men in intimate relationships. In A. J. Reiss, Jr. and J. A. Roth (Eds.), *Understanding and Preventing Violence* (Vol. 3, 115–292). Washington, DC: National Academy Press.

Finkelhor, D. (1983). Common features of family abuse. In D. Finkelhor, R. J. Gelles, G. T. Hotaling, and M. A. Straus (Eds.), *The Dark Side of Families: Current Family Violence Research* (17–28). Newbury Park, CA: Sage.

Flitcraft, A. (1977). Battered women: An emergency room epidemiology and description of a clinical syndrome and critique of present therapeutics. Unpublished master's thesis, Yale Medical School.

Gayford, J. J. (1975). Wife battering: A preliminary survey of 100 cases. *British Medical Journal, 1,* 194–197.

Gazmararian, J. A., Lazorick, S., Spitz, A., Ballard, T., Saltzman, L. E., and Marks, J. S. (1996). Prevalence of violence against pregnant women. *Journal of the American Medical Association, 275,* 1915–1920.

Gelles, R. J. (1974). *The Violent Home.* Newbury Park, CA: Sage.

Gelles, R. J. (1975). Violence and pregnancy: A note on the extent of the problem and needed services. *Family Coordinator, 24,* 81–86.

Gelles, R. J. (1988). Violence and pregnancy: Are pregnant women at greater risk of abuse? *Journal of Marriage and the Family, 50* 841–847.

Gelles, R. J. (1995). *Contemporary Families: A Sociological View.* Thousand Oaks, CA: Sage.

Gelles, R. (1997). *Intimate Violence in Families* (3rd ed.). Thousand Oaks, CA: Sage.

Gelles, R. J. (1998). *The Relationship Between Husband-wife Violence and Violence Toward Children.* Kingston, RI: Mimeographed.

Gelles, R. J., Lackner, R., and Wolfner, G. D. (1994). Men who batter: The risk markers. *Violence Update, 4,* 1.

Gelles, R., and Loseke, D. (Eds.). (1993). *Current Controversies on Family Violence.* Newbury Park, CA: Sage.

Gelles, R. J., and Straus, M. A. (1979). Determinants of violence in the family: Toward a theoretical integration. In W. R. Burr, R. Hill, F. I. Nye, and I. L. Reiss (Eds.), *Contemporary Theories about the Family* (Vol. 1, 549–581). New York: Free Press.

Gelles, R. J., and Wolfner, G. (1994). Sexual offending and victimization: A life course perspective. In A. Rossi (Ed.), *Sexuality Across the Life Course* (363–388). Chicago: The University of Chicago Press.

Giles-Sims, J. (1985). A longitudinal study of battered children of battered wives. *Family Relations, 34,* 205–210.

Hughes, H. M., Parkinson, D., and Vargo, M. (1989). Witnessing spouse abuse and experiencing physical abuse: A "Double Whammy?" *Journal of Family Violence, 4*, 197–209.

Hwalek, M., Senstock, M. C., and Lawrence, R. (1984). Assessing the probability of abuse of the elderly. Paper presented at the Annual Meetings of the Gerontological Society of America, San Antonio, Texas.

Jacobson, N., and Gottman, J. (1998). *When Men Batter Women: New Insights Into Ending Abusive Relationships*. New York: Simon and Schuster.

Kalmuss, D., and Seltzer, J. (1986). Continuity of marital behavior in remarriage: The case of spouse abuse. *Journal of Marriage and the Family, 48*, 113–120.

Lane, K. E., and Gwartney-Gibbs, P. A. (1985). Violence in the context of dating and sex. *Journal of Family Issues, 6*, 45–59.

Levine, M., Compaan, C., and Freeman, J. (1994). *The Prevention of Child Fatalities Associated with Child Maltreatment*. Buffalo NY: State University of New York.

Levine, M., Compaan, C., and Freeman, J. (1995). Maltreatment-related fatalities: Issues of policy and prevention. *Law and Policy, 16*, 449–471.

McClain, P., Sacks, J., and Frohlke, R. (1993). Estimates of fatal child abuse and neglect, United States, 1979–1988. *Pediatrics, 91*, 338–343.

National Center of Child Abuse and Neglect. (1997). *Study Findings: Study of National Incidence and Prevalence of Child Abuse and Neglect: 1995*. Washington, DC: U.S. Department of Health and Human Services.

National Research Council. (1993a). *Understanding and Preventing Violence*. Washington, DC: National Academy Press.

National Research Council. (1993b). *Understanding Child Abuse and Neglect*. Washington, DC: National Academy Press.

National Research Council. (1996). *Understanding Violence Against Women*. Washington, DC: National Academy Press.

National Research Council. (1998). *Violence in Families: Assessing Prevention and Treatment Programs*. Washington, DC: National Academy Press.

Nock, S. (1992). *Sociology of the Family* (2nd ed.). Englewood Cliffs, NJ: Prentice-Hall.

Ohlin, L., and Tonry, M. (Eds.). (1989). *Family Violence*. Chicago: University of Chicago Press.

Pagelow, M. (1984). *Family Violence*. New York: Praeger.

Pagelow, M. (1989). The incidence and prevalence of criminal abuse of other family members. In L. Ohlin and M. Tonry (Eds.), *Family Violence* (263–313). Chicago: University of Chicago Press.

Pillemer, K. (1985). The dangers of dependency: New findings on domestic violence against the elderly. *Social Problems, 33*, 146–158.

Pillemer, K. (1993). The abused offspring are dependent: Abuse is caused by the deviance and dependency of abusive caretakers. In R. J. Gelles and D. Loseke (Eds.), *Current Controversies on Family Violence* (237–249). Newbury Park, CA: Sage.

Pillemer, K., and Finkelhor, D. (1988). The prevalence of elder abuse: A random sample survey. *The Gerontologist, 28*, 51–57.

Renzetti, C. (1992). *Intimate Betrayal: Partner Abuse in Lesbian Relationships*. Newbury Park, CA: Sage.

Smith, M. (1991a). Male peer support of wife abuse: An exploratory study. *Journal of Interpersonal Violence, 6*, 512–519.

Smith, M. (1991b). Patriarchal ideology and wife beating: A test of a feminist hypothesis. *Violence and Victims, 5*, 257–273.

Steinmetz, S. K. (1993). The abused elderly are dependent: Abuse is caused by the perception of stress associated with providing care. In R. J. Gelles and D. Loseke (Eds.), *Current Controversies on Family Violence* (222–236). Newbury Park, CA: Sage.

Stets, J. E. and Straus, M. A. (1990). Gender differences in reporting marital violence and its medical and psychological consequences. In M. A. Straus and R. J. Gelles (Eds.), *Physical Violence in American Families* (151–166). New Brunswick, NJ: Transaction.

Straus, M. (1975, July). Cultural Approval and Structural Necessity of Intrafamily Assaults in Sexist Societies. Paper presented at the International Institute of Victimology, Bellagio, Italy.

Straus, M. A., Gelles, R. J., and Steinmetz, S. K. (1980). *Behind Closed Doors: Violence in the American Family*. Garden City, NY: Anchor Press.

Sugarman, D., and Hotaling, G. T. (1989). Dating violence: Prevalence, context, and risk markers. In M. A. Pirog-Good and J. E. Stets (Eds.), *Violence in Dating Relationships: Emerging Issues* (3–32). New York: Praeger.

Suiter, J., Pillemer, K., and Straus, M. (1990). Marital violence in a life course perspective. In M. A. Straus and R. J. Gelles (Eds.), *Physical Violence in American Families* (305–317). New Brunswick, NJ: Transaction.

U.S. Bureau of the Census. (1992). *Statistical Abstract of the United States.* Washington, DC: Government Printing Office.

U.S. Department of Health and Human Services. (1996). *The Third National Incidence Study of Child Abuse and Neglect (NIS–3).* Washington, DC: U.S. Department of Health and Human Services.

Van Hasselt, V. B., Morrison, R. L., Bellack, A. S., and Hersen, M. (Eds.). (1988). *Handbook of Family Violence.* New York: Plenum.

Walker, L. (1979). *The Battered Woman.* New York: Harper and Row.

Walker, L. (1984). *The Battered Woman Syndrome.* New York: Springer.

Wauchope, B., and Straus, M. A. (1990). Physical punishment and physical abuse of American children: Incidence rates by age, gender, and occupational status. In M. Straus and R. J. Gelles (Eds.), *Physical Violence in American Families: Risk Factors and Adaptations to Violence in 8145 Families* (113–148). New Brunswick, NJ: Transaction.

Wilson, M., and Daly, M. (1993). Spousal homicide risk and estrangement. *Violence and Victims, 8,* 3–16.

Wilt, S. A., Illman, S. M., and BrodyField, M. (1997). *Female Homicide Victims in New York City: 1990–1994.* New York: NYC Department of Health. Mimeographed.

Wolf, R. (1995). Abuse of the elderly. In R. Gelles (Ed.), *Visions 2010: Families and Violence, Abuse, and Neglect* (8–10). Minneapolis: National Council on Family Relations.

Wolf, R., Strugnell, C., and Godkin, M. (1982). *Preliminary Findings from Three Model Projects on Elderly Abuse.* University of Massachusetts Medical Center, University Center on Aging.

Wolfner, G., and Gelles, R. (1993). A profile of violence toward children: A national study. *Child Abuse and Neglect: The International Journal, 17,* 197–212.

Yllo, K. (1983). Using a feminist approach in quantitative research. In D. Finkelhor, R. Gelles, M. Straus, and G. Hotaling (Eds.), *The Dark Side of Families: Current Family Violence Research* (277–288). Beverly Hills, CA: Sage.

Yllo, K. (1988). Political and methodological debates in wife abuse research. In K. Yllo and M. Bograd (Eds.), *Feminist Perspectives on Wife Abuse* (28–50). Newbury Park, CA: Sage.

Yllo, K. (1993). Through a feminist lens: Gender, power, and violence. In R. Gelles and D. Loseke, (Eds.), *Current Controversies on Family Violence* (47–62). Newbury Park, CA: Sage.

Yllo, K., and Straus, M.A. (1981). Interpersonal violence among married and cohabiting couples. *Family Relations, 30,* 339–347.

Note

1. Men make up 89 percent of all people arrested for violent crimes. The percentages discussed in the text are for males. However, the same age–related trend exists for female homicidal and nonnegligent homicide offenders. ✦

Chapter 9
Families in the Context of Communities Across Time

Gary L. Bowen
Jack M. Richman
Natasha K. Bowen
University of North Carolina at Chapel Hill

All families are embedded in a sociohistorical and cultural context that influences the structure of families, the timing and sequencing of life events, and the demands on time and energy of family members and that operates as a potential resource in meeting the needs of the families and their members. Consistent with a contextual view, families are seen as dynamic agents constantly interacting with their environment. Proponents of life course theory and family development theory have long conceptualized family boundaries as being permeable to societal influences, especially social norms about the timing and sequencing of events by age and stage (Klein and White 1996). However, studies of families across time have generally neglected the relationship between the family system and the larger social structure.

This chapter draws both the structural and interactional perspectives of family development theory. We discuss how structural and normative properties in local communi-

ties and neighborhoods influence patterns of family functioning and interaction over time. "Family-environment fit" describes the interface between families at particular stages in the life course and the community in which they are embedded. Next, we give considerable attention to the "social capacity" of communities and the variables that strengthen or obstruct this potential resource for families. Finally, we conclude the chapter by proposing a model of family life processes that attempts to explain the diversity in the timing and sequencing of family transitions in the context of community.

Communities, Neighborhoods, and Family-Environment Fit

Communities can be viewed in two ways: as geographic communities and as functional communities. Communities defined by geographical boundaries differ from functional communities that form around common interests or activities (Gusfield 1975). Geographic communities and functional communities are not necessarily independent. Both types can be described on a continuum that reflects the extent to which their residents come together in either a deliberate or a spontaneous manner to (a) develop a psychological sense of connection, (b) acquire external resources and create opportunities for meeting the individual and collective needs and goals of their residents, (c) offer opportunities for meaningful participation, (d) provide instrumental and expressive social support, (e) solve problems and manage conflicts as a collective unit, (f) affirm and enforce prosocial norms, (g) respond to internal and external threats, and (h) maintain stability and order (Bogenschneider 1996; Bowen 1998; McMillan and Chavis 1986).

In this chapter, "community" refers to the spatial setting in which a family resides, specifically the neighborhood. While "neighborhood" is a familiar term, it has proved difficult to define in research studies. Sampson, Raudenbush, and Earls (1997) defined a neighborhood as "a collection of people and institutions occupying a subsection of a larger community" (919).

The Concept of Family-Environment Fit

In thinking about the relationship between families and communities, we find the concept of family-environment fit to be useful. Extending the concept of *person-environment fit* from the work of French and associates (Caplan 1983; French, Caplan, and Harrison 1982; Harrison 1978) to the family level, Bowen and Pittman (1993) proposed two types of family-environment fit. The first type has to do with how well communities meet families' needs. Some of these needs are universal and constant over time, while others vary depending on the developmental stage and individual characteristics of the families (Melson 1983). Examples of family needs include shelter, safety, social support, transportation, educational facilities, and social and recreational facilities for individuals of different ages. Family-environment fit is considered *high* when communities provide families with opportunities and resources that match their needs.

The second type of fit has to do with how well families meet the demands and requirements of the community. Thus, family-environment fit also reflects the extent to which the capabilities and competencies (social skills, parenting style, problem-solving ability) of families are responsive to community needs. For example, communities may demand participation of members in community events and the vigilance of members to monitor children's activities and help maintain public order.

These two types of family-environment fit are interrelated (Kulik, Oldham, and Hackman 1987). Communities that place too little demand on families may actually lower their capacity to meet the families' needs in the future. In addition, families are considered better able to achieve higher levels of maturity and competence in environments that challenge them (Moos 1987).

Family Adaptation and Family Resiliency

For purposes of discussion, it is important to define two concepts used to describe family functioning from a family-environment fit perspective: *family adaptation* and *family resiliency*. Family adaptation reflects the outcome of the interplay between families and

their environments at any one point in time (McCubbin and McCubbin 1987; McCubbin and Patterson 1983). From this perspective, family adaptation is defined as the outcome of efforts by families to effect changes in themselves or their environments so as to meet their needs and to confront life demands successfully (Bowen, Orthner, and Bell 1997). Members in adaptive families cooperate in accomplishing their collective goals as a family as well as their personal goals as individuals in such a way that neither the needs of the collective nor the needs of the individual are systematically neglected (Bowen 1991; Constantine 1986; Kantor and Lehr 1975).

The concept of *family resiliency* captures changes in the level of family adaptation over time in the context of stressor events and situations. It is the pattern of adaptation *over time* in the context of stressor events and situations that distinguishes resiliency from adaptation (DeHaan, Hawley, and Deal 1995; Hawley and DeHaan 1996; Silliman 1997). Resilient families are those who are able to establish, maintain, or regain an expected or satisfactory range of adaptation in the context of developmental transitions, positive challenges, or life adversities (DeHaan et al. 1995; Hawley and DeHaan 1996). As a source of both protective factors and risks, the community can serve as either an ally or an adversary in this process.

According to Silliman (1997), families work to maximize their level of fit with their environment by adapting their functioning or by finding a context that is more supportive of their needs and goals. When families are unable to negotiate a better context, they may actively disengage from their community of residence to protect the family and its interests. Family members may also work to arrive at a new consensus about their presenting situation. For instance, Boss (1988) discussed how family members use denial as a collective strategy in an attempt to manage situations of poor fit. It is likely that families will be more prone to distort their interpretations of fit when they are overwhelmed by demands or when they perceive low levels of control over their presenting situation.

Social Capacity in Communities

Social capacity in a community reflects the informal system of social care and social control in that community. It is the extent to which community members are able to generate psychological, social, and material resources and opportunities; enforce prosocial norms; and maintain order and safety. The social capacity of a community is thus assumed to directly influence families' abilities to manage developmental transitions and to evidence adaptation and resiliency over time. Because communities have varying levels of social capacity, some are better able than others to meet the needs of families and promote the successful development and functioning of families and their members.

Both academic and social commentators generally conclude that the social capacity of communities in the United States has declined (Bellah 1990; Coleman 1988; Schorr 1989; 1997). An important task for informing community practitioners is to identify features that reflect a community's social capacity as a resource for families at different stages of development, such as when children are added to the family through birth, adoption, or marriage or when adult family members grow older or suffer disabilities.

Social capacity may be reflected in both informal and formal relationships among individual community members and between individuals and institutions. McKnight (1997) uses the term *association* to describe how citizens may work informally together to solve problems and to care for community members. McKnight contrasts associations with *systems*: formal institutions in society that provide services and supports on a contractual basis. Policymakers and practitioners struggle with the question of the best way to generate community responsiveness to family needs: should it be through institutions and formal support mechanisms, or through the promotion of informal networks of support? For example, is it better to place children who have been permanently removed from their homes in paid foster care settings until they can be placed in new families, or to support willing extended family members as care providers by providing them with financial and other assistance? McKnight concludes that formal systems have evolved at the expense of group associations over the last century. When formal systems provide benefits that could have been provided through informal relationships, residents are denied an opportunity to engage in the types of exchanges that promote the development of informal ties and obligations.

Three features of communities that reflect their social capacity have emerged in the literature in recent years: social capital (Coleman 1988), collective efficacy (Bandura 1986; Sampson et al. 1997), and value consensus (Coleman and Hoffer 1987). These features primarily reflect informal relationships among community members, although at times they involve relationships of community members with formal systems. We discuss each in the following sections, along with selected community features that may limit their development. Understanding these three aspects of social capacity can help community practitioners identify aspects of communities that need to be enhanced to promote the healthy development of families and their members.

Social Capital

James Coleman (1988) introduced the concept of social capital into the literature as one of three types of family capital, or resources within the family. *Social capital* refers to the quality and support of family relationships. Financial capital is the family's economic or physical resources, including possessions and income. Human capital includes knowledge and skill possessed by parents and the capabilities and competencies of children. Social capital is perhaps the most important of the three types, for without it, financial capital may assume little meaning and human capital may not be translated into positive outcomes for family members. Coleman emphasized that social capital, like other forms of capital, makes it possible to achieve certain outcomes that would not be attainable without it.

Coleman (1988) also described social capital as an asset that is embedded in the nature of relationships among persons outside the family. Social capital outside the family includes the level to which the family system is embedded in an integrative network of people and institutions in the community that share common values. Our discussion here is concerned with the social capital that lies in the community outside the family. Extra-familial social capital is considered to promote the ability of families to make successful adaptations and to demonstrate resiliency in the face of normative and non-normative stressors. Coleman discussed three related forms of social capital that can be applied to the community as indicators of its social capacity: "obligations and expectations, information channels, and social norms" (95).

Obligations and expectations. The first form of social capital, obligations and expectations, may be applied to communities in which reciprocal patterns of exchange among residents create a sense of indebtedness that is regulated by norms of trust and cooperation. Social capital is likely to be greater in communities with dense patterns of social exchange and in which transactions evolve from short-term exchanges to long-term commitments. The social capital that is available to a family increases as it is able to incur credits from exchange relationships in the community. For example, a parent builds "credit" among neighbors when she provides a ride or child care to another parent or links a neighbor child to an adult friend who has the expertise to help with a school project. Using formal systems of support in a community may actually decrease the fund of social capital that results from these types of informal exchanges between residents.

Information channels. The second form of social capital discussed by Coleman, information channels, includes information from others that facilitates the family's ability to meet its needs and to accomplish its goals. For example, for a single parent who needs child care to work a job with a split shift, getting information from others in the community about flexible child care alternatives may mean the difference between employment and unemployment. Communities vary in the extent to which residents share varied and specific information across a range of topics.

Social norms. Coleman discusses social norms as the third form of informal community social capital. A product of social interaction over time, norms constitute expectations for behavior that both facilitate and constrain behavior. Norms in a community that promote prosocial and altruistic behavior and constrain antisocial and self-centered behavior are likely to provide a positive context for family life. For example, in some communities, norms exist that encourage neighbors to look out for one another, such as through community watch programs. In others, neighbors may call parents of children in the neighborhood when they see the children engaged in problem behavior, such as skipping school. Such behavior sends a message to youth that parents in the neighborhood work together. Communities may vary in the strength of feedback mechanisms among residents that affirm or enforce a range of acceptable behavior. Community networks in which residents know and interact with one another over an extended period of time are most likely to develop consensus about expectations for behavior and the collective ability to promote and constrain the behavior of those in the network through differential rewards and punishments. As noted by Coleman, the potential power of these networks to shape behavior increases as these relationships extend across different contexts (e.g., family members live in the same neighborhood, attend the same church, shop at the same stores, work for the same employer).

In summary, communities vary in their social capital, which is one of three components of social capacity. Social capital is a community's ability to promote reciprocal obligations and expectations, information exchanges, and shared norms among members. Coleman's components of social capital suggest community characteristics that may be targeted in neighborhood-level interventions. A useful starting point for these interventions is to provide opportunities, such as community events and activities, for neighbors to get to know one another.

Collective Efficacy

The second component of social capacity, collective efficacy, evolved from the work of Albert Bandura (1986, 1993, 1995). Collective efficacy is defined by Sampson and associates as "social cohesion among neighbors combined with the willingness to intervene on behalf of the common good" (918). Collective efficacy includes social capital as an important dimension but adds a second dimension that involves the willingness of members to mobilize their efforts to promote the public good. Collective efficacy is thus an important component of the community's social capacity that functions as an asset for families by promoting adaptation. As an example, Sampson et al. (1997), in a large-scale survey of 343 neighborhoods in Chicago, found that the extent to which neighbors evidenced social bonds and trust and assumed collective responsibility for the welfare of children was a more important predictor of neighborhood violence than either poverty or residential instability. When residents in impoverished neighborhoods with high immigrant concentrations and residential instability demonstrated a sense of community consciousness and collective action, violence levels declined.

Thus, the concept of collective efficacy, like social capital, suggests variables for community practitioners to target in interventions. Collective efficacy is enhanced when neighborhood efforts to organize and to request resources or assistance from community institutions and local community resources, such as the city council, police department, or area churches, are successful. Real-life examples of collective efficacy include residents demanding and receiving city help in cleaning up a vacant lot for establishing a playground; supporting a police crackdown on neighborhood traffic related to drug dealing, weapons, and drunk driving through a surprise random license checkpoint; and working with a white, elderly church in a predominant African-American neighborhood on its declining to open its doors to neighbors and provide afterschool and mentoring programs for youth. Community practitioners can work with community groups as a coaches, role models, cata-

lysts, and advocates in accomplishing such results.

Common Values

The third community feature that reflects social capacity is a sense of common values that encourage and affirm supportive interaction patterns within and between families and the enforcement of prosocial norms (Coleman and Hoffer 1987). Consistent with the work of Bowen (1991) and others (Christensen 1964; Kluchhohn and Strodtbeck 1961; Parsons and Shils 1951), *values* are defined as characteristics of individuals that reflect organized sets of preferences that inform choices among alternatives and strategies for achieving desired results. Patterns of interaction among residents over time that reflect cooperation, trust, and mutual support facilitate the development of core community values and the willingness of neighbors to accommodate their individual priorities and wishes to the needs and interests of the collective.

The extent to which residents share common values that inform more specific goals, aims, interests, ambitions, and aspirations may also encourage the development of social capital and collective efficacy in a community. For example, shared values among members of a community about the importance of education to children's success in life are likely to reinforce norms (which constitute expectations in social relations) that encourage neighbors to tell parents when they see their children engaging in problem behavior.

Shared community values are not always positive and affirming to family adaptation and resiliency (Steinberg, Darling, Fletcher, Brown, and Dornbusch 1995). The most positive context for a family's level of adaptation and resiliency is the situation in which the focal values have positive significance for family outcomes, the values of the family align with community values (value congruency), and values are highly crystallized in a community (value consensus). In examining the relationship between parent monitoring and adolescent performance in school, Steinberg et al. (1995) reported an important caveat in the operation of value consensus in a community: The level of value consensus has positive effects on youth development only to the extent to which the values promote positive developmental goals for youth. These findings suggest the importance of considering not only the extent to which values are shared by residents in a community but also the content of its values in assessing its social capacity.

Community practitioners need to be aware that common community values help set the standard for behavior and behavioral norms among residents. A lack of value consensus among community residents may subvert citizen participation and collective mobilization efforts around social problems and issues that challenge family adaptation. Greater outreach by practitioners to help residents better understand their values and the values of their neighbors about community and family life may promote efforts to identify core community values.

Variations in the Social Capacity of Communities

Some communities face particular difficulties and challenges in building social capacity. Furstenberg and Hughes (1997) discuss several community-level features that may influence a community level of social capacity, each of which can be targeted for community intervention. The first is the nature of the *physical infrastructure* of the community. Communities vary in their level of isolation, ranging from isolated farming communities to densely populated urban centers; the type, quality, and density of housing that residents have available; the presence of parks and recreational facilities for families and children; their proximity to local agencies and resources; and the design of roads and patterns of access within and between communities. Such physical features are likely to frame opportunities for social interaction in the community.

Second, according to Furstenberg and Hughes (1997), communities vary in their social and demographic composition. Such collective attributes reflect the *social infrastructure* of the community and are likely to inform the nature of sociocultural risks and opportunities in neighborhood settings. For

example, consistent with social disorganization theory (Shaw and McKay 1942), works by Wilson (1987, 1996), Coulton and Pandey (1992), and Sampson et al. (1997) demonstrate how the presence of concentrated disadvantage in communities (poverty, welfare dependency, joblessness, segregation, crime, oppression, social isolation) provides a poor context for the development of social capacity. In addition, high levels of residential instability in communities may prevent the development of interactions that build social capital. For example, Sampson et al. (1997) found that residential stability (percentage of residents living in the same house at least five years; percentage of owner-occupied dwellings) was positively associated with supportive patterns of interaction among residents and effective mechanisms of informal social control, which they conceptualized as collective efficacy. Riger and Lavrakas (1981) developed a similar measure of residential stability that they defined as "behavioral rootedness." Research by McAuley and Nutty (1985) suggests that, as families move through the life cycle, they become more rooted in their communities, experience greater community integration, and associate more risk with moving.

Third, Furstenberg and Hughes (1997) discuss how the operation of *institutional resources*, including those inside and outside of the community's boundaries (mental health center, police department, churches, community development initiatives), influence the nature of community life. These institutional resources function as instruments of socialization, social control, and social support.

The next section offers an integrative summary of key concepts that have been introduced in this chapter. A case study by Brodsky (1996) shows the importance of considering families in this community context. In the case study, ten single-parent families struggle with raising school-age children in a context of danger and peril, a situation in which the social capacity of the community is too weak to compensate for its social risks. This case study demonstrates the astute parenting skills and, in some cases, harsh parenting practices it takes to protect children from noxious realities.

Single-Parent Families in Peril: A Case Example

Brodsky (1996) conducted a qualitative study of the protective strategies of ten single mothers raising fourth- to sixth-grade daughters in "risky"neighborhoods. The mothers, who were described as "resilient" by key informants, used strategies such as distancing themselves and their children psychologically and physically from their neighbors. *Psychological distance* was achieved by viewing themselves as having different values and behaviors than others in the community. The mothers conveyed to their children that they were not true members of the community and used other youths in the neighborhood as examples for their children of how *not* to be. One mother went so far as to tell her son she would "kill him" before allowing him to engage in the behaviors common to young men in their neighborhood—using drugs and alcohol on street corners. *Physical distance* was achieved by locking doors, keeping children inside, avoiding sitting out in front of the residence, and being a "homebody." One woman saw her home as a totally separate place from the neighborhood: "It's my world. And. . . when you close that door, leave the world out there" (351).

Another strategy demonstrated by the mothers in Brodsky's study was to limit their community involvement to only those roles that directly benefited their own children, such as volunteering at the school. One mother in the sample maintained involvement in a local resident council primarily to receive early notices of upcoming youth activities, which benefited her child. This strategy represented a deliberate, sometimes reluctant, abandonment of a community orientation because of a perceived lack of shared values and a sense of hopelessness about the possibility of improving neighborhood conditions.

Some women in Brodsky's sample placed an emphasis on involvements *outside* their residential community. Church involvement sustained more than one woman, and church was considered a "community" separate from the neighborhood. One mother worried about her child's negative perceptions of their neighborhood and hoped the girl would know she did not have to live "that way": "If I can put her in a different environment where it's a different culture or whatever, I don't care, I'll do it" (356).

Brodsky (1996) suggests that maintaining what she calls a negative psychological sense of community represented a deliberate, adaptive strategy of the women in her sample to protect themselves and their children from the threatening characteristics of their communities. This may be the best available strategy for families in communities that have the least to offer families with negligible levels of family-environment. However, the strategy is likely to have its disadvantages. In neighborhoods where selected opportunities and resources do exist, such as supervised activities for children, it might prevent parents from exploiting existing supports. Furthermore, Pretty et al. (1996), found that adolescents' perceptions of a lack of sense of community in their neighborhood contributed to loneliness and a lower sense of well-being. Brodsky also points out that parents' wariness of peers and community sites may be especially stressful on family relationships when children reach the adolescent stage of separation and individuation (Erikson 1959). The potential for parent-adolescent conflict is illustrated by two mothers' comments about how they refused to indulge children's requests for popular items of clothing or jewelry out of fear of having them draw the attention of drug dealers, gang members, or robbers or the sexual attention of men on the street.

This case study illustrates ways in which social risks present in a community may overwhelm its resources for social capacity and consequently detract from the community's ability to serve as a context for healthy family and human development. In such circumstances, both family adaptation and family resiliency may be threatened or constrained. However, Brodsky's case study also illustrates the actions families may undertake in an effort to achieve a desirable family-environment fit. As for the children in the study, perceptions of an "inhospitable" community may impede participation and the development of social connections and social skills that would normally occur as youths become more involved in the community (Pretty, Conroy, Dugay, Fowler, and Williams 1996). In sum, in dangerous communities and communities that fail to provide a sense of community, the needs of both the developing individual and the family are not met by the community; the lack of family-environment fit can affect both parenting behavior and child social development.

Conclusion

As indicated in the example we have discussed, the importance and implications of social capacity as a resource may vary over the life course of the family. Yet studies of the effects of community environments on family outcomes have tended to neglect variations in the level of fit between families at particular stages of life and the communities in which they are embedded. In addition, studies of variations in family processes and outcomes over the family life course have tended to treat community context as a constant.

Models of family development are needed that recognize today's diversity in family structures and variation in the timing and sequencing of family statuses, as well as capture the community context in which these family transitions and processes take place. A model that is considered to have implications for guiding practice interventions and informing research efforts is depicted in Figure 9.1. This model includes three major components: (a) stages of the life course, (b) the social capacity of the community, and (c) external community context.

Five stages of family life processes define the central aspect of the model: (a) establishing a family, (b) addition of family members, (c) family members pursing independence, (d) separation of family members, and (e) adults developing dependence (Richman and Caye 1995). Each stage, which is represented metaphorically as a step on life's staircase, is delineated by a central family

Figure 9.1
Combining Research, Interventions, and Families

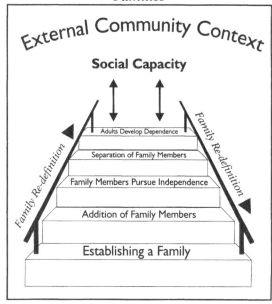

life task. At any one time, families demonstrate a level of internal family adaptation, which ranges from maladaptation to "bonadaptation." Over time and in the context of developmental transitions and challenges, families demonstrate a pattern of adaptation that represents their level of resiliency, which ranges from low to high.

In the first stage, the family is established. This may happen in traditional ways through courtship and marriage, but it also could occur through other means, including remarriage, birth, adoption, and cohabitation involving either a heterosexual or a gay or lesbian couple. The establishment of the family, broadly defined, occurs when any two individuals define themselves as a family (Hartman and Laird 1983).

In the second stage, members are added. Most often, this occurs through birth. However, family members can be added through adopting, providing kinship care for a child, or having parents move in with adult children.

In the third stage, family members pursue independence to the extent that they are capable. Typically, children begin to develop relationships in the wider community. As they move through adolescence, they generally begin the launching process from the family of origin. However, this process toward independence may not always be possible for all children. Some children have physical, intellectual, or psychological challenges that restrict their ability to function independently from their family of origin. Although there is a tendency to associate this stage with children growing older, centrifugal forces in the family also may be initiated by adult members who occupy positions in systems outside the family. For example, a parent may return to school in order to pursue a new career field.

Families may revisit the fourth stage, separation of family members, multiple times. In the traditional trajectory, families launch young adult children. The process of separation may also be dealt with when adults in the family separate or divorce, when a family member dies, or when a family member moves to a residential facility, such as a nursing home. Family separation can also be more temporary, such as when a family member lives apart from the family system as a consequence of job demands.

In the last stage, adult members of the family grow older or suffer disabilities or circumstance that may make them dependent on the other member of the family for assistance. These situations may be either permanent or temporary. In such cases, one partner may develop dependence on the other or both partners may become dependent on other family members.

These family life steps can vary in their sequence and timing, can be skipped, and can be revisited as the family changes over time. In addition, families may be challenged by more than one task at any one time. For example, in situations of divorce and remarriage in which the new couple has children from a previous marriage who are pursuing independence as well as preschool children from the current marriage, the family system can be described as "stretching" or "straddling" steps.

The process of family redefinition within and between stages is depicted as informed and constrained by the social capacity of the community: the second component of the model. Families are considered to have some influence over the level of social capacity present in the community. As discussed previously, the level of fit between the family system and the community influences the success of the family in making transitions, in fulfilling the individual and collective needs of family members, and in responding to external demands.

Research is needed that addresses the level and types of social capacity that the family system may need at different stages of the life course. For example, a socially integrative neighborhood may be a particularly important asset for parents with children in the early and middle adolescent years—a period in development when children begin to spend an increasing amount of time in the wider community. An important task for researchers is to better understand the minimum threshold of social capacity below which families become systematically disabled and fail to demonstrate adaptation and resiliency. Research by Crane (1991) suggests that neighborhoods have breaking points below which residents experience sharp increases in problem behavior.

The external community context is the last component of the model. Families who reside in the community typically exert less control over its external context than they do its social capacity. As discussed in a previous section, the external context includes the physical infrastructure of the community, its sociodemographic characteristics, and its institutional resources (see Furstenberg and Hughes 1997). These community features influence the degree to which residents are able to build the community's social capacity. Additional research is needed that examines how the relationship between these contextual features and family outcomes are mediated by the level of social capacity in the community.

In his campaign for nomination as the Democratic candidate for president of the United States in 1968, Robert F. Kennedy summoned Americans to join together to restore community as "a place where people can see and know each other, where children play and adults work together and join in the pleasures and responsibilities of the place where they live" (cited in Schorr 1997, 305). Unfortunately, Kennedy's call remains unanswered in too many communities. And too many families continue to be plagued by inadequate housing, concentrated disadvantage, joblessness, and crime and violence. Such conditions seriously jeopardize the ability of communities to develop the kind of social capacity that Kennedy felt had been lost in many American communities and that represents the type of context that promotes family adaptation and resiliency in the face of developmental transitions, positive challenges, and life adversities.

Discussion Questions

1. What are some behavioral indicators in families that would suggest a "goodness of fit" with their community?

2. In what ways do shared values among community residents provide a means to affirm or enforce norms that govern social relations in the community?

3. Why is it important in assessing the social capacity of a community to focus not only on the level of value consensus among residents but also on the content of this consensus?

4. What are examples of community-level features that may influence the level of social capacity in a community?

5. In what ways may the social capacity in the community influence the ability of families to successfully make developmental transitions?

Glossary

Collective efficacy A pattern of social relations among members of a group in which members evidence solidarity, a sense of responsibility for promoting the collective interests of the group, and belief in the ability of the group to organize to achieve specific aims and goals.

External community context Physical, demographic, and institutional features of the community, including its opportunity structure and its formal systems of care, that influence the degree to which residents are able to build the community's social capacity.

Family adaptation The outcome of efforts by families to effect needed changes in themselves and their environments so as to meet their needs and to confront life demands.

Family-environment fit The level of congruence in the relationship between the family and the larger community.

Family resiliency Describes families who are able to establish, maintain, or regain an expected or satisfactory range of adaptation when faced with developmental transitions, positive challenges, or life adversities.

Social capacity The extent to which community members come together in either a deliberate or a spontaneous manner to develop a psychological sense of connection, acquire external resources and create opportunities for meeting the individual and collective needs and goals of their members, offer opportunities for meaningful participation, provide instrumental and expressive social support, solve problems and manage conflicts as a collective unit, affirm and enforce prosocial norms, respond to internal and external threats, and maintain stability and order.

Social capital The level to which the family system is embedded in an integrative network of people and institutions that share common values.

Values Characteristics of individuals that reflect organized sets of preferences that inform choices among alternatives and strategies for achieving desired results.

Suggested Readings

Brodsky, A. E. (1996). Resilient single mothers in risky neighborhoods. *Journal of Community Psychology, 24,* 347–363.

Brooks-Gunn, J., Duncan, G. J., and Aber, J. L. (Eds.). (1997). *Neighborhood Poverty*(Vols. 1–2). New York: Russell Sage Foundation.

Coleman, J. (1988). Social capital in the creation of human capital. *American Journal of Sociology, 94,* 95–120.

McKnight, J. L. (1997). A 21st–century map for healthy communities and families. *Families in Society, 78* 117–127.

Sampson, R. J., Raudenbush, S. W., and Earls, F. (1997). Neighborhoods and violent crime: A multilevel study of collective efficacy. *Science, 277*, 918–924.

Bibliography

Bandura, A. (1977). Self-efficacy: Toward a unifying theory of behavioral change. *Psychological Review, 84*, 191–215.

Bandura, A. (1993). Perceived self-efficacy in cognitive development and functioning. *Educational Psychologist, 28*, 117–148.

Bandura, A. (1986). *Social Foundations of Thought and Action: A Social Cognitive Theory*. Englewood Cliffs: Prentice-Hall.

Bandura, A. (1995). Reflections on human agency. In J. Georgas, M. Manthouli, E. Besevegis, and A. Kokkevi (Eds.), *Contemporary Psychology in Europe* (194–210). Seattle: Hogrefe and Huber.

Bellah, R. N. (1990). The invasion of the money world. In D. Blankenhorn, S. Bayme, and J. B. Elshtain (Eds.), *Rebuilding the Nest: A New Commitment to the American Family* (227–236). Milwaukee: Family Service America.

Bogenschneider, K. (1996). An ecological risk/protective theory for building prevention programs, policies, and community capacity to support youth. *Family Relations, 45*, 127–138.

Boss, P. (1988). *Family Stress Management*. Newbury Park, CA: Sage.

Bowen, G. L. (1991). *Navigating the Marital Journey*. New York: Praeger.

Bowen, G. L. (1998). *Community Resiliency: A Research Roadmap*. Chapel Hill, NC.: The University of North Carolina at Chapel Hill.

Bowen, G. L., Orthner, D. K., and Bell, D. B. (1997). Differences in spouses' perceptions of family adaptation. *Journal of Social Behavior and Personality, 12*, 53–72.

Bowen, G. L., and Pittman, J. F. (1993). *Family Adaptation to Relocation in the U.S. Air Force: Implications for Policy and Practice*. Washington, DC: U.S. Air Force.

Brodsky, A. E. (1996). Resilient single mothers in risky neighborhoods. *Journal of Community Psychology, 24*, 347–363.

Caplan, R. D. (1983). Person-environment fit: Past, present, and future. In C. L. Cooper (Ed.), *Stress Research* (35–78). New York: Wiley.

Christensen, H. T. (1964). The intrusion of values. In H. T. Christensen (Ed.), *Handbook of Marriage and the Family* (969–1006). Chicago: Rand McNally.

Coleman, J. (1988). Social capital in the creation of human capital. *American Journal of Sociology, 94*, 95–120.

Coleman, J., and Hoffer, T. (1987). *Public and Private High Schools: The Impact of Communities*. New York: Basic Books.

Constantine, L. L. (1986). *Family Paradigms: The Practice of Theory in Family Therapy*. New York: Guilford Press.

Coulton, C. J., and Pandey, S. (1992). Geographic concentration of poverty and risk to children in urban neighborhoods. *American Behavioral Scientist, 35*, 238–257.

Crane, J. (1991). The epidemic theory of ghettos and neighborhood effects on dropping out and teenage childbearing. *American Journal of Sociology, 96*, 1226–1259.

DeHaan, L., Hawley, D. R., and Deal, J. E. (1995). Operationalizing family resilience: Methodological considerations and recommendations. Paper presented in the Theory Construction and Research Methodology Workshop at the National Council on Family Relations Annual Meeting, Portland, Oregon.

Erikson, E. (1959). *Childhood and Society* (2nd ed.). New York: Norton.

Forehand, R., and Wierson, M. (1993). The role of developmental factors in planning behavioral interventions for children: Disruptive behavior as an example. *Behavior Therapy, 24*, 117–141.

French, J. R. P., Jr., Caplan, R. D., and Harrison, R. V. (1982). *The Mechanisms of Job Stress and Strain*. Chichester, England: John Wiley and Sons.

Furstenberg, F. F., Jr., and Hughes, M. E. (1997). The influence of neighborhoods on children's development: A theoretical perspective and a research agenda. In J. Brooks-Gunn, G. J. Duncan, and J. L. Aber (Eds.), *Neighborhood Poverty* (Vol. II, 23–47). New York: Russell Sage Foundation.

Gusfield, J. R. (1975). *The Community: A Critical Response*. New York: HarperCollins.

Harrison, R. V. (1978). Person–environment fit and job stress. In C. L. Cooper and R. Payne (Eds.), *Stress at Work* (175–205). Chichester, England: John Wiley and Sons.

Hartman, A., and Laird, J. (1983). *Family-centered Social Work Practice*. New York: Free Press.

Hawley, D. R., and DeHaan, L. (1996). Toward a definition of family resilience: Integrating life–span and family perspectives. *Family Process, 335*, 283–298.

Kantor, D., and Lehr, W. (1975). *Inside the Family: Toward a Theory of Family Process.* San Francisco: Jossey-Bass.

Klein, D. M., and White, J. M. (1996). *Family Theories: An Introduction.* Thousand Oaks: Sage.

Kluckhohn, F. R., and Strodtbeck, F. L. (1961). *Variations in Value Orientations.* Evanston: Row, Peterson.

Kulik, C. T., Oldham, G. R., and Hackman, J. R. (1987). Work design as an approach to person-environment fit. *Journal of Vocational Behavior, 31,* 278–296.

McAuley, W. J., and Nutty, C. L. (1985). Residential satisfaction, community integration, and risk across the family life cycle. *Journal of Marriage and the Family, 47,* 125–130.

McCubbin, H. I., and Patterson, J. M. (1983). The family stress process: The double ABC-X model of adjustment and adaptation. In H. I. McCubbin and J. M. Patterson (Eds.), *Social Stress and the Family: Advances and Developments in Family Stress Theory and Research* (7–37). New York: Haworth Press.

McCubbin, M. A., and McCubbin, H. I. (1987). Family stress theory and assessment: The T-double ABC-X model of family adjustment and adaptation. In H. I. McCubbin and A. I. Thompson (Eds.), *Family Assessment Inventories for Research and Practice* (3–32). Madison: The University of Wisconsin.

McKnight, J. L. (1997). A 21st-century map for healthy communities and families. *Families in Society, 78,* 117–127.

McMillan, D. W., and Chavis, D. M. (1986). Sense of community: A definition and theory. *Journal of Community Psychology, 14,* 6–23.

Melson, G. F. (1983). Family adaptation to environmental demands. In H. I. McCubbin and C. R. Figley (Eds.), *Stress and the Family: Coping with Normative Transitions* (Vol. 1, 149–162). New York: Brunner/Mazel.

Moos, R. H. (1987). Person–environment congruence in work, school, and health care settings. *Journal of Vocational Behavior, 31,* 231–247.

Parsons, T., and Shils, E. A. (Eds.). (1951). *Toward a General Theory of Action.* Cambridge: Harvard University Press.

Pretty, G. M. H., Conroy, C., Dugay, J., Fowler, K., and Williams, D. (1996). Sense of community and its relevance to adolescents of all ages. *Journal of Community Psychology, 24,* 365–379.

Richman, J. M., and Caye, J. S. (1995). *Family Centered Practice Curriculum.* Chapel Hill: University of North Carolina School of Social Work.

Riger, S., and Lavrakas, P. J. (1981). Community ties: Patterns of attachment and social interaction in urban neighborhoods. *American Journal of Community Psychology, 9,* 55–66.

Sampson, R. J., Raudenbush, S. W., and Earls, F. (1997). Neighborhoods and violent crime: A multilevel study of collective efficacy. *Science, 277,* 918–924.

Schorr, L. B. (1989). *Within Our Reach: Breaking the Cycle of Disadvantage.* New York: Anchor Books.

Schorr, L. B. (1997). *Common Purpose: Strengthening Families and Neighborhoods to Rebuild America.* New York: Anchor Books.

Shaw, C. R., and McKay, H. D. (1942). *Juvenile Delinquency and Urban Areas.* Chicago: University of Chicago Press.

Silliman, B. (1997). Resiliency in family systems. Paper presented in the Theory Construction and Research Methodology Workshop at the National Council on Family Relations Annual Meeting, Washington, DC.

Steinberg, L., Darling, N. E., Fletcher, A. C., Brown, B. B., and Dornbusch, S. M. (1995). Authoritative parenting and adolescent adjustment: An ecological journey. In P. Moen, G. H. Elder, Jr., and K. Luscher (Eds.), *Examining Lives in Context: Perspectives on the Ecology of Human Development* (423–466). Washington, DC: American Psychological Association.

Wilson, W. J. (1987). *The Truly Disadvantaged: The Inner City, the Underclass, and Public Policy.* Chicago: The University of Chicago Press.

Wilson, W. J. (1996). *When Work Disappears: The World of the New Urban Poor.* New York: Alfred A. Knopf. ✦

Chapter 10
Health and Illness in Families Through the Life Cycle

Thomas L. Campbell
University of Rochester School of Medicine

Families are the primary context within which most health problems and illnesses occur. Physical and mental illnesses have a strong influence and impose enormous burdens on families. Family members, not health care providers, are the primary caretakers for individuals with the most illnesses. Conversely, research has shown that family relationships can have a powerful adverse impact on health, as important as any biological factors (Campbell 1986).

Despite this link between family and health, family social scientists and health professionals have only recently shown interest in this relationship. Most of the research on families and health issues has been conducted over the past two decades. The lack of attention to family and health issues can be attributed in large part to our cultural split between mind and body. For example, medical professionals have largely focused on biomedical issues and ignored psychological and social ones, whereas social scientists have neglected the biological aspects of social interactions.

This chapter uses the biopsychosocial model as a framework for integrating family and health issues and reviews the research on families and health across the life span. The developmental tasks and pertinent health issues and illnesses for each stage of the life cycle are reviewed. Emphasis is placed on some of the clinical issues that arise at each stage and the research that supports family interventions for specific health problems. Many of the health problems seen in medical settings are addressed in other chapters, including mental illness, substance abuse, sexual dysfunction, and family caregiving. This chapter focuses on those physical health issues not addressed elsewhere in the book.

Engel (1977) first developed the biopsychosocial model from general systems theory. He described the interactions among various levels of living systems from the molecular to global and how changes at one level influence every other level. This systems approach emphasizes that health and illness occur within a social context and that the family can influence an individual's physical health and vice versa.

One principle of a biopsychosocial systems approach is that somatic symptoms and physical illnesses can serve adaptive functions within families and be maintained by family patterns. Dym and Berman illustrate this systemic interaction between family and physical illness with a case of childhood asthma:

> In John and Mary's relationship, John drinks frequently. When he drinks, Mary criticizes him. Their son, Harry, 14, unable to deal with the stress leaves the house. As the fight continues, George, 11, becomes more anxious and has an asthma attack. Mary shifts her focus to George and gives him an inhaler. She then blames John, who feels guilty. He leaves and the fight stops. The next day he drinks again and the cycle continues. (Dym and Berman 1986, 15)

From a biopsychosocial systems perspective, the problem is not simply the asthma but a problem-maintaining relational pattern within the family.

Couples, Marriage, and Health Care

George and Susan had been together as a couple for over eight years but have been undecided as to whether to get married or have children. Over the past few years, Susan had become increasingly concerned about George's health as he approached 40. George was overweight, smoked a pack of cigarettes a day, and exercised little. When Susan urged him to exercise, stop smoking, or eat less, he would become angry, and they would argue. George agreed to see their family physician for a checkup before his 40th birthday.

At his physical, George's physician quickly recognized that George had little motivation to change any of his risky health behaviors. When the doctor asked why George had scheduled the appointment he learned about George's struggles with his partner about his health. Dr. C. asked George to return with Susan in several weeks. At that visit, Dr. C. helped George identify one lifestyle change that he would like to make. George decided to start playing tennis regularly with some friends, an activity that he used to enjoy. Dr. C. discussed with Susan ways that she could be supportive of George's healthy behaviors and how to avoid nagging or criticizing him.

When they returned several months later, George reported that he stopped playing tennis after a month and had gained an additional ten pounds. Susan had become more angry with his smoking and obesity. It became apparent to Dr. C. that these struggles over George's health represented deeper couple conflicts that had been simmering for several years. He recommended that they see a couples therapist to help them negotiate these issues. The couple accepted the referral.

Most families, whether traditional or nontraditional, usually begin with coupling—the coming together of two individuals to form a family. This is usually the unit that produces, nurtures, and rears the next generation. There are many variations in couples, including same-sex couples, married and unmarried couples, and couples who stay together only briefly, sometimes only long enough to conceive a child. Most couples have children and move to another stage of the family life cycle, but some remain as couples without children. The major developmental tasks for couples are to form a committed relationship and to realign relationships with extended family to include the partner.

Marriage is the social relationship that has the most powerful influence on health. Long before there was any systematic investigation of the relationship between marriage and health, it was recognized that married individuals tend to be healthier and live longer than unmarried people. In 1853, William Farr, the registrar general for England and Wales, commented: "Marriage is a healthy state. The single individual is more likely to be wrecked on his voyage than the lives joined together in matrimony" (Wyke and Ford 1992, 523). Subsequent epidemiological research has confirmed and clarified Farr's observation. For both sexes, and at different ages, married individuals have lower death rates and report better health than those who are unmarried. Among the unmarried, however, those who have never married survive longer than those who are widowed, while divorced individuals have the shortest life span (Burman and Margolin 1992).

Cross-sectional surveys are unable to determine causal links between marriage and health. Individuals may be unmarried because they are unhealthy or vice versa. Prospective studies of the health effects of widowhood have clearly demonstrated that men are at significantly greater risk of dying during the first 6 to 24 months after the death of a spouse (Martikainen and Valkonen 1996). Studies focusing on social support demonstrate that a spouse is the most important source of support and has the strongest effect on mortality and morbidity (House, Landis, and Umberson 1988). The process by which marriage influences health is poorly understood, but it seems to be the result of several factors (Wyke and Ford 1992), including married persons' tendency to experience lower levels of stress and greater social support. In contrast, unmarried persons engage in more unhealthy lifestyles, including higher rates of smoking, obesity, and excess alcohol consumption.

More recently, researchers have examined the physiological effects of marital relationships and interactions. Research in psychoimmunology has shown that individuals who are divorced or unhappily married have poorer immune functioning than happily married persons, which may place them at higher risk for infections and cancer (Kiecolt-Glaser et al. 1987). Again, it is unknown whether this relationship is a result of the stress in the marital relationship or the result of individuals with poor immune function selecting each other as partners—that is, a selection effect. Ewart, Burnett, and Taylor (1983) found an increase in blood pressure in couples who engage in hostile interactions, leading the researchers to hypothesize that chronic marital conflict may cause persistent autonomic arousal, hypertension, and long-term harmful health effects. In a series of studies, Levenson and Gottman (1983, 1985) have examined links between physiological variables and marital interaction. Using direct observations of marital interactions combined with concurrent measurements of physiological data (heart rate, skin conductance, general somatic activity), Levenson and Gottman demonstrated that the more physiologically aroused a couple became during marital conflict, the more their marital satisfaction declined over the next three years. The researchers hypothesized that physiological arousal plays an important role in marital satisfaction and that men have difficulty tolerating this physiologic stimulation. Studies on the physiological effects of interpersonal relationships are one of the most promising areas for future family and health research.

Couples and Health Care Behaviors

Most individuals manage the majority of physical symptoms at home with family and friends, without consulting a health professional. The decision to consult a medical professional is often influenced by other family members, usually the spouse. One study of middle-aged couples found that when a decision was made to consult a physician about a symptom, it was more often initiated by the spouse. In contrast, if the decision was to wait or delay medical consulta-tion, it was usually the symptomatic member of the couple who made the decision, sometimes against the spouse's advice or wishes (Dowds and Bibace 1996). Prior experiences with similar symptoms often influence such decision making.

Many families have a "family health expert" who assumes this role in health matters. In most families, it is the wife or mother, and she is consulted by other family members when a physical symptom develops. It is often helpful for the clinician to identify and consult with the family health expert so as not to erroneously contradict her advice.

It is important to understand that the customer is the person who desires health care and may not be the same person as the patient. Young and middle-aged men tend to avoid physicians and other health care professionals and usually seek care only at a later stage of an illness. When these men do present for routine care or health maintenance, they often are sent by their wives, who may be concerned that they are overworking or are not paying attention to their health. Eliciting and addressing the customer's concerns may be crucial for understanding a presenting complaint or the reason for the visit.

Lack of compliance or adherence with medical treatments is a major public health problem. It has been estimated that only one-third of patients with hypertension are under treatment, and only half of those patients have their blood pressure adequately controlled. Patients' compliance with treatment often depends on whether the spouse or other important family members agree with prescribed treatments. In one large study, providing family support to assist with compliance with blood pressure medication resulted in improved compliance, reduced blood pressure, and a 50 percent reduction in cardiac mortality (Morisky et al. 1983). Based on this and similar compliance research, the National Heart, Lung, and Blood Institute (1982) recommended that all physicians use the following as one of three basic strategies for increasing compliance with antihypertensive regimens:

Enhance support from family members—identifying and involving one influential person, preferably someone living with the patients, who can provide encouragement, help support the behavior change, and, if necessary, remind the patient about the specifics of the regimen. (10)

Couples and Health Promotion

Couples play an important role in health care promotion and risk reduction. Most health care behaviors are developed, maintained, or changed within a family setting. Couples have a high concordance for most health behaviors, such as smoking, diet, and physical activity, and for some physiological variables, such as weight, cholesterol level, and blood pressure (Doherty and Campbell 1988). Some of these similarities are a result of assortative mating, or the tendency for individuals to marry someone with similar habits and appearance. Also, health behaviors tend to become more similar the longer a couple stays together.

The initiation, maintenance, and cessation of smoking is strongly influenced by marital and family relationships. Smokers are much more likely to marry other smokers, to smoke the same number of cigarettes a day, and to quit at the same time (Venters, Jacobs, Luepker, Maiman, and Gillum 1984). Smokers who are married to nonsmokers or ex-smokers are more likely to quit and remain abstinent than smokers who are married to smokers. Support from the spouse or partner is associated with successful smoking cessation (Cohen and Lichtenstein 1990). In particular, supportive behaviors involving cooperative participation, such as talking a smoker out of smoking a cigarette, and reinforcement, such as expressing pleasure at the smoker's efforts to quit, predict successful quitting. Negative behaviors, such as nagging the smoker and complaining about the spouse's smoking, predict relapse (Coppotelli and Orleans 1985).

Based on this research, a number of smoking cessation studies have attempted to use partner support as an adjunct to their programs. These studies have tried to combine or integrate a social support intervention with standard cognitive-behavioral programs to increase abstinence from smoking. Several studies involving a total of over 250 subjects have tested a partner-support program in randomized trials (Lichtenstein, Glasgow, and Abrams 1986). Most of these programs were individual smoking cessation programs, involving nicotine replacement, self-management training, and relapse prevention. In the partner support groups, the partner (usually the spouse) participated in all the treatment sessions, and the couples were given suggestions and feedback on helpful and unhelpful behaviors.

The results of these trials are quite consistent and discouraging. The smoking cessation rates in the partner-support groups were not significantly different from those for the standard individually treated subjects—either at the end of the trials or at 6 to 12 months follow-up. In each of the studies, the amount of spousal or partner support reported by the smokers was predictive of the successful cessation, and the absence of negative or unsupportive behaviors generally was more important than the presence of supportive behaviors. However, these interventions failed to significantly increase the amount of support provided by the spouse. Thus, these studies confirm the hypothesis that spousal support and the absence of spousal criticisms are important for smoking cessation, but they also indicate that these behaviors are not easily changed through education and problem solving.

The failure of these interventions to increase smoking cessation may be partly the result of a lack of systemic orientation. Smoking is a complex behavior that is influenced by biological factors (nicotine addiction), individual psychological issues, and extrafamilial social relationships and pressures, as well as the marital relationship. Supportive behaviors by the spouse are part of a complex marital relationship and are probably related to overall marital quality and satisfaction. Unfortunately, none of these observational or experimental studies of smoking cessation has measured any marital variables (other than spousal support), such as marital communication or satisfaction. Some of these studies do support the general finding in marital research that negative spousal interactions have a greater impact on outcomes than positive interactions

(Billings and Moos 1983; Coppotelli and Orleans 1985).

The research on family involvement in weight reduction programs for adults parallels that for smoking cessation programs. Observational studies have shown that spousal support predicts successful weight loss (Streja, Boyko, and Rabkin 1982) and that criticism and nagging (including high levels of expressed emotion) from the spouse are associated with poor outcomes (Fischmann-Havstad and Marston 1984). A number of randomized controlled trials have examined the effect of spousal involvement in weight reduction programs (Brownell, Heckerman, Westlake, Hayes, and Monti 1978; Brownell and Stunkard 1981; Pearce, LeBow, and Orchard 1981; Saccone and Israel 1978; Wilson and Brownell 1978). As with the smoking studies, these trials have been based on a cognitive behavioral model in which the spouse is seen as a reinforcer of the desired behavior. In general, spouses attend all training sessions, varying from 6 to 18 sessions, and are instructed in basic behavior modification techniques. They are trained to give positive reinforcement and instructed not to criticize their partner's weight or eating behaviors.

The results of these studies have been mixed, with approximately half of the studies demonstrating that spousal involvement had a positive effect, particularly on the maintenance of weight loss after the end of the intervention. The most successful programs (Brownell et al. 1978) have reported two to three times greater weight loss in the spouse-involved groups at three-month and three-year follow-ups. Pearce, LeBow, and Orchard (1981) demonstrated the greatest weight loss occurred in the group in which the spouses were asked not to nag or otherwise participate in their partners' weight loss efforts. This study emphasizes the importance of spousal criticism in weight reduction and suggests that blocking negative marital interactions may be more important than promoting supportive behaviors.

Black, Gleser, and Kooyers (1990) conducted a meta-analysis of couples' weight loss programs and found that, based on effect sizes, the couples programs were slightly but significantly superior to subject-alone programs at post-treatment. At two- to three-month follow-up, the couples programs maintained a nearly significant ($p = .06$) improvement that disappeared at lengthier follow-up.

This research on marriage and health demonstrates that the marital relationship has a powerful impact on all aspects of health and illness, ranging from health promotion and health care utilization to effects on chronic illness and survival. The impact of nonmarital couple relationships on health has not been studied, but it is likely to be similar, depending on the length of the relationship and degree of commitment. These findings have important implications for family and health professionals who care for couples.

Pregnancy and Childbirth

Jill is a 17-year-old high school student who became pregnant when her boyfriend "forgot" to use a condom. Her mother initially was very upset and angry with her, but over several months she came to accept Jill's pregnancy. The pregnancy was complicated by recurrent urinary tract infections and anemia. Jill's boyfriend and mother came to different prenatal medical appointments, and both were present at the delivery. The labor was long but uncomplicated. At the time of delivery, the boyfriend cut the umbilical cord, and Jill's mother helped her with breastfeeding. Both of them joined her at her infant's two-week well child visit.

Pregnancy and the birth of the first child are nodal points in the family life cycle and create important interactions with the health care system. Most women develop a close relationship with a health care provider (midwife, family physician, or obstetrician) during the pregnancy and must make numerous decisions about prenatal care, labor, and delivery.

With the birth of the first child, a couple must accommodate a new member to a three-person family. For many couples, the birth of their first baby is considered the beginning of their family. It is also a time in which couples reassess their commitment and responsibility not only to each other but to the new child. The couple must make room in their relationship for the new infant while maintaining the intimacy and sexuality of their marriage. The dyad becomes a triad, and the triangle illustrates the complexities of these new relationships. In addition, there are opportunities for alliances (e.g., parents working together to care for the child) and risks of coalitions (one parent and child against the other parent). As each new child is added, the family constellation becomes forever changed.

The birth of a first child affects the extended family as well. Everyone moves up a generation; parents of the couple become grandparents; sisters and brothers become aunts and uncles. Combrinck-Graham (1985) calls this a centripetal phase in which the family comes closer together and the connectedness or cohesion between family members strengthens, while interpersonal boundaries become diffuse. Becoming parents encourages couples to reflect on their relationship with their own parents and offers opportunities for reworking that relationship.

The absence of fathers in many families has been identified as a major public health issue (Doherty, Kouneski, and Erickson 1996). With the increase in nonmarital childbearing and divorce, the number of single-parent households and absent fathers has increased dramatically. If a father does not live with the mother of his child at the time of birth, he is unlikely to become involved in his child's life. After divorce, many fathers visit their children less and less as time passes. One national study of divorced families found that 65 percent of 18- to 22-year-olds reported a poor relationship with their fathers, compared to 29 percent of those whose parents had not divorced (Zill, Morrison, and Coiro 1993).

One recommendation for increasing fathers' involvement in their children's lives is to involve them in parental roles as early as possible. This is best done by inviting them to prenatal visits, involving them in labor and delivery, and including them in childbirth and child-care classes. Many fathers who attend and participate in the birth of their child report strong bonding with the infant and more involvement in child care. Involving fathers should be a part of every prenatal program.

One study examined the impact of early contact by fathers on preterm infants. Levy-Shiff and colleagues (1990) followed 50 preterm infants and their parents during the hospital stay and for 18 months afterward. The frequency of paternal visits significantly correlated with more intensive and positive patterns of fathering at discharge and at later periods. These visits also predicted better weight gain in these infants. The researchers concluded that "the findings emphasize the central role which fathers play in the families of preterm infants. It would seem that the frequency of paternal visits highlights fathers who continue to be positively involved in their children's growth and development" (292).

Research has demonstrated that family stress, family supports, and aspects of family interaction can influence the course of pregnancy, including obstetrical and perinatal complications and birth weight. Women who receive emotional support and practical help from their spouse and other family members experience less depression during pregnancy and the postpartum period. Highly stressed women with low family and other social supports have higher rates of obstetric complications (Norbeck and Tilden 1983; Nuckolls, Kaplan, and Cassel 1972). High levels of family support can buffer the impact of psychosocial stressors. The family can also be a source of stress and have a negative impact on pregnancy outcome. Poor family functioning has been associated with labor complications and lower birth weight (Pagel, Smilkstein, Regen, and Montano 1990; Reeb, Graham, Zyzanski, and Kitson 1987; Smilkstein, Helsper-Lucas, Ashworth, Montano, and Pagel 1984). Women who live apart from their families deliver smaller babies than those who live with their partners or families of origin (Abell, Baker, Clover, and Ramsey 1991). However, those women who are excessively close to or enmeshed with their extended families also tend to deliver smaller babies, suggesting that the quality as well as the quantity of family support influences health. Ramsey and colleagues (1986) have hypothesized that the extended family's overinvolvement during pregnancy may be detrimental by not allowing enough autonomy or psychological space for a new family member.

Although there are no randomized controlled trials of family-centered maternity care, Kennel, Klaus, and their colleagues have examined the effects of a supportive companion or "doula" on the course of labor. In randomized controlled trials in Guatemala and the United States, they demonstrated that women who had a labor companion had shorter labors and fewer obstetric complications, including caesarean sections (Kennell, Klaus, McGrath, Robertson, and Hinkley 1991; Sosa, Kennell, Klaus, Robertson, and Urrutia 1980). Although it is likely that supportive family members have a similar effect, it has not been studied in a systematic manner.

Breastfeeding also is strongly influenced by family relationships and attitudes. Breastfeeding has been shown to improve an infant's immune functioning and reduce newborn allergies and infection. If a woman's mother breastfed her children and is supportive of breastfeeding, she is much more likely to breastfeed her babies. However, if the father of the newborn is not supportive of breastfeeding, the mother is unlikely to breastfeed. Thus, fathers need to be included in discussions about the benefits of breastfeeding for infants, and mothers who have breastfed can be a valuable resource.

Families With Young Children

Jim and Larry had been partners for ten years before they decided to adopt a child. Jim's father had died from multiple sclerosis, and Jim had been impressed by how much others had done for him. As a result, Jim wanted to adopt a child with developmental disabilities. They chose a four-year-old boy who was wheelchair-bound with spina bifida. Over the next several years, the boy had numerous surgeries and hospitalizations. Jim and Larry attended each medical visit, slept by his bedside in the hospital, and shared in his home medical care. Despite his medical prob-lems, their son did well and attended regular grade school.

Fortunately, most families with young children lead healthy lives, and their contact with the health care system usually involves well-child visits and minor illnesses. Most serious illnesses in childhood are preventable or easily treated. Much of well-child care provided by pediatricians, family physicians, and nurse practitioners consists of parental education and advice. As couples have become more isolated from their extended families, new parents increasingly rely on health professionals for advice and support in parenting. The developmental tasks of this stage are to form a parental team and negotiate relationships with extended family that include parenting and grandparenting roles.

Children are often a barometer of family stress. In response to stress or conflict in the family, they may misbehave or "act out," develop physical or emotional symptoms, or have an exacerbation of a chronic condition. Parents may become more aware of or worried about a child's health problems during periods of stress. A study of 500 families found that family stress dramatically increased use of health services for the children and that in one-third of the health visits, the practitioner found no evidence of any physical health problem. Highly stressed mothers were more likely to seek care for their children and less likely to see a health care provider for themselves. The researchers interpreted this finding as follows:

> Mothers, especially, may recognize stress as a cause of their own illness and do not regard it as legitimate to take the sick role for such illness. They do, however, regard it legitimate to assign the sick role to their children for stress-related illness and actually do so more frequently for such illness than for stress-unrelated illness. (Roghmann and Haggerty 1973, 524)

Family stress can not only increase health care utilization by children but also result in higher rates of illness. A number of studies have examined the relationship between family life events and child health. An early study by Meyer and Haggerty (1962) found chronic stress to be associated with higher rates of streptococcal pharyngitis, and 30 percent of the strep infections were preceded by a stressful family event. In a study conducted in a day care center, children who experienced more stressful life events had longer, but not more frequent, respiratory illnesses (Boyce and Chesterman 1990). A prospective study of over 1,000 preschoolers found that family life events were strongly correlated with subsequent visits to the physician and hospital admissions for a wide range of conditions. Children from families with more than 12 recent stressful life events during the four-year study period were six times more likely to be hospitalized (Beautrais, Fergusson, and Shannon 1982).

Unfortunately, not all children remain healthy throughout childhood, and a significant percentage develop a chronic illness such as asthma or diabetes. A large body of research has documented a strong relationship between family structure and functioning and health outcomes in families with chronic illness. Most of the early literature focused on family dysfunction and its association with poor outcomes in children with chronic illness.

In a seminal study, Minuchin and his colleagues (1975, 1978b) at the Philadelphia Child Guidance Clinic studied poorly controlled diabetic children from families with high cohesion or emotional closeness. These children had recurrent episodes of diabetic ketoacidosis despite adherence to diet and insulin. When these children were hospitalized and removed from the family environment, their diabetes was easily managed. It appears that stress and emotional arousal within the family directly affected the child's blood sugar. In studying these families and the families of children with severe asthma and anorexia nervosa, Minuchin discovered a specific pattern of interaction, characterized by enmeshment (high cohesion), overprotectiveness, rigidity, and conflict avoidance. He called these families "psychosomatic families."

To determine how family interactions can affect diabetes, Minuchin studied the physiologic responses of diabetic children to a stressful family interview (Minuchin et al. 1975). During the interview, the children from psychosomatic families had a rapid rise in free fatty acids (a precursor to diabetic ketoacidosis), which persisted beyond the interview. The parents of these children exhibited an initial rise in free fatty acid levels, which fell to normal when the diabetic child entered the room. Minuchin hypothesized that in psychosomatic families, parental conflict is detoured or defused through the chronically ill child, and the resulting stress leads to exacerbations of the illness. Minuchin and his colleagues (1975) have also reported the successful treatment of these young diabetics by using structural family therapy to help disengage the diabetic and establish more appropriate family boundaries. In all 15 cases, the pattern of recurrent ketoacidosis ceased, and insulin doses were reduced.

Although there are no controlled studies to examine the effectiveness of family therapy for diabetes, two randomized controlled trials have used family therapy in the treatment of severe childhood asthma. In the first study, 37 children with severe asthma were randomly assigned to family or individual therapy in addition to their usual medical care (Lask and Matthew 1979). Family therapy was used to reduce stress by encouraging the family to deal with their emotional reactions to asthma and to develop more realistic attitudes. Children in the family therapy group showed significant improvement in symptomatic wheezing and several aspects of objectively measured lung functioning. In another study, 18 asthmatic children were randomly assigned to family therapy in which the focus was on changing family patterns in which time and energy were disproportionately organized around illness-related needs and strong emotional reactions were repressed out of fear of provoking asthma attacks (Gustafsson, Kjellman, and Cederblad 1986). The treatment group showed significant improvements in health status, school attendance, and daily activities.

Although these studies demonstrate some effectiveness of family therapy for a childhood illness, they are focused on a small subset of children with severe illness and significant family dysfunction. In contrast, the majority of families with chronically ill children cope quite well with the illness and are unlikely to benefit from family therapy. Thus, more recent research has focused on family strengths that are associated with positive outcomes. In one particularly noteworthy study, Patterson and her colleagues at the University of Minnesota Cystic Fibrosis Center followed 90 children with CF to examine the impact of family variables on health outcomes. They found that balanced family coping (a measure of how well the family maintains family optimism and self-esteem), measured at baseline, predicted compliance with medical treatment and pulmonary health as measured by pulmonary function testing ten years later (Patterson, Budd, Goetz, and Warwick 1993). Because the medical management of cystic fibrosis is so demanding, the ability of the family to comply with treatment has an enormous impact on the course of the illness and survival rates of these children.

In an integrative review of this literature, Patterson (1991) identified nine aspects of resilient family process associated with positive outcomes in children with chronic illnesses and disabilities: (a) balancing the illness with other family needs, (b) maintaining clear family boundaries, (c) developing communication competence, (d) attributing positive meanings to the situation, (e) maintaining family flexibility, (f) maintaining family cohesiveness, (f) engaging in active coping efforts, (g) maintaining social support, and (h) developing collaborative relationships with professionals.

Based on descriptive studies, interventions have been developed to help families more effectively cope with chronic childhood illnesses. Unlike family therapy interventions, which focus on treating family dysfunction, these psychoeducational programs provide support for families and teach specific skills for coping with the illness. The focus is on the illness rather than the family, and on developing family strengths rather than treating family pathology. As a result, psychoeducational programs tend to be applicable to a wider group of families and are better accepted by these families.

Several randomized controlled trials have studied the effectiveness of family psychoeducational interventions for various disorders. In a study of families of diabetic children, a multifamily group intervention resulted in significant improvement in their attitudes, self-care, and diabetic control (as measured by glycosylated hemoglobin), as compared to a control group (Satin, La Greca, Zigo, and Skyler 1989). Similar studies have been conducted with families of children with asthma (Tal, Gil-Spielberg, Antonovsky, Tal, and Moaz 1990), chronic abdominal pain (Sanders, Shepherd, Cleghorn, and Woolford 1994), and developmental disabilities (Hawkins, Singer, and Nixon 1993; Nixon and Singer 1993), and with preterm infants (Affleck, Tennen, Rowe, Roscher, and Walker 1989; Pokorni, Katz, and Long 1991). These studies show consistent improvement in psychosocial outcomes such as depression, anxiety, and overall stress in the parents.

Psychoeducational programs offer the greatest promise for helping families cope with childhood chronic illness. More research is needed to determine what the essential elements of these programs are, whether a single-family or multifamily group format is more effective, and what impact the programs have on disease processes. This is an area of research where family social scientists and health professionals need to collaborate to develop and test the most effective interventions.

Families with Adolescents

Kate had always been a model student and skilled athlete. As a 10-year old, she became seriously interested in modern dance. Although she was not overweight, her dance instructor suggested that she lose some weight so that she would be a more attractive dancer. Over the next few years, she lost over 30 pounds, until she collapsed after a strenuous dance rehearsal. She was briefly hospitalized and diagnosed with anorexia nervosa. Her parents were bewildered and concerned. They participated in a parents' group for eating disorders and began family therapy with Kate and her younger brother. With the help of a structured eating disorder program and the support of her family, Kate was able to gain back 15 pounds. She decided to give up her dancing.

Adolescence is a tumultuous period in a family's life. As teenagers develop a sense of self and begin to separate from their families, new and unpredictable stresses and strains occur. Although most teenagers remain healthy throughout their adolescence and young adulthood, they often engage in risky behaviors, including smoking, drinking, drug use, and unsafe sexual practices. Most of the health care of adolescents is focused on identifying these risky behaviors and counseling teens about their health risks.

Despite the rising influence of peer groups on adolescents, families continue to be the primary influence on adolescent development and well-being. A recent national study found that positive family relationships were the strongest predictor of healthy development in adolescents. A strong relationship with parents and family was protective against most health risk behaviors, including substance abuse, depression, violence, and early sexual behaviors. Parents' expectations regarding school achievement were also associated with lower rates of these risky behaviors (Resnick et al. 1997).

Parents' health behaviors strongly influence whether an adolescent will adopt healthful behaviors. Adolescents are much more likely to smoke if either parent or a sibling smokes. A teenager who has a parent and an older sibling who smoke is five times more likely to smoke than a teenager from a nonsmoking family (Bewley and Bland 1977).

Interventions directed at adolescents need to be designed quite differently from those for younger children. In several studies of preadolescent obese children, involvement of parents in structured behavior modification programs resulted in better weight loss in both the children and the involved parents (Campbell and Patterson 1995). Brownell, Kelman, and Stunkard (1983) compared three groups in a cognitive-behavioral weight reduction program: parent-adolescent trained together, parent-adolescent trained separately, and the adolescent trained alone. The teenagers whose parents trained separately had the greatest weight loss and were the only group that maintained their weight loss at one-year follow-up. This finding suggests that obese adolescents benefit from a moderate level of parental involvement with the parents supportive of the weight reduction program while also supporting the adolescent's age-appropriate independence. This study can serve as a model to determine whether similar approaches are effective with other disorders.

Eating disorders are a common problem in adolescents, particularly in females, and are thought to be related to various elements of family dysfunction. Early work suggested that girls with anorexia nervosa tend to come from families that are enmeshed, rigid, and avoidant of conflict (Minuchin, Rosman, and Baker 1978a). Subsequent research has not been able to confirm these observations and shows that anorexia can be present in a wide range of family types. Three randomized controlled trials have examined the effectiveness of family therapy in the treatment of anorexia and bulimia (Crisp et al. 1991; Robin, Siegel, and Moye 1995; Russell, Szmukler, Dare, and Eisler 1987). Overall these studies show that family therapy appears to be more effective than individual therapy for adolescents with anorexia of less than three years' duration, and equally effective for most other anorexic patients. Older patients with more severe anorexia or bulimia may not benefit from family therapy.

The challenge for health care providers who care for adolescents is to respect the adolescent's growing autonomy and need to individuate while recognizing the parents' vital role in the adolescent's overall health and development. There is a danger in treating the teenager as either a child or an adult. Most clinicians deal with this problem by seeing the adolescent both alone and with a parent during medical visits. Having an alliance with both the adolescent and his or her parents allows the clinician to be most effective in dealing with the common health problems and risk behaviors of this stage of the life cycle.

Elderly and Family Caregiving

Mrs. R. is an 82-year-old woman who has been living with her daughter Susan since Mr. R. died eight years ago. Over the past three years, her cognitive abilities have been declining. She has become increasingly forgetful and confused at times. Her physician recently diagnosed her with Alzheimer's disease. Susan works full time and is a single mother with two teenage daughters living at home. The living arrangements worked well until Mrs. R's mental decline. Susan is reluctant to leave her mother alone, but her daughters resent "babysitting" her. With the help of the local chapter of the Alzheimer's Disease and Related Disorders Association (ADRDA), Susan was able to get help in the home and participate in a support group for family caregivers.

Family members, not professionals, are the primary health care providers for most patients. Outside the hospital, health care professionals give advice and suggestions for the care of acute and chronic illnesses, but the actual care is usually provided by the patient (self-care) or by family members. With the aging of the population, there has been a significant increase in the prevalence of chronic illness and disability. Nearly half of all noninstitutionalized elderly persons over age 65 are limited by at least one chronic condition. In addition, managed care has dramatically shortened hospital stays, so that patients are returning home with more health care needs than ever before. Many acute and chronic illnesses that were previously treated in the hospital are now managed in the "outpatient setting," which usually means at home by the family.

The aging of the population and changes in our health care delivery system have resulted in a dramatic increase in family caregiving. Over 40 percent of the elderly over the age of 85 have some form of dementia, and half of those individuals are cared for by family members in their own communities (Evans et al. 1989). Unfortunately, adequate services have not been provided to families to manage these increased demands, and it has become more challenging for families to cope with chronic illness. An extensive body of research on family care-

givers has documented the enormous burden and strain they experience in caring for impaired older adult family members (see Chapter 11). Overall, family caregivers have poorer emotional and physical health than age-matched controls (Biegel, Sales, and Schulz 1991). The incidence of depression is estimated to be between 40 and 50 percent, with high self-reported levels of anger, hostility, and guilt (Gallagher, Wrabetz, Lovett, Del Maestro, and Rose 1989). Only recently has family caregiving been recognized as a major public health issue. Several national organizations and government agencies are beginning to address such family issues.

A wide variety of interventions have been developed and tested to assist family caregivers, including psychoeducational and family counseling interventions, family support and education groups, and the direct provision of services, such as respite care, to caregiving families. Studies have found high levels of satisfaction by the family caregivers. The interventions have had variable impact on other outcomes, including caregiver burden and depression, the caregivers' physical health, and the length of time the elderly family member remains in the community. A number of family psychoeducational programs have taught family caregivers the skills to deal with many of the common problems presented by older adults with dementia (Chiverton and Caine 1989; Goodman and Pynoos 1990; Mittelman et al. 1995; Toseland, Rossiter, Peak, and Smith 1990). These interventions usually involved group sessions led by a trained professional (nurse, social worker, but not family therapist) that meet weekly for eight to ten weeks. These controlled trials have consistently shown an improvement in the emotional distress and level of depression in the family caregivers who received the intervention. Findings regarding the impact on the caregivers' subjective and objective sense of burden have been less consistent and not as great. A few studies that have provided psychoeducational interventions for individual families have had a greater impact on both emotional distress and burden (Toseland et al. 1990).

Family support groups for caregivers have become very popular and are being actively promoted by advocacy groups such as the ADRDA. These are usually open-ended groups that are professionally or peer led and provide information and emotional support to families. Several controlled studies of support groups for family caregivers of dementia patients have examined the impact of these groups (Farran, Keane-Hagerty, Tatarowicz, and Scorza 1993; Haley, Brown, and Levine 1987; Haley, Levine, Brown, and Bartolucci 1987; Kahan, Kemp, Staples, and Brummel-Smith 1985). All participants have reported high levels of satisfaction with the group and increased knowledge about dementia. The impact on caregiver well-being is less consistent. Thus, although family support groups are well received by participants and result in higher levels of knowledge, they have had an inconsistent impact on caregivers' emotional distress and sense of burden and do not appear to be as effective as more intensive and focused family psychoeducational interventions.

The most impressive study of family intervention in Alzheimer's disease was conducted by Mittelman and her colleagues at NYU (Mittelman et al. 1995; Mittelman, Ferris, Shulman, Steinberg, and Levin 1996). They conducted a randomized controlled trial of a multifaceted, structured intervention for spouse-caregivers of AD patients. The intervention included an initial series of individual and family education and counseling sessions, a weekly caregiver support group, and ongoing crisis counseling. They enrolled 205 subjects over a three-year period and followed them for eight years. The intervention resulted in an improvement in both the physical and mental health of the caregivers and a significant delay in nursing home placement for the AD patients (average of 329-day delay). With the cost of nursing homes being at least $30,000 per year, cost savings of this type of intervention are enormous.

In one study of families caring for stroke patients, researchers compared the impact of providing information about the illness to the family to a more comprehensive family psychoeducation and counseling program (Evans, Matlock, Bishop, Stranahan, and Pederson 1988). Although both interventions resulted in less deterioration of family functioning for the AD groups than the control group, only the more comprehensive program that involved counseling showed any effect on family behavior or sustained benefits on family functioning. The authors concluded that family education alone is a "necessary but not a sufficient criterion for influencing families" (Evans et al. 1992, 1247). This conclusion seems to be supported by similar studies of caregivers of Alzheimer's patients.

From this research, we can conclude that family psychoeducational interventions for the caregivers of dementia and stroke patients can improve the mental and physical health of the caregivers and delay institutionalization. These psychoeducational programs are quite similar to those that have been developed and tested for schizophrenia. Family support groups are well received by family caregivers, but their effect on caregivers is less clear.

Conclusions

This chapter documents the importance of the family in health and illness throughout the life cycle. Health problems at all stages of the life cycle have an enormous impact on other family members. Family members, in turn, can influence the development and course of many physical illnesses. Research is beginning to demonstrate that family interventions can improve medical and psychosocial outcomes.

The challenge for health care professionals is to develop and implement more family-oriented approaches to health care. Unfortunately, most medical care remains focused on the individual, with little attention to families. Guidelines for family-oriented approaches have been published (McDaniel, Campbell, and Seaburn 1992) but are not widely accepted. Interventions are needed at all levels of medical training (medical school, residencies, and continuing medical education for practicing physicians) as well as in health care organizations. Effective models of family-oriented health care involve close collaboration between medical providers and mental health providers, especially family therapists. These biopsychosocial approaches attend to both the physical and psychological needs of families throughout the life cycle.

Discussion Questions

1. Describe the role of the family in health promotion and disease prevention, including nutrition and smoking cessation.

2. Discuss how family members may influence health care utilization patterns.

3. What is the relationship between marital status and health measures? Discuss some of the proposed explanations for this relationship.

4. Discuss the role of the family in the management of chronic illness. Describe several family interventions that have been demonstrated to be effective.

5. What are some of the differences in programs that focus on families and health of adolescents compared to families and health of young children? Single persons compared to married persons?

Glossary

Assortative mating The tendency for an individual to marry someone with similar appearance or habits, including health-related behaviors.

Biopsychosocial model An approach developed by George Engel that is based on systems theory and that emphasizes the interrelationships between psychosocial and biological factors in health and illness.

Family-oriented health care An approach to health care that emphasizes the primary importance of the family in health and illness.

Family psychoeducation An effective family intervention in physical illness that provides families with psychological support and teaches them specific skills to cope with the medical illness.

Psychoimmunology The field of science that studies the relationship between psychological, neurological, immunological, and endocrinologic processes in human and animal systems.

Psychosomatic families A term used by Salvador Minuchin to describe the families of children with poorly controlled diabetes, asthma, and anorexia nervosa. These families are characterized by enmeshment (high cohesion), overprotectiveness, rigidity, and conflict avoidance.

Suggested Readings

Campbell, T. L., and Patterson, J. M. (1995). The effectiveness of family interventions in the treatment of physical illness. *Journal of Marital and Family Therapy, 21,* 545–584.

Christie-Seely, J. (Ed.). (1984). *Working With the Family in Primary Care: A Systems Approach to Health and Illness.* New York: Praeger.

Doherty, W. J., and Baird, M. A. (1983). *Family Therapy and Family Medicine: Toward the Primary Care of Families.* New York: Guilford.

Doherty, W. J., and Campbell, T. L. (1988). *Families and Health.* Beverly Hills, CA: Sage.

McDaniel, S., Campbell, T., and Seaburn, D. (1990). *Family-oriented Primary Care: A Manual for Medical Providers.* New York: Springer-Verlag.

Ramsey, C. N. (1989). *Family Systems in Medicine.* New York: Guilford.

Bibliography

Abell, T. D., Baker, L. C., Clover, R. D., and Ramsey, C. N., Jr. (1991). The effects of family functioning on infant birthweight. *Journal of Family Practice, 32,* 37–44.

Affleck, G., Tennen, H., Rowe, J., Roscher, B., and Walker, L. (1989). Effects of formal support on mothers' adaptation to the hospital-to-home transition of high-risk infants: The benefits and costs of helping. *Child Development, 60,* 488–501.

Beautrais, A. L., Fergusson, D. M., and Shannon, F. T. (1982). Life events and childhood morbidity: A prospective study. *Pediatrics, 70,* 935–940.

Bewley, B. R., and Bland, J. M. (1977). Academic performance and social factors related to cigarette smoking by schoolchildren. *British Journal of Preventive and Social Medicine, 31,* 18–24.

Biegel, D. E., Sales, E., and Schulz, R. (1991). *Family Caregiving in Chronic Illness.* Newbury Park, CA: Sage.

Billings, A. G., and Moos, R. H. (1983). Social-environmental factors among light and heavy cigarette smokers: A controlled comparison with nonsmokers. *Addictive Behaviors, 8,* 381–391.

Black, D. R., Gleser, L. J., and Kooyers, K. J. (1990). A meta-analytic evaluation of couples weight-loss programs. *Health Psychology, 9,* 330–347.

Boyce, W. T., and Chesterman, E. (1990). Life events, social support, and cardiovascular reactivity in adolescence. *Journal of Developmental and Behavioral Pediatrics, 11,* 105–111.

Brownell, K. D., Heckerman, C. L., Westlake, R. J., Hayes, S. C., and Monti, P. M. (1978). The effect of couples training and partner co-operativeness in the behavioral treatment of obesity. *Behaviour Research and Therapy, 16,* 323–333.

Brownell, K. D., Kelman, J. H., and Stunkard, A. J. (1983). Treatment of obese children with and without their mothers: Changes in weight and blood pressure. *Pediatrics, 71,* 515–523.

Brownell, K. D., and Stunkard, A. J. (1981). Couples training, pharmacotherapy, and behavior therapy in the treatment of obesity. *Archives of General Psychiatry, 38,* 1224–1229.

Burman, B., and Margolin, G. (1992). Analysis of the association between marital relationships and health problems: An interactional perspective. *Psychological Bulletin, 112,* 39–63.

Campbell, T. L. (1986). Family's impact on health: A critical review. *Family Systems Medicine, 4,* 135–327.

Campbell, T. L., and Patterson, J. M. (1995). The effectiveness of family interventions in the treatment of physical illness. *Journal of Marital and Family Therapy, 21,* 545–584.

Chiverton, P., and Caine, E. D. (1989). Education to assist spouses in coping with Alzheimer's disease: A controlled trial. *Journal of the American Geriatrics Society, 37,* 593–598.

Cohen, S., and Lichtenstein, E. (1990). Partner behaviors that support quitting smoking. *Journal of Consulting and Clinical Psychology, 58,* 304–309.

Combrinck-Graham, L. (1985). A developmental model for family systems. *Family Process, 24,* 139–150.

Coppotelli, H. C., and Orleans, C. T. (1985). Partner support and other determinants of smoking cessation maintenance among women. *Journal of Consulting and Clinical Psychology, 53,* 455–460.

Crisp, A. H., Norton, K., Gowers, S., Halek, C., Bowyer, C., Yeldham, D., Levett, G., and Bhat, A. (1991). A controlled study of the effect of therapies aimed at adolescent and family psychopathology in anorexia nervosa. *British Journal of Psychiatry, 159,* 325–333.

Doherty, W. A., and Campbell, T. L. (1988). *Families and Health.* Beverly Hills, CA: Sage.

Doherty, W. J., Kouneski, E. F., and Erickson, M. F. (1996). *Responsible Fathering: An Overview and Conceptual Framework.* Washington, DC: Department of Health and Human Services.

Dowds, B. N., and Bibace, R. (1996). Entry into the health care system: The family's decision-making process. *Family Medicine, 28,* 114–118.

Dym, B., and Berman, S. (1986). The primary health care team: Family physician and family therapist in joint practice. *Family Systems Medicine, 4,* 9–21.

Engel, G. (1977). The need for a new medical model: A challenge for biomedicine. *Science, 196,* 129–136.

Evans, D. A., Funkenstein, H. H., Albert, M. S., Scherr, P. A., Cook, N. R., Chown, M. J., Hebert, L. E., Hennekens, C. H., and Taylor, J. O. (1989). Prevalence of Alzheimer's disease in a community population of older persons: Higher than previously reported. *Journal of the American Medical Association, 262,* 2551–2556.

Evans, R. L., Griffith, J., Haselkorn, J. K., Hendricks, R. D., Baldwin, D., and Bishop, D. S. (1992). Poststroke family function: An evaluation of the family's role in rehabilitation. *Rehabilitation Nursing, 17,* 127–131.

Evans, R. L., Matlock, A. L., Bishop, D. S., Stranahan, S., and Pederson, C. (1988). Family intervention after stroke: Does counseling or education help? *Stroke, 19,* 1243–1249.

Ewart, C. K., Burnett, K. F., and Taylor, C. B. (1983). Communication behaviors that affect blood pressure: An A-B-A-B analysis of marital interaction. *Behavior Modification, 7,* 331–344.

Farran, C. J., Keane-Hagerty, E., Tatarowicz, L., and Scorza, E. (1993). Dementia care-receiver needs and their impact on caregivers. *Clinical Nursing Research, 2,* 86–97.

Fischmann-Havstad, L., and Marston, A. R. (1984). Weight loss maintenance as an aspect of family emotion and process. *British Journal of Clinical Psychology, 23,* 265–271.

Gallagher, D., Wrabetz, A., Lovett, S., Del Maestro, S., and Rose, J. (1989). Depression and other negative affects in family caregivers. In E. Light and B. Lebowitz (Eds.), *Alzheimer's Disease and Family Stress: Directions for Research* (218–244). Rockville, MD: National Institute of Mental Health.

Goodman, C. C., and Pynoos, J. (1990). A model telephone information and support program for caregivers of Alzheimer's patients. *Gerontologist, 30,* 399–404.

Gustafsson, P. A., Kjellman, N. I., and Cederblad, M. (1986). Family therapy in the treatment of severe childhood asthma. *Journal of Psychosomatic Research, 30*, 369–374.

Haley, W. E., Brown, S., and Levine, E. G. (1987). Family caregiver appraisals of patient behavioral disturbance in senile dementia. *Clinical Gerontologist, 6*, 25–34.

Haley, W. E., Levine, E. G., Brown, S., and Bartolucci, A. A. (1987). Stress, appraisal, coping, and social support as predictors of adaptational outcome among dementia caregivers. *Psychology and Aging, 2*, 323–330.

Hawkins, N. E., Singer, G. H., and Nixon, C. D. (1993). *Short-term Behavioral Counseling for Families of Persons with Disabilities*. Baltimore, MD: Paul H. Brookes Publishing.

House, J. S., Landis, K. R., and Umberson, D. (1988). Social relationships and health. *Science, 241*, 540–545.

Kahan, J., Kemp, B., Staples, F. R., and Brummel-Smith, K. (1985). Decreasing the burden in families caring for a relative with a dementing illness: A controlled study. *Journal of the American Geriatrics Society, 33*, 664–670.

Kennell, J., Klaus, M., McGrath, S., Robertson, S., and Hinkley, C. (1991). Continuous emotional support during labor in a US hospital: A randomized controlled trial. *Journal of the American Medical Association, 265*, 2197–2201.

Kiecolt-Glaser, J. K., Fisher, L. D., Ogrocki, P., Stout, J. C., Speicher, C. E., and Glaser, R. (1987). Marital quality, marital disruption, and immune function. *Psychosomatic Medicine, 49*, 13–34.

Lask, B., and Matthew, D. (1979). Childhood asthma: A controlled trial of family psychotherapy. *Archives of Disease in Childhood, 54*, 116–119.

Levenson, R. W., and Gottman, J. M. (1983). Marital interaction: Physiological linkage and affective exchange. *Journal of Personality and Social Psychology, 45*, 587–597.

Levenson, R. W., and Gottman, J. M. (1985). Physiological and affective predictors of change in relationship satisfaction. *Journal of Personality and Social Psychology, 49*, 85–94.

Levy-Shiff, R., Hoffman, M. A., Mogilner, S., Levinger, S., and Mogilner, M. B. (1990). Fathers' hospital visits to their preterm infants as a predictor of father-infant relationship and infant development. *Pediatrics, 86*, 289–293.

Lichtenstein, E., Glasgow, R. E., and Abrams, D. B. (1986). Social support in smoking cessation: In search of effective interventions. *Behavior Therapy, 17*, 606–619.

Martikainen, P., and Valkonen, T. (1996). Mortality after death of spouse in relation to duration of bereavement in Finland. *Journal of Epidemiology and Community Health, 50*, 264–268.

McDaniel, S., Campbell, T., and Seaburn, D. (1992). *Family-oriented Primary Care: A Manual for Medical Providers*. New York: Springer-Verlag.

Meyer, R. J., and Haggerty, R. J. (1962). Streptococcal infections in families: Factors altering individual susceptibility. *Pediatrics, 29*, 539–549.

Minuchin, S., Baker, L., Rosman, B. L., Liebman, R., Milman, L., and Todd, T. C. (1975). A conceptual model of psychosomatic illness in children: Family organization and family therapy. *Archives of General Psychiatry, 32*, 1031–1038.

Minuchin, S., Rosman, B. L., and Baker, L. (1978a). *Psychosomatic Families*. Cambridge, MA: Harvard University Press.

Minuchin, S., Rosman, B. L., and Baker, L. (1978b). *Psychosomatic Families: Anorexia Nervosa in Context*. Cambridge, MA: Harvard University Press.

Mittelman, M. S., Ferris, S. H., Shulman, E., Steinberg, G., Ambinder, A., Mackell, J. A., and Cohen, J. (1995). A comprehensive support program: Effect on depression in spouse-caregivers of AD patients. *Gerontologist, 35*, 792–802.

Mittelman, M. S., Ferris, S. H., Shulman, E., Steinberg, G., and Levin, B. (1996). A family intervention to delay nursing home placement of patients with Alzheimer disease: A randomized controlled trial. *Journal of the American Medical Association, 276*, 1725–1731.

Morisky, D. E., Levine, D. M., Green, L. W., Shapiro, S., Russell, R. P., and Smith, C. R. (1983). Five-year blood pressure control and mortality following health education for hypertensive patients. *American Journal of Public Health, 73*, 153–162.

National Heart, Lung, and Blood Institute. (1982). Management of patient compliance in the treatment of hypertension. *Hypertension, 4*, 415-423.

Nixon, C. D., and Singer, G. H. (1993). Group cognitive-behavioral treatment for excessive self-blame and guilt. *American Journal of Mental Retardation, 97*, 665–672.

Norbeck, J. S., and Tilden, V. P. (1983). Life stress, social support, and emotional disequilibrium in complications of pregnancy: A prospective, multivariate study. *Journal of Health and Social Behavior, 24*, 30–46.

Nuckolls, K. B., Kaplan, B. H., and Cassel, J. (1972). Psychosocial assets, life crisis and the prognosis of pregnancy. *American Journal of Epidemiology, 95* 431–441.

Pagel, M. D., Smilkstein, G., Regen, H., and Montano, D. (1990). Psychosocial influences on newborn outcomes: A controlled prospective study. *Social Science and Medicine, 30,* 597–604.

Patterson, J. M. (1991). Family resilience to the challenge of a child's disability. *Pediatric Annals, 20,* 491–499.

Patterson, J. M., Budd, J., Goetz, D., and Warwick, W. J. (1993). Family correlates of a 10-year pulmonary health trend in cystic fibrosis. *Pediatrics, 91,* 383–389.

Pearce, J. W., LeBow, M. D., and Orchard, J. (1981). Role of spouse involvement in the behavioral treatment of overweight women. *Journal of Consulting and Clinical Psychology, 49,* 236–244.

Pokorni, J. L., Katz, K. S., and Long, T. M. (1991). Chronic illness and preterm infants: Family stress and support issues. *Early Education and Development, 2,* 227–239.

Ramsey, C. N., Jr., Abell, T. D., and Baker, L. C. (1986). The relationship between family functioning, life events, family structure, and the outcome of pregnancy. *Journal of Family Practice, 22,* 521–527.

Reeb, K. G., Graham, A. V., Zyzanski, S. J., and Kitson, G. C. (1987). Predicting low birth weight and complicated labor in urban black women: A biopsychosocial perspective. *Social Science and Medicine, 25,* 1321–1327.

Resnick, M. D., Bearman, P. S., Blum, R. W., Bauman, K. E., Harris, K. M., Jones, J., Tabor, J., Beuhring, T., Sieving, R. E., Shew, M., Ireland, M., Bearinger, L. H., and Udry, J. R. (1997). Protecting adolescents from harm: Findings from the National Longitudinal Study on Adolescent Health. *Journal of the American Medical Association, 278,* 823–832.

Robin, A. L., Siegel, P. T., and Moye, A. (1995). Family versus individual therapy for anorexia: Impact on family conflict. Topical section: Treatment and therapeutic processes. *International Journal of Eating Disorders, 17,* 313–322.

Roghmann, K. J., and Haggerty, R. J. (1973). Daily stress, illness, and use of health service in young families. *Pediatric Research, 7,* 520–526.

Russell, G. F., Szmukler, G.I., Dare, C. and Eisler, I. (1987). An evaluation of family therapy in anorexia nervosa and bulimia nervosa. *Archives of General Psychiatry, 44,* 1047–1056.

Saccone, A. J., and Israel, A. C. (1978). Effects of experimental versus significant other controlled reinforcement and choice of target behavior on weight loss. *Behavior Therapy, 9,* 271–278.

Sanders, M. R., Shepherd, R. W., Cleghorn, G., and Woolford, H. (1994). The treatment of recurrent abdominal pain in children: A controlled comparison of cognitive-behavioral family intervention and standard pediatric care. *Journal of Consulting and Clinical Psychology, 62,* 306–314.

Satin, W., La Greca, A. M., Zigo, M. A., and Skyler, J. S. (1989). Diabetes in adolescence: Effects of multifamily group intervention and parent simulation of diabetes. *Journal of Pediatric Psychology, 14,* 259–275.

Smilkstein, G., Helsper-Lucas, A., Ashworth, C., Montano, D., and Pagel, M. (1984). Prediction of pregnancy complications: An application of the biopsychosocial model. *Social Science and Medicine, 18,* 315–321.

Sosa, R., Kennell, J., Klaus, M., Robertson, S., and Urrutia, J. (1980). The effect of a supportive companion on perinatal problems, length of labor, and mother-infant interaction. *New England Journal of Medicine, 303,* 597–600.

Streja, D. A., Boyko, E., and Rabkin, S. W. (1982). Predictors of outcome in a risk factor intervention trial using behavior modification. *Preventive Medicine, 11,* 291–303.

Tal, D., Gil-Spielberg, R., Antonovsky, H., Tal, A., and Moaz, B. (1990). Teaching families to cope with childhood asthma. *Family Systems Medicine, 8,* 135–144.

Toseland, R. W., Rossiter, C. M., Peak, T., and Smith, G. C. (1990). Comparative effectiveness of individual and group interventions to support family caregivers. *Social Work, 35,* 209–217.

Venters, M. H., Jacobs, D. R., Jr., Luepker, R. V., Maiman, L. A., and Gillum, R. F. (1984). Spouse concordance of smoking patterns: The Minnesota Heart Survey. *American Journal of Epidemiology, 120,* 608–616.

Wilson, G. T., and Brownell, K. (1978). Behavioral therapy for obesity: Including family members in the treatment process. *Behavior Therapy, 9,* 943–945.

Wyke, S., and Ford, G. (1992). Competing explanations for associations between marital status and health. *Social Science and Medicine, 34* 523–532.

Zill, N., Morrison, D. R., and Coiro, M. J. (1993). Long-term effects of parental divorce on parent-child relationships, adjustment, and achievement in young adulthood. *Journal of Family Psychology, 7,* 91–103. ✦

Chapter 11
Caregiving Over the Life Course of Families

Christine A. Price
Southwest Missouri State University

Hilary A. Rose
Washington State University

Susan (age 74) and Nick (78) Thompson have been married 51 years and have two children, Nancy (49) and David (45). Nancy lives in Oregon and is married to Bill Marshall (50), the oldest son of Elaine (70) and Frank (72) Marshall. Nancy and Bill have four children: Sarah (24), who had a child at 17 and works full-time in town; Dana (18), a freshman in college; Joe (14); and Kelly (10). Susan and Nick's son David is a successful accountant who is gay and lives with his partner in Boston. Because of his hectic schedule, David and his partner are only able to visit David's family once a year. Elaine and Frank's youngest son, Tad (40), has a substance abuse problem and was widowed at age 35 with two young children, now 4 and 7. As a result of Tad's inability to care consistently for his children, Elaine and Frank are raising their two young grandchildren.

Most caregiving occurs within and over the life course of families. In fact, a curvilinear pattern of caregiving across the life span is evident in most families. That is, there are high levels of caregiving when children are small and again when the older members of families need assistance. Fur-

thermore, the responsibilities of providing care for family members are ongoing despite differences in racial background, socioeconomic status, and lifestyle choice.

Experts have devised numerous definitions for *caregiving*, including Travis' (1995) delineation of "functional assistance" compared to "affective assistance." For the purposes of this chapter, however, *caregiving* refers to the emotional and instrumental support provided to family members by other family members, regardless of age, life stage, or motivation.

Most caregiving behaviors are motivated by a mixture of duty combined with love and affection (Doty 1986, cited in Dwyer 1995). For example, for the parents of young children caregiving may involve both love and a sense of parental obligation, whereas for adult children of aging parents, caregiving may be a mixture of duty and the desire to reciprocate for previous care. Regardless of motivation, however, caregiving within the context of family life is often emotionally charged and physically demanding.

Several theoretical perspectives have been used to help explain caregiving activities over the life course of families. These include, among others, family development theory, the feminist perspective, and attachment theory. For example, many feminist writers argue that family work is highly "gendered," with caregiving work being no exception (Allen and Baber 1994; Ferree 1990; Thompson and Walker 1989). Attachment theory contributes significantly to our understanding of parent-child relationships over the life course (Hagestad 1987). The parent-child relationship exhibits unique characteristics (Maccoby and Martin 1983) because it is an enduring relationship marked by initial asymmetry in terms of both competence and power, yet it must accommodate dramatic changes over the life course. In addition, attachment between parents and children has been described as the most salient construct that applies to all stages of parent-child relationships (Rossi and Rossi 1990) and helps explain reciprocity in intergenerational relations (Norris and Tindale 1994). Therefore, it is assumed that any discussion of caregiving across the life course is based, at least in part, on recognition of the importance of this attachment relationship.

Caring For and Caring About

When considering caregiving among family members, it is important to make the distinction between caring *for* and caring *about* someone (Bengtson, Rosenthal, and Burton 1996). Caring *about* someone is primarily an emotional act (i.e., attachment), whereas caring *for* someone is primarily a physical act. These two concepts are related, as most families members care *about* the people they care *for*.

The information presented in Table 11.1 shows which generations of family members are cared *for* versus cared *about* by different family members at each stage of family development over the life course. Bill and Nancy Marshall's family is at Stage VI (Launching) of the family life cycle. Their daughters, Sarah and Dana, have moved out of the home into their own apartment. Given the Marshalls' status as a Stage VI family, we can use the table to analyze Nancy Marshall's caregiving responsibilities with respect to the other members of her family. For example, although Nancy cares *about* her parents (and her in-laws), she is not yet actively involved in daily care *for* them (although she may soon take over the caregiver role of her aging mother). Likewise, she cares *about* her husband, Bill, but she does not actively provide caregiving for him. She cares *about* her four children, but she is only actively caring *for* the youngest two (who are still at home). Finally, Nancy cares *about* her 7-year-old granddaughter, but she rarely cares *for* her. Thus, we can see that although Nancy is very involved in the lives of other family members (as well as having a full-time job and running the household) at this stage of the family life cycle, her direct caregiving responsibilities (i.e., caring *for*) is limited to her two youngest children.

Gender and Family Caregiving

Despite the increase in the number and proportion of women in the workforce, caregiving responsibilities across the life course remain primarily the domain of women (Allen and Baber 1994; Ferree 1990; Thompson and Walker 1989). Providing care to loved ones, whether they are children, disabled spouses, or aging parents, is viewed in this and other cultures as "women's work." Children are raised primarily by women, whether it is by their own mothers, female siblings, or their grandmothers. Similarly, as family members get older and need help, this pattern continues, with women assuming the primary responsibility for providing care.

Pointing to the interplay of power and socialization, feminist scholars direct attention to the inequality that exists in families and society concerning the division of labor related to caregiving. Females are socialized, from a very young age to be nurturing, empathetic, and altruistic. Not only are young girls encouraged to be nurturant, but in many cases older siblings, and especially girls, are given full responsibility for looking after younger children. The result is that young girls and female adolescents have more experience spending time with and taking care of younger children than boys and male adolescents do (Frodi and Lamb 1978), and this pattern continues over the life course. In addition, models of gender development for women emphasize how girls are taught to define themselves in reference to their attachment to others (Chodorow 1978), as well as to satisfy the needs of others, often in place of their own needs (Gilligan 1982). The outcome of this socialization is that caregiving holds a central place in women's lives.

In spite of the strong gender socialization of women, not all women desire to become mothers or caregivers. Additionally, many men are competent and nurturing caregivers (Parke 1996). There are several explanations as to why, when men and women are both competent and proficient caregivers, women provide most care for family members. One explanation is that women are often reluctant to relinquish control of traditional responsibilities that provide them with a central role and power in the family (Allen and Baber 1994; Parke 1996). At the same time, men may be reluctant to disrupt

Table 11.1

Delineation of Changes in Caring About Someone and Caring For Someone Over the Life Course of Families.

	Generation 1	Generation 2	Generation 3	Generation 4	Generation 5
STAGE I: Couple					
Caring *about:*	grandparents	parents	spouse	—	—
Caring *for:*	—	—	—	—	—
STAGE II: Childbearing					
Caring *about:*	grandparents	parents	spouse	children	—
Caring *for:*	—	—	—	children	—
STAGE III: Preschool age					
Caring *about:*	grandparents	parents	spouse	children	—
Caring *for:*	—	—	—	children	—
STAGE IV: School age					
Caring *about:*	grandparents	parents	spouse	children	—
Caring *for:*	—	—	—	children	—
STAGE V: Teenage					
Caring *about:*	grandparents	parents	spouse	children	—
Caring *for:*	—	—	—	children	—
STAGE VI: Launching					
Caring *about:*	—	parents	spouse	children	grandchildren
Caring *for:*	—	parents	—	—	—
STAGE VII: Retirement					
Caring *about:*	—	parents	spouse	children	grandchildren
Caring *for:*	—	parents	—	—	—
STAGE VIII: Aging family					
Caring *about:*	—	—	spouse	children	grandchildren
Caring *for:*	—	—	spouse	—	—

the traditional caregiving arrangements that clearly benefit them. Finally, women may not view men as competent caregivers (Parke 1996) or may feel guilty about not fulfilling duties that have been socially labeled as "women's work" (Allen and Baber 1994).

The gendered nature of employment and paid work also contributes to the increased likelihood that women will perform most caregiving duties in families (Ferree 1990; Walker 1992). Women who are employed outside the home typically make less money than their male counterparts, and their work is often viewed as expendable. Therefore, women are more likely to leave paid work in order to care for young, ill, or elderly family members.

Another explanation as to why women provide a disproportionate amount of care to family members is based on attachment theory. Women are viewed as having greater emotional ties to loved ones, regardless of their life stage (Bowlby 1951) and therefore are depicted as "kin-keepers" of the family both within and between generations. For example, women's attachments to loved ones are more often "vertical" as opposed to "horizontal," whereas men's attachments are the reverse (Troll 1987). In other words, women are more likely to feel responsible for both younger and older family members and, as a result, to provide more intergenerational care.

Society rarely acknowledges the costs of caregiving to women. Over the life course, the unpaid labor of women is seldom valued or often viewed as "low cost." However, the costs of caregiving for women are many, including loss of income, loss of retirement benefits (including Social Security), loss of career advancement, psychological stress, physical exhaustion, and the loss of freedom for social and other pleasurable activities (Walker 1992).

Attachment Over the Life Course

Attachment refers to "species-characteristic behaviors that promote *proximity to a caregiver*" (Ainsworth 1989, 70). Maintaining proximity is crucial for survival in species such as humans that bear neotenous offspring—young who cannot survive independent of their caregivers. Furthermore, attachment behaviors are not limited to the early stages of the life course but actually "characterize human beings from the cradle to the grave" (Bowlby 1979, 129). Beginning at about six months of age, infants develop specific attachments and become distressed on separation (i.e., suffer separation anxiety) from primary caregivers. As toddlers and preschoolers, children maintain proximity by means of clinging to and following their caregivers.

As children get older, the characteristics of attachment change. In the case of a young adult living away from home, proximity may be maintained by calling home, writing letters, or e-mailing parents, especially under stressful circumstances (Bee 1987; Cicirelli 1983, 1991). In adulthood "symbolic attachment" emerges—that is, an individual creates a mental representation of the specific attachment figure (Bowlby 1969; Cicirelli 1983, 1991), so that even over distance and time, the attachment figure can still provide a sense of security and comfort. Symbolic attachment is illustrated in the Marshall family. For example, Dana, a college freshman, displays her ongoing attachment to her parents by calling home. In fact, on particularly stressful days she is reminded of how much she misses her mother and frequently calls home just to hear her mother's voice.

Parent-child attachment undergoes a qualitative shift as the child becomes an adult and as parents age to the degree that a role reversal often takes place when parents are impaired as a result of aging or illness (Ainsworth 1989). This crossover in type of attachment occurs over the life course (Cicirelli 1991). In early life, children's attachment takes the form of dependency, while parental attachment takes the form of protectiveness. Later, adult children's feelings for their parents shift from feelings of dependency to feelings of protectiveness. Parental attachment also shifts from feelings of protectiveness when children are younger to feelings of dependency as the parents age. Much negotiation, however, is required in order for parent-child dyads to shift from the child being dependent on the parent during infancy and childhood to the potential dependency of an older parent on the child (Rossi and Rossi 1990).

Caregiving in the Early Stages of Family Development

Kelly Marshall is the 10-year-old daughter of Bill and Nancy Marshall. Kelly has been anxious lately because of her parents' repeated arguments. At night, after she has gone to bed, Kelly can hear her mother complaining to her father that he needs to help more with the housework and the care of the children. Her mom cries sometimes and says she simply cannot continue working full-time, assisting with her in-laws, transporting Joe and Kelly to all their activities, and doing the cooking, cleaning, and laundry. Kelly can hear her dad argue that he does work around the house but admit he rarely is involved with the children's activities. Actually, Kelly is hoping her dad will start doing more things with her, like taking her to soccer practice or to the movies with friends. At least that way she could spend more time with him. Kelly loves her mom but misses spending time with her dad the way they did when she was little.

During the early stages of the life course of families, caregiving consists primarily of hands-on care of infants, toddlers, preschoolers, children, and, to some degree, adolescents. During these early stages, caregiving is typically not reciprocal; rather, parent-child relations are characterized by asymmetry—including asymmetry of caregiving (Maccoby and Martin 1983). Although older children and adolescents may perform household chores, including providing care for younger siblings (McHale and Gamble 1989), it is rare that children provide care for their parents during the early stages of family development. An exception may occur with divorced, single-parent families in which children may temporarily take over adult caregiving because of their parents' diminished capacity to parent (Wallerstein and Kelly 1980).

Attachment During the Early Stages of the Family Development

Almost all infants become attached to their caregivers; however, individual differences exist in the quality of this attachment (Ainsworth, Blehar, Waters, and Wall 1978; Ainsworth and Marvin 1995). Ainsworth and her colleagues documented three types of attachment in infants: secure attachment, insecure-avoidant attachment, and insecure-ambivalent attachment. Infants classified as *securely* attached missed their mothers when separated and were glad to see them on reunion. In addition, these infants used their mothers as a "secure base" from which to explore the environment. Infants who were *in-*

securely attached either ignored their mothers (*insecure-avoidant*), or were ambivalent toward them (*insecure-ambivalent*). A fourth category—*insecure-disorganized attachment*—was added later (Main and Solomon 1986).

It has been suggested that a continuity of attachment style exists between infancy and adulthood. Support for this hypothesis would demonstrate a "meaningful developmental link between the attachment-related experiences of the child and how that child behaves in attachment relationships when s/he grows up to be an adult" (Ainsworth and Marvin 1995, 19). For example, college students who recalled being securely attached to their parents were rated as less anxious and less hostile by their peers than students who recalled being insecurely attached (Kobak and Sceery 1988). Furthermore, there is a high rate of agreement between an individual's early attachment style and their attachment to romantic partners (Owens et al. 1995). Such continuity of attachment has clear implications for caregiving over the life course—for one's spouse or partner, as well as children and parents.

Gendered Caregiving in the Early Stages of Family Development

By all estimates, mothers perform at least two to three times as much child care as fathers, even when both parents work outside the home (Parke 1996; Thompson and Walker 1989). When fathers perform child care, it is typically in a "helping" capacity; rarely do they take full responsibility for children (Lamb 1987; Thompson and Walker 1989). For example, fathers are infrequently left alone with their young children, and it is typically mothers who manage and monitor fathers' care of infants and young children. At the same time, fathers are the primary caregivers during mothers' work hours in 20 percent of dual-career families (Pleck 1993). Clearly, fathers today are spending more time caregiving than they did in the 1950s and 1960s, but the increase is small. For instance, one study of family work found that between 1966 and 1988 the time that fathers spent with their children increased from a little over an hour a day to almost two hours a day (Robinson 1988). Mothers, even those who work outside the home, still perform the majority of caregiving tasks associated with children.

Many factors influence parents' involvement in caregiving. One of the key factors is the societal belief that caregiving is mandatory for mothers but optional for fathers (Thompson and Walker 1989). Women, if they have children, do not have a choice about caregiving, yet men do. It could be argued that fathers are not as competent as mothers at caregiving. Parke (1996), however, reported that fathers were just as capable as mothers at caregiving (e.g., feeding babies) but were simply less involved. Furthermore, fathers appear to have less external support for the caregiving role than mothers do. For example, employers are less tolerant of men taking time off from work to care for children than they are of women taking time off. In addition, mothers may play a *gatekeeper* role in limiting fathers' involvement in caregiving (Allen and Baber 1994; Parke 1996). In fact, research shows that a majority of mothers are satisfied with the amount of child care their husbands perform.

Another factor that seems to influence parents' involvement in caregiving is the sex of the child. A strong preference exists for male children in many countries, including the United States. At the same time, there is a clear pattern that both parents—mothers and fathers—interact more with their same-sex infants; mothers touch and vocalize more with female infants and fathers touch and vocalize more with male infants (Parke 1996). Kotelchuck (1976) found that American fathers played half an hour longer a day with their infant sons than with their infant daughters, and Israeli men living on kibbutzim visited longer in the infant nursery if their baby was a boy (Gewirtz and Gewirtz 1968). In contrast, Hossain and Roopnarine (1993) found no pattern of same-sex involvement in African-American men. Rather, these fathers played just as much with their daughters as they did with their sons.

Fathers typically spend a greater proportion of their time playing with children, yet mothers play with children more than fathers do. Nevertheless, because mothers also do the majority of the caregiving, they spend a smaller proportion of their time playing with children—25 percent of their time compared to fathers' 40 percent (Kotelchuck 1976; Parke 1996); in the case of African-American parents, mothers spend 38 percent of their time playing with children while fathers spend 54 percent (Hossain and Roopnarine 1993). Not surprisingly, fathers are often their children's preferred playmates, although this preference may be related to the different styles of play; fathers' play is more unpredictable and physical, whereas mothers' play is more predictable and verbal. The roles of father as playmate and mother as caregiver continue as the child gets older—that is, most of the time fathers spend with their teenage children is in leisure activities (Larson and Richards 1993), while mothers' time with teens reflects a wider range of activities, including personal care, shared housework, and leisure activities.

Caregiving in the Middle Stages of Family Development

Nancy Thompson Marshall is 49 and feels exhausted. She works full time as an elementary school teacher, is active in her children's and grandchild's schedules, provides occasional support to her in-laws (who are raising two grandchildren), and has been providing assistance to her own parents, who live out of state. Her mother has been recently diagnosed with probable Alzheimer's disease, and Nancy is frequently on the phone arranging for services or talking to her father about her mother's condition. Nancy loves her parents and her children and even her in-laws, but she sometimes feels overwhelmed by all her responsibilities. She also feels increasing resentment at the minimal assistance her brother is providing for their parents. She realizes he is busy, but so is she! Just because she is the daughter is no reason for her to be completely responsible for the care of her parents and her in-laws.

During the middle stages of family development, family caregiving consists primarily of the exchange of assistance between either middle-aged parents and their young-adult children, or middle-aged adult children and their young-old parents. In either case, the typical pattern of assistance (i.e., financial, emotional, and instrumental) is from the older generation to the younger generation (Spitz and Logan 1992; Zarit and Eggebeen 1995). Regardless of whether parents are in their 40s, 50s, or 60s, they typically give more assistance (1.92 hours per week on average) to their adult children than they receive (.52 hours per week on average) (Spitz and Logan 1992).

Researchers have pointed out that research on parent-child relationships over the life course focuses primarily on the early and later life stages of development, dismissing the important years during the middle stages (Hagestad 1984; Rossi and Rossi 1991). Nevertheless, the middle stages of family development are characterized by a number of special cases of caregiving. For example, in one study, almost 30 percent of middle-aged parents reported having a co-resident adult child, usually a single adult male (Aquilino 1990). Sometimes labeled "boomerang children," these adult children often encounter unemployment, divorce, or other personal challenges that require them to return home to live with parents (Okimoto and Stegall 1987). In the Thompson family described earlier, David encountered financial difficulties early in his career and spent two years as an adult child living with his parents. Additionally, 15 percent of middle-aged adults reported being "sandwiched" between two generations—one older, one younger—that both require caregiving (Loomis and Booth 1995), as evidenced by the experience of Nancy Thompson Marshall. Finally, 5 percent of grandparents are the primary caregivers for their grandchildren (Fuller-Thompson, Minkler, and Driver 1997), often because of teen pregnancy, substance abuse, psychological instability, incarceration, AIDS, or death. Elaine and Frank Marshall are examples of such caregiving grandparents. In addition, it is not unusual that at this stage of the family life cycle (as well as at later stages) one spouse will experience illness to the degree that the other spouse becomes a caregiver for them. Other families may be involved with caregiving of extended family members or nonrelated individuals who are in need of help.

The 'Sandwich' Generation Family

There has been much speculation about the burden of being caught in the middle of two (or more) generations—a situation commonly referred to as being a member of the "sandwich generation" (Bengtson et al. 1996; Loomis and Booth 1995). The perceived burden comes as a result of *multigenerational* caregiving, or caregiving not only to one's children but also to one's parents. The possibility of being caught in the middle of two or more generations is becoming greater as a result of the aging of the population. Four- and five-generation families, with fewer members in each generation (i.e., "beanpole" families) are becoming more common as life expectancy increases and fertility rates decline (Bengtson, Rosenthal, and Burton 1990); thus, the likelihood that a middle-aged adult will be a member of the sandwich generation is growing.

Several issues are yet to be resolved with respect to the sandwich generation and multigenerational caregiving. According to Loomis and Booth (1995), most of the research on caregiving to elderly parents has used convenience samples of older parents with greater needs (e.g., recruited through social service agencies), which are not representative of the population as a whole. Such samples have negatively biased the results of studies addressing the effects of caregiving on the caregiver. For example, most authors have viewed caregiving as a burden while ignoring the benefits that may be associated with it (Bengtson et al. 1996), as well as the reciprocal aspects of caregiving. In addition, there is little information regarding how often multigenerational caregiving actually takes place in families.

At least two studies have used representative national samples (Loomis and Booth 1995; Rosenthal, Martin-Matthews, and Matthews 1996) to study the prevalence of the sandwich generation. Using liberal requirements (child at home, one living parent), Loomis and Booth found that 55 percent of their longitudinal sample (mean age 44 years) qualified as members of this group.

Four years later (mean age 48), 44 percent of their sample qualified. Rosenthal et al. (1989) used more stringent requirements in their study (child at home, paid work, one living parent), and found that 42 percent of the sample in their early 40s met the requirements, whereas only 35 percent of the sample in their late 40s met the requirements. Finally, in terms of actual caregiving, only 15 percent of Loomis and Booth's sample (in 1988 and 1992) were responsible for caregiving for more than one generation. Therefore, it may be concluded that most middle-aged women do not experience multigenerational caregiving because they do not have both a child still living at home and a living parent who needs care (Rosenthal et al. 1996; Rosenthal, Matthews, and Marshall 1989; Spitz and Logan 1990).

Still, many people (especially women) can expect to provide care to aging parents or in-laws at some point in their lives (Bengtson et al. 1996; Rosenthal et al. 1989). In contrast to the assumption that serving as a caregiver to an older parent is a burden, Loomis and Booth (1995) found that taking on multigenerational caregiving responsibilities had little to no effect on caregivers' well-being and concluded that the burden of multigenerational caregiving is largely a myth. Rather, caregiving to children was more stressful than caregiving to elderly parents. There are several reasons for this lack of stress, including the fact that until parents reach 75 years old, they consistently give more help to their adult children than they receive (Spitz and Logan 1992). For example, over half of parents up to age 75 give an average of two hours help to their adult children per week; only 13 percent of adult children give help to their parents—at an average of half an hour per week. Parents who are older than 75, however, require more help from their adult children than they give in return, but by this time most of the children in the youngest generation would be less likely to require care themselves. Thus, it seems that multigenerational caregiving is neither widespread nor, for the most part, particularly burdensome.

The 'Skip-Generation' Family

Another increasing family caregiving trend involves grandparents raising grandchildren. Labeled *skip-generation* families, this new caregiving arrangement involves young-old and middle-old adults taking full or partial parental responsibility for their grandchild(ren). Although grandparents have cared for grandchildren for centuries, recent Census data indicate that the number of grandchildren living with grandparents increased 44 percent between 1980 and 1990; the Census Bureau estimated that, as of 1991, 3.3 million grandchildren resided with grandparents (Fuller-Thompson et al. 1997; Jendrek 1994). Furthermore, two-thirds of these families consisted of three-generation households; in other words, grandparents were providing care for grandchildren despite the presence of at least one parent (Fuller-Thompson et al. 1997).

Based on the variables of physical custody and legal rights, Jendrek (1994) classified caregiving grandparents into three categories. *Custodial* grandparents have a legally recognized relationship with their grandchild(ren). These grandparents have adopted, established guardianship of, or obtained full or temporary custody of their grandchildren and therefore have full parental authority. In contrast, *living-with* grandparents reside with their grandchildren (usually in the grandparents' home), providing daily physical care. These grandparents, however, have not obtained legal authority of their grandchildren and cannot make legal decisions about them. *Day-care* grandparents do not have legally recognized authority, yet they do provide daily care to their grandchildren for extended periods of time. Therefore, many grandchildren spend a majority of the day in their grandparents' care yet officially live with their parents.

In a recent study attempting to profile grandparent caregivers, Fuller-Thompson et al. (1997) found that for many caregiving grandparents, the arrangement was a "long-term and labor-intensive commitment" (409). Of the 3,477 grandparents included in this study, 380 (10.9 percent) had responsibility for a grandchild for six months or more. Of those who had reported caregiving responsibilities, 77 percent were women, 62 percent were Non-Hispanic white, 56 percent had provided care for at least three years, 72 percent had begun their role of custodial grandparent before the grandchild was 5 years of age, and 39 percent were raising a daughter's child rather than a son's child (31 percent). Compared to grandparents who had not cared for grandchildren, 60 percent of caregiving grandparents reported incomes below the poverty line. Because of the representative nature of the sample, these profile results have significant implications for the social, economic, and policy needs of this caregiving population.

Skip-generation grandparents often face many challenges related to the "legal, financial, medical, educational, and emotional issues that come with this new role" (Grandparent Information Center 1993). Studies examining the experience of caregiving grandparents have depicted this role as "off-time" (i.e., a role that is not expected for the current life stage) and therefore the cause of considerable stress. The challenges experienced by skip-generation seniors are many, including having a limited income, locating health care and insurance resources, and exploring legal avenues for establishing parental visitation rights and/or authority. Additionally, these seniors must refresh their parenting skills, and they sometimes encounter challenges related to the social context in which they now live (e.g., media influence, crime, drugs). For example, Elaine and Frank Marshall are in their 70s and raising two granddaughters ages 4 and 7. Originally, they had planned to spend their retirement years traveling the country; now they find themselves attending parent-teacher conferences, reading about nonpunitive discipline techniques, and singing songs with a purple dinosaur. Despite the many unexpected challenges, Elaine and Frank, as well as many caregiving grandparents, report considerable fulfillment and joy from providing for their grandchildren (Burton 1992).

Caregiving in the Late Stages of Family Development

Susan Thompson, Nancy's mother, has been recently diagnosed with probable Alzheimer's disease. For the past six months she has been showing signs of memory loss and disorientation. Last month, she got lost while driving home from the grocery store. Her husband, Nick, is devastated. He had suspected his wife was ill for the past year but would not admit it to himself or his children. He is concerned he will not be able to care for his wife adequately as the disease progresses, but he is determined not to place her in a nursing home. Currently, he is depending a great deal on his daughter, Nancy, for assistance in making decisions and arrangements for respite care providers and home health personnel. His son, David, attempts to be supportive but lives in Boston with his partner and is simply not as involved. Nick is thinking that he and his wife may need to move to be near Nancy and her family.

Three generalizations about family caregiving in later life are consistently supported by empirical research (Dwyer and Coward 1992). First, families are the primary source of care for aging family members; as much as 80 percent of informal support received by aging family members is provided by family and friends (Dwyer 1995; Dwyer, Folts, and Rosenberg 1994). Second, as previously discussed, women are much more likely to fill the role of caregiver than are their male counterparts (Dwyer et al. 1994; Montgomery and Datwyler 1990), to the degree that *family care* and *informal care* are simply "euphemisms for female family members" (Dwyer and Seccombe 1991, 231). Finally, because women are usually widowed, live longer than men, and thus have higher rates of disability, most seniors in need of care are women (Chappell 1990; Dwyer and Coward 1992).

As a result of increased life expectancy, family mobility, and participation of women in the workforce, caregiving tasks in later life have become increasingly complex and sometimes stressful for family members. Because individuals are living longer, there is greater incidence of chronic and degenerative illnesses as opposed to acute illnesses that result in immediate death (Coward, Horne, and Dwyer 1992; Dwyer et al. 1994; Kinsella 1995). Chronic and degenerative diseases result in greater physical disability among older adults, and thus greater needs for assistance with activities of daily living (ADLs), such as tasks of personal care, bathing, dressing, eating, and instrumental activities of daily living (IADLs), such as shopping, financial management, and housework (Chappell 1990; Dwyer 1995; Travis 1995).

Family as the Primary Source of Care

Despite the common stereotype that a majority of older adults live in nursing facilities, only 5 percent of individuals over age 65 reside in a skilled-care residence. The remaining 95 percent of seniors live independently in the community, with only 10 percent as functionally impaired as those in skilled-care institutions (Chappell 1990). Types of care usually required by aging individuals are categorized as *formal* or *informal*. Formal care usually consists of "hands-on care" provided for a fee and for a limited period by individuals with no significant emotional connection to the care recipient (Travis 1995). *Informal* care, on the other hand, is usually provided on an "as needed" basis by family members and friends. This type of care, usually given by a spouse or child, is free of charge and is most often motivated by love, commitment, and a need to reciprocate for past care, but it may also involve feelings of obligation or guilt (Cicirelli 1986; Travis 1995).

Researchers have consistently found that most caregiving for older adults is provided by family members (Chappell 1990; Dwyer 1995). The Thompson family serves as an example of how families assign caregiving responsibilities. When Susan Thompson began showing signs of dementia, Nick, her husband, provided more assistance by helping her dress, reminding her of appointments, and often driving her places. Now that Susan's symptoms are requiring increased care, the adult daughter, Nancy, is becoming more involved. Nancy lives out of state, works full-time, and cares for the two of her four children who are in the home. David, the adult son, lives further from his family than Nancy and is working full-time; however, he has no children or in-laws. David also has the financial resources to travel home. Despite these factors, there was never any expectation that David would be involved in arranging for or providing care to his mother. He does call home every week and visit once a year. Often, such caregiving decisions are influenced by gender rather than the availability of time or resources.

In order to determine who plays the role of primary caregiver, families often conform to a caregiving hierarchy (Chappell 1990; Dwyer 1995; Horowitz 1985). The first to provide support to an older ill family member is typically a spouse. Assuming they have no disabilities of their own, spouses of either gender usually provide the necessary care. In cases where a spouse is not available, an adult daughter or daughter-in-law is most likely to provide care (Dwyer 1995; Dwyer and Seccombe 1991; Enright 1991). When an adult daughter or daughter-in-law is not available, another female relative, such as a niece, sister, or granddaughter, is likely to assume caregiving responsibilities. Finally, in the absence of a spouse, adult daughter, daughter-in-law, or another female relative, an adult son provides care (Enright 1991; Soldo and Myllyluoma 1983).

Researchers have compared two primary types of caregivers: spousal caregivers and adult-child caregivers. Spousal and adult-child caregivers exist in relatively equal proportion; however, their experiences of caregiving are different. Spousal caregivers are likely to be older than adult-child caregivers, to have lower incomes, to provide care for extended periods, to provide care in the home, and to receive little outside assistance (Chappell 1990; Enright 1991; Montgomery and Datwyler 1990). Additionally, spousal caregivers have been found to be more depressed, to be in poorer health than adult-child caregivers, and to be in urgent need of respite services (Smerglia and Deimling 1997). In contrast, adult-child caregivers are more likely to have knowledge of available support resources and to take advantage of formal and informal assistance (Enright 1991). In fact, employed adult-child caregivers are much more likely to receive paid assistance than are spousal caregivers.

What motivates adult children to provide care for their aging parents? Various theoretical approaches have been used to explain and predict caregiving behaviors, including Bengtson's model of intergenerational solidarity (Bengtson, Olander, and Haddad 1976; Treas and Bengtson 1987), models of filial obligation (Jarrett 1985), and attachment theory (Cicirelli 1983, 1991). Jarrett (1985) has argued that positive affect (i.e., attachment) weakens under the strain of caregiving for aging parents; obligation, on the other hand, remains a motivating force in spite of the burden of caregiving. Cicirelli (1983) used both attachment and obligation to predict adult children's caregiving and future caregiving behaviors. Results showed that filial obligation did not directly predict either caregiving behavior or future caregiving behavior, although there was an indirect effect through attachment behaviors. There was, however, a direct effect of attachment behaviors on both caregiving and future caregiving behaviors. Thus, the overall effect was stronger for attachment than for filial obligation.

Gendered Caregiving in Late Life

Most researchers investigating the experiences of family caregivers have examined caregiving experiences of both genders (Allen 1994; Ingersoll-Dayton, Starrels, and Dowler 1996; Kramer and Kipnis 1995). A majority of these findings have pointed to gender differences in the adjustment and experience of caregiving for men and women, whether spousal or adult-child. Generally, consistent with previous stages, women have been found to provide "hands-on" types of care such as personal care, laundry, household cleaning, and meal preparation (Dwyer et al. 1994; Horowitz 1985; Kramer and Kipnis 1995; Montgomery and Datwyler 1990). In contrast, male caregivers are more likely to be "care managers," for example, by managing the finances, providing transportation, performing home maintenance, and arranging for formal care services (Dwyer et al. 1994; Horowitz 1985; Kramer and Kipnis 1995).

Female caregivers, specifically adult daughters, are more likely to experience caregiver burden as a result of their caregiving responsibilities than are male caregivers, especially adult sons (Chappell 1990; Ingersoll-Dayton et al. 1996; Kramer and Kipnis 1995). This may be attributed to women experiencing conflict between work responsibilities and caregiving responsibilities more often than men do (Kramer and Kipnis 1995). Caregiving women have been found to continue working despite dramatic increases in caregiving responsibilities. In fact, when researchers compared the effect of employment on the care provided by adult sons and daughters, they found that employment reduced the involvement of sons but not of daughters (Enright 1991; Stoller 1983). Additionally, when caregiving crises occur, it is caregiving women who are more likely to miss work, reduce their hours to part-time, or quit their jobs (Chappell 1990; Kramer and Kipnis 1995).

Because women often marry men older than themselves, have longer life expectancies, and are socialized to fulfill caregiving tasks, most spousal caregivers are women (Dwyer et al. 1994). Typically, caregiving wives receive considerably less assistance from family and friends than do caregiving husbands (Enright 1991). Adult-child caregivers are also predominantly women; adult daughters and daughters-in-law provide a disproportionate amount of care to aging relatives. Furthermore, as in earlier stages of family development, there is some evidence of a same-sex pattern of caregiving for women (Lee, Dwyer, and Coward 1993). More older women than men are the recipients of caregiving, and it is primarily their daughters (or daughters-in-law) who provide the care. Finally, female adult-child caregivers may have responsibilities to their family of procreation as well and can have difficulty balancing the multiple roles of caregiver, parent, spouse, and employee.

Conclusions

Caregiving across the life span takes place within the family. From birth to death, family members care *for* and *about* their loved ones. Because most families experience consistent life cycle transitions that require the exchange of assistance between family members and affect multiple generations, a broad conceptualization of "caregiving" within the family should include providing support and exchanging resources at multiple stages over the life course. This includes the care parents provide to growing children, adolescents, and young adults; the support exchanged between mature parents and middle-aged children; and finally, the increasingly intensive care provided to aging parents by adult children.

The nature of the resources available to family members and the types of assistance exchanged between family members vary widely and evolve as the family develops. The purpose of this chapter has been to describe the nature of family caregiving over the life course using a life course perspective. Additionally, we used the feminist perspective to illustrate the gendered nature of family caregiving and attachment theory to emphasize the importance of emotional ties at all stages of the life course.

Although viewing families over time is a valuable framework for obtaining a longitudinal understanding of family functioning, it is important to recognize one serious limitation of this framework. Because the level of analysis is most often the nuclear family form, nontraditional family forms are often not represented, including gay and lesbian families, step families, childless families, and "boomerang-child" families (adult children returning to live at home). It is important to recognize these family forms and consider that caregiving takes place in all types of families at all stages of the life course.

In conclusion, there are still a number of issues in the area of family caregiving that need to be explored more fully. They include:

1. A better understanding of the antecedents of men's involvement in family caregiving.

2. More research focusing on caregiving during the middle stages of family development rather than focusing on only early and later stages of family life.

3. More studies of caregiving in later life that are grounded in attachment theory.

4. Increased attention to the implications of demographic trends (e.g., delayed childbearing and low fertility) on the sandwich generation phenomenon.

5. Increased recognition of the role of older adult siblings in the exchange of care in later life.

6. Future studies that address caregiving roles and responsibilities from a life course perspective should target less conventional family forms.

Discussion Questions

1. Family development theory describes the traditional trajectory of family development. What criticisms do you have of this approach with regard to caregiving?

2. Define caring "for" and caring "about." What is the relationship between the two?

3. Why are men in families typically less involved in caregiving than women are? List several possible reasons.

4. How would you predict that children's early quality of attachment to parents might affect later caregiving to aging parents? Give an example.

5. Define the different types of skip-generation grandparents. What makes each of these grandparenting roles unique?

6. Compare and contrast adult-child caregivers with spousal caregivers.

Glossary

Beanpole family Four- and five-generation families with few members in each generation.

Boomerang children Adult children who return to live in the home of their parents.

Caregiving Emotional and instrumental support provided to family members by other family members, regardless of age.

Neotenous offspring Young who cannot survive independent of their caregivers.

Sandwich generation Adults between two generations in need of caregiving—usually middle-aged persons who have children still living at home and who also have aging parents.

Skip-generation families Families in which grandparents are caring for grandchildren.

Suggested Readings

Bretherton, I. (1992). The origins of attachment theory: John Bowlby and Mary Ainsworth. *Developmental Psychology, 28*, 759–775.

Dwyer, J. W., and Coward, R. T. (1992). *Gender, Families and Elder Care*. Newbury Park, CA: Sage.

Parke, R. D. (1996). *Fatherhood*. Cambridge. MA: Harvard University Press.

Pillemer, K., and McCartney, K. (1991). *Parent-child Relations Throughout Life*. Hillsdale, NJ: Erlbaum.

Thompson, L., and Walker, A. J. (1989). Gender in families: Women and men in marriage, work, and parenthood. *Journal of Marriage and the Family, 51*, 845–871.

Zarit, S. T., and Eggebeen, D. J. (1995). Parent-child relationships in adulthood and old age. In M. H. Bornstein (Ed.), *Handbook of Parenting* (Vol. 1, 119–140). Mahwah, NJ: Erlbaum.

Bibliography

Ainsworth, M. D. S. (1989). Attachments beyond infancy. *American Psychologist, 44*, 709–716.

Ainsworth, M. D. S., Blehar, M. C., Waters, E., and Wall, S. (1978). *Patterns of Attachment: A Psychological Study of the Strange Situation*. Hillsdale, NJ: Erlbaum.

Ainsworth, M. D. S., and Marvin, R. S. (1995). On the shaping of attachment theory and research: An interview with Mary D. S. Ainsworth. In E. Waters, B. E. Vaughn, G. Posada, and K. Kondo-Ikemura (Eds.), *Caregiving, Cultural, and Cognitive Perspectives on Secure-base Behavior and Working Models: New Growing Points of Attachment Theory and Research. Monographs of the Society for Research in Child Development, 60* 2–3, Serial No. 244), 3–21.

Allen, K. R., and Baber, K. M. (1994). Issues of gender. In P. C. McKenry and S. J. Price (Eds.), *Families and Change* (21–39). Thousand Oaks, CA: Sage.

Allen, S. M. (1994) Gender differences in spousal caregiving and unmet need for care. *Journals of Gerontology: Social Sciences, 49*, S187–S195.

Aquilino, W. S. (1990). The likelihood of parent-adult child co-residence: Effects of family structure and parental characteristics. *Journal of Marriage and the Family, 52*, 405–419.

Bee, H. L. (1987). *The Journey of Adulthood*. New York: Macmillan.

Bengtson, V. L., Olander, E., and Haddad, A. (1976). The "generation gap" and aging family members: Toward a conceptual model. In J. F. Gubrium (Ed.), *Time, Roles, and Self in Old Age* (237–263). New York: Human Sciences Press.

Bengtson, V. L., Rosenthal, C., and Burton, L. (1990). Families and aging: Diversity and heterogeneity. In R. H. Binstock and L. K. George (Eds.), *Handbook of Aging and the Social Sciences* (3rd ed., 263–287). San Diego, CA: Academic.

Bengtson, V. L., Rosenthal, C., and Burton, L. (1996). Paradoxes of families and aging. In R. H. Binstock and L. K. George (Eds.), *Handbook of Aging and the Social Sciences* (4th ed., 253–282). San Diego, CA: Academic.

Bowlby, J. (1951). *Maternal Care and Mental Health*. Geneva: World Health Organization.

Bowlby, J. (1969). *Attachment and Loss: Vol., 1 Attachment*. New York: Basic Books.

Bowlby, J. (1979). *The Making and Breaking of Affectional Bonds*. London: Tavistock.

Burton, L. M. (1992). Black grandparents rearing children of drug-addicted parents: Stressors, outcomes, and social service needs. *The Gerontologist, 32*, 744–751.

Chappell, N. L. (1990). Aging and social care. In R. H. Binstock and L. K. George (Eds.), *Handbook of Aging and the Social Sciences* (3rd ed., 438–454). San Diego, CA: Academic.

Chodorow, N. (1978). *The Reproduction of Mothering*. Berkeley: University of California Press.

Cicirelli, V. G. (1983). Adult children's attachment and helping behavior to elderly parents: A path model. *Journal of Marriage and the Family, 45*, 815-825.

Cicirelli, V. G. (1986). The relationship of divorced adult children with their elderly parents. *Journal of Divorce, 9*, 39–54.

Cicirelli, V. G. (1991). Attachment theory in old age: Protection of the attached figure. In K. Pillemer and K. McCartney (Eds.), *Parent-Child Relations Throughout Life* (25–42). Hillsdale, NJ: Erlbaum.

Coward, R. T., Horne, C., and Dwyer, J. W. (1992). Demographic perspectives on gender and family caregiving. In J. W. Dwyer and R.

T. Coward (Eds.), *Gender, Families, and Elder Care* (18–33). Newbury Park, CA: Sage.

Dwyer, J. W. (1995). The effects of illness on the family. In R. Blieszner and V. H. Bedford (Eds.), *Handbook of Aging and the Family* (401–421). Westport, CT: Greenwood Press.

Dwyer, J. W., and Coward, R. T. (1992). *Gender, Families, and Elder Care*. Newbury Park, CA: Sage.

Dwyer, J. W., Folts, W. E., and Rosenberg, E. (1994). Caregiving in a social context. *Educational Gerontology, 20*, 615–631.

Dwyer, J. W., and Seccombe, K. (1991). Elder care as family labor. *Journal of Family Issues, 12*, 229–247.

Enright, R. B. (1991). Time spent caregiving and help received by spouses and adult children of brain-impaired adults. *The Gerontologist, 31*, 375-383.

Ferree, M. M. (1990). Beyond separate spheres: Feminism and family research. *Journal of Marriage and the Family, 52*, 866–884.

Frodi, A. M., and Lamb, M. E. (1978). Sex differences in responsiveness to infants: A developmental study of psychophysiological and behavioral responses. *Child Development, 49*, 1182–1188.

Fuller-Thompson, E., Minkler, M., and Driver, D. (1997). A profile of grandparents raising grandchildren in the United States. *The Gerontologist, 37*, 406–411.

Gewirtz, H. B., and Gewirtz, J. G. (1968). Visiting and caretaking patterns for kibbutz infants: Age and sex trends. *American Journal of Orthopsychiatry, 38*, 427–443.

Gilligan, C. (1982). *In a Different Voice*. Cambridge, MA: Harvard University Press.

Grandparent Information Center. (1993). *Grandparents Raising Their Grandchildren*. Washington, DC: American Association of Retired Persons.

Hagestad, G. O. (1984). The continuous bond: A dynamic multigenerational perspective on parent-child relations between adults. In M. Perlmutter (Ed.), *Parent-Child Relations in Child Development: The Minnesota Symposium on Child Psychology* (Vol. 17, 129–158). Hillsdale, NJ: Erlbaum.

Hagestad, G. O. (1987). Parent-child relations in later life: Trends and gaps in past research. In J. B. Lancaster, J. Altmann, A. S. Rossi, and L. R. Sherrod (Eds.), *Parenting Across the Life Span: Biosocial Dimensions* (405–433). New York: Aldine de Gruyter.

Horowitz, A. (1985). Sons and daughters as caregivers to older parents: Differences in role performance and consequences. *The Gerontologist, 25*, 612-617.

Hossain, Z., and Roopnarine, J. L. (1993). Division of labor and child care in dual-earner African-American families with infants. *Sex Roles, 29*, 571–583.

Ingersoll-Dayton, B., Starrels, M. E., and Dowler, D. (1996). Caregiving for parents and parents-in-law: Is gender important? *The Gerontologist, 36*, 483–491.

Jarrett, W. H. (1985). Caregiving within kinship systems: Is affection really necessary? *The Gerontologist, 25*, 5–10.

Jendrek, M. P. (1994). Grandparents who parent their grandchildren: Circumstances and decisions. *The Gerontologist, 34*, 206–216.

Kinsella, K. (1995). Aging and the family: Present and future demographic issues. In R. Blieszner and V. H. Bedford (Eds.), *Handbook of Aging and the Family* (32–56). Westport, CT: Greenwood Press.

Kobak, R. R., and Sceery, A. (1988). Attachment in late adolescence: Working models, affect regulation, and representations of self and others. *Child Development, 59*, 135–146.

Kotelchuck, M. (1976). The infant's relationship to the father: Experimental evidence. In M. Lamb (Ed.), *The Role of the Father in Child Development* (123–157). New York: Wiley.

Kramer, B. J., and Kipnis, S. (1995). Eldercare and work-role conflict: Toward an understanding of gender differences in caregiver burden. *The Gerontologist, 35*, 340–348.

Lamb, M. E. (1987). *The Father's Role: Cross-cultural Perspectives*. Hillsdale, NJ: Erlbaum.

Larson, R., and Richards, M. H. (1993). *Divergent Realities: The Emotional Lives of Mothers, Fathers, and Adolescents*. New York: Basic Books.

Lee, G. R., Dwyer, J. W., and Coward, R. T. (1993). Gender differences in parent care: Demographic factors and same-gender preferences. *Journals of Gerontology: Social Sciences, 48*, S9–S16.

Loomis, L. S., and Booth, A. (1995). Multigenerational caregiving and well-being: The myth of the beleaguered sandwich generation. *Journal of Family Issues, 16*, 131–148.

Maccoby, E. E., and Martin, J. A. (1983). Socialization in the context of the family: Parent-child interaction. In E. M. Hetherington (Ed.), *Handbook of Child Psychology, 4*, 1–101. New York: Wiley.

Main, M., and Solomon, J. (1986). Discovery of a new, insecure-disorganized/disoriented attachment pattern. In M. Yogman and T. B.

Brazelton (Eds.), *Affective Development in Infancy* (95–124). Norwood, NJ: Ablex.

McHale, S. M., and Gamble, W. C. (1989). Sibling relationships of children with disabled and nondisabled brothers and sisters. *Developmental Psychology, 25*, 421–429.

Montgomery, R. J. V., and Datwyler, M. M. (1990). Women and men in the caregiving role. *Generations, 14*, 34–38.

Norris, J. E., and Tindale, J. A. (1994). *Among Generations: The Cycle of Adult Relationships.* New York: Freeman.

Okimoto, J. D., and Stegall, P. J. (1987). *Boomerang Kids: How to Live With Adult Children Who Return Home.* Boston: Little, Brown.

Owens, G., Crowell, J. A., Pan, H., Treboux, D., O'Connor, E., and Waters, E. (1995). The prototype hypothesis and the origins of attachment working models: Adult relationships with parents and romantic partners. In E. Waters, B. E. Vaughn, G. Posada, and K. Kondo-Ikemura (Eds.), *Caregiving, cultural, and cognitive perspectives on secure-base behavior and working models: New growing points of attachment theory and research. Monographs of the Society for Research in Child Development, 60* (2–3, Serial No. 244), 216–233.

Parke, R. D. (1996). *Fatherhood.* Cambridge, MA: Harvard University Press.

Pleck, J. (1993). Are 'family supportive' employer policies relevant to men? In J. Hood (Ed.), *Men, Work, and Family* (221–222). Newbury Park, CA: Sage.

Robinson, J. (1988). "Who's doing the housework?" *American Demographics, 12*, 24ff.

Rosenthal, C. J., Martin-Matthews, A., and Matthews, S. H. (1996). Caught in the middle? Occupancy in multiple roles and help to parents in a national probability sample of Canadian adults. *Journal of Gerontology: Social Sciences, 51B*, S274–S283.

Rosenthal, C. J., Matthews, S. H., and Marshall, V. W. (1989). Is parent care normative? The experience of a sample of middle-aged women. *Research on Aging, 11*, 244–260.

Rossi, A. S., and Rossi, P. H. (1990). *Of Human Bonding: Parent-Child Relations Across the Life Course.* Hawthorne, NY: Aldine de Gruyter.

Rossi, A. S., and Rossi, P. H. (1991). Normative obligations and parent-child help exchange across the life course. In K. Pillemer and K. McCartney (Eds.), *Parent-Child Relations Throughout Life* (201–224). Hillsdale, NJ: Erlbaum.

Smerglia, V. L., and Deimling, G. T. (1997). Care-related decision-making satisfaction and caregiver well-being in families caring for older members. *The Gerontologist, 37*, 658–665.

Soldo, B. J., and Myllyluoma, J. (1983). Caregivers who live with dependent elderly. *The Gerontologist, 23*, 605–611.

Spitz, G., and Logan, H. (1990). Sons, daughters, and intergenerational support. *Journal of Marriage and the Family, 52*, 420–430.

Spitz, G., and Logan, J. (1992). Helping as a component of parent-adult child relations. *Research on Aging, 14*, 291–312.

Stoller, E .P. (1983). Parental caregiving by adult children. *Journal of Marriage and the Family, 45*, 851–858.

Thompson, L., and Walker, A. J. (1989). Gender in families: Women and men in marriage, work, and parenthood. *Journal of Marriage and the Family, 51*, 845–871.

Travis, S. S. (1995). Families and formal networks. In R. Blieszner and V. H. Bedford (Eds.), *Handbook of Aging and the Family* (459–473). Westport, CT: Greenwood Press.

Treas, J., and Bengtson, V. L. (1987). The family in later years. In M. B. Sussman and S. K. Steinmetz (Eds.), *Handbook of Marriage and the Family* (626–648). New York: Plenum.

Troll, L. E. (1987). Gender difference in cross-generational networks. *Sex Roles, 17*, 751–766.

Walker, A. J. (1992). Conceptual perspectives on gender and family caregiving. In J. W. Dwyer and R. T. Coward (Eds.), *Gender, Families, and Elder Care* (34–46). Newbury Park, CA: Sage.

Wallerstein, J. S., and Kelly, J. B. (1980). *Surviving the Breakup: How Children and Parents Cope With Divorce.* New York: Basic Books.

Zarit, S. H., and Eggebeen, D. J. (1995). Parent-child relationships in adulthood and old age. In M. H. Bornstein (Ed.), *Handbook of Parenting* (Vol. 1, 119–140). Mahwah, NJ: Erlbaum. ✦

Chapter 12
Family Economic Issues Across Time

Kathryn D. Rettig
University of Minnesota-Twin Cities

Ronit D. Leichtenbritt
Tel Aviv University

The following case study highlights economic issues across the life course by reviewing the lives of Andy and Kate Johnson, a couple who were included in a study conducted from 1986 to 1996. The study examined 1,153 divorce cases, finalized in 1986, that involved minor children, and followed the parents by two mail surveys and one telephone interview during the five years after the final divorce decree was granted (Rettig, Tam, and Yellowthunder 1995). The personal facts about the couple have been changed to protect their privacy, but their economic situation is accurately represented. They married on August 27, 1955 and lived together for 31 years while raising five children. Their divorce decree was finalized when Andy was 54 and Kate was 51, and they still had two children living at home, one of whom was 15 and eligible to receive child support. Andy and Kate are now in the last stage of the family life cycle, which begins at retirement and ends with death of both spouses. The Johnson case is representative of middle-income couples with mothers who stayed home to provide full-time care for their children and who divorced in their late middle years (Rettig, Yellowthunder, Christensen, and Dahl 1989, 1990, 1991).

The chapter begins by defining the economic concepts demonstrated in the case study, including economics, economic resources, economic unit, economic activities of economic units, the kinds of income and wealth that result from these economic activities, economic well-being, financial well-being, and financial developmental tasks. The chapter continues by explaining family economic issues across the life cycle of the Johnson family using three family-life stages as they were first conceptualized by Bigelow (1931) and placing emphasis on the contracting phase when divorce occurred.

Economic Perspectives of Family Life

Economics is the art of choosing the best ways to organize and combine limited resources to meet specific needs; it is the "science of choice among scarce resources" (Hoyt, Reid, McConnell, and Hooks 1954, 3), or decision making under conditions of scarcity (Blau and Ferber 1986). Families are among the groups that must make economic decisions about what should be produced and how various kinds of resources should be used, in both the present and the future.

Resources are anything that can be used to attain desired ends or goals (means to ends). Resources have also been defined as "any commodity, material or symbol, that is transmitted through interpersonal behavior and is available as a means of positive or negative needs satisfaction" (Foa and Foa 1974, 36). Resources include love, status (respect and esteem), services, information, goods, and money, and they are exchanged between persons within the environments of time, space, and social institutions. Economic resources include time, human energy, fossil fuel energy, goods, and money. These economic resources are scarce, can be objectively measured, and can be combined for use in a variety of ways (Diesing 1976).

Economic resources that are used in one way cannot be simultaneously used in another way. Each decision may involve using the resource of time for reaching one goal but at the expense of another, an *opportunity cost*. Most people who hear the word *economics* immediately think only about money resources. However, *time* is the ultimate scarce economic resource. Time cannot be "saved," because each minute comes only once and is gone forever, and the way time is used affects the kinds of income, wealth, and leisure available to family members.

Economic Units and Their Economic Activities

Family groups are important economic units in society. An *economic unit* is any social system that is able to hold together a set of goals, a "common good" for its members (Diesing 1976, 19). The *economic activities* of any economic unit are the managerial decisions and actions that are needed for coordinating production, consumption, distribution, allocation, investment, and exchange. This chapter places special emphasis on the family economic activities of *production* of human resources; *investments* in human capital, with mention of *allocation* of time, energy, and money resources; and *consumption* of goods and services.

Types of Income and Wealth Resulting From Family Economic Activities

The way *time is allocated* will affect the various kinds of income (flow resources) and assets/wealth (stocks of resources) that are the components of family economic well-being. Time can be allocated in only a few ways. First, people allocate time to working for *money income in the market production activities* that lead to the accumulation of financial wealth (*financial capital*). Second, people allocate time to working for *nonmoney income (in-kind income)* by producing goods and services for the use of family members in the *household production activities* that may lead to the accumulation of things (*physical capital*) (Morgan and Duncan 1982).

Third, people allocate time to *investment activities* in the form of learning and personal maintenance, producing and teaching children, and assisting family members to acquire an education and to maintain their health and well-being. These investment activities result in the development and maintenance of human resources and in a wealth of marketable skills (*human capital*) that will provide money income in the future. Fourth, people allocate time to working with others in *exchange activities* that establish family and community support groups and improve the usefulness of existing social institutions that contribute to their social wealth (*social capital*) (Coleman 1988). In addition, time is devoted to eating, leisure pursuits, and transit time between activities (*consumption*). The combination of all of these economic activities, and the resulting types of income and wealth, provides a sense of satisfaction (psychic income) that also contributes to economic well-being.

Components of Family Economic and Financial Well-Being

Family economic well-being is an indication of the status of all the types of income and wealth for the family group at one point in time. A true measure of economic well-being would take into account many factors, including family composition, money, and leisure time. Money income is an inadequate measure of family economic well-being (Morgan and Duncan 1982) because economic well-being is defined (for individuals) as the access to goods, services, and leisure (Fuchs 1986). Financial well-being refers to only money resources, including income and accumulated financial assets (financial capital or wealth).

Financial well-being, compared to economic well-being, is easier to define and measure and is a central concern for decision making in legal separations and divorces. There are many ways to measure financial well-being. For example, the courts use wealth-based measures such as the net worth statement that indicates financial *wealth* on a particular date. The courts also use income-based measures of financial well-being, such as income per person in the household (per capita income). A third way to measure financial well-being is with ratio-based measures; for instance, an income-to-needs ratio would indicate whether the money income is sufficient to meet the consumption needs of the household. These measures are seldom used in courts or during divorce negotiations (Christensen and Rettig 1991).

The income-to-needs ratio is calculated by comparing the household gross (or net) income in the numerator to a denominator consisting of an amount of money needed for an appropriate level of consumption. One possible denominator would be the poverty-level income guidelines in the United States, which represent a minimal subsistence level of consumption. An income-to-needs ratio with a value of 1.00 would mean the income is equal to poverty-level income for a household of that particular size. The extent to which a family has "financial well-being" is a value judgment, but most parents would hope for an income-to-needs ratio that is at least twice poverty level (2.0) when using net rather than gross income in the numerator.

Economic Approaches to Family Studies and Developmental Tasks

Macro family economics explores questions about "what adjustments can be made between society and the household that will give better family life and a better society" (Andrews 1935). *Micro* family economics explores questions about "how a family can best allocate time, energy, and money to carry on all of its activities in order to maintain a quality of life that is consistent with desired goals and central values" (Andrews 1935). This chapter places greater emphasis on *micro* family economics in order to focus on internal family transitions and developmental tasks of one nuclear family. In addition, the Johnson family case study provides more factual information about money rather than about time resources.

Early family economists described the stages of the family life cycle by explaining differing demands on time, energy, and money present at each stage and suggesting alternative strategies for meeting these demands (Gross and Crandall 1963). A more recent version of family economic and financial tasks was developed by the American Council of Life Insurance and its Extension Advisory Committee (1979) in educational materials called the "Adult Financial Management Matrix." The matrix outlined financial tasks, desired outcomes, and common financial errors by ages of adults. The overall

tasks, however, were to (a) manage financial resources to meet changing responsibilities for self and others over the life cycle, (b) cover financial risks, (c) provide for life-long learning needs, (d) build a satisfying life, (e) assess public systems and institutions to increase nonmoney income, (f) utilize professional and legal counsel, and (g) increase consumer proficiency. Many of these economic developmental tasks will be evident in examining the life course of the Johnsons.

People who write about the life course of families do recognize the importance of time and the varying influences of environmental contexts that alter family processes and affect human development (Rodgers and White 1993). *Historical time*, which refers to the "events in the broader social context that alter the roles or values of individuals and families" (Bengtson and Allen 1993, 471), is a particularly important influence on the economic issues of family life. Forces in the larger economy affect employment for family members and the income stability for the group. The economy also affects the prices of needed goods and services and, therefore, family expenditures. The economic climate further shapes personal attitudes and values, as well as the way parents socialize their children.

Examining The Life Course of the Johnsons

The divorce study that was used as a basis for this chapter did not investigate Andy's or Kate's family of origin or their early years of marriage. However, the historical cohort in which they were born provides important clues concerning their economic decisions. Andy Johnson was born in October 1932 in the rock-bottom phase of the Great Depression when over 12 million people were unemployed (Morrison 1965). Kate was born in 1935, the same year the Social Security Act was passed by Congress and the policies of Roosevelt's bold New Deal were starting to alleviate some of the worst conditions of the Depression (Morrison 1965). Several studies have concluded that parents and children of this era were significantly affected by the economic deprivation they experienced, evidenced in their attitudes and behaviors about time and money use. Boys of school age in 1932 were particularly industrious in their time use and possessed a greater sense of financial responsibility and a tendency to save money than those in later cohorts (Elder 1974).

Andy may have acquired such values of industriousness and responsibility because we know he began working for his company at age 23 and had worked there for 31 years at the time of his divorce in 1986. He had accumulated substantial savings, pension benefits, and life insurance, and he owned both stocks and bonds that were individually purchased. His wife, when reporting on marital difficulties, said there was *no difficulty* with his ability to earn or save money, but they had some difficulties talking about money issues. Another important historical event in Andy's early years was World War II. He was only nine years old at the time of the Pearl Harbor bombing, so he was not entitled to the educational benefits that enabled many veterans to attend college. Andy was only able to complete a high school education.

The Beginning Family from 1955 to 1958

The Johnsons were married in 1955 when she was 20 and he was 23. Their marriage ages were consistent with that time period; girls who completed high school usually married by the time they were 20 (Duvall 1971), and boys married at about age 22. Kate and Andy were married for three years before their first child was born, a year longer than the average period for the beginning (Stage I) of the family life cycle (Duvall 1971).

The establishment phase of this family took place during the Eisenhower presidency in 1955 when jobs were plentiful, workers tended to remain with the same company for a lifetime, and the economy was growing. Andy worked for a corporations that offered job security with income stability and excellent fringe benefits that facilitated continued health and long-term financial security for families.

Research suggests the Johnsons satisfactorily accomplished several developmental tasks of Stage I, based on Duvall's (1971)

model. Andy became established in his occupation by assuming responsibility for getting and holding a job and supporting his family. He planned for the long-term support of his family with his insurance, savings, and investments. Kate was making a home and managing the household, but it is not known whether she continued to work in the labor market at a time when only 34 percent of Caucasian women in the United States were employed (Blau and Ferber 1986).

The American Council of Life Insurance (1979) guidelines suggested the desired financial outcomes for 18- to 24-year-olds were to assess financial needs; determine short- and long-term economic and social goals; develop consumer skills and plans for spending, borrowing, and saving; keep accessible financial and legal records; and use professional expertise when needed. Kate's life represents one of the common financial errors of this age group. She did not seek additional schooling or on-the-job education in order to develop her marketable skills.

The Expanding Family From 1958 to 1971

The expanding stage of the Johnson family life cycle lasted for 13 years, from the birth of the first to the fifth child. Andy and Kate were only a year older in 1958 than the average ages for new parents (22 and 25 years), (Duvall 1971) when their first son was born (John). A second son was born (Jordan) one year later, and a daughter in 1961 (Jennifer), the year in which President Kennedy authorized an experimental food stamp program. Jennifer's birth was followed by the birth of James in 1968 and Jeffrey in 1971. The Johnson family was larger than most for that time period (1.4 persons under age 18 years), (Duvall 1971).

The 31 years between 1958 and 1989 were child-bearing and -rearing years for Kate (ages 23 to 54 years), who had a heavy workload as a full-time homemaker. Mothers with infants spent about 9.4 to 12.4 hours daily in housework (Walker 1969; Walker and Woods 1976). In 1968, Andy and Kate's children were 10, 9, and 7, and they had a new infant. Walker and Woods (1976) reported that the total time in household work for families with four children was 12.3 hours per day for nonemployed wives. Husbands contributed about 1.6 hours per day, regardless of the number and ages of children or the employment status of wives. We do not know the extent to which Andy contributed to the household work, but we do know that Kate made substantial time investments in human capital. When her youngest child was 18 (1989), she had invested 57 percent of the time of her life (31 out of 54 years) in the human resource development of her husband and children.

Kate's decision to stay home to care for family members (specializing in household rather than market production activities) may not have been carefully deliberated, with thought given to the long-term economic consequences; however, the decision probably made economic sense at the time. Commercial child-care facilities were limited in those years; her earning capacity was low because of her limited education and work experience; and the dollar value of the goods and services she produced for the family (an estimated time investment of approximately 70 hours weekly) was an important economic contribution to family well-being.

Kate decided on the *time-intensive* rather than the *goods-intensive* method of child-rearing (Becker 1991; Peters 1995). Economic theories describe goods-intensive methods of child-rearing as the child-care services that are purchased. This method is most often chosen by women who make enough money in their jobs that they are able to meet the added expenses of earning income, including child-care services, and still have additional money. Time-intensive methods are chosen when the mother cares for her own children, usually because the value of her time in the labor market is low and her economic contribution to the family is higher when she provides the services of care for her own children (Peters 1995).

The expanding stage of the family life cycle is a time of rising expenses as the number of children increases and as children become old enough to develop their special talents and interests. Family economists refer to these stages as centering on "accumulation" of physical capital because there are increasing needs for housing space, household furnishings, and equipment. The major family concerns in the expanding stages of the life cycle are meeting the direct and indirect costs of parenting (Gross and Crandall 1963). The total amount of time that Andy and Kate invested in their five children is unknown, but research indicates that money expenditures per child decrease as the number of children in a family increases (Espenshade 1984). Economists also conceptualize family size decisions in terms of investments in quantity versus quality of children (Haveman and Wolfe 1994). As the costs of parenting have increased over the last decades, the tendency has been for parents to have fewer children in order to provide them with more resources that will result in a better life for them in the future.

Direct costs of parenting. Direct costs are the out-of-pocket money expenditures on children for food, clothing, housing, transportation, health care, child care, and education. The Johnson children were growing toward their most expensive years (ages 15–24) during a time of rapid inflation (between 1968 and 1975) when prices rose at the fastest rate since 1947. Andy and Kate must have experienced significant challenges in meeting the expenses of their growing family when Jeffrey was born in 1971.

Indirect costs of parenting. The money costs of children are high, but the indirect costs must be added in order to arrive at a realistic estimate of total costs of parenting. The indirect costs of children are indicated by the time and energy required for the increased workload at home and the income-earning opportunities lost by the caretakers of children when they must miss work, take lower-paying jobs that are more flexible, are unable to invest in the social networking that professional careers demand, cannot participate in on-the-job training experiences for personal growth, or migrate to jobs elsewhere. The indirect costs of family life are highest for women like Kate if their marriages later end in divorce (Holden and Smock 1991). Researchers have concluded that the sum of all money costs of raising children are lower than the indirect costs, which amount to two-thirds of the total cost of raising a child (Culley, Van Name, and Settles 1976). Bryant (1990) estimated the total money and time costs of raising a single son born in 1980 to the age of 22 years and educated in a four-year residential college to be $243,819 in 1982 dollars and $326,371 in 1990 dollars. What is the dollar value of a mother's time spent in caring for her own children? A conservative estimate, using a federal minimum wage of $5.15 per hour for the 24-hour care that mothers provide, would indicate a value of $123.60 per day, $865.20 per week, and $44,990.40 per year in 1997. The minimum wage was lower when Kate was raising her children, but at $4.25 per hour she would have provided for the family in 1986 the equivalent of an annual income of $37,128, and she had worked at this child-rearing job for 28 years, making a sizable economic contribution to her family and society (Rettig 1993).

Developmental and financial tasks. One of the developmental tasks for parents of school-age and teenage children is continuing to satisfy each other as married partners (Duvall 1971). Some of the indirect costs of parenting five children may have been the loss of time and money for Andy and Kate as a couple and for their shared activities. The concerns of keeping financially solvent and establishing patterns for getting and spending income (Duvall 1971) were present. We do know that money resources had to be used for current needs, and their savings did not include plans for continuing education of the parents, postsecondary education for the children, or disability income protection or retirement savings for the homemaker. These are common financial errors of adults from ages 25 to 54 (American Council of Life Insurance 1979).

The Contracting Family From 1976 to 1989

The Johnson family experienced several overlapping stages of the family life cycle. John, the oldest child, reached 18 years in 1976, only five years after his youngest brother was born. The parents thus had both school-age and adolescent children and were also launching young adults. Like the expanding phase, the contracting phase of their family life cycle lasted 13 years, which

was double the amount of time (6–7 years) typical of most families (Duvall 1971, 358). The family was also atypical because the parents divorced in 1986, prior to the launching of all children. The immediate and longer-term economic and financial consequences of the divorce transition in the contracting stage of the family life cycle are discussed next.

The divorce decree decisions. There are three transitions in family life when rights to physical and financial assets are legally transferred. The first transition is the date of marriage, the second occurs at death of one of the partners, and the third is on the date of divorce, if it occurs. The final divorce decree involves legal decisions about child custody and visitation rights; parental income allocations for child support, spousal maintenance, debt payment responsibilities; and division of physical and financial capital assets. These legal decisions have long-term economic consequences for both partners.

The Johnson's final divorce decree was entered on July 22, 1986, and on that date Andy earned a monthly gross income of $3,767 (annual gross income $45,204). His monthly net income after taxes was listed as $2,221 (annual net income $26,652). Kate was employed as a cook and waitress at a restaurant, where she earned a biweekly gross income of $211 ($5,486 annually). Her biweekly net income was listed as $176 ($4,576 annually). Her monthly expenses for herself and two children were listed as $2,031—an amount almost half of her annual income. Andy was to pay child support, spousal maintenance, and $10,000 in debts the couple had accumulated. Kate was allowed to continue her health insurance on her husband's policy but would be required to pay the additional premium cost, which she could not afford to pay, and so it was an asset she lost at divorce.

The Johnson's decree awarded joint legal custody of Jeffrey (age 15) to both parents, sole physical custody to Kate, with liberal visitation granted to Andy. The child support award was set at $400 monthly ($4,800 annually), which was $157 a month below the state child support guidelines formula. Health insurance for Jeffrey was to be provided by his father, but no mention was made concerning out-of-pocket costs for medical or dental care, and no dental insurance was mentioned. No provisions were made for postsecondary education. James had reached the age of majority (18 years) and was not eligible to receive child support, although it was unlikely that he had received any vocational education to prepare him for the labor market. Spousal maintenance income was awarded to Kate at $400 monthly for three years and four months until child support ceased, and then $500 monthly until Andy's retirement, when spousal maintenance was to be terminated. Termination would also occur upon the death or remarriage of either party.

The distribution of physical capital assets included the house, furnishings, and vehicles. The house had a market value of $60,300, with a mortgage debt of $17,400, and equity of $42,900. Kate was to be responsible for the mortgage payments, and sale costs and was to receive credit for payments reducing the principal of the mortgage and any capital improvements to the house over $500 prior to the sale. The remainder of the equity was to be divided 50/50. The 1981 Ford Escort with an estimated market value of $2,500 was awarded to Kate. The 1976 Ford van (valued $750) was awarded to Andy, who also received a 1980 Honda motorcycle, a 1983 all-terrain vehicle, and such goods as a painting of his father, an eight-horsepower tiller, a drill press, a grinder, and a radial arm saw.

The final decree listed the financial capital of the husband's pension (estimated current value of $191,614) and the couple's savings, stocks, and bonds, which had an estimated value of $21,000. Kate was awarded an immediate cash settlement of $750 and a portion of Andy's pension to be awarded in the future if he survived to receive it. The amount was 50 percent of the marital interest. (Marital interest is the total accumulation amount during the marriage that was owned by the employee, and that amount is divided by two.) Kate was also awarded Series E Savings Bonds for an undisclosed face amount and several shares of three different companies' stock. Andy was awarded the cash value of the life insurance policy and

many shares of eight different companies' stock. This divorce was typical of many others because the wife received a settlement with higher value in physical capital and the husband received higher value in financial capital (Baker 1987; Rowe 1991; Weitzman 1985; Wishik 1986).

Human capital assets are seldom mentioned in divorce decrees unless a case is contested and goes to trial. No information was provided in the Johnsons' decree concerning occupations or earnings of the partners at the time of the marriage, and thus it would not be possible to estimate the appreciation or depreciation of the dollar value in human capital assets for each person. The following sections demonstrate the financial consequences of divorce that are frequently experienced by full-time homemakers who divorce in their middle years. Kate's financial well-being steadily declined over time, despite the fact that her former husband lived to retirement age so she received a portion of his pension, she was eligible for spousal Social Security retirement benefits, he did not remarry, and her spousal maintenance and child support awards were paid in full amounts.

Immediate financial consequences of the divorce decree. The final divorce decree specified that an annual amount of $9,600 be transferred from the nonresidential parent to the custodial parent, which was 21 percent of Andy's gross annual income. It reduced his net income ($26,652) to $17,052 for the support of one person and increased Kate's net income ($4,576) to $14,176 for the support of three people. If Kate had received the amount of child support income that the state guidelines suggested, she would have received $16,069, and Andy would have had $15,189. Discrepancies in levels of living between the two households would have been reduced.

Intermediate financial consequences of divorce. When Kate responded to a 1989 mail survey, she reported that her income supported three people in 1986 and now supported two, herself and a "problem teenager." She stated that the no-fault divorce law treats homemakers unjustly and that meeting the expenses of obtaining an attorney were impossible (Rettig and Dahl 1993). Kate's assessment of her financial condition was that it was worse and now paid for necessities only. She could not afford major repairs to her house, and she had learned to go without furniture and many other things. She felt her finances in three years would be about the same. Kate's income sources were from work (25–30 hours weekly), child support, spousal maintenance, savings interest, and investment dividends. She had held her job for less than one year; it provided no health, disability, or pension benefits, and she had no vacation or sick leave time.

Her monthly household income for September, 1989 was $1,200, and her estimated annual gross income of $14,400 was 1.79 times the poverty level ($8,020) for two persons. The change in Kate's financial well-being could also be calculated by changes in per person (per capita) income (Weitzman 1985). Kate's per capita income decline of minus 43 percent from prior to divorce to 1989 was similar to the declines experienced by young women who divorced between 1980 and 1987, which ranged from 30 to 55 percent (Duncan and Hoffman 1985; Morgan 1991; Smock 1993; Weiss 1984).

The child support was completely paid at the time of the survey, and it amounted to $4,800 per year for 1986, 1987, and 1989. Kate said the amount was "not at all adequate for the necessities and that the person paying could afford to pay more." The amount of money received for child support was 80 percent of the poverty level income for one person (Family Economics Review 1986a) in 1989 ($5,980) which was a decline from 90 percent in 1986 (Rettig, Christensen, and Dahl 1991). The expenses of raising children increase in the teenage years (Family Economics Review 1986a), but mothers like Kate find that the fixed income of child support meets a lower percentage of these consumption needs over time. Her weekly child support income ($92.31) must first be spent for the necessity of food, and the amount of money required for food steadily increased from 34 percent of the child support income in 1986 to 36 percent in 1987, and to 41 percent in 1989 (Family Economics Review 1986b, 1987, 1988,

1989). These figures demonstrate the effects of moderate inflationary increases in food costs and modest changes in food needs.

Longer-term financial consequences of divorce, 1990 to present. Kate also responded to the 1990 survey, but her former husband did not. There were no children living at home, so child support had terminated. Kate was 55 years old and her income sources were personal wages, spousal maintenance, pension income, and savings interest. She worked 28 hours each week at the same job and still received no fringe benefits. She listed her gross monthly household income as $900 ($10,800 annually) and her net monthly household income as $750 ($9,000 annually). Her gross annual income was 1.72 times poverty level of $6,280 (compared to 1.79 in 1989 and 4.61 prior to divorce). Her net annual income was 1.43 times poverty level (compared to 1.55 in 1986 and 2.84 prior to divorce). According to these indicators, Kate's financial well-being was steadily declining.

Kate reported that her most serious financial problems (rated 7 on a seven-point scale) were having to work at a minimum-wage job and the fact that her worries had reduced her productivity at work. She could not afford medical care or health insurance. She had to take a lower-paying job, had no opportunities for new training at work, could not afford to make a career change, and was unable to pay for more education for herself or her children. She was unable to save money (Rettig 1990).

Fortunately for Kate, she had remained married for more than ten years. This meant she could qualify for Social Security Retirement Benefits as a dependent spouse because her husband was a worker with eligibility, and she did not remarry before she reached the minimum age of eligibility of 62 years in 1997. Spousal benefits are lower amounts than worker benefits, and if she elects to receive benefits at age 62 years, the monthly amount she receives will be lower than if she waits until age 65. When she receives Social Security, her Medicare insurance will need to be supplemented with another health insurance policy to fill the gaps in coverage, and this will be a difficult (perhaps an impossible) expense for her to meet. Kate will find it difficult to accomplish the chief developmental task of aging women and families: adjusting to retirement income.

Human Capital Investments in Families and Returns at Divorce

Kate has allocated most of the time of her life (31 of 55 years, or 56 percent) to investing in the human resource development of her family members, and the return on this human capital investment is now being received by family members and society. Her substantial economic contributions are recognized in economic theories and theories of law, but seldom in the practical realities of divorce court. Her time investments in children have been mostly invisible to a society that more highly values the money earned from market production than in-kind income generated from household production. The income from household production contributes significantly to improving the levels and standards of living for family members and to their ultimate satisfactions and economic well-being. Kate's opportunity cost of lost labor market experiences, earnings, pension benefits, and financial assets have set the stage for living near poverty in her retirement years.

Human capital formed during marriage has important consequences for partners at divorce (Bryant 1992). Investments in human capital are both general and marriage-specific. General human capital consists of experiences and abilities, such as human relations and management competencies, that can be transferred to any family or to labor market jobs. Marriage-specific human capital includes experiences and abilities that yield economic returns only in the context that is specific to the marriage within which it was accumulated, but in no other marriage or context (Bryant 1990). Examples are the particular skills in handling the personality of the spouse and the children of the marriage, who are more important to their parents than to anyone else (Weiss and Willis 1985).

The economic returns on the general human capital developed within marriage are received outside the marriage by the person who possesses it. Thus, a wife who has invested in her husband's education and career will leave a marriage without a return on this investment, while her former husband will be eligible for better jobs and opportunities. When a marriage ends, the costs of depreciated earnings of one spouse, which were previously absorbed by the partnership, are now carried by the partner whose paid work was interrupted (Funder 1992). Marriage-specific human capital formed within the household is lost to both the investor and the possessor at divorce (Bryant 1990).

Economic opportunity cost can be defined as the dollar value of the income-earning opportunities lost when market labor production activities (for money income) are reduced or given up for the substitute activities of family care (household production for in-kind income). The dollar value of the opportunity costs of parenting are ultimately impossible to measure with any degree of precision. However, previous studies document that motherhood has resulted in permanent reductions in lifetime earnings and pension benefits. Mincer and Polacheck (1978) estimated that each year out of the labor force would reduce a woman's income by 1.2 percent or as much as 4.3 percent for college-educated women. A time break of 2 to 4 years would reduce earnings by 13 percent, and a 5-year break would reduce earnings by 19 percent. Divorcing women also face a labor market that is occupationally segregated, wage discriminatory, and highly technical (Fuchs 1989). Cramer (1979) estimated that the average net effect of having one baby is the loss of over 400 work hours of market work, considering both short- and long-term losses.

The loss of a parent through divorce or death also presents economic opportunity costs for children, who may grow up to be less dependable or productive workers or be less prepared for parenthood because of less education or less parental guidance (Wyrick 1993). The absence of a parent has been found to affect cognitive development and academic achievement, resulting in lower lifetime career earnings (Beller and Graham 1993; Haveman and Wolfe 1994; Krein and Beller 1988).

Fuchs (1986) indicated that the greatest barrier to economic equality for women is children. Rutherford (1990) notes that when an economic partnership is dissolved, the law tends to favor the economically powerful party by protecting property interests of capital at the expense of labor. Therefore, when one partner furnishes most of the financial capital and another most of the labor services, the financial partner is more likely to recover his or her investment, whereas the hard worker is likely to lose. Rutherford then suggests a solution to the problem: income sharing for several years following the divorce. This alternative would benefit traditional homemakers in divorce courts, but it is highly controversial and unlikely to be adopted because of lack of political support.

Conclusion

Economics assumes that individuals will make better decisions if they have more accurate information on which to base their judgments. Whether or not you agree with this assumption, it may be worthwhile to develop better educational programs for young people concerning family economic issues across the life span. If we have better estimates of the direct and indirect costs for caretakers of children, we are better able to make informed decisions about family size. Family educators need to assist young people in understanding the possible long-term economic consequences of deciding about time allocations when balancing the demands of work and family.

Several questions need answers from researchers and discussion by parents: What would be the dollar value estimate of the opportunity cost of parenting in present times? How would this dollar estimate vary, depending on the education, employment, and geographical location of the parents? How would the dollar estimate vary with the number of children in the family, their health, and their talents? How can families best plan for meeting current and future economic needs of all members? What public laws, policies, and practices can assist families in providing the best caretakers and educators for children without sacrificing the economic stability and security of their caretakers? Some researchers have worked on answering these questions, but more attention could be given to these important family economics issues in future research, in policy analysis, and in educational settings.

Discussion Questions

1. What are the long-term economic consequences for adults who allocate a major portion of their lives to the economic activities of household production instead of market production?

2. What are the economic benefits to families of having a person who is involved in full-time work in the household and who makes significant investments in the human resource development of other family members?

3. What are the costs of rearing children? What benefits may accrue to parents?

Glossary

Comparative advantage The special ability of a person to provide one product or service less expensively than other products or services or other persons. When time spent in production of goods and services at home results in a higher dollar value than time spent in market earnings, or one's labor market earnings are higher relative to one's partner (Blau and Ferber 1986).

Human capital A resource pool of personal capabilities, talents, skills, and traits that have resulted from investments in health, education, on-the-job training, and migration and that are instrumental in providing access to higher future income. The measure of human capital for divorce settlements is the current value of the future income stream. In other words, you add each year of expected earnings until retirement and then calculate the present value (Parkman 1987).

Human resources All the physical-biological and social-psychological characteristics internal to an individual that enables him or her to fulfill the varying roles required by society (North Central Strategy Committee on Community and Human Resource Development 1975).

Marriage-specific human capital Experiences and abilities that yield economic returns only in the context of marriage. This is in contrast to general human capital that consists of experiences and abilities, such as human relations and management competencies, that can be transferred to any family or labor market job.

Opportunity cost The dollar value of the income-earning opportunities that are lost when market labor production activities are reduced or given up for the substitute activities of family care (household production for in-kind income).

Present value The value today of an amount of money to be received in the future; it is the amount that would have to be invested today at a given interest rate over a specified time period to accumulate the future amount (Gitman and Joehnk 1996).

Social capital Social structures and the way they facilitate persons within the structures to achieve certain things that would not be possible without the structures. Social capital is created by changes in relations among persons that facilitate actions (Coleman 1988).

Total or full income Purchasing power, plus the wealth, goods, and services created and used within a specific time period. The value of a combination of money and nonmoney incomes and leisure time, as well as all of the various kinds of wealth: financial, physical, human, and social capital within a specified time period.

Suggested Readings

Beller, A. H., and Graham, J. W. (1993). *Small Change: The Economics of Child Support*. New Haven, CT: Yale University Press.

Brooks-Gunn, J., Duncan, G. J., and Aber, J. L. (Eds.). (1997). *Neighborhood Poverty: Context and Consequences for Children*. New York: Russell Sage Foundation.

Edin, K., and Lein, L. (1997). *Making Ends Meet: How Single Mothers Survive Welfare and Low-wage Work*. New York: Russell Sage Foundation.

Hauser, R. M., Brown, B. V., and Prosser, W. R. (Eds.). (1997). *Indicators of Children's Well-being*. New York: Russell Sage Foundation.

Haveman, R., and Wolfe, B. (1994). *Succeeding Generations: On the Effects of Investments in children*. New York: Russell Sage Foundation.

Bibliography

American Council of Life Insurance Extension Advisory Committee. (1979). *Adult Financial Management Matrix*. Washington, DC: Science and Education Administration-Extension, U.S. Department of Agriculture.

Andrews, B. (1935). *Economics of the Household: Its Administration and Finance*. New York: Macmillan.

Baker, B. (1987). *Family Equity at Issue: A Study of the Economic Consequences of Divorce on Women and Children*. Anchorage: Alaska Women's Commission.

Becker, G. S. (1991). *A Treatise on the Family* (enlarged ed.). Cambridge, MA: Harvard University Press.

Beller, A. H., and Graham, J. (1993). *Small Change: The Economics of Child Support*. New Haven, CT: Yale University Press.

Bengtson, V. L., and Allen, K. R. (1993). The life course perspective applied to families over time. In P. G. Boss, W. J. Doherty, R. LaRossa, W. R. Schumm, and S. K. Steinmetz (Eds.), *Sourcebook of Family Theories and Methods: A Contextual Approach* (469–499). New York: Plenum.

Bigelow, A. F. (1931). Toward a theory of family finance. *Journal of Home Economics, 23,* 325–332.

Blau, F. D., and Ferber, M. A. (1986). *The Economics of Women, Men, and Work*. Englewood Cliffs, NJ: Prentice-Hall.

Bryant, W. K. (1990). *The Economic Organization of the Household*. New York: Cambridge University Press.

Bryant, W. K. (1992). Human capital, time use, and other family behavior. *Journal of Family and Economic Issues, 13,* 395–405.

Christensen, D. H., and Rettig, K. D. (1991). Standards of adequacy for child support awards. *Journal of Divorce and Remarriage, 16,* 19–45.

Coleman, J. S. (1988). Social capital in the creation of human capital. *American Journal of Sociology, 94,* S95–120.

Cramer, J. C. (1979). Employment trends of young mothers and the opportunity costs of babies in the United States. *Demography, 16,* 177–197.

Culley, J. D., Van Name, J. B., and Settles, B. H. (1976). Measuring the indirect costs of child care. *Public Welfare, 10,* 7–13.

Diesing, P. (1976). *Reason in Society: Five Types of Decisions and Their Social Conditions.* Westport, CT: Greenwood Press.

Duncan, G. J., and Hoffman, S. D. (1985). Economic consequences of marital instability. In J. D. Smeeding and T. Smeeding (Eds.), *Horizontal Equity, Uncertainty, and Well-being* (427–467). Chicago: University of Chicago Press.

Duvall, E. M. (1971). *Family Development* (4th ed.). Philadelphia: Lippincott.

Elder, G. H., Jr. (1974). *Children of the Great Depression: Social Change in Life Experience.* Chicago: University of Chicago Press.

Espenshade, T. (1984). *Investing in Children: New Estimates of Parental Expenditures.* Washington, DC: The Urban Institute Press.

Family Economics Review a. (1986). 1986 Revision of poverty income guidelines, 3, 23.

Family Economics Review b. (1986). Updated estimates of the cost of raising a child, 4, 28–29.

Family Economics Review. (1987). Cost of food at home, 1, 32.

Family Economics Review. (1988), 2(2), 24.

Family Economics Review. (1989), 2(4), 32.

Foa, U. G., and Foa, E. B. (1974). *Societal Structures of the Mind.* Springfield, IL: Charles Thomas.

Fuchs, V. R. (1986). Sex differences in economic well-being. *Science, 232,* 459–464.

Fuchs, V. R. (1989). Women's quest for economic equality. *Journal of Economic Perspectives, 3,* 25–41.

Funder, K. (1992). Australia: A proposal for reform. In L. Weitzman and M. Maclean (Eds.), *The Economic Consequences of Divorce: The International Perspective* (175–191). Oxford: Clarendon Press.

Gitman, L. J., and Joehnk, M. D. (1996). *Personal Financial Planning* (7th ed.). Fort Worth: The Dryden Press.

Gross, I. H., and Crandall, E. W. (1963). *Management for Modern Families* (2nd ed.). New York: Appleton-Century Crofts.

Haveman, R., and Wolfe, B. (1994). *Succeeding Generations: On the Effects of Investments in Children.* New York: Russell Sage Foundation.

Holden, K. C., and Smock, P. J. (1991). The economic costs of marital disruption: Why do women bear a disproportionate cost? *Annual Review of Sociology, 17,* 51–78.

Hoyt, E. E., Reid, M. G., McConnell, J. L., and Hooks, J. M. (1954). *American Income and Its Use.* New York: Harper and Row.

Krein, S. F., and Beller, A. H. (1988). Educational attainment of children from single-parent families: Differences by exposure, gender, and race. *Demography, 25,* 221–234.

Mincer, J., and Polacheck, S. (1978). Women's earnings re-examined. *Journal of Human Resources, 13,* 118–134.

Morgan, J. N., and Duncan, G. J. (1982). *Making Your Choices Count: Economic Principles for Everyday Decisions.* Ann Arbor: The University of Michigan Press.

Morgan, L. A. (1991). *After Marriage Ends: Economic Consequences for Midlife Women.* Newbury Park, CA: Sage.

Morrison, S. E. (1965). *The Oxford History of the American People.* New York: Oxford University Press.

North Central Strategy Committee on Community and Human Resource Development, NCRS-3. (1975). *Human Resources and Community.* Ames: Iowa State University.

Parkman, A. M. (1987). The recognition of human capital as property in divorce settlements. *Arkansas Law Review, 40,* 439–467.

Peters, H. E. (1995). An economic approach to the study of child well-being. *Journal of Family Issues, 16,* 587–608.

Rettig, K. D. (1990). Financial problems following divorce. Unpublished scale. St. Paul, MN: Department of Family Social Science, University of Minnesota.

Rettig, K. D. (1993). The cost of traditional parenting. *Proceedings of the Minnesota Matrimonial Trial Lawyers Conference on the Art, Science, and Mythology of Spousal Maintenance.* Deerwood, MN.

Rettig, K. D., Christensen, D. H., and Dahl, C. M. (1991). Impact of child support guidelines on the economic well-being of children. *Family Relations, 40,* 167–175.

Rettig, K. D., and Dahl, C. M. (1993). Impact of procedural factors on perceived justice in divorce settlements. *Social Justice Research, 6,* 301–324.

Rettig, K. D., Tam, V. C., and Yellowthunder, Y. (1995). Family policy and critical science research: Facilitating change. *Journal of Family and Economic Issues, 16,* 109–143.

Rettig, K. D., Yellowthunder, L., Christensen, D. H., and Dahl, C. M. (1989, 1990, 1991). *Economic Consequences of Divorce in Minnesota for Men, Women, and Children.* Unpublished research reports I, II, III. St. Paul: Department of Family Social Science, University of Minnesota.

Rodgers, R. H., and White, J. M. (1993). Family development theory. In P. G. Boss, W. J. Doherty, R. LaRossa, W. R. Schumm, and S. K. Steinmetz (Eds.), *Sourcebook of Family Theories and Methods: A Contextual Approach* (225–257). New York: Plenum.

Rowe, B. R. (1991). The economics of divorce: Findings from seven states. *Journal of Divorce and Remarriage, 16,* 5–18.

Rutherford, J. (1990). Duty in divorce: Shared income as a path to equality. *Fordham Law Review, 58, (4),* 539–562.

Smock, P. J. (1993). The economic costs of marital disruption for young women over the past two decades. *Demography, 30,* 353–371.

U.S. Bureau of the Census. (1987). *Child Support and Alimony, 1985* (Series P-23, No. 152). Washington, DC: U.S. Government Printing Office.

Walker, K. E. (1969, September). Time spent in household work by homemakers. *Family Economics Review,* 5–6.

Walker, K. E., and Woods, M. E. (1976). *Time Use: A Measure of Household Production of Family Goods and Services.* Washington, DC: American Home Economics Association.

Weiss, R. (1984). The impact of marital dissolution on income and consumption in single-parent households. *Journal of Marriage and the Family, 46,* 115–127.

Weiss, Y., and Willis, R. J. (1985). Children as collective goods and divorce settlements. *Journal of Labor Economics, 3,* 268–292.

Weitzman, L. (1985). *The Divorce Revolution.* New York: Free Press.

Wishik, H. R. (1986). Economics of divorce: An exploratory study. *Family Law Quarterly, 20,* 79–107.

Wyrick, R. L. (1993). The economic value of parental guidance. *Journal of Legal Economics, 3,* 81–94. ✦

Chapter 13

Religion and Families Over the Life Course

J. Elizabeth Miller
Northern Illinois University

David Hoffman and Kathleen McKinney met in the first grade in 1930 in Detroit, Michigan. David's family was one of the few Jewish families in Detroit; Kathleen came from a large Irish Catholic community. David's parents, Joseph and Ida, immigrated from Germany in 1928 and joined a small community of immigrant Jews who were active in the Beth Israel congregation. Joseph financially provided for the family, and Ida took care of the home.

Kathleen's family was active in St. Mary's Catholic church, but she attended Jefferson Memorial Elementary School, the same school David Hoffman attended. David also attended Wednesday afternoon and Saturday religious classes, where he learned to read Hebrew and memorized selections from the Talmud. Kathleen attended Catechism classes. Some of Kathleen's prayers were in Latin, so David and Kathleen used to teach each other Latin and Hebrew words.

During high school, Kathleen and David started dating. They did not tell their siblings, families, or friends, but they saw each other at school whenever they could. As their relationship became more serious, they anticipated their families would be against their union. Nevertheless, they felt very strongly about staying together, and just be-

fore David was to leave for college, they eloped.

Religion is a powerful and pervasive force in shaping families. The 1997 World Values Survey indicates that Americans are among the most religious in the world (Americans Are Churchgoers 1998); over 90 percent of Americans indicate some religious identification (Gallup and Castelli 1989). In addition, over 44 percent of Americans, compared to about one quarter of British and French, attend church regularly (Americans Are Churchgoers 1998). In the United States and Canada, 86 percent describe themselves as Christian, 2 percent Jewish, and 2 percent Mormon; other faiths, including Islam, Buddhism, and Hindi, are also represented (Bibby, Hewitt, and Roof 1998; Yearbook of American and Canadian Churches 1997). Over half of the American membership in the Christian faith is found in three denominations: Roman Catholics, Southern Baptists, and United Methodists (Yearbook of American and Canadian Churches 1997).

Religions differ in the degree to which they emphasize intellectualism, formal belief systems, and religious education as opposed to personal experiences and meanings ascribed to events (McGuire 1992). Religion may be analyzed from a behavioral perspective (extrinsic) or an emotional, spiritual perspective (intrinsic) (Allport 1966). In addition, some religions are more conservative than others, some place higher authority in their leaders, and all differ in the degree to which they are enculturated or isolated from the larger society (Bellah, Madsen, Sullivan, Swidler, and Tipton 1985). These values and beliefs affect families who worship within the religious community, and they produce very different expectations.

Religion and Spirituality

The role of religion is multifaceted. It provides rituals that mark important milestones in the lives of individuals and families, such as birth, puberty, marriage, and death. It also provides a sense of community—a sort of "extended family" that witnesses the milestones and provides support and guidance, especially during times of crises. Perhaps most important, religion provides and helps shape values, morality, and family structure, even when family members may not be aware of this influence.

People who would not consider themselves to be religious are also influenced by religion. For example, although church attendance has dropped in recent years, both Americans and Canadians continue to utilize religious institutions for rites of passage. Over two-thirds of the respondents in the Bibby et al. (1998) study reported they were baptized or married in a church or synagogue, and over 80 percent reported plans to return to a religious group for ritualistic services in the future. Today, religious participation appears to reflect a modern consumerist approach—people pick and choose what services and programs they participate in—or "religion à la carte" (Bibby 1997; Bibby et al. 1998). This change in religious participation also signals needed changes in the way family scholars consider the impact of religion on families; that is, they need to diversify definitions of religious involvement to include more personal and autonomous spiritual beliefs and move beyond traditional assessments of church attendance.

Religion is not the same as spirituality, although these concepts are frequently related. *Spirituality* is described as a personal experience that transcends human experience and connects the human to a greater power or being (Maslow 1964, 1968). While spirituality is not necessarily perceived through the senses (Abbott, Schumm, and Hatch 1990), it governs individuals in making decisions consistent with their values while believing in the strength of a higher power to overcome human needs and difficulties. People's spirituality is often evident in their praying, meditating, honoring the forces of nature, listening to instinctive responses, and seeking harmony within the self, the family, and the larger society. Spirituality has been linked to enhanced physiological and psychosocial health (Sorensen 1989) and is important to a holistic approach to family functioning (Friedman 1985).

Religiosity, in contrast, has been measured in terms of its meanings (how important it is), beliefs (how conservative or liberal), activities (how frequently one attends church or prays), and attitudes (pronatalist versus pro-environmentalist). Historically, religiosity in family studies has been defined operationally as religious activity—specifically, church attendance and behavioral connections to family of origin (attending church together, family prayers). More recently, investigations have focused on meanings associated with religiosity (a belief in God or higher power), prayer, and the importance of social connectedness to a community, spiritual values (such as caring for others and/or the earth), and the importance of human dignity and freedom.

For the purposes of this chapter, the term *religion* is used to reflect an organized and creedal orientation toward a belief system. Further, religion is conceptualized from an institutional perspective, as found in churches, synagogues, and mosques. Within religions, people hold certain beliefs collectively, as members of a community of faith. The term *denomination* refers to groups that share primary creedal beliefs but that differ on specific values. For example, Southern Baptists and United Methodists are both Protestant denominations, but they differ on their social polity and the importance of a personal conversion experience. *Spirituality* and *faith* are used to refer to the more individualistic, less creedal belief system that one may hold without an institutional commitment. Spirituality also encompasses belief in a higher power, but one that may not meet the traditional view of a specific Godlike being. Both religion and spirituality, however, influence individual and family development.

Religion and Families

At every stage in the family life cycle—marriage, childbearing, adolescence, adulthood, old age, and death—the interplay of religion and family life is evident. Newborns are christened; parents frequently send their children to Sunday school; most couples have church weddings; hospitals have names such as Good Samaritan and St. Luke's; and the dying may be given last rites.

In every part of the family life cycle, from marriage to birth to the death of a spouse, religion plays a part for most people. This impact is more often seen by (a) providing rituals to celebrate normative passages/transitions, (b) defining a sense of community, and (c) providing support to families in need. Further, religion and spirituality affect individual development, particularly one's moral values and identity, which influences relationships.

Formation of Marriages and Partnerships

Both families were upset by Kathleen and David's marriage, but the couple cherished each other's differences and thought of their differing faiths as deepening their commitment. Both wanted to rear their children so they would be exposed to different faiths, and even though the task was difficult, David and Kathleen worked hard at their interfaith marriage. Neither family would accept the other, so extended family relations were strained. The couple celebrated both religions, observing the Sabbath prayers on Saturday and attending Mass on Sunday. However, the birth of their first child, Jonathan, brought about conflict. After much discussion, Kathleen and David compromised—the sons would follow the religion of their father, and any daughters would be raised Catholic; both sons and daughters would attend worship services of each religion with their parents on alternating weeks.

Initiation of a family through marriage or partnership is the first stage of the family life cycle. Two individuals come from different families to create a new family, historically for the purposes of procreation and economy and, more recently, for companionship. In the traditional model of religious family formation, sexual intercourse does not occur until the marriage has been legalized and sanctified. The state has the legal authority to form a union; the religious institution holds the moral and spiritual authority to form a family. Through the sacrament of marriage, the religious body gives permission to form this new union, reflecting the beliefs that marriage is a holy way to exist, that the bond is for life, and that the union takes precedence over individual interests.

The developmental tasks at this stage of the family life cycle include creating a home, establishing joint patterns of interaction and social behavior, developing systems for accruing financial resources, and planning for the future. For example, couples who share religious beliefs usually share other family values as well. These values influence how money is earned and spent, the kind of neighborhood where the couple lives, the types of relationships they have with extended families, and their desire for children. These decisions may be less a function of religious beliefs and more of the expectations of the religious community.

Weddings. Weddings are the formal sanctification of the bond between two persons. Many who are not devout or who do not regularly attend religious services seek a wedding within a religious community. In a recent review of American "baby boomers" (adults born between 1946 and 1964), 69 percent were married in churches or synagogues (Bibby et al. 1998). The demand for professional services by clergy, rabbis, and priests reflects a desire among individuals to stay connected to their familial and religious belief systems. The rituals associated with marriage symbolize the commitment of two persons, and for Judeo-Christian believers, this covenant parallels the covenant between God and humans; it is sacred, not lightly considered, and is supposed to last for a lifetime.

Lesbian and gay couples can also find acknowledgment and support in some religious communities. While legal sanctions for marrying gay or lesbian couples do not currently exist, more religious groups are recognizing the desire of these couples to establish families and make lifetime commitments. These ceremonies are usually called "commitment ceremonies" or "unions," and they convey that gay and lesbian couples have made a lifetime and monogamous commitment to one another within the context of and support of their religious community.

Some faiths encourage the couple to see the marriage as the beginning of a family, and the couple is expected to be responsible parents. For these persons, the wedding ceremony specifically addresses the individuals' roles as partners. Wedding rituals define the kind of relationship the couple should seek and institute clear expectations from the religious community about how married couples should behave. For example, the Catholic ceremony includes a question: "Will you accept children lovingly from God, and bring them up according to the law of Christ and his Church?" The Catholic Nuptial Blessing also includes the request that God "help them create a home together and give them children to be formed by the gospel and to have a place in your family" (*The Rite of Marriage*, 1970, 24, 78). In Protestant and Catholic ceremonies, couples are asked to promise to be faithful to each other, in good times and bad, in sickness and in health, and forsaking all others, to live wholly unto one another. The tradition of breaking the glass at Jewish weddings is based on the premise the marriage will last as long as it takes to put the glass together again.

Early marriages and marital roles. Many religious institutions require some form of premarital counseling, conducted by clergy or others in the religious community. This counseling is designed to facilitate the union by (a) outlining areas of communication and conflict management, (b) seeking to minimize difficulties in establishing new relationships, and (c) demonstrating support for the new couple (Summers and Cunningham 1989).

Religious groups have belief systems that place value on how males and females should behave. For example, the recent amendment to the Southern Baptists' Faith and Message statement that a wife should "submit herself graciously" to her husband made a clear connection between the authority of the husband and the authority of Christ as head of the Church (Niebuhr 1998). Likewise, the long-standing inclusion of the word "obey" (as in "the wife should obey her husband") has been omitted in many liberal churches but is frequently included in more conservative wedding ceremonies.

Beliefs regarding male and female roles as well as attitudes toward fertility seem to be moderated by the particular cultural heritage of the believers. For example, conserva-

tive Protestants and Catholics of Latin American descent seem to be more authoritarian and male-dominant than Catholics of European descent (Mindel, Habenstein, and Wright 1998). In contrast, more liberal Protestant churches and Jewish communities promote a more egalitarian attitude toward gender roles (Heaton and Cornwall 1989).

Religious beliefs may influence a couple's decision regarding family planning and the use of birth control. For example, if their religion is pronatalist, they may believe that having children is their religious obligation or an opportunity to rear as many religious children as possible. For example, Roman Catholics, Amish, and many Mormons practice only natural forms of birth control, and Mormons who use modern contraception more typically do so after the birth of the first child in order to space children rather than limit family size (Campbell and Campbell 1998). However, if a couple's religious beliefs support them, they may choose to limit the number of children they have. Many Protestant churches have no formal doctrines regarding birth control; therefore, the decision is left to the individuals.

Religion plays a role in the sexual behavior of individuals and families. Sex outside of marriage (premarital or extramarital sex) is prohibited and considered sinful by many faiths. Also, religiosity has been found to be related to sexual behavior. For example, the onset of sexual intercourse is later among youths who report higher levels of religiosity (Herold and Goodwin 1981; Langer, Zimmerman, and McNeal 1992; Miller and Simon 1974), and religious conservatives are more likely to enter marriage as virgins (Brewster, Cooksey, Guilkey, and Rindfuss 1998). The basic belief in many religious communities is that sexual relationships should only be a part of a relationship where love is predominant, and sexual intercourse is appropriate only when it communicates that love. Additionally, some religions, notably Catholic and Mormon, hold that love should naturally lead to the procreation of children—which, of course, should only be done in the context of marriage (D'Antonio 1985).

One task for newly married couples is to develop patterns of decision making, communication, and conflict management. Depending on the couple's beliefs, the definition of these roles may be based on gender. Similarly, the religious belief systems may provide options for couples in crisis. For example, divorce is seen by some as wicked and sinful and therefore is rarely considered as an option. For others, divorce is seen as an unfortunate but inevitable part of intimate human interaction. They believe that God would not want someone to remain in a relationship that is abusive, stifling, or demoralizing. The inevitable adjustments to newly married life, then, may be met with differing outcomes depending in part on one's religious ideology.

Making a commitment to a partner with the support of the religious community affords many resources to assist the newly formed relationship. Premarital counseling often includes sessions on financial management and family planning; younger couples may find older couples and clergy who can provide advice on coping with the challenges that come when establishing a home and family; and church or temple activities can help create a community where the couple can establish relationships with friends who share their values and enable them to participate as a couple.

It is also important to consider the ways in which religion affects marital satisfaction. First, religious proscription against divorce and the concomitant importance of parenting may encourage couples to find ways to overcome marital problems and renew their commitment to each other at many times during their married life. Religious beliefs may also be related to personal happiness, which contributes to marital happiness, and religious beliefs and values that encourage individual change and acceptance of others may help couples accommodate each other's differences (Filsinger and Wilson 1984).

Interfaith marriages. Not all members of religious communities marry someone of the same faith. In fact, *religious exogamy,* or marriage to someone of a different religion, has increased in recent decades. Although estimates are difficult to gather, as many as 10 to 20 percent of religious individuals are thought to marry outside their faith. Few differences in marital happiness have been reported among those married to other religious individuals, regardless of their faith. However, intermarriage between a religious individual and a nonreligious one is less likely to be regarded as "very happy" (Glenn 1982).

Interfaith marriages can bring a sense of richness to a marriage but may result in conflict between the partners as well as between the couple and their families and religious communities. It can be difficult for the couple to make decisions regarding the faith in which to rear children, which congregation receives offerings and/or tithes, what rituals to practice in the home, and which services to attend. These issues, if not resolved, can develop into problems that the family must deal with across the family life cycle (Sousa 1995).

Families With Children

Religion has been found to affect family relationships and marital quality. For example, six qualities that have been identified as characteristic of strong families include, (a) appreciation of one another, (b) spending time together, (c) commitment to one another, (d) good communication patterns, (e) the ability to deal with crises in a positive manner, and (f) a high degree of religious orientation. Specifically, Stinnett and DeFrain (1985) found that strong families attended church and participated in religious activities together; their commitment to one another included a spiritual lifestyle, a purpose for living, and more compassionate behavior toward one another.

Marital satisfaction has also been positively linked with religiosity, congruence of religious beliefs, church attendance, family worship, and tolerance of others (Bahr and Chadwick 1985; Dudley and Kosinski 1990; Glenn 1982; Larson 1989). Among women, religiosity has been related to a lesser likelihood of consideration of divorce (Booth and White 1980) and increased marital commitment. In addition, enhanced intimacy has been reported by married couples with similar faith beliefs (Robinson and Blanton 1993), although higher levels of religious activity do not appear to lead to an improvement in marital quality (Booth, Johnson, Branaman, and Sica 1995).

Childbearing. Tasks for this second stage of the traditional family life cycle include the transition to parenthood. The physical, emotional, and financial demands on new parents are high, and the transition to parenthood is considered to be one of life's most stressful tasks.

Many churches and synagogues have well-established structural processes by which children are welcomed into the religious community. Infants are brought into religious communities through baptisms, christenings, dedications or blessings, and, in the Jewish faith, the Bris (circumcision ceremony seven days after birth). Again, these rituals most frequently take place within the church or home as a part of the worship experience, and they enlist the community's participation and support.

For couples who have "strayed" from religious participation in the earlier phase of their relationship, having children frequently brings them back "into the flock" (Wilson and Sherkat 1994). Religious communities are seen as vital resources for helping young families adapt to their changing needs and meeting the tasks associated with creating an atmosphere of love and support. Religious communities often provide a wide range of activities for young children. Religious institutions also provide additional adults who share similar values to help train and educate children.

Families who are involved in religious institutions have been observed to establish more supportive and cohesive relationships at home (Brody, Stoneman, Flor, and McCrary 1994), thereby providing a place for both children and adults to develop their capacities for unconditional love. In addition, families are encouraged to foster an environment of mercy, acceptance, forgiveness, and intimacy.

Socialization of children. David and Kathleen had three girls and three boys, and for several years, everything went smoothly. However, the Hoffman family's attendance at religious services began to decline. With six children and two sets of grandparents, many weekends focused on family responsibilities. Jonathan, the oldest child, continued to identify as a Jew and participated in the activities of the youth group, including his Bar Mitzvah. Kathy, the oldest daughter, occasionally attended the Catholic church but refused to go through Confirmation classes. The next youngest daughter wanted to be a nun. The rest of the children attended services with their parents and studied their lessons but did not indicate a strong identity with either Judaism or Catholicism.

The task of families with school-aged and adolescent children is to maintain an environment that enriches the development of children while respecting individual needs. As children age, they learn to contribute to the family's functioning, share responsibilities for family living, and enlarge the family's environment (schools, community groups). Religious institutions contribute to enriching children's and adolescents' development through education and by providing activities with others who share the same values. Religious communities support families by assisting parents in the socialization and education of their children; at the same time, parents socialize children into the beliefs of the religious community (Strayhorn, Weidman, and Larson 1990; Weihe 1990).

Religious beliefs of children are merged with their understanding of their parents and families. For example, many young children fuse the concept of God with their concept of parents; their parents and God are both viewed as omnipotent, wise, and in control and as nurturing or punishing (Heller 1986). The family serves as an agent of religious socialization, wherein children learn how to relate to others, treat others with respect, and understand relationships between nurturance, justice, mercy, and power. The incorporation of these values assists families in their development of a balanced and healthy style of interaction with one another.

The socialization of children into religion is a gradual process, largely dependent on the child's cognitive ability. For example, preschoolers might learn about the God who loves everyone and might punish only humans who sin (this is Kohlberg's preconventional stage, which emphasizes obtaining rewards and avoiding punishment). School-aged children's religious lessons might focus on emphasizing social rules (Kohlberg's conventional stage) by learning the Ten Commandments, the Golden Rule, or catechism. The postconventional stage emphasizes moral principles and includes the development of social contracts and universal ethical principles (Kohlberg 1981).

Families with adolescents. A major task of adolescence is the achievement of identity (Erikson 1968), which occurs within families and in a larger societal context. Gaining a sense of self requires exploring, questioning, developing a sense of purpose, and understanding oneself. Family tasks include developing respect for the needs of "independent" youths. Adolescents are generally granted more responsibility for family life and may be expected to work in or outside the home.

In families and religious institutions where individual exploration and responsibility is supported, adolescents can achieve healthy identities. However, in settings where exploration and questioning are devalued or discouraged, differences between adolescents and authority figures could present problems, with the adolescent eventually eschewing all beliefs related to authority figures (parents, teachers, clergy) or deciding on an identity without appropriate time for experimentation (moratorium).

Based on Erikson, Piaget, and Kohlberg, Fowler (1981) asserted that the concept of faith and the belief in a higher power is based on the transference of trust and faith in one's parents to the care for oneself. As family relationships develop, so does the development of faith. Thus, in childhood, the development of faith begins with a sense of trust ("God will take care of me"), which leads to a sense of industry ("I will do good works in order to please God"), which then becomes part of one's identity in adolescence ("I am a good person because I do good works").

Likewise, the development of a sense of self may be rooted in the notion of God or a higher power. Christians, for example, believe themselves to be created in the image of God; thus, to understand themselves, they must begin to understand the nature of God (Westerhoff 1976). This credo moves the faithful into action, to seek connection with others, serve others, and find ways to alleviate their needs. It further develops the sense of self by encouraging adolescents to view themselves as important to the world and by giving direction to their life goals.

The value of identity seeking is influenced by religious beliefs. Some religious communities tolerate doubting believers better than others do. Religious communities that place high value on the authority of clergy and share fundamentalist beliefs are less likely to tolerate adolescents who challenge these beliefs. For example, the Amish use "excommunication" (being banned from the religious community) and "shunning" (avoiding all normal interaction with the excommunicated member) to enforce the discipline and to encourage the shunned member to realize the gravity of his or her sins (Huntington 1998).

In contrast, some religious communities encourage the development of faith by accepting periods of doubt and speculation. Although most religious organizations prefer that their young not leave their particular religious community, it is commonly accepted that youth should have a time for religious moratorium—that is, some religious communities seek to include such experiences as a part of adolescent youth programs. For example, one common activity is the opportunity to visit other religious communities and faiths, including interviews with clergy, priests, and rabbis, so young people may ask questions and challenge their personal religious assumptions.

Some religious communities use formal rituals to affirm the transition from childhood into adolescence and adulthood. Through established rituals, including baptism, confirmation, and Catechism classes and Bar/Bat Mitzvah, adolescents are supported in the process of becoming adult members of their congregations. These ceremonies, as well as others, are the outgrowth of general and specific religious education.

For example, in Catholic and Protestant churches that practice infant baptism, religious education begins during the preschool years. However, special sacramental classes precede the first communion (typically in the first or second grade) and confirmation (personal acceptance of the blessing of baptism) in adolescence. Furthermore, in Protestant denominations that do not practice infant baptism, baptism after the age of accountability (when the child/adolescent understands the difference between right and wrong) demonstrates the personal acceptance of God. Once these rites of passage are completed, young people have full membership in their churches or synagogues, with the rights and responsibilities of adult members to vote, tithe, and provide relief, education, and support for others.

The most formal of these ceremonies is the Bar Mitzvah (for boys) or Bat Mitzah (for girls). This ceremony involves the young adolescent (usually on his or her thirteenth birthday) performing the ritualistic prayers and scripture readings before members of the congregation. Preceding this event is a six-month period of intensive training with a Bar Mitzvah elder who mentors the adolescent in the ritual. However, much of the practice takes place in the home, and "ceremony lessons" become a daily family event. The extended family is expected to attend the event and the celebration that follows the Bar/Bat Mitzvah. This ritual changes the young person's position in the religious community, as they (a) are considered full participants in synagogue worship services, (b) can read the Scriptures and prayers, and (c) participate in other aspects of the community. In Orthodox synagogues, to denote the change in identity from child to adult, clothing and behavior change as well. For example, after the Bat/Bar Mitzvah in Orthodox communities, females may no longer wear pants, and males must cover their heads at all times.

Middle Age and Older Families

David and Kathleen, in their fifties, are experiencing the "empty nest" stage of their family life cycle. At this time they find their involvement in each other and their spiritual life has increased. In fact, they often attend social events, religious education classes, and marital enrichment classes, in both religious communities.

Over time, the needs of families change. Therefore, most religious communities seek to provide programs for persons across the life span, including middle and older adulthood. Through social and educational programs, religious institutions create outlets for developing relationships classes, dinners, and recreational activities for single persons and young married couples. Middle-aged adults may meet their Eriksonian challenge of generativity versus stagnation by developing avenues of caring for others through volunteer work, leading worship and religious education, mentoring young couples, and providing financial support for the church.

While not as structured as classes for children, most congregations offer religious education in the form of Bible study classes and special sessions on issues that improve human development and interaction. Some religious communities also offer activities that encourage participation by entire families. Children and adolescents may go to their religious classes, while adults explore contemporary issues such as family financial planning, communication, stress management, parenting strategies, or current events. These programs provide child care while parents have an opportunity to pursue their interests and enhance their commitment to their religious beliefs.

Adults in middle age must cope with the tasks involved in maintaining a comfortable home and assuring security for their retirement years while also responding to the needs of their extended families. Their energies are often divided among work, family, needs of their children, and needs of aging parents.

Many religious communities provide support for their members (and gain new members) through groups for middle-aged populations. Single members may find dating partners or support for dating in a "Single Again" social group or receive a form of therapy in a "Separated and Divorced" support group. Support groups are also available for individuals considering remarriage, stepfamilies, gays and lesbians, and those with substance abuse problems. In addition, churches frequently provide space for community support groups such as Alcoholics Anonymous, Resolve (infertility support group), La Leche (breast feeding support group), Amnesty International, and adult literacy tutoring.

As family members age, they must adjust to retirement, maintain satisfactory and safe housing, adjust household routines, and cope with the physical challenges of aging. Older married persons must also cope with the deaths of spouses, siblings, and friends.

One of the primary social outlets for many older persons is their religious community. In our society, many have made lifelong commitments to this community (Atchley 1997) and find the social/spiritual activities increase in importance as other social and familial circles decline (Crohan and Antonucci 1989). For example, religious communities frequently provide special programs for senior citizens, including dinners, activities, day trips, and vacation tours, as well as regular programs.

As people age, they tend to place less emphasis on the institutional aspects and more on the personal components of religion (Koenig, Kvale, and Ferrel 1988; Thibault, Ellor, and Netting 1991). This is probably a result of a number of factors, including physical disabilities that hamper a person's ability to go outside the home, travel, and participate in social interactions (Brubaker 1983; Fowler 1981; Friedman 1985). Such disabilities limit the accessibility to worship services and other activities offered by the church.

Although many older persons cannot attend religious activities as frequently as desired, they often turn toward internal spiritual support mechanisms as a way of coping with life changes and losses (Ellor 1990; Koenig 1993; Koenig, Kvale and Ferrel 1988; Thibault et al. 1991). It would appear that for many, religious beliefs provide them with coping mechanisms such as prayer and hope (Courtenay, Poon, Martin, Clayton, and Johnson 1992; Koenig 1993; Myers 1978). Older persons who are religious report that

their daily Bible study and prayer give them a sense of connection—both to their past lives and to their future (Koenig 1993). For example, religious commitment has been found to be a strong predictor of happiness among seniors (Coke and Twaite 1995; Holt and Dellman 1992; Kehn 1995; Nye 1993) and among black seniors who view their role as passing on spiritual values to the younger community and family members (Dancy and Wynn-Dancy 1994; Shenk, Zablotsky, and Croom 1998).

Activities in the religious community may also provide a comfortable type of social interaction for older persons. For example, leadership roles are often available to retirees, thereby providing opportunities for social interaction (Atchley 1985). In addition, the religious community is a place where roles (committee member, church school teacher, choir member) do not dramatically alter when one ages, so continued participation may heighten one's sense of ego integrity.

Both religious and spiritual factors have been linked to physical and mental health status for all ages. Religiosity has been associated with prevention of disease and coping with and recuperating from illness (Matthews 1998); higher morale (Koenig, George, and Siegler 1988; Koenig, Kvale and Ferrel 1988); lowered blood pressure; and lower levels of depression and anxiety (Koenig 1993). Many older people use spiritual beliefs to cope with physical and mental problems (now known as "religious coping behavior"). The majority of these persons cope with problems through prayer and faith in God (Courtenay et al. 1992; Koenig 1993; Koenig, George and Siegler 1988; Koenig, Kvale and Ferrel 1988). The constancy of their beliefs may be one of the few aspects of their lives that is not changing (Ellor 1990).

Although older persons are less likely to attend a church/synagogue than younger persons, not all their religious experiences take place in private. Rather, it is common for religious leaders to visit and lead worship where seniors congregate—in nursing and retirement homes as well as hospitals. Communion, confession, and ritual prayers are often a part of these gatherings. At other times, members of the religious community provide educational and musical programs or make personal visits to places where older persons live. Thus, the connection to the congregation continues.

Death and Dying

Life for the Hoffmans changed dramatically when two of their children were hit by a drunk driver. Mary Margaret was killed instantly, and Jonathan was in critical condition. Both families gathered at the hospital; the priest of St. Mary's said last rites for Mary Margaret. It was the first time the Hoffmans and the McKinneys had shared prayers, and while they were in both Hebrew and Latin, the request for healing was the same—to save Jonathan.

In the days that followed, family members stayed at the hospital near Jonathan as other family members prepared for Mary Margaret's funeral. Jonathan died the day of Mary Margaret's funeral, and the family immediately began funeral preparations for him. Members of St. Mary's Church and Beth Israel Synagogue brought food and gave comfort to the family before and after each funeral; Shiva prayers were offered after Jonathan's death.

After the deaths of their two children, the familys' faith systems both supported them and caused conflict. While one daughter, Kathy, became more devout, a son stopped attending synagogue, feeling that God had abandoned him and his family.

A person's life is acknowledged through various rituals. The rituals surrounding death have been found to provide comfort to families. Members of the religious community often visit the home and provide food and companionship, and clergy and rabbis play a major role in assisting the family in planning the memorial service. Most religious training involves education on Kübler-Ross's stages of death and dying, so trained clergy, rabbis, and laypersons in the religious community are often resources for individuals and families at this time.

Funeral services are typically religious ceremonies, and these services are meaningful because they convey a sense of continu-ance of their being. For example, saying prayers for the departed, wearing special clothing, preparing and eating special foods, and receiving visits by friends and family are often part of the funeral process and help the grieving family. For most Protestants and Catholics, funeral services occur within three days of death, and the days between the death and the funeral are filled with visits from family and friends. In the Catholic church, there is usually a wake, or a celebration of the life of the departed one. In the Jewish faith, the funeral is frequently within a day of the death, but Shiva begins after the burial. Shiva is a highly structured period of mourning in which the religious community gathers at the family home. Evening services are held at the home, and the religious community supports the immediate family of mourners in their roles as they participate in the ritual prayers. In some communities, prayer and memorial services continue throughout the year as a part of communal worship experiences (e.g., Yom Kippur, All Saint's Day) and through individual rites for the family of mourners on the anniversary of the death of their loved one.

The rituals surrounding death and dying provide meaning to those who participate, reconnecting them to their beliefs about God. The rituals also provide a set of expectations that alleviate some of the stress of losing someone; the predictability of the process as well as being surrounded by a caring community provides a sense of comfort in a time of loss.

Divorce and Religion

Religiosity is related to the decision to divorce, and rates of divorce vary among different religious groups. For instance, less religious individuals have a greater likelihood of divorce (Glenn and Supancic 1984; Teachman 1983), but more liberal denominations have lower divorce rates than conservative and fundamentalist ones (Brodbar-Nemzer 1986; Raschke 1987). This finding may be more a function of economics than religion, however, as lower socioeconomic groups are more likely to be members of religiously conservative groups and also more likely to divorce. In addition, nonreligious couples have the highest divorce rates and Jews have the lowest (Glenn and Supancic 1984).

The response of religious communities to troubled marriages varies according to religion, denomination, location, and even the specific congregation. For example, churches and synagogues in large urban settings are more likely to develop support groups for divorcing members, whereas in smaller communities members may feel embarrassed and drop out of the religious community. Catholic and conservative Protestant churches frequently have less developed mechanisms for support and at times have refused remarriage to persons who were divorced. Most religious leaders consider their own values, the policies of the larger organization, and the circumstances surrounding the request to remarry. Although the case can be made that most faiths would prefer that (a) marriages continue, (b) families remain stable, and (c) sex be limited to marriage, most religious leaders understand that to truly minister to their congregations, support of all their participants is necessary and appropriate.

Conclusions

The influence of religion on families and individuals is complex and powerful and may be seen through both structural effects and interpersonal interaction. These influences may include rituals, religious education, social support, and community support, which form connections to the family and provide meanings throughout the life course of families. Religious processes help families and individuals cope with changes in the family life cycle by providing organizational structure and moral guidance, a sense of community and extended family, and some sense of external authority or internal empowerment.

Conversely, family processes—communication, discipline, negotiation of gender roles and division of labor, parenting, socialization—influence perceptions of religious structure. Depending on an individual's environment, he or she may cling tightly to prescribed religious boundaries or may question

tion or even dismiss them, all of which have consequences for that individual's development.

Kohlberg's studies on moral development demonstrate how the growth of religious awareness parallels the growth of the individual's identity. As the individual and family relationships develop, so can faith. This development can be enhanced if an individual is encouraged to question and develop beliefs on his or her own, or it may be hampered by the development of a negative identity or a prematurely foreclosed identity.

Religious "identity-seeking" stages in the individual are moderated by religious beliefs and the beliefs of the religious community to which the individual belongs.

These beliefs are put into action at the adult stage through outreach programs, social charities, and community leadership. Religious communities support the elderly by providing a social outlet and a sense of community during crises such as major illnesses or the death of a loved one. The final stage of the family life cycle, death, is marked by ritual, just as the first stage, marriage, is marked by ritual. The members of the religious community offer their support and bear witness to these milestones—providing support and encouragement at the beginning and consolation for the bereaved at the end. In these various ways, the religious community supports and maintains the family life cycle and can be integrally related to the major transitions of individual and family life.

Discussion Questions

1. What are the major differences between spirituality and religion? Why is knowing these differences important to the study of families?

2. What are the major developmental issues for children and adolescents, and how can religious groups support successful resolution of these issues?

3. How might one's understanding of gender roles and sexual behavior be affected by religious traditions?

4. What are Kohlberg's three stages of moral development? Why are these important to family development?

5. How do religious groups support families in their communities?

Glossary

Bris Jewish circumcision ceremony seven days after birth.

Denominations Groups that share primary creedal beliefs but that differ on specific values.

Religion An organized and creedal orientation toward a belief system.

Religious exogamy Marriage to someone of another religion.

Spirituality/faith Individualistic, less creedal belief system that one may hold without an institutional commitment.

Suggested Readings

Bellah, R. N., Madsen, R., Sullivan, W. M., Swidler, A., and Tipton, S. M. (1985). *Habits of the Heart: Individualism and Commitment in American Life.* Berkeley: University of California.

D'Antonio, W. V., and Aldous, J. (1983). *Families and Religions: Conflict and Change in Modern Society.* Beverly Hills, CA: Sage.

Duvall, E. M. (1970). *Faith in Families.* New York: Abingdon.

Fowler, J. W. (1981). *Stages of Faith: The Psychology of Human Development and the Quest for Meaning.* San Francisco: Harper and Row.

Greeley, A. M. (1982). *Religion: A Secular Theory.* New York: Free Press.

Bibliography

Abbott, D. A., Schumm, W. R., and Hatch, R. (1990, November). *Into the Lion's Den: Christian Family Theory as a Contemporary Family Theory?* Paper presented at National Council on Family Relations, Seattle, WA.

Allport, G. (1966). The religious context of prejudice. *Journal for the Scientific Study of Religion, 5,* 447–457.

Americans Are Churchgoers. (1998, July–August). *Society, 35,* 2–3.

Atchley, R. (1985). *Social Forces and Aging.* Belmont, CA: Wadsworth.

Atchley, R. (1997). The subjective importance of being religious and its effect on health and morale fourteen years later. *Journal of Aging Studies, 11,* 131–142.

Bahr, H., and Chadwick, B. A. (1985). Religion and family in Middletown, USA. *Journal of Marriage and the Family, 47,* 407–414.

Bellah, R. N., Madsen, R., Sullivan, W. M., Swidler, A., and Tipton, S. M. (1985). *Habits of the Heart: Individualism and Commitment in American Life.* Berkeley: University of California.

Bibby, R.W. (1997). The persistence of Christian religious identification in Canada. *Canadian Social Trends, 44,* 24–29.

Bibby, R. W., Hewitt, W. E., and Roof, W. C. (1998). Religion and identity: The Canadian, American, and Brazilian cases. *International Journal of Comparative Sociology, 39,* 237–271.

Booth, A., Johnson, D. R., Branaman, A., and Sica, A. (1995). Belief and behavior: Does religion matter? *Journal of Marriage and the Family, 57,* 661–671.

Booth, A., and White, L. (1980). Thinking about divorce. *Journal of Marriage and the Family, 42,* 605–616.

Brewster, K. L, Cooksey, E. C., Guilkey, D. K., and Rindfuss, R. R. (1998). The changing impact of religion on the sexual and contraceptive behavior of adolescent women in the United States. *Journal of Marriage and the Family, 60,* 493–505.

Brodbar-Nemzer, J. Y. (1986). Divorce and group commitment: The case of Jews. *Journal of Marriage and the Family, 48,* 329–340.

Brody, G. H., Stoneman, Z., Flor, D., and McCrary, C. (1994). Religion's role in organizing family relationships: Family process in rural, two-parent African American families. *Journal of Marriage and the Family, 56,* 878–888.

Brubaker, T. H. (1983). *Family Relationships in Later Life.* Beverly Hills: Sage.

Campbell, B. L., and Campbell, E. E. (1998). The Mormon family. In R. W. Habenstein, C. H. Mindel, and R. Wright (Eds.), *Ethnic Families in America* (480–507). Upper Saddle River, NJ: Prentice Hall.

Coke, M., and Twaite, J. A. (1995). *The Black Elderly: Satisfaction and Quality of Later Life.* New York: Haworth.

Courtenay, B. C., Poon, L. W., Martin, P., Clayton, G. M., and Johnson, M. A. (1992). Religiosity and adaptation in the oldest-old. *International Journal of Aging and Human Development, 34,* 47–56.

Crohan, S. E., and Antonucci, T. C. (1989). Friends as a source of social support in old age. In R. G. Adams and R. Blieszner (Eds.), *Older Adult Friendship: Structure and Process* (283–299). Newbury Park: Sage.

Dancy, J., and Wynn-Dancy, M. L. (1994). Faith of our fathers (mothers) living still: Spirituality as a force for the transmission of family values within the black community. *Activities, Adaptation, and Aging, 19*, 87–105.

D'Antonio, W. V. (1985). The American Catholic family: Signs of cohesion and polarization. *Journal of Marriage and the Family, 47*, 395–405.

Dudley, M. G., and Kosinski, F. A., Jr. (1990). Religiosity and marital satisfaction: A research note. *Review of Religious Research, 26*, 59–72.

Ellor, J. W. (1990). The role of religion in the lives of older adults and their families. *The Journal of Aging and Judaism, 5*, 97–106.

Erikson, E. (1968). *Identity: Youth and Crisis.* New York: Norton.

Filsinger, E. E., and Wilson, M. R. (1984). Religiosity, socioeconomic rewards, and family development: Predictors of marital adjustment. *Journal of Marriage and the Family, 46*, 663–670.

Fowler, J. W. (1981). *Stages of Faith: The Psychology of Human Development and the Quest for Meaning.* San Francisco: Harper and Row.

Friedman, E. H. (1985). *Generation to Generation.* New York: Guilford.

Gallup, G., Jr., and Castelli, J. (1989). *The People's Religion: American Faith in the 90s.* New York: Macmillan.

Glenn, N. D. (1982). Interreligious marriage in the United States: Patterns and recent trends. *Journal of Marriage and the Family, 44*, 555–566.

Glenn, N. D., and Supancic, M. (1984). The social and the demographic correlates of divorce and separation in the United States: An update and reconsideration. *Journal of Marriage and the Family, 46*, 563–575.

Heaton, T. B., and Cornwall, T. B. (1989). Religious group variation in the socioeconomic status and family behavior of women. *Journal of the Scientific Study of Religion, 28*, 283–299.

Heller, D. (1986). *The Children's God.* Chicago: University of Chicago.

Herold, E. S., and Goodwin, M. S. (1981). Premarital sexual guilt. *Canadian Journal of Behavior Science, 13*, 65–75.

Holt, M. K., and Dellman, M. (1992). Research and implications for practice: Religion, well-being/morale, and coping behavior in later life. *Journal of Applied Gerontology, 11*, 101–110.

Huntington, G. (1998). The Amish family. In R. W. Habenstein, C. H. Mindel, and R. Wright (Eds.), *Ethnic Families in America* (450–479). Upper Saddle River: Prentice Hall.

Kehn, D. J. (1995). Predictors of elderly happiness. *Activities, Adaptation and Aging, 19*, 11–30.

Koenig, H. G. (1993). Religion and aging. *Reviews in Clinical Gerontology, 3*, 195–203.

Koenig, H. G., George, L. K., and Siegler, I. C. (1988). The use of religion and other emotion-regulating coping strategies among older adults. *The Gerontologist, 28*, 303–310

Koenig, H. G., Kvale, J. N., and Ferrel, C. (1988). Religion and well-being in later life. *The Gerontologist, 28*, 18–28.

Kohlberg, L. (1981). *Essays on Moral Development* (Vol. 1). New York: Harper and Row.

Langer, L. M., Zimmerman, R. S., and McNeal, R. (1992). Explaining the association of race and ethnicity with the HIV/AIDS-related attitudes, behaviors and skills of high school students. *Population Research and Policy Review, 11*, 233–247.

Larson, L. E. (1989). Religious and marital commitment: "Until death do us part" revisited. *Family Science Review, 2*, 303–316.

Maslow, A. (1964). *Religions, Values, and Peak Experiences.* Columbus: Ohio State University.

Maslow, A. (1968). *Toward a Psychology of Being* (2nd ed.). Princeton: Van Nostrand.

Matthews, D. (1998). Religious commitment and the health status: A review of the research and implications for family medicine. *The Journal of the American Medical Association, 279*, 19–30.

McGuire, M. B. (1992). *Religion: The Social Context* (3rd ed.). Belmont: Wadsworth.

Miller, P. Y., and Simon, W. (1974). Adolescent sexual behavior: Context and change. *Social Problems, 22*, 58–76.

Mindel, C. H., Habenstein, R. W., and Wright, R. (Eds.). (1998). *Ethnic Families in America.* Upper Saddle River: Prentice Hall.

Myers, L. W. (1978). Elderly black women and stress resolution: An exploratory study. *The Black Sociologist, 8*, 29–37.

Niebuhr, G. (1998, June 10). Southern Baptists Declare Wife Should 'Submit' to Her Husband. *The New York Times*, p. A1.

Nye, W. P. (1993). Amazing grace: Religion and identity among elderly black individuals. *International Journal of Aging and Human Development, 36*, 103–114.

Raschke, H. (1987). Divorce. In M. Sussman and S. Steinmetz (eds.). *Handbook of Marriage and the Family* (597–620). New York: Plenum.

The Rite of Marriage. (1970). New York: Catholic Book Publishing.

Robinson, L. C., and Blanton, P. W. (1993). Marital strengths in enduring marriages. *Family Relations, 42,* 38–45.

Shenk, D., Zablotsky, D., and Croom, M. (1998). Thriving older African American women: Aging after Jim Crow. *Journal of Women and Aging, 10,* 75–97.

Sorensen, E. S. (1989). Religion and family health: A need for study. *Family Science Review, 2,* 303–316.

Sousa, L. A. (1995). Interfaith marriage and the individual and family life cycle. *Family Therapy, 22,* 97–104.

Stinnett, N., and DeFrain, J. (1985). *Secrets of Strong Families.* New York: Berkley.

Strayhorn, J. M., Weidman, C. S., and Larson, D. (1990). A measure of religiousness, and its relation to parent and child mental health variables. *Journal of Community Psychology, 18,* 34–43.

Summers, J. R., and Cunningham, J. L. (1989). Premarital counseling by clergy: A key link between church and family. *Family Science Review, 2,* 327–336.

Teachman, J. (1983). Early marriage, premarital fertility, and marital dissolution: Results of blacks and whites. *Journal of Family Issues, 4,* 105–126.

Thibault, J. M., Ellor, J. W., and Netting, F. E. (1991). A conceptual framework for assessing the spiritual functioning and fulfillment of older adults in long-term care settings. *Journal of Religious Gerontology, 7,* 29–43.

Weihe, V. R. (1990). Religious influence on parental attitudes toward the use of corporal punishment. *Journal of Family Violence, 5,* 173–186.

Westerhoff, J. H., III. (1976). *Will Our Children Have Faith?* New York: Saber.

Wilson, J., and Sherkat, D. E. (1994). Returning to the fold. *Journal for the Scientific Study of Religion, 33,* 148–161.

Yearbook of American and Canadian Churches. (1997). Nashville: Abingdon. ✦

Chapter 14
Parent-Child Relations Across the Life Course

Autonomy Within the Context of Connectedness

Gary W. Peterson
Debra Madden-Derdich
Stacie A. Leonard
Arizona State University

Sam is a 50-year-old attorney with a prosperous law practice and a very busy life, a major portion of which involves being someone's parent and someone's child. When he was 34, Sam married Carol, an elementary school teacher, who was 31 at the time. During the next three years, Carol and Sam had two daughters, Erika and Tanya, who kept them both very busy balancing family and career interests. Eventually, however, Sam and Carol developed marital problems and divorced when Erika was 6 and Tanya was 4. Despite some initial problems, both Sam and Carol were committed to helping each other remain involved with the girls and to working together as parents. As a result, they agreed to a flexible joint custody arrangement in which Erika and Tanya lived with each of them for half of each week.

Sam remained single for several years, but when he was 45 he met and married Diane, a social worker, who was 33 at the time.

Three years later and somewhat surprisingly, Sam and Diane had a son, Michael. So, at 50, Sam now finds himself fathering two teenagers (Erika age 16 and Tanya age 14) and doing his best to chase around a toddler (Michael age 2), all at a later age than is typical for most men today. He is, as he likes to say, "up to his ears in parenting, the most demanding, but wonderful experience in life!"

Sam also has experienced some difficult transitions in parent-child relationships during recent years. When asked, he always says that the most influential person on how he deals with life was his mother, who died three years ago after a long battle with cancer. Sam often turned to his mother in times of trouble, and he credits her with teaching him many of the values and beliefs he now holds dearly. Despite his mother's death, he says that she still "gives him advice" almost every day through cherished memories, the values she taught, some mistakes she made, and the love she communicated during her life. He has come to realize that people and relationships remain alive not simply through their physical presence, but in our memories, thoughts, and feelings.

During the early years of establishing his law practice, Sam's parents helped him with practical things like financing his first home. He increasingly has realized that, in some ways, he would always remain his parents' child and often affirmed this by seeking their views about important life decisions. Sometimes he disagreed with their opinions and went his own way, but in hindsight he appreciated their steadfast willingness to listen, provide input, and offer help.

Sam remains close to his 78-year-old father and finds himself providing increased help and emotional support to assist his dad through the loneliness following his mother's death, with problems of declining health, and with the onset of forgetfulness. His father spends a lot of time at Sam and Diane's home now, and Sam runs all sorts of errands for his father and tries to be a good companion for him.

A person who spends time with Sam for a few days might observe the following parent-child activities: dropping off and picking up Michael at day care, driving Tanya to her night-time acting class, taking his father to the grocery store, reading Michael a bedtime story, attending a high school football game to watch Erika play in the marching band, stopping off to have lunch with dad and chat, phoning home from work to ensure that Erika and Tanya are home from school and doing their homework, having a "tickle match" with Michael, worrying about and consulting with physicians about his dad's cardiovascular problems, and discussing with Tanya why her grade in math slipped from a B to a C. As we can see, a large portion of Sam's life is spent in efforts to cope with all the changes that have occurred in his parent-child roles, and sometimes he feels overwhelmed. Specific issues will change and some new troubles may show up, but Sam certainly recognizes that he will always be someone's parent and someone's child.

A fundamental idea for understanding relationships between parents and children is that "nothing is so constant as the process of change." The intense relationships between mothers, fathers, sons, and daughters undergo dramatic changes as the young progress from infancy through adulthood. Complex transitions involve moving from being dependent on parents for survival during infancy to a time when conditions reverse and aged parents must turn to adult children for their care. The totality of these changes involves virtually every aspect of individual and relationship development in the lives of parents and children.

Although change in parent-child relationships is virtually inevitable, these transitions should not be viewed as chaotic, but rather as patterned and predictable. Parent-child relationships involve both constancy and change across time, within the context of an underlying developmental pattern. These assumptions about pattern and continuity are useful, despite the observable, everyday aspects of behavior change.

Consistent with these ideas, the purpose of this paper is to describe some of the major transitions, continuities, and themes that are common within American society across the life course of parent-children relationships. We give particular attention to those issues that have broad application across a variety of family structures and ethnic-minority communities. We draw on concepts from the life course perspective (Bengtson and Allen 1993) to guide our discussion. The common social themes we use to describe successive periods of development across the parent-child life course are fundamental aspects of human interpersonal associations referred to as "autonomy," "connectedness," and "interdependence" within relationships (Peterson 1995). These concepts refer to fundamental aspects of intimate relationships and recognize that a person's human existence is largely a product of defining a sense of individuality, but often in terms of social meanings and evaluations experienced during interactions with others (Blumer 1969). As a result, the developmental experiences of "becoming one's own person" and "being connected to others" might best be viewed as only somewhat distinct, and even complementary, sides of the same coin.

The Parent-Child Life Course

We use concepts from the family life course perspective to conceptualize development within parent-child relationships for a variety of reasons. First, a life course perspective is applicable because of its attention to critical transitions and change across time, both at the individual and relationship levels of development. We maintain this focus on patterned development while not becoming preoccupied with conventional sets of family stages or structures that only some families experience. Consequently, we are able to give recognition to the ideas that a great diversity of family structures have become increasingly normative and that social change is a constant force that shapes families and parent-child relationships (Bengtson and Allen 1993).

The life course perspective gives ample recognition to the fact that family and parent-child development are subject to influences from the larger society, such as socioeconomic forces, historic events, membership in a particular cohort or generational group, general cultural values, age norms, and role expectations. As a result, the life course perspective recognizes that development in family and parent-child relationships may vary substantially across historic time, social class distinctions, and ethnic-cultural membership (Bengtson and Allen 1993).

Another important aspect of the life course perspective is that family members, including parents and children, engage in interdependent, reciprocal relationships. Thus, how parents or children respond to particular social environments, historic events, or cultural values, will affect the developmental course of both persons in a relationship. The behavior of parents and children is a function not only of each individual's developmental attributes but also of the other person's developmental attributes within the context of their relationship (Bengtson and Allen 1993).

A central focus of this chapter, therefore, is to demonstrate how two general cultural values, *individualism* and *collectivism*, are manifested within the parent-child life course as specific relationship dimensions referred to as *autonomy* and *connectedness* (Peterson 1995). Individualism has a long history in Western civilization, with its modern form emerging in England and America from the seventeenth through the nineteenth centuries in the writings of Thomas Hobbes, Adam Smith, John Locke, Thomas Jefferson, and Thomas Paine. Its emphasis is on the self-directed, self-contained, and comparatively unrestrained person or ego. Person-centered values and individual goals take precedence over the interest of social groups. Individualism includes the idea that society is best served when individuals can maximize their freedoms, choose their objectives, and pursue their own interests (Kim 1994). The parent-child relationship level of this value, referred to as autonomy, is defined as mechanisms within families (or parent-child relationships) that allow each person to assert his or her individuality in reference to family obligations, control attempts, rules, beliefs, and emotional processes (Peterson 1995).

The modern form of collectivism, on the other hand, first emerged in the eighteenth-century writings of Jean-Jacques Rousseau, G. W. F. Hegel, and Karl Marx. Collectivism emphasizes the community and its rights, not the rights of isolated persons. This cultural orientation underscores the importance of relationships based on trust, cooperation, harmony, common ownership, and group loyalty (Kim 1994; Triandis 1994). Individuals are viewed as being bound by ascribed relationships and encouraged to put the interests of the group before their personal priorities (Kim 1994). The parent-child version of this cultural value, referred to as connectedness, designates relationship components characterized by togetherness in the form of mutual obligations, conformity to expectations, continuing influence, cooperative behavior, strong family bonds, and emotional ties (Peterson 1995).

The precise relationship between autonomy and connectedness consists of two possibilities: (1) that growth in autonomy will occur at the expense of connectedness, or (2) that autonomy and connectedness are complementary (and compatible) concepts that develop together. In the first case, autonomy and connectedness are portrayed as being at opposite ends of the same continuum—respective locations that make them mutually exclusive (see Figure 14.1). Thus, any movement up this continuum toward higher autonomy necessarily means that proportionate decreases will occur in relationship connectedness. The contrasting perspective is that autonomy and connectedness are separate dimensions, each of which varies independently of the other (from high amounts to low), but as components of the same parent-child relationships (Peterson 1995) (see Figure 14.1). This latter conception proposes that autonomy and connectedness coexist, develop together, and become at least partially reconciled as connectedness becomes the secure base from which competent autonomy arises. The result is that variable amounts of autonomy and connectedness become components of the concept of *interdependence*—or the idea that parent-child relationships involve the development of individuality as well as the formation of intense interpersonal connections (Triandis 1994; Peterson 1995).

Although parent-child relationships in all cultures and ethnic groups must accommo-

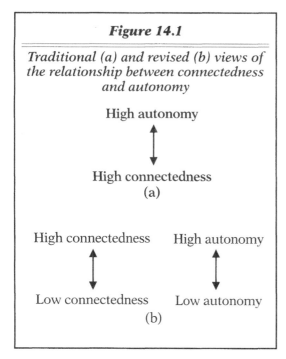

Figure 14.1

Traditional (a) and revised (b) views of the relationship between connectedness and autonomy

High autonomy

↕

High connectedness
(a)

High connectedness   High autonomy

↕   ↕

Low connectedness   Low autonomy
(b)

date both *autonomy* and *connectedness,* each societal group strikes a somewhat unique balance in emphasizing one or the other of these socialization goals. For example, parent-child relationships in many other countries (Chinese, Korean, and Indian families) and within certain ethnic groups in American society (Mexican-American and Chinese-American families) emphasize collectivism or connectedness more extensively than socialization approaches used within the dominant American culture (Arnett 1995; Kim 1994; Triandis 1994). Despite the fact that American parents do place considerable emphasis on connectedness, American socialization practices tend to foster such autonomous goals as personal achievement, independence, self-determination, and the centrality of the separate self, as an outgrowth of cultural individualism. In contrast, collectivistic cultures and certain ethnic groups place greater emphasis on cooperation, close ties, achievement of group purposes, and the subordination of the self to group interests. The point here is that parent-child relationships can be characterized in terms of both autonomy and connectedness, but the exact balance between the

two varies widely across cultural and ethnic group contexts.

Parent-Child Relationships During Infancy and Early Childhood

The period of infancy through early childhood provides substantial support for the idea that connectedness and autonomy are separate dimensions that develop together and become complementary aspects of relationship interdependence (Peterson 1995). Healthy connectedness between infants and parents (or caregivers) involves a need for physical proximity and an emotional bond that is developed and maintained through mutually satisfying interaction. Healthy autonomy, in turn, emerges out of relationship connectedness as infants begin to use parents as secure bases from which to explore the environment. Thus, as development proceeds, connectedness and autonomy are separate relationship dimensions that together help to define increasingly complex forms of interdependence.

The development of "connected" relationships with parents is a fundamental achievement for infants and young children. From a biological perspective, Bowlby (1988) contends that infants initially have an innate set of goal-directed attachment behaviors, such as crying, looking, and smiling, that promote proximity between babies and caregivers. Conversely, adults acquire similar proximity-seeking behaviors by adapting responses to the child's behavioral cues. For example, when a baby cries, parents are likely to pick them up and comfort them. These rudimentary infant behaviors and parental responses are thought to be reciprocal behaviors that facilitate secure attachments or an elementary form of relationship connectedness (Bretherton 1990).

The biological propensity to seek proximity, however, is only part of a developing sense of connectedness between parents and children. Many additional aspects of connectedness are social in nature and rapidly become central to parent-child relations as development proceeds. Qualities such as maternal warmth, sensitive responsiveness, and children's temperament, as well as appropriate signaling and response behaviors all contribute to degrees of connectedness between the young and their parents. These components of parent-child relationships are subject to both individual differences and substantial variability resulting from social influences (Sroufe and Fleeson 1986).

Sensitivity and support are aspects of parental behavior that play important roles in determining the nature of connectedness within parent-child relationships (Ainsworth et al. 1978; Peterson and Hann 1999). Parental sensitivity consists of being responsive to infant cues, interpreting signals appropriately, being flexible, and having abilities to negotiate conflicting goals, whereas parental support involves verbal and physical affection, warmth, and acceptance (Bretherton 1990; Peterson and Hann 1999). Parents facilitate connectedness by acquiring a working knowledge of infant goals and behavior (i.e., reading infant signals), while acquiring abilities to assist infants in reaching goals through supportive (nurturant) behavior and sensitive responsiveness.

Infants also contribute to connectedness through such characteristics as their own temperament and their abilities to signal caregivers effectively. Temperament includes such attributes as adaptability, approach/withdrawal behavior, and quality of mood, all of which may influence parents' levels of responsiveness (Bates 1987). Children with difficult temperaments, for example, may elicit less affectionate and sensitive responses from mothers because it is difficult and frustrating to try to soothe them.

Connectedness is also influenced by the abilities of infants to effectively signal caregivers. During the first year of life, infants increasingly use their own abilities to elicit responses from caregivers and differentiate their behavior according to specific needs. Infants who are highly irritable and easily aroused may have greater difficulty in clearly expressing their own needs to caregivers, with the consequence being that parents are less able to read the child's signals and respond. Parents who demonstrate ineffective responses and inabilities to soothe

their infants are more likely to feel a sense of failure, with the infants often seeming less competent to affect their social environment. Consequently, relationship connectedness is inhibited because both members of the dyad feel less capable of conducting successful interaction.

As previously indicated, progress toward autonomy also begins early in the parent-child relationship. Bowlby (1988) proposed, for example, that parent-child relationships begin to change when infants/toddlers become mobile and begin to explore. Young children are naturally curious about the world around them, and caregivers often provide a secure base from which infants and toddlers can safely venture and explore their surrounding environment (Bowlby 1988). As a result, the focus of relationships between parents and children begins to change from an emphasis on proximity or connectedness to one where increasing priority is placed on exploratory or autonomous behaviors. Children who have a caregiver that is consistently available and responsive often tend to experience feelings of security that encourage exploratory behavior. Infants who are ineffectively connected (or attached) to parents may either (a) experience fear of abandonment and become excessively dependent or (b) develop feelings of being separated from a parent who is either low or inconsistent in responsiveness (Barnard and Martell 1995).

A key component of early social competence, therefore, is to begin structuring a balance between the bonds of connectedness and initial strivings toward autonomy—referred to as relationship *interdependence*. Early success in structuring this balance between connectedness and autonomy forms the basis for an "internal working model" that helps shape how the young may conduct future relationships during early childhood (or even later periods of development). Children develop internal representations of themselves and their relationships (or a kind of "relationship template") that they subsequently generalize to later associations with parents and other social agents.

Some evidence suggests, however, that, even as early as the parent-infant relationship, the particular balance between the two dimensions of interdependence may be subject to cross-cultural variation. For example, infants from Western societies tend to demonstrate exploratory or autonomous behavior, whereas Japanese infants are reported to display a higher incidence of "clinging" or proximity-seeking behaviors in reference to caregivers (Vanijzendoorn and Kronenberg 1988). An interpretation of these outcomes might be that even as early as infancy, cultures vary in terms of their desirable "endpoints" for parent-child relationships (Haywood et al. 1995). In contrast with Western societies, Japanese families may place less emphasis on exploratory behavior (i.e., autonomy) in the service of such cultural priorities as relationship connectedness, strong family bonds, and extended family ties.

The emergence of relationship interdependence during infancy and toddlerhood sets the stage during early childhood for the development of new dimensions of autonomy and connectedness. The major challenges for the period immediately beyond infancy are drives toward expanded forms of autonomy, which include such activities as feeding and dressing oneself and playing separately without parental participation. Such indicators of individuality do not suggest, however, that most youngsters are becoming extensively separated from parents; rather they represent the emergence of capacities that are only "one step removed" (in both a physical and psychological sense) from parents (Edwards 1995).

Another key aspect of relationship autonomy during early childhood is the progress made toward independence from parents through the emergence and growth of peer relationships. Here again, the most successful peer relationships during early childhood seem to be accomplished by those youngsters who are connected to parents through secure attachment relationships. Proponents of attachment theory often posit that securely attached infants and toddlers have acquired internal working models that provide them somewhat later in early childhood with greater competencies for interacting with their social environment (Ainsworth

1989). In contrast, children who exhibit more insecure forms of attachment to parents during infancy are more likely to have internal working models that may predispose them to display incompetent behavior with peers (Rose-Krasnor, Rubin, Booth, and Coplan 1996).

The increased role of peers during early childhood does not occur exclusively within the context of autonomy to the exclusion of connectedness. Instead, the centrality of interdependence is again demonstrated by the fact that mothers often play a key role in mediating the entry of young children into these wider social relationships and associations (Barnard and Martell 1995). Mothers influence this process by providing their young with opportunities for making friends or by supervising their child's play and coaching them in sharing, entering groups, and solving disputes. These aspects of the parent-child relationship indicate that progress toward autonomy is often managed within the context of close parental and interpersonal ties (i.e., connectedness).

Another means of fostering connectedness in early childhood is through the initial assertion of parental influence aimed at instilling in youngsters both the family's and the larger community's standards of behavior (Peterson and Hann 1999). Parents who exercise influence that fosters connectedness must seek to establish their authority without disrupting affectionate bonds with young children or inhibiting competent progress toward autonomy. The most effective strategies that balance these outcomes are the use of firm control, effective monitoring, nonintrusive guidance, and redirection of behavior within an overall context of warmth and acceptance.

Parent-Child Relationships During Middle Childhood

Changes in the parent-child relationships of middle childhood originate in both individual development and changing social expectations. These developments include the child's (a) increased cognitive abilities for solving concrete problems, (b) greater physical and social knowledge, (c) more involvement with peers and societal contexts outside family boundaries, (d) increased emphasis on school adjustment and academic achievement, and (e) greater capacities for self-conceptualization, self-evaluation, self-regulation, and social responsibility. Such developmental changes require parents to initiate new child-rearing behaviors that are aimed at the socialization goals of autonomy and connectedness (Collins, Harris, and Susman 1995). For example, parents and school-age children must face new issues and alter previous ways of dealing with an important aspect of connectedness: emotional closeness in relationships. A major challenge for relationship closeness is the tendency for children to spend only half as much time with parents during middle as compared to early childhood (Maccoby 1984). Moreover, expressions of physical affection between parents and children decline, although there is little evidence of change in other indicators of closeness (Ambert 1997; Roberts, Block, and Block 1984). Relationship closeness simply becomes more verbal (rather than physical) and indirect, while declines occur in overt expressions of negative emotions (emotional outbursts and temper tantrums) and conflict (Patterson 1982).

Connectedness also becomes evident during this period through the relative similarity that often develops in parents' and children's cognitions about each other and about issues of mutual interest. For example, research indicates that parents and 10- to 11-year-olds often agree about many issues relating to parental authority, especially when compared to later periods of development (adolescence) (Smetana 1989). Parental competence and authority is fostered by children's perceptions that parents use reason, are supportive, apply fairness, reject punitiveness, and have expertise and skill (Braine, Pomerantz, Lorber, and Krantz 1991; Maccoby 1984; Peterson and Hann 1999).

Closer bonds or connectedness are also fostered by parents who use socialization approaches that encourage children to internalize certain beliefs and expectations. Instead of emphasizing the power of parents through force and punitiveness, more effective ways of gaining internalized influence include fostering voluntary acceptance, promoting developmental achievements, and rejecting intrusiveness. A pattern of parental behaviors that fosters these goals, "authoritative" parenting, consists of reasoning, clear communication of expectations, moderate levels of monitoring, deprivation of privileges, and expressions of warmth and affection (Baumrind 1989; Peterson and Rollins 1987; Peterson and Hann 1999).

An important qualification to these ideas, however, is that ethnic-minority and social class differences may exist in how connectedness is encouraged within the parent-child relationship. Some of the current research on low-income African-American families, for example, indicates that black parents tend to place greater emphasis on obedience to authority and the use of physical discipline (Portes, Dunham, and Williams 1986; Staples and Johnson 1993). This approach to parenting has sometimes been referred to as parent-centered rather than child-centered, because its primary focus is not the interests of children but rather the needs of mothers and fathers (Petersen and Hann 1999). Another explanation is that more strict or direct forms of parenting may be prevalent in African-American families, simply because disproportionate numbers have lower incomes and are compelled to live in more dangerous, inner-city neighborhoods. Under these circumstances, children are placed at greater risk for becoming involved in or victims of antisocial behavior (Ambert 1997). Strict obedience to parental authority is an adaptive strategy that parents may pursue by using more direct, rigid, and physical forms of discipline.

Changes also occur in how autonomy, the second socialization goal, is pursued during middle childhood. The key task for parents is to recognize the increased abilities of school-age children for self-regulation, goal directedness, and for communication of plans and wishes. These new capacities often require parents to be less directly controlling and to encourage children to regulate their own behavior for increasingly longer periods of time (Collins, Harris, and

Susman 1995). Parents remain very much involved, but they must now begin monitoring, guiding, dialoguing with, and supporting their children at a somewhat greater distance. An intermediate circumstance of "coregulation" often develops, especially when compared to the greater movement toward self-regulation that will soon emerge during adolescence. According to this concept, parents continue to function in general supervisory roles, use reason, and provide support, while expecting children gradually to assume more responsibilities for moment-to-moment self-management. Coregulation is a significant step in a long process of gaining autonomy that continues throughout the remainder of childhood, adolescence, and early adulthood (Collins, et al. 1995; Grotevant 1998; Hill and Holmbeck 1986).

Greater emphasis on relationship autonomy is necessary during middle childhood because children of this age are faced with more complicated peer relationships and the importance of being successful in school. Peer relationships require that children develop effective social skills, cooperative behavior, and self-assertiveness to gain acceptance by other youngsters. Both peer relationships and success in school, defined in terms of higher grades and the lower incidence of classroom misbehavior, is predicted by components of authoritative parenting, as opposed to either authoritarian or permissive strategies.

Parent-Child Relationships During Adolescence

The classic view of parent-adolescent relationships, which is deeply rooted in psychoanalytic theory, proposes that greater autonomy by teenagers is virtually inevitable and develops at the expense of relationship connectedness in families. Greater autonomy was supposed to be achieved primarily through a process of psychological "separation" or emotional distancing (i.e., becoming disconnected) from parents. This disengagement process was expected to involve unpredictable emotional disturbances and relationship turmoil in the form of disagreements, conflicts, and rebellion against the regulatory influences of parents (Blos 1979; Freud 1958).

More recent research and theory on adolescent autonomy, however, provides a view that does not require substantial declines in parent-child connectedness. Instead, similar to what occurs in earlier periods of development, healthy adolescent autonomy is viewed as being compatible with continued connections with parents as part of the larger construct of interdependence (Grotevant 1998; Hill and Holmbeck 1986; Silverberg and Gondoli 1996; Steinberg 1990). The granting of autonomy by parents is a process of allowing for greater parent-youth reciprocity as patterns of responsibility are redefined. Mothers and fathers of teenagers must engage in a gradual process of renegotiation that involves "letting go." This involves a long transition that originates in childhood and accelerates during adolescence until adulthood is achieved.

Several individual and social developments during the period of adolescence help to make autonomy a central issue within the parent-adolescent relationship. An important influence on this issue in American society is the social definition assigned to adolescence as an extended time of preparation for adulthood in a culture that values individuality, personal freedom, self-reliance, and individual success (Peterson 1995). Consequently, autonomy becomes an increasingly prominent issue during the later years of adolescence as the young become "launched" or prepared to leave home, begin careers (or higher education), and look toward establishing families of their own (Grotevant 1998).

The physiological changes of puberty and abstract thinking abilities are additional sources of autonomy. That is, acquiring the physical characteristics of adulthood often means that parents will view the young as more mature and grant them greater autonomy. These responses by parents may, in turn, change how adolescents view themselves as being both capable and deserving of greater self-responsibility. Moreover, abstract thinking abilities are sources of flexibility in thought, independent decision making, and personal value choices that pave the way for teenagers to define their own sense of individuality in reference to parents (Grotevant 1998).

Greater autonomy also results from the increased involvement of adolescents beyond family boundaries within peer groups, part-time jobs, and school activities. Becoming more involved in these settings exposes teenagers to different viewpoints, diverse values, and alternative lifestyle possibilities that may differ from those within their families. Social experiences resulting from increased ties outside family boundaries include differences over such areas as hairstyles, clothing, curfews, money, dating, and use of a car (Silverberg and Gondoli 1996). Adolescents often use these social experiences and lifestyle issues to negotiate greater autonomy from parents (Steinberg 1990).

Progress toward autonomy during adolescence is not a simple process, but rather a complex achievement composed of more than one way of becoming self-responsible. The first component, *emotional autonomy,* involves adolescents becoming more in charge of their own feelings separate from others, as well as assessing their parents' strengths and limitations more realistically. The major result is that adolescents retain close ties with parents but become more capable of managing their own emotional experiences when faced with the variety of challenges that are part of the life course (Hill and Holmbeck 1986; Silverberg and Gondoli 1996).

A second component of becoming more self-responsible, *behavioral autonomy,* involves becoming more self-governing about one's personal conduct within such areas as family decision making, choice of friends, dating, use of leisure time, selection of clothes, use of spending money, choice of lifestyle characteristics (e.g., body piercing, tattoos, hairstyles), and restrictions on personal freedom (e.g., curfews and personal mobility). Behavioral autonomy is the aspect of self-regulation that adolescents are most aware of and about which conflict with parents occurs most frequently (Smetana 1988a, 1988b; Steinberg 1990).

The third component of being self-responsible, *value autonomy,* refers to making judgments and choices about personal belief systems and principles, rather than having them imposed by others. Attaining value autonomy means that adolescents do not merely adopt the opinions and values of parents but become committed to their own principled belief systems that they have voluntarily chosen (Douvan and Adelson 1966). These autonomous belief systems (religious, ethical, philosophical, or political) may range from being the same as to being substantially different from those of their parents. The important thing is that adolescents choose specific values through their own judgment and commitment, rather than having them imposed by others.

Besides these general patterns of autonomy development, however, evidence is also emerging that certain ethnic groups may differ somewhat in the way that autonomy is granted to adolescents (Grotevant 1998; Cooper 1994). African-American families, for example, may socialize older adolescents for autonomy by placing greater emphasis on communalism than Anglo families do. That is, these families tend to foster self-responsibility by allowing greater ties between teenagers and surrounding elements of the immediate community, such as neighborhood peer groups. In contrast, Hispanic families often resist pressures toward autonomy and peer influences through cultural traditions emphasizing the importance of strong family bonds (Grotevant 1998). These patterns of communalism and strong family bonds suggest that ethnic varieties of parent-adolescent relationships may lean more toward connectedness than is the norm within the dominant culture.

In the dominant culture, pressures for greater adolescent autonomy also require that parents are expected to change. Mothers and fathers must do so by increasingly recognizing that, by the end of the adolescent years, the young will enter adulthood and require essentially equal relationships with them. This means that adolescents and parents are constantly negotiating with each other to gradually change the rules of families. Parents who foster competent progress toward autonomy often practice "enabling behaviors" such as encouraging adolescents to express their own ideas, ask questions, and challenge parental viewpoints (Hauser, Powers, Noam, Jacobson, Weiss, and Follansbee 1984; Hauser, Powers, and Noam 1991). Competent autonomy is best facilitated by parents who use noncoercive forms of control, reason, moderate degrees of monitoring, and two-way communication and who gradually relinquish authority. Supportive behavior by parents that fosters autonomy includes encouragement, acceptance, and empathy (Grotevant 1998). Consistent with the concept of interdependence, one must continue to keep in mind that progress toward autonomy for most adolescents remains rooted in connectedness with parents. A large majority of adolescents feel close to their parents, value their parents' opinions, agree with parents about basic values, believe that their parents love them, respect their parents as authority figures, and share their parents' aspirations for educational and occupational progress (Holmbeck, Paikoff, and Brooks-Gunn 1995; Steinberg 1990). According to recent studies, differences of opinion are greater among adolescents than between teenagers and their parents (Gecas and Seff 1990; Holmbeck, Paikoff, and Brooks-Gunn 1995). A general result, therefore, is that adolescent autonomy often develops within a secure base of affectionate ties and shared beliefs with parents, the essential ingredients of interdependence.

Adult Child-Parent Relationships

Relationships involving both children and parents often continue, even when the younger generation enters adulthood and the older generation becomes elderly. Although current research on adult child-parent relationships has focused primarily on relationship connectedness, the dimension of autonomy continues to be an important relationship issue, especially when the young are entering early adulthood and generational boundaries are being formed (McCullough and Rutenberg 1989). Compared to more collectivistic societies, for example, cultural traditions in the United States lean considerably in the directions of individualism, with the result being that independence is encouraged on both sides of the generational boundary throughout the development of adult child-parent relationships.

The transitions to adulthood by the young, for example, involve the reciprocal challenges of "being released" on the part of adult children and "letting go" on the part of parents. These transitions entail gradual changes in the family's authority structure, from a circumstance in which the parental subsystem is clearly dominant to a condition in which greater equality exists between parents and adult children.

With the advent of adulthood, the autonomy of the younger generation is demonstrated in a behavioral, emotional, and cognitive sense by the establishment of intimate relationships, career avenues, independent living arrangements, and financial independence (McCullough and Rutenberg 1989). Although adult children and their parents often feel obligated to assist each other, both parties often prefer exchanges of support that do not compromise the independence of each recipient (Lye 1996). Most older adults, for example, prefer to maintain their own households separate from their children (Walsh 1989), a preference reflective of the emphasis in American society on individuality, independence, and the privacy of small, immediate family units.

Despite the importance of autonomy, as previously indicated, much of the research dealing with relationships between adult children and their parents tends to explore aspects of connectedness. Concerns have been raised that individualistic and nuclear family values might lead to the abandonment, alienation, and isolation of parents by their adult children (Lye 1996), but most research conducted on American samples indicates that enduring associations involving love, affection, and trust are characteristic of these relationships (Lewis and Lin 1996; Zarit and Eggebeen 1995). Studies on intergenerational contact and proximity during this lengthy period indicate that (a) half of adult children live within a one-hour drive of their parents, (b) 40 percent have face-to-face contact with a parent at least once a week (Lye 1996), and (c) only 3 percent of parents report that they never see an adult child (Walsh 1989). Moreover, an increase in life expectancy over the last century (Mancini and Bliezner 1989) has given parents and children greater opportunities to continue developing their relationships throughout the later stages of the life course. These statistics support the idea that ongoing connectedness in the form of frequent contact and the exchange of support continues throughout the lives of adult children and their parents (Mancini and Blieszner 1989).

An important aspect of connectedness during this period is the reciprocal nature of the relationships. As a result, both the continuing influence of parents on adult children and the growing influence of adult children on aging parents must be given careful consideration across the life course (Zarit and Eggebeen 1995). A central aspect of this ongoing connectedness between adult children and their parents is the reciprocal exchange of both instrumental (child care, household help, financial aid) and emotional support (advice giving, encouragement, expressions of love) (Lye 1996). Beginning in early adulthood, for example, children are more likely to receive support from their parents rather than offer assistance to them (Cooney and Uhlenberg 1992; Lawton et al. 1994). The type and amount of support offered adult children, however, depends on the life cycle stage of the adult child, the quality of the parent-child relationship, and the geographic distance between adult children and their parents. For example, parents often give the greatest amounts of practical and financial help to children during early adulthood for such things as college expenses and purchasing a home (Cooney and Uhlenberg 1992; Lawton et al. 1994). Research findings also suggest that emotional support and advice are the most frequent types of support exchanged by adult children and parents (Eggebeen 1992; Lye 1996).

Another important factor is parental age, with research indicating that the older generation gradually receives a growing proportion of assistance from adult children

(Mancini and Bleizner 1989; Spitze and Logan 1992) in response to advanced age, declining physical abilities, worsening health, or death of a spouse. The age of 70 appears to be a point at which greater assistance is required (Spitze and Logan 1992). The amount and type of help needed can range from minimal assistance with household maintenance to long-term assistance with chronic disabilities. Help for elderly parents is most often provided by family members, with one person commonly assuming primary responsibility for this care.

If a surviving spouse is present, the norm is for adult children to play secondary roles in providing care for the elderly. When a spouse is not in the picture, however, daughters are the most likely persons to assume the role of primary caregiver (Zarit and Eggebeen 1995). Subsequently, when an adult child becomes a caregiver, the balance between relationship autonomy and connectedness may be influenced as elderly parents become increasingly dependent on their children for instrumental or financial assistance. Despite normative support and personal preferences for separate households, a loss of autonomy often occurs as elderly parents become more dependent on adult offspring for their well-being.

Connectedness is also influenced by the type of challenges and disabilities that elderly parents may be experiencing. When they are struggling with Alzheimer's or related disorders, the resulting emotional distress for adult children tends to be high (Pearson, Verma, and Nellett 1988). Mental incapacities often translate into greater dependency and a diminished quality in the emotional connectedness that occurs within the adult child-parent relationship. When elderly parents are afflicted with physical challenges, however, reciprocal exchanges of emotional connectedness often do remain possible, despite the loss of physical autonomy. Evidence indicates that less than 5 percent of families choose the option of institutionalized care in the form of nursing home facilities. Although placing an elderly parent in a nursing home often provides some physical and emotional relief for adult children, feelings of guilt and depression may result (Zarit and Eggebeen 1995).

Recent studies also indicate that gender differences exist in how support is given and received across generations. Women are often the primary kinkeepers in families, with adult children reporting closer relationships with mothers than fathers, and mothers reporting the receipt of greater amounts of emotional support than fathers (Lawton et al. 1994; Silverstein, Parrott, and Bengtson 1995; Umberson 1992). Daughters assume disproportionate kinkeeper roles in the form of more frequent contact with parents (Spitze and Logan 1992) and the provision of routine help to them (Eggebeen and Hogan 1990). The types of support provided by men and women tend to follow traditional gender roles, with women being more likely to provide child care and emotional help, whereas men are more likely to provide financial assistance (McCullough and Rutenberg 1989).

Another possible influence on connectedness, ethnic differences in adult child-parent relationships, has demonstrated increasingly mixed findings and suggests that further research is needed. Studies conducted in the 1970s, for example, indicated that African Americans were more likely than whites to live in extended families, experience stronger kinship ties, and exchange assistance (Lye 1996). Two recent national surveys, however, have not supported these earlier findings indicating that African-American parents and adult children are less likely to exchange assistance than are white parents and children and that African-American parents often provide help that is less practical (Lawton et al. 1994). Recent interpretations of these results propose that such changes may reflect the impact of socioeconomic circumstances on the adult child-parent relationships within African-American families. Specifically, the erosion of neighborhood circumstances, diminished employment opportunities for males, and changes in family structure may partially explain the declines in certain aspects of connectedness within African-American communities (Wilson 1987).

Additional life course circumstances that affect the nature of interdependence within the parent-child relationship are transitions brought about by the marriage, parenthood, and divorce of adult children. The transition to marriage, for example, is a challenging process for the increasingly complex social relationships of adult children. When adult children marry, they often find themselves in the circumstance of holding positions of adult children in their families of origin and of spouses within their new marital subsystems. Consequently, becoming married often requires a complicated process of bringing together two complex family systems (McGoldrick 1989) that, in turn, help shape the nature of autonomy and connectedness (or interdependence) within the adult child-parent relationship.

As a result, the adult child and his or her new partner must now define and create what is important to them as a family unit, with the result being that the couple's beliefs and values may or may not match those of their parents. Discrepancies between these perspectives may result in tension and a decrease in cross-generational connectedness during this transition. New marital partners must now become the most significant persons in the lives of adult children while also attempting to be incorporated into each partner's family of origin. Married couples increasingly find themselves faced with the challenge of accommodating quite different expectations from each partner's family of origin.

These transitions associated with marriage often proceed smoothly for those parents and children who have been successful in the "letting go" process and have established a healthy balance of autonomy and connectedness (i.e., interdependence). However, for those relationships in which adult children are not sufficiently autonomous, the younger generation's marital relationships may pose a threat to the development of healthy forms of connectedness within the parent-child dyad. Specifically, generational boundaries in these families have not been defined sufficiently so that parents remain in a hierarchical position of power leading to overcontrol and intrusions into the lives of their children. As a result, family structures with these qualities may not be sufficiently flexible to accommodate the entrance of marital partners into the family system. That is, if parents perceive the entrance of a marital partner as threatening their control and involvement, they may react either by interfering in the younger couple's relationship or, at the other extreme, by emotionally cutting off their child (McGoldrick 1989).

Life course events experienced by the parent generation also have important implications for the pattern of interdependence between adult children and their elders. As adults age, for example, they typically experience three major life course transitions: retirement, widowhood, and the transition to "old age," which is often accompanied by a decline in health. The interrelatedness of these transitions for parents with those of adult children plays a crucial role in defining the nature of parent-child relationships, such that the developmental needs of adult children and aging parents may either coincide nicely or be in conflict. For example, the parent may be reaching later stages of the life course during which increases in assistance are required at a time when the younger generation needs more autonomy to establish their own careers and marital relationships. If a lack of fit exists, increased conflict may result, putting strain on the existing nature of relationship interdependence. In contrast, if aging parents require assistance after adult children have launched their own young and now have additional time, the life course transitions of the two generations are likely to be complementary (Zarit and Eggebeen 1995).

Another important transition for the parent generation, retirement from a career, often leads to an increase in the importance of relationship connectedness between adult children and parents. This process may lead to greater involvement by parents in the lives of adult children and again highlights the interrelatedness of life course transitions between adult children and parents. If aging parents expect closer relationships during a time when adult children are occupying many roles (and have little time), conflicts may grow, reducing connectedness. In contrast, if adult children have sufficient time available to spend with aging parents, an increase in connectedness may result (Zarit and Eggebeen 1995).

Finally, changes that parents experience in their relationships with marital partners, such as divorce and widowhood, also have implications for interdependence within the adult child-parent relationship. The rise of divorce rates in American society has meant for example, that more parents make the transition to old age without a spouse and live alone. Compared to married parents, those who divorce (and especially fathers) both offer less support to and receive less support from adult children (Cooney and Uhlenberg 1992; Eggebeen 1992), with the result being that connectedness is diminished. In the case of widowhood, however, somewhat different patterns of relationship interdependence are common. That is, some research indicates that widowed mothers from the older generation are more likely than married parents to receive assistance from adult children but are less likely to offer support (Eggebeen 1992). Although these widowed mothers experience greater connectedness with adult children, widowed fathers often experience decreased support, a pattern that again reflects the tendency of women to be the primary "kinkeepers" in families (Walsh 1989).

Conclusions

As transitions occur in the parent-child relationship, a central theme across the life course is the shifting balance between autonomy and connectedness that constantly defines and redefines the precise nature of interdependence. This complex process involves changes in connectedness that vary from the infant's immediate proximity-seeking behaviors directed toward a caregiver, to an adult child's emotional support given to an aged father at the death of his partner, the adult child's mother. Indicators of autonomy, in turn, vary from a toddler venturing away from a mother into the next room to the moment that an 18-year-old boards a plane to leave home to attend college. Such changes in the nature of interdependence can best be viewed as continual elaborations on a theme, complete with growing complications, shades of subtlety, and diversifying social ties that define how people assert their individuality and relate to others. Individuals are faced with these fundamental issues in diverse situations and in ever more complex forms from birth to death.

Despite variation across societies, ethnic groups, social class, family traditions, and individuals, most, if not all, parents and children must deal with autonomy and connectedness and structure some kind of balance among these relationship issues. The choices that are made often shape important patterns of development within parent-child relationships. In the most complete sense, therefore, "becoming one's own person" and "being connected to others" are really somewhat different but complementary sides of the same coin.

Discussion Questions

1. Describe how culture can influence the development of autonomy and connectedness throughout the life span.

2. How might the quality of an infant's relationship with a caregiver influence later social relationships in childhood, adolescence, and adulthood?

3. In what ways do parents contribute to a child's developing sense of autonomy and connectedness before adolescence? How does the onset of adolescence change the parent-child relationship?

4. Describe the ways in which gender may influence the development of autonomy and connectedness between caregivers and children. (Consider the gender of the parent as well as the child.)

5. Explain the statement, "Connectedness and autonomy are separate relationship dimensions that help to define complex forms of interdependence." Refer to the periods of infancy and toddlerhood.

6. How do parent-child relationships change when children become adults?

7. Do you feel that American culture places too much value on autonomy at the expense of connectedness? Why or why not?

Glossary

Life course perspective A theoretical perspective that focuses on critical transitions across time at the individual and relationship levels of development. This perspective recognizes that family and parent-child development are influenced by the larger society.

Individualism A cultural orientation that is person centered—individual interests and goals take precedence over the interest of social groups.

Autonomy Mechanisms within families (or parent-child relationships) that allow each person to assert his or her individuality in reference to family obligations, control attempts, rules, beliefs, and emotional processes.

Collectivism A cultural orientation that emphasizes community and its rights, rather than the rights of isolated persons.

Interdependence The idea that parent-child relationships involve both the development of individuality and the formation of intense interpersonal connections.

Internal working model The idea that children develop internal representations of themselves and their relationships that they later generalize to other relationships.

Authoritative parenting A child-centered parenting style that emphasizes the use of reasoning, clear communication of expectations, moderate levels of monitoring, deprivation of privileges, and expressions of warmth and affection.

Emotional autonomy Becoming more self-governing about one's own feelings separate from others.

Behavioral autonomy Becoming more self-governing about one's own personal conduct and behavior.

Value autonomy Making judgments and choices about one's own personal belief systems and principles that one has chosen voluntarily.

Instrumental support Refers to practical forms of assistance, such as child care, household help, and financial aid.

Emotional support Refers to behavior such as advice-giving, expressing love, and providing encouragement.

Suggested Readings

Ainsworth, M. S., Blehar, M., Walters, E., and Wall, S. (1978). *Patterns of Attachment.* Hillsdale, NJ: Lawrence Erlbaum Associates.

Grotevant, H. D. (1998). Adolescent development in family contexts. In W. Damon and N. Eisenberg (Eds.), *Handbook of Child Psychology,* 5th ed., (1097–1149). New York: John Wiley and Sons, Inc.

Lawton, L., Siverstein, M., and Bengtson, V. L. (1994). Solidarity between generations in families. In V. Bengtson and R. Harootyan (Eds.), *Intergenerational Linkages: Hidden Connections in American Society.* (19–42). New York: Springer.

Peterson G.W., and Hann, D. (1999). Socializing children and parents in families. In M. Sussman, S. Steinmetz, and G. W. Peterson (Eds.), *Handbook of Marriage and the Family,* Rev. ed. New York: Plenum.

Bibliography

Ainsworth, M. S. (1989). Attachments beyond infancy. *American Psychologist, 44,* 709–716.

Ainsworth, M. S., Blehar, M., Walters, E., and Wall, S. (1978). *Patterns of Attachment.* Hillsdale, NJ: Lawrence Erlbaum Associates.

Ambert, A. (1997). *Parents, Children, and Adolescents: Interactive Relationships and Development in Context.* New York: Haworth.

Arnett, J. (1995). Broad and narrow socialization: The family in the context of a cultural theory. *Journal of Marriage and the Family, 54,* 339–373.

Barnard, K. E., and Martell, L. K. (1995). Mothering. In M. H. Bornstein (Ed.), *Handbook of Parenting,* Vol. 3. (3–26). Mahwah, NJ: Lawrence Erlbaum Associates.

Bates, J. E. (1987). Temperament in infancy. In J. D. Osofsky (Ed.), *Handbook of Infant Development,* 2nd ed., (1101–1149). New York: Wiley.

Baumrind, D. (1989). Rearing competent children. In W. Damon (Ed.), *Child Development Today and Tomorrow* (349–378). San Francisco: Jossey-Bass.

Bengtson, V. L., and Allen, K. R. (1993). The life course perspective applied to families over time. In B. G Boss, W. J. Doherty, R. LaRossa, W. R. Schumm, and S. K. Steinmetz (Eds.), *Sourcebook of Family Theories and Methods: A Contextual Approach* (469–499). New York: Plenium Press.

Blos, P. (1979). *The Adolescent Passage.* New York: International Universities Press.

Blumer, H. (1969). *Symbolic Interaction.* Englewood Cliffs, NJ: Prentice-Hall.

Bowlby, J. A. (1988). *A Secure Base: Parent-Child Attachment and Healthy Human Development.* New York: Basic Books.

Braine, L. G., Pomerantz, E., Lorber, D., and Krantz, D. H. (1991). Conflicts with authority: Children's feelings, actions and justifications. *Developmental Psychology, 27,* (829–840).

Bretherton, I., (1990). Open communication and internal working models: Their role in the development of attachment relationships. In R. A. Thompson (Ed.), *Socioemotional Development* (57–113). Lincoln: University of Nebraska Press.

Bretherton, I., Biringen, Z., and Ridgeway, D. (1991). The parental side of attachment. In K. Pillemer and K. McCartney (Eds.), *Parent-Child Relations Throughout Life* (1–24). Hillsdale, NJ: Lawrence Erlbaum Associates.

Collins, W. A., Harris, M. L., and Susman, A. (1995). Parenting during middle childhood. In M. H. Bornstein (Ed.), *Handbook of Parenting: Children and Parenting,* Vol. 1, (65–89). Mahwah, NJ: Lawrence Erlbaum Associates.

Cooney, T. M., and Uhlenberg, P. (1992). Support from parents over the life course: The adult child's perspective. *Social Forces, 71,* (63–84).

Cooper, C. R. (1994). Cultural perspectives on continuity and change in adolescents' relationships. In R. Montemayor, G. R. Adams and T. P. Gullotta (Eds.), *Advances in Adolescent development: Vol 6. Personal Relationships During Adolescence* (78–100). Newbury Park, CA: Sage.

Douvan, E., and Adelson, J. (1966). *The Adolescent Experience.* New York: Wiley.

Edwards, C. P. (1995). Parenting toddlers. In M. H. Bornstein (Ed.), *Handbook of Parenting: Children and Parenting* Vol. 1, (41–63). Mahwah, NJ: Lawrence Erlbaum Associates.

Eggebeen, D. J. (1992). Family structure and intergenerational exchanges. *Research on Aging, 14,* 427–447.

Eggebeen, D. J., and Hogan, D. P. (1990). Giving between generations in American families. *Human Nature, 1,* 211–232.

Freud, S. (1958). *A General Introduction to Psychoanalysis.* New York: Permabooks.

Gecas, V., and Seff, M. A. (1990). Adolescents and families: A review of the 1980's. *Journal of Marriage and the Family, 52,* 941–958.

Grotevant, H. D. (1998). Adolescent development in family contexts. In W. Damon and N. Eisenberg (Eds.), *Handbook of Child Psychology,* 5th ed. (1097–1149). New York: John Wiley and Sons, Inc.

Hauser, S., Powers, S., and Noam, G. (1991). *Adolescents and Their Families: Paths of Ego Development.* New York: Free Press.

Hauser, S., Powers, S., Noam, G., Jacobson, A., Weiss, B., and Follansbee, D. (1984). Familial contexts of adolescent ego development. *Child Development, 55,* 195–213.

Haywood, R. L., Miller, J. G., and Irizarrz, N. L. (1995). *Culture and Attachment: Perspectives of the Child in Context.* London: Guilford Press.

Hill, J. P., and Holmbeck, G. N. (1986). Attachment and autonomy during adolescence. In G. J. Whitehurst (Ed.), *Annals of Child Development,* Vol. 3, (145–189). Greenwich, CT: JAI Press.

Holmbeck, G. N., Paikoff, R. L., and Brooks-Gunn, J. (1995). Parenting adolescents. In M. H. Bornstein (Ed.), *Handbook of Parenting: Vol. 1. Children and Parenting* (41–63). Mahwah, NJ: Lawrence Erlbaum Associates.

Kim, U. (1994). Individuation and connectedness: Conceptual clarification and elaboration. In U. Kim, H. C. Triandis, C. Kagitcibasi, S. Choi, and G. Yoon (Eds.), *Individuation and Collectivism: Theory, Method, and Applications* (19–40). Thousand Oaks, CA: Sage.

Lawton, L., Siverstein, M., and Bengtson, V. L. (1994). Solidarity between generations in families. In V. Bengtson and R. Harootyan (Eds.), *Intergenerational Linkages: Hidden Connections in American Society.* New York: Springer.

Lewis, R. A., and Lin, L. W. (1996). Adults and their midlife parents. In N. Vanzetti and S. Duck (Eds.), *A Lifetime of Relationships.* Pacific Grove, CA: Brooks/Cole.

Lye, D. N. (1996). Adult-child-parent relationships. *Annual Review of Sociology, 22,* 79–102.

Maccoby, E. E. (1984). Middle childhood in the context of the family. In W. A. Collins (Ed.), *Development During Middle Childhood: The Years from Six to Twelve* (184–239). Washington, DC: National Academy of Sciences Press.

Mancini, J. A., and Bliezner, R. (1989). Aging parents and adult children: Research themes in intergenerational relations. *Journal of Marriage and the Family, 51,* 275–290.

McCullough, P. G., and Rutenberg, S. K. (1989). Launching children and moving on. In B. Carter and M. McGoldrick (Eds.), *The Changing Family Life Cycle: A Framework for Family Therapy,* 2nd ed. (287–311). Boston: Allyn and Bacon.

McGoldrick, M. (1989). The joining of families through marriage: The new couple. In B. Carter and M. McGoldrick (Eds.), *The Changing Family Life Cycle: A Framework for Family Therapy,* 2nd ed. (41–43). Boston: Allyn and Bacon.

Patterson, G. R. (1982). *Coercive Family Processes.* Eugene, OR: Castalia Press.

Pearson, J., Verma, S., and Nellett, C. (1988). Elderly psychiatric patient status and caregiver perceptions as predictors of caregiver burden. *Gerontologist, 28,* 79–83.

Peterson, G. W. (1995). Autonomy and connectedness in families. In R. G. Day, K. R. Gilbert, B. H. Settles and W. R. Burr (Eds.), *Research and Theory in Family Science* (20–41). Pacific Grove, CA: Brooks/Cole.

Peterson, G. W., and Hann, D. (1999). Socializing children and parents in families. In M. Sussman, S. Steinmetz and G. W. Peterson (Eds.), *Handbook of Marriage and the Family,* (327–370). New York: Plenum Press.

Peterson, G. W., and Rollins, B. C. (1987). Parent-child socialization. In M. B. Sussman, and S. K. Steinmetz (Eds.), *Handbook of Marriage and the Family.* (471–538). New York: Plenum Press.

Portes, P. R., Dunham, R. M., and Williams, S. (1986). Assessing childrearing style in ecological settings: In relation to culture, social class, early age intervention and scholastic achievement. *Adolescence, 21,* 723–725.

Roberts, G. C., Block, J. H., and Block, J. (1984). Continuity and change in parents' child-rearing. *Child Development, 55,* 586–597.

Rose-Krasnor, L., Rubin, K. H., Booth, C. L., and Coplan, R. (1996). The relation of maternal-directiveness and child attachment security to social competence in preschoolers. *International Journal of Behavioral Development, 19,* 309–325.

Silverberg, S. B., and Gondoli, D. M. (1996). Autonomy in adolescence: A contextualized perspective. In G. R. Adams, R. Montemayor and T. P. Gullotta (Eds.), *Psychosocial Development During Adolescence: Progress in Developmental Contextualization* (12–61). Thousand Oaks, CA: Sage.

Silverstein, M., Parrott, T. M., and Bengtson, V. L. (1995). Factors that predispose middle-aged sons and daughters to provide social support to older parents. *Journal of Marriage and the Family, 57*, 465–475.

Smetana, J. G. (1988a). Adolescents' and parents' conceptions of parental authority. *Child Development, 59*, 321–335.

Smetana, J. G. (1988b). Concepts of self and social convention: Adolescents' and parents' reasoning about hypothetical and actual family conflicts. In M. R. Gunnar and W. A. Collins (Eds.), *Minnesota Symposia on Child Psychology* Vol. 21, (79–122). Hillsdale, NJ: Lawrence Erlbaum Associates.

Smetana, J. (1989). Adolescents' and parents' reasoning about actual family conflict. *Child Development, 60*, 1052–1067.

Spitze, G., and Logan, J. (1992). Helping as a component of parent-child relations. *Research on Aging, 14*, 291–312.

Sroufe, L. A., and Fleeson, J. (1986). Attachment and the construction of relationships. In W. Hartup and Z. Rubin (Eds.), *Relationships and Development* (51–71). New York: Cambridge University Press.

Sroufe, L. A. (1990). Considering normal and abnormal together: The essence of developmental psychopathology. *Development and Psychopathology, 2*, 335–347.

Staples, R., and Johnson, L. B. (1993). *Black Families at the Crossroads*. San Francisco: Jossey-Bass.

Steinberg, L. (1990). Interdependence in the family: Autonomy, conflict, and harmony in the parent-adolescent relationship. In S. S. Feldman and G. L. Elliot (Eds.), *At the Threshold: The Developing Adolescent* (255–276). Cambridge: Harvard University Press.

Triandis, H. C. (1994). Theoretical and methodological approaches to the study of collectivism and individualism. In U. Kim, H. C. Triandis, C. Kagitcibasi, S. Choi, and G. Yoon (Eds.), *Individuation and Collectivism: Theory, Method, and Applications* (41–51). Thousand Oaks, CA: Sage.

Umberson, D. (1992). Relationships between adult children and their parents: Psychological consequences for both generations. *Journal of Marriage and the Family, 54*, 664–674.

Vanijzendoorn, M. H., and Kroonenberg, P. M. (1988). Cross-cultural patterns of attachment: A meta-analysis of the strange situation. *Child Development, 59*, 147–156.

Walsh, F. (1989). The family later in life. In B. Carter and M. McGoldrick (Eds.), *The Changing Family Life Cycle: A Framework for Family Therapy*, 2nd ed.(311–332). Boston: Allyn and Bacon.

Wilson, W. J. (1987). *The Truly Disadvantaged*. Chicago: University of Chicago Press.

Zarit, S. H., and Eggebeen, D. J. (1995). Parent-child relationships in adulthood and old age. In M. Bornstein (Ed.), *Handbook of Parenting: Children and Parenting*, Vol. 1. Mahwah, NJ: Lawrence Erlbaum Associates, Inc. ✦

Chapter 15
Family Life Education Over the Life Course

Margaret E. Arcus
University of British Columbia

Preparing individuals and families for the roles, responsibilities, and transitions of family living is nothing new. Humans have no built-in knowledge about life span development, interpersonal relationships, and family living, and thus they must learn about these things from somewhere. Over time, all societies have developed ways through which they transmit their societal wisdom and experience regarding family living from one generation to the next. In some societies and in some eras, knowledge about certain family matters has been transmitted through formal means such as puberty or initiation rites. For the most part, however, most individuals have informally learned about family living in the family setting itself, as they have observed and participated in activities and interactions within their own families and in other families around them.

As societies change and become more complex, however, reliance on informal methods of learning about living in families appears inadequate. Changes in wider society (such as advances in technology, the development of new knowledge, and changing social and economic conditions) create circumstances where the teachings of previous generations are no longer appropriate or sufficient. These changes may lead to strains or tensions in individuals and families, resulting in family dissatisfaction and disruption. According to Kirkendall (1973), an increased divorce rate, increased strife between parents and children, and shifts in marital and familial roles have commonly occurred as societies have become industrialized and urbanized. In these circumstances, societies must find or create new ways through which to prepare individuals for their family roles and transitions.

Family Life Education

One of the ways used for transmitting such knowledge has been the movement called family life education (Arcus, Schvaneveldt, and Moss 1993). This movement developed as an educational specialty early in the twentieth century in response to changing social conditions of the time that were perceived to have negative impacts not only on individuals and their families, but also on wider society. Because families appeared to be inadequately prepared to deal with these changing conditions, attempts were made to support and strengthen families through the efforts of agencies and institutions outside the family. In particular, the early founders of family life education believed that the development of formal educational programs, specifically focused on family tasks and transitions, would help improve family living and ameliorate or reduce family-related social problems.

The purpose of family life education is to strengthen and enrich individual and family well-being, and its programs are intended to be preventive and educational rather than therapeutic. That is, family life programs are intended to equip individuals for their family roles and transitions rather than to repair individual or family dysfunction. General goals include (a) learning about human development and behavior in the family setting over the life course, (b) learning about the patterns and processes of marriage and family living, (c) gaining insight into oneself and others, (d) acquiring personal and interpersonal skills to enhance family living, (e) developing capacities for both present and future family roles, and (f) building strengths in individuals and their families. To accomplish these goals, a program may include a wide range of content, such as understanding and improving relationships; providing and managing the resources of the family; balancing family, work, and community roles; meeting individual needs within the family, interacting with and caring for family members; and engaging with social institutions such as the legal, religious, educational, and governmental systems. It is assumed that if these and other related goals and objectives are met through family life education programs, families will be better equipped to deal with and possibly even to prevent family-related problems (both those within the family and in wider society) and will become empowered to live their family lives in ways that are both personally satisfying and socially responsible.

In family life education, it is also assumed that education for family living is relevant to all individuals and families, whatever their family structure, stage of the life course, or special individual or family circumstances. The various normative developments for individuals and families, such as getting married or becoming a parent, have been the impetus for the development of certain family life education programs (marriage education, parent education). Some programs may be age related (sexuality education during puberty), whereas others are event related (death education with the loss of a family member). Still other family life education programs address family needs and transitions that are non-normative, reflecting special needs or transitions that affect some, but not all, individuals and families (parenting children with special needs, getting divorced, facing unemployment or underemployment). Responses to both normative and non-normative events and transitions have resulted in the emergence of a number of specialty areas within family life education, with some well established (parent education, sexuality education, marriage preparation) and others emerging (parent education for adolescent parents, sexual abuse education, remarriage education).

In keeping with the theme of this text, *Families Across Time*, this chapter examines family life education programs designed to meet the needs of families as they form, develop, and change over time. Relationships in families, rather than family structure, are used as the organizing theme, focusing on two major kinds of family relationships: couple relationships and parent-child relationships. Within each of these, the major forms of family life education programs are discussed, including how these programs may or may not address issues of individual and family diversity. Although historically, most programs have been based on white, middle-class models, many of the major concepts and principles are relevant to other family forms as well (single-parent families, gay-lesbian families, ethnic/minority families).

Most family life course models begin with the formation of the couple relationship during young adulthood; in this chapter we thus emphasize family life education programs designed for adults. To facilitate discussion, the chapter will follow a couple, Deborah and Dave, and the family life education opportunities potentially available to them over their family life course. Deborah and Dave have recently become engaged and plan to marry within the year. They are in their mid-twenties, and each has completed at least some post-secondary education. Both are Caucasian and Protestant and plan to marry in the church attended by Deborah's family.

Family Life Education for Couple Relationships

Dave and Deborah have been informed by the minister who will marry them that they are required to participate in a marriage preparation experience. Although this kind of requirement is relatively recent, marriage preparation was one of the earliest forms of family life education, having appeared in North America in the 1920s and 1930s (Stahmann and Salts 1993). At least in Westernized societies, the emergence of marriage preparation (also called premarital education or premarital counseling) was influenced in part by the shift from institutional to companionate marriages. In an institutional marriage, authority and discipline were vested in the head of the family and re-inforced by external forces such as the law, social mores, tradition, and public opinion. Thus, there was little perceived need for any educational support to help the couple develop their relationship. With the emergence of companionate marriages, however, greater emphasis was placed on the marital relationship, including the development of mutual affection and intimacy between the partners and of shared authority, interests, and activities. This shared rather than authoritarian model required substantial interpersonal relationship skills and abilities, and programs in marriage preparation were developed as one means to assist couples in preparing for these new kinds of relationships.

Marriage preparation is based on the premise that becoming a couple is one of the most difficult and complex transitions of the family life course (Stahmann and Salts 1993). In this transition, couples must not only negotiate individual, interpersonal, and family-of-origin issues, but they must also address contemporary social issues (such as the changing roles of women and men) that may influence their relationship. The formation of a couple relationship may be even more difficult or complex when the partners come from different ethnic, religious, or social class backgrounds or when they are geographically distant from the support of their families of origin.

Initially, emphasis in family life education was placed on the formation of the couple relationship. However, the recognition that relationships are not only formed but must also be maintained and must eventually end (either through separation/divorce or through death) has led to the development of additional educational programs relevant to the ongoing nature of relationships (marriage enrichment, divorce education). The term *marriage education* is sometimes used to refer this broad spectrum of programs for relationship education across time (forming, maintaining, and ending relationships).

Forming Relationships

Marriage preparation is specific rather than generalized education—that is, it is de-signed to help couples like Deborah and Dave prepare for their own marriage. Through this experience, couples gain knowledge about and discuss the critical issues and tasks of marriage; acquire the communication, problem-solving, and other behavioral skills that might enhance their marital relationship; and examine, evaluate, and possibly in some cases, reconsider their relationship. The experience may also be designed to challenge the romanticism of the couple and to help them examine their untested assumptions and unrealistic expectations. Marriage preparation takes one of two forms: (a) programs provided to groups of couples or (b) private premarital counseling sessions offered to individual couples.

If Deborah and Dave decide to participate in a marriage preparation program, they will be involved in a series of eight to ten educational sessions that will address the following kinds of topics: marriage as a commitment, marital roles, the perceived strengths of their relationship, family-of-origin experiences and issues, patterns of interaction including communication styles and conflict resolution, sexuality and intimacy, expectations regarding children and parenting, financial resources and resource management, religious or spiritual values and expectations, and issues related to educational and career goals and leisure and recreational interests. During these sessions, they will participate in a variety of educational experiences, such as didactic presentations by the program leaders or guest speakers (which may include modeling specific couple behaviors), skill development exercises, written assessment instruments such as PRE-PARE (Olson, Fournier, and Druckman 1982), and various structured and unstructured couple or group discussions and activities such as role-playing exercises (Bagarozzi and Rauen 1981; Miller, Nunnally, and Wackman 1979; Stanley, Markman, St. Peters, and Leger 1995). It has been suggested that at least some of these sessions might be more beneficial after, rather than before, the wedding, as couples would then have a more realistic understanding of their relationship strengths and issues (Bader, Microys, Sinclair, Willett, and

Conway 1980). However, most marriage preparation continues to be offered prior to the marriage.

Marriage preparation programs differ not only in how much the format, curricula, and activities are predetermined by the program developer rather than input from the participating couples, but also in their theoretical foundations. Some programs place greater emphasis on the feelings and emotions of the couple, others on the development of relevant skills and abilities, and still others on the development of knowledge and understanding about relationships (see Ulrici, L'Abate, and Wagner 1981). Because of these differences, the particular experience of Dave and Deborah and their preparation for their own marriage will depend in part on the nature and focus of the particular program they attend. The advantages of marriage preparation programs include the opportunity to observe other couples and learn from their interactions, to obtain feedback from others on their own relationship, and to observe each other as they interact with others in the group. Because of time constraints, however, not all of the needs of a particular couple may be met. Some couples may also be tempted to work on the problems of other couples rather than focus on their own issues.

If Dave and Deborah decide on premarital counseling, they will be involved in a series of private sessions with a trained marriage educator or a member of the clergy. These sessions will address goals and topics similar to those in marriage preparation programs, but the specific focus will be determined by their own needs and interests, by the goals and expertise of their counselor, and by the number of sessions required. Couple discussion will be emphasized, and questionnaires and assessment instruments such as PREPARE (Olson et al. 1982) may be used to assist with and enhance their learning. The advantage of premarital counseling is that topics and discussion are personalized to focus on the couple's specific needs and issues. However, not all couples may be aware of some of their needs and issues that require discussion, or the counselor may not be adequately prepared to help them address

some important topics. There is also no opportunity to observe how other couples might interact or solve problems, and thus no opportunity to learn from a group experience (e.g., Stahmann and Hiebert 1987).

Early programs in marriage preparation were developed as generic education, based on the assumption that the same kind of educational experience was appropriate for all couples. Over time, however, these generic models have been modified to be more sensitive to issues of family diversity. To date, the greatest attention has been given to religious diversity, with many marriage preparation programs and premarital counseling experiences developed by religious groups specifically for their own members and offered through their own religious settings. Few programs, however, have given attention to issues of ethnic diversity, to gay and lesbian families, or to variation in educational levels. In fact, not all groups may value the companionate model of marriage on which marriage preparation is based and thus may not see this form of family life education as appropriate (see Hildreth and Sugawara 1993, regarding ethnicity and diversity in family life education). In addition, the typical educational strategies of marriage preparation (the use of written materials, open-ended and peer-led discussion groups) may not be equally appropriate or effective for those with lower levels of literacy or different educational backgrounds. The issue of age variation also has not been addressed—that is, do the educational needs of couples differ, depending on whether they are in their 20s, their 30s, or their 50s?

Marriage preparation originally was designed for young couples like Deborah and Dave who are preparing to marry for the first time, but this is not the only audience for which such education is relevant. Although few programs have been specifically designed for couples who are cohabiting rather than planning to marry, these couples may also be interested in relationship issues and in enhancing their own relationship. Thus they may benefit from participation in those family life education programs or counseling experiences that focus on relationship issues. More recently, influenced by a rising divorce rate, marriage preparation programs have been developed for couples in which at least one partner has been married before (education for remarriage). In addition to the typical goals of marriage preparation, these programs also include issues specific to remarried families (combining two families in ways that meet everyone's needs, deciding on stepparent roles, coping with unique economic issues) (Price and Burnett 1993). Attention is directed to the structural complexity and diversity of remarried families and to key differences between first marriages and second or third ones.

Will marriage preparation help Deborah and Dave? Evidence to date suggests that most marriage preparation programs meet at least some of their goals, helping couples learn the intended skills or content. However, not all programs are effective or are equally effective for all participants. Also, it is not clear how long the learnings from marriage preparation last.

Maintaining Relationships

After several years of marriage, Dave and Deborah are now concerned that their relationship is not as satisfying as it once was. The challenges of raising their family, the difficulties of making ends meet, strains generated in the workplace, and even the monotony of living with each other every day have taken a toll on their relationship. Deborah and Dave still care for each other and want to improve their relationship. Friends have suggested that they consider taking a marriage enrichment program.

The marriage and family enrichment movement emerged in the 1960s as a means of helping couples like Deborah and Dave who want to maintain and strengthen their relationship. These programs are based on the human potential hypothesis that all persons and all relationships have a need for growth; all have strengths, resources, and unused potential that can be tapped and developed; and, given appropriate conditions, all can learn to maintain significant interpersonal relationships. For the most part, enrichment programs were designed for well-functioning couples rather than for those in marital distress (see Mace and Mace 1986).

Two marital enrichment options are available to Dave and Deborah: participating in an intensive weekend retreat or enrolling in a series of six to eight weekly enrichment sessions. Some enrichment programs are highly structured and follow a specified curriculum, whereas others are relatively unstructured in order to meet the emerging needs of the participants. Programs will differ in how much emphasis they place on didactic presentations from leaders or guests, group discussion and interaction, and couple and individual work. Despite considerable diversity in these programs, however, all appear to have the following features: (a) they are dynamic, experiential, educational, and preventive; (b) they typically promote a balance between growth in the relationship and growth for the individual; (c) they are ongoing, viewing enrichment as the beginning rather than the end for marital growth; (d) they focus on identifying, sharing, and developing the positive aspects of the relationship; and (e) they emphasize the ability to communicate effectively (Hof and Miller 1980). Most programs are designed for married couples, but some have also been used with premarital couples. Some programs have been developed for specific audiences, such as dual-career couples, remarried couples, alcoholics, and wife batterers (see Stahmann and Salts 1993).

In general, evaluations indicate that marriage enrichment programs can make a difference. Programs reporting the greatest change tend to be longer and to involve experiential activities, including behavioral rehearsal. The effects of enrichment programs appear to diminish over time, lending support to those who advocate booster programs (Guerney and Maxson 1990). Although most enrichment programs are designed for well-functioning couples, interestingly, they appear to attract slightly distressed or preclinical couples. Most participants in marriage enrichment programs tend to be middle class and well educated; little specific attention appears to have been given to issues of family or ethnic diversity (Wampler 1990).

Ending Relationships

Eventually the relationship of Deborah and Dave must end, either through separation/divorce or through death. Because the loss of a partner, for whatever reason, brings about significant changes in the life circumstances of all involved, including other family members, these transitions require considerable emotional and social adjustment. A number of family life education programs have been developed to assist individuals and couples (and sometimes their families) with these complex transitions.

If Dave and Deborah become increasingly dissatisfied with their relationship, and their level of interpersonal conflict increases, they may decide to separate and eventually may divorce. If this happens, a number of issues will require their attention: their continuing responsibilities for child rearing (if any); the reactions of their children; the nature of their ongoing relationship as former spouses; changes in their social networks (both friends and family); and changes in their finances, household management, personal habits, and lifestyles (including dating and sexuality issues). In general, educational programs for those who have separated or divorced are designed to help individuals adjust to the status and roles of singlehood and to change their attitudes, feelings, and/or behaviors toward themselves (self-acceptance, personal growth, development of autonomy), toward others (children, the former spouse, friends, relatives), and toward other aspects of their life (sex, dating, work, recreation). Attention to these issues is particularly important if the individual intends to remarry because the quality of a subsequent remarriage will be influenced by the quality of the dissolution of the previous marriage. Salts (1989) cautions, however, that divorce education groups are not for everyone and that some may find therapy to be more relevant and more helpful than education. In her view, individuals need first to resolve basic needs such as finances, housing, food, and child care before they can fully benefit from divorce education programs. In a growing number of communities, a short, specifically designed educational course for parents who

are divorcing has been mandated by the court system to assist them in minimizing any negative effects of the divorce on their children (Emery 1995; Geasler and Blaisure 1998).

The death of the spouse also marks the end of the couple relationship, and this loss has a major impact on the life situation of the survivor. It may influence his or her health and well-being, and widows, in particular, may face a substantial reduction in their income. Deborah will likely be the survivor, as wives are typically younger than their husbands and women typically live longer than men. Regardless of whether the survivor is Deborah or Dave, the loss will be a difficult one, with a number of emotional, economic, and relational issues to be addressed: fulfilling everyday household needs, maintaining physical and emotional health, maintaining family and other relationships, and developing a lifestyle as a single person. In some cases, the surviving spouse may also need to deal with continued occupational and childrearing responsibilities.

Educational support for those who have lost their spouse includes support services for individuals, group educational programs, or a combination of individual and group support. In the Widow-to-Widow program (Silverman 1977), individual support services are provided to the newly widowed by someone who has already faced that experience. This program is based on the assumption that individuals who have already faced this kind of loss are in the best position to respond to the emotional and other needs of those who are newly widowed. The Grief Workshop (Wood 1987) combines an educational seminar experience with the development of a support system to help individuals deal with their loss and grief. Through the seminar, participants gain information, interact with others facing a similar experience, and develop a support network with other participants. This workshop is typically organized around holidays—a time that is especially difficult for those who have lost a loved one.

The issue of family diversity is seldom discussed in either the divorce adjustment or death/grief education literature. This is not surprising, as these bodies of literature are relatively new and comparatively limited. However, some important diversity issues need attention. For example, are a person's educational needs different if the loss of a spouse from death occurs "off time" (during young adulthood) rather than "on time" (during later adulthood)? Does a person's involvement in a strong social support network (family or extended family, ethnic or religious group) influence the need for these forms of family life education? Given the difficulties associated with the ending of relationships, how might someone find an appropriate balance between family life education, social support services, and therapy, and how might needs differ depending on individual life circumstances and experiences?

Family Life Education for Parent-Child Relationships

Deborah and Dave have three children, two boys and a girl. Although both parents have siblings, had experience as babysitters, and had worked with youth groups during their adolescence, neither felt adequately prepared for their role as parents. Becoming a parent is one of the major roles of adulthood, a role that has significant social and cultural meanings. Couples may feel considerable pressure to assume this role, with these pressures typically greater on women than on men. The majority of adults become parents, and most of them, like Deborah and Dave, take this role seriously and want to succeed. They recognize that good parenting is essential for the survival and development of the child and that, as parents, they will be an important influence on the child's life. At the same time, Deborah and Dave lack specific training for parenting, and they may have taken on the role with unrealistic or romantic notions of what is required to be a successful parent.

The life course of the parent-child relationship (parenting across time) differs in several ways from the life course of a couple relationship. According to Bigner (1989), the parental role is not always voluntarily assumed (as marriage is presumed to be), but

once assumed, this role is irrevocable (there is no alternative comparable to divorce). More important, the developmental nature of parenting is unique in that parents must continually modify their parenting activities and behaviors in keeping with the developmental changes that occur in each of their children. From their intensive involvement and responsibility during the early childhood years, parents must gradually relinquish this involvement in order to facilitate the development of independence in their adolescent children and to establish a pattern of friendship and colleagueship with their adult children. Deborah and Dave may also need to come to terms with their own potential dependence on their children as they themselves age. Not only are these shifts in parenting difficult, but their nature and timing will differ with each child.

Parent education is designed to improve or enhance parental role performance by helping parents such as Dave and Deborah (or other primary caregivers) to increase their knowledge of child growth and development, expand their repertoire of skills and strategies for carrying out their parental tasks, and increase their understanding of patterns of parent-child interaction (Brock, Oertwein, and Coufal 1993). Two modes of parent education are particularly relevant to Deborah and Dave: the mass mode and the group mode. The mass mode includes the many books, magazines, newsletters, pamphlets, radio and television programs, and, more recently, internet sites that provide information and advice on a wide range of topics of concern to parents (Harmin and Brim 1980). Many parents prefer and rely on this "do it yourself" mode of parent education, finding it to be cost-effective, nonthreatening, and convenient (no time constraints). Both Deborah and Dave have used at least some of these mass mode sources as they seek to become better parents.

However, they have also become aware of the second mode of parent education, the group mode (Harmin and Brim 1980), which they feel might better meet some of their ongoing needs for parenting education. When parent education first emerged in the late 1800s, it tended to be discussion groups and was primarily mother education provided by women for women (Lewis-Rowley, Brasher, Moss, Duncan, and Stiles 1993). Group parenting programs involving discussions continue to be an important mode of parent education, and participants continue to be primarily mothers such as Deborah.

A wide variety of these programs have been developed in recent years (Brock et al. 1993; Fine and Henry 1989). Theoretically, most are based on Baumrind's (1971) authoritative parenting model of providing structure for children, although different programs may emphasize different aspects of the model. In addition to the focus on structure (making and enforcing rules, setting limits, controlling, following through), most programs also incorporate other major themes of parenting such as nurturance (providing warmth and support, having developmentally appropriate expectations), empathetic listening, the processes of parent-child interaction, and techniques of discipline. Typical educational activities in parent education programs include group discussions and experiential learning activities, including the practice of parenting skills.

Some parent education programs are locally developed, but several are well established and widely disseminated and illustrate the kinds of programs available to Deborah (and possibly Dave). Both *Parent Effectiveness Training* (PET) (Gordon 1975) and *Systematic Training for Effective Parenting* (STEP) (Dinkmeyer and McKay 1976) reflect Baumrind's authoritative parenting model and emphasize experiential learning and the direct involvement of children in the process (Fine 1989). In these programs, parenting skills are demonstrated and modeled, and parents are given the opportunity to practice and refine these skills. Unique elements of PET include ownership of the problem, flexibility rather than consistency in parenting, and no-lose conflict resolution. STEP focuses on children's misbehaviors, such as attention getting, power, revenge, and expressions of inadequacy, and it promotes the use of family meetings for the democratic discussion of family problems and activities. These programs have served as models for newer parent education programs, including *How to Talk So Kids Will Listen and Listen So Kids Will Talk* (Faber and Mazlich 1980) and *Active Parenting* (Popkin 1989). *Active Parenting* uses a video format to present vignettes of parent-child interaction, which are then reinforced with weekly enrichment activities at home. This delivery system would be particularly appropriate for audiences where literacy may be an issue. Although being a parent is a lifetime role, most parent education programs focus on the early and middle childhood years, with few programs for parents of adolescents and even fewer addressing parents and their adult children.

Many parent education programs were originally developed as generic, appropriate for all parents. Over time, two kinds of modifications have been made. In some cases, curricular and format modifications have been made at the local level to meet the specific needs of a specific group of parents. Not all parents can or will commit the time required to complete the program as designed by its developers; the lifestyles of some parents may make it difficult for them to attend the typical weekly series of eight to ten sessions; and some parents are more interested in addressing their own specific parenting issues rather than learning about the general issues and skills promoted in the program (Brock et al. 1993).

In addition, the general trend in parent education has been to move away from generic programs toward those with greater specificity in order to more adequately meet the needs of specific target audiences. For example, the contemporary roles and responsibilities of fathers such as Dave are changing, with shared parenting more likely in two-parent families and an increasing number of fathers taking on single-parenting roles following divorce or the death of their spouse (Levant and Kelly 1989; Meyers 1993). Because fathers may lack both the formal education for parenting and the informal socialization and experience that mothers may have, these parenting programs need to address the greater needs of fathers for knowledge about child development and child-rearing, the external barriers that may hinder their involvement with children, and their typically smaller social support networks.

Attention is also being given to designing culturally responsive parent education programs. These programs should be based on the specific needs, expectations, and strengths of the target families (Hildreth and Sugawara 1993), but for some cultural groups, there may be limited empirical data on their parenting needs and interests and a limited understanding of their cultural backgrounds (Powell, Zambrana, and Silva-Palacios 1990; The Rural and Appalachian Youth and Families Consortium 1996). In some cases, programs may need to address the bicultural or intergenerational conflicts that emerge as a consequence of migration and immigration, resulting in different values and beliefs being held by parents and their children, particularly during the adolescent years (Jim and Suen 1990). Dumka, Roosa, Michaels, and Suh (1995) suggested that it may not be necessary to develop specialized programs for each subgroup but rather to ensure that programs have built-in flexibility to accommodate the individual needs of the subgroup. In parent education, an important question will need to be addressed: Is the Baumrind model of authoritative parenting equally effective for all families (Brock et al. 1993)?

Other parent education programs designed for specific audiences include those for single parents, stepparents, parents of adolescents, adolescent parents, and parents at risk for abuse. As yet, little attention has been given in the literature to other unique groups, such as grandparents, who may become the primary caregivers for their grandchildren.

Conclusions

As discussed in this chapter, there are many opportunities and needs for family life education for families as they grow, develop, and change across time, whether one is concerned with education for the couple relationship or for the parent-child relationship. In both cases, attention has typically focused primarily on family educational needs at the entry or early stages of these relationships.

Parenting programs, for the most part, continue to focus on these early stages when parental involvement and responsibilities are greatest and most demanding, but in couple education, programs in marriage enrichment and divorce education have extended this form of family education across time.

To provide family life education for all families across the life span, two major challenges are significant. First, efforts to address issues of family diversity must continue and expand to be relevant to additional groups, and second, greater attention must be given to the family life education needs of later-life individuals and families (Arcus et al. 1993). This large and growing proportion of the population faces new and different issues in marital and intimate relationships (influenced by the aging process) and in parenting (influenced by patterns of family expansion and contraction). If these challenges are met, not only will family life education be relevant to all individuals and families, whatever their circumstances or stage of the life course, but family life education programs will likely be more available.

Discussion Questions

1. The emergence of family life education programs historically has been influenced by changing social and economic conditions. What major social and economic conditions influenced marriage education in the past? Identify two or three current social or economic conditions, and speculate how they might influence the need for marriage education.

2. Other chapters in this text discuss various kinds of families. Select one of these chapters, and identify the key normative needs for family life education for the families discussed in that chapter.

3. Imagine your personal family life situation ten years from now (marital status, number and ages of family members, stage of the family life course, socioeconomic status). What family life education needs would your family likely

have at this time? What special circumstances might change these needs?

4. Suppose you are the leader or co-leader of a marriage preparation program in a community where participation in these programs is required by law. Your current group includes four couples who are in their early 20s and married for the first time, two couples who are in their late 30s where one of the couple has been married before, and one couple in their 50s, with each partner being married for the first time. How might the educational needs of these couples be different?

Glossary

Family life education Preventive and educational programs designed to strengthen and enrich individual and family well-being.

Marriage preparation Specific education designed to help couples prepare for their own marriage.

Parent education Programs designed to improve or enhance parental role performance by helping parents increase their knowledge of child growth and development, expand their repertoire of skills and strategies for carrying out their parental tasks, and increase their understanding of patterns of parent-child interaction.

Premarital counseling Private sessions with a trained counselor, addressing the specific needs and interests of the couple and the counselor.

Suggested Readings

Arcus, M. E. (1992). Family life education: Toward the 21st century. *Family Relations, 41,* 390–393.

Arcus, M. E., Schvaneveldt, J. D., and Moss, J. J. (1993). *Handbook of Family Life Education: The Practice of Family Life Education*, Vol. 2, Newbury Park, CA: Sage.

Hughes, R., Jr. (1994). A framework for developing family life education programs. *Family Relations, 43,* 74–80.

Morgaine, C. A. (1992). Alternative paradigms for helping families change themselves. *Family Relations, 41,* 12–17.

Bibliography

Arcus, M. E., Schvaneveldt, J. D., and Moss, J. J. (1993). The nature of family life education. In M. E. Arcus, J. D. Schvaneveldt, and J. J. Moss (Eds.), *Handbook of Family Life Education: Vol. 1. Foundations of Family Life Education* (1–25). Newbury Park, CA: Sage.

Bader, E., Microys, G., Sinclair, C., Willett, E., and Conway, B. (1980). Do marriage preparation programs really work? A Canadian experiment. *Journal of Marital and Family Therapy, 6,* 171–179.

Bagarozzi, D., and Rauen, P. (1981). Premarital counseling: Appraisal and status. *American Journal of Family Therapy, 9,* 13–28.

Baumrind, D. (1971). Current patterns of parental authority. *Developmental Psychology Monographs, 4,* 1–103.

Bigner, J. J. (1989). *Parent-child Relations: An Introduction to Parenting,* 3rd ed. New York: Macmillan.

Brock, G. W., Oertwein, M., and Coufal, J. D. (1993). Parent education: Theory, research, and practice. In M. E. Arcus, J. D. Schvaneveldt, and J. J. Moss (Eds.), *Handbook of Family Life Education: The Practice of Family Life Education,* Vol. 2 (87–114). Newbury Park, CA: Sage.

Dinkmeyer, D., and McKay, G. (1976). *Systematic Training for Effective Parenting: Parent's Handbook.* Circle Pines, MN: American Guidance Service.

Dumka, L. E., Roosa, M. W., Michaels, M. L., and Suh, K. W. (1995). Using research and theory to develop prevention programs for high-risk families. *Family Relations, 44,* 78–86.

Emery, R. E. (1995). Divorce mediation: Negotiating agreements and renegotiating relationships. *Family Relations, 44,* 377–383.

Faber, A., and Mazlich, E. (1980). *How to Talk so Kids Will Listen and Listen so Kids Will Talk.* New York: Avon.

Fine, M. J. (Ed.). (1989). *The Second Handbook on Parent Education: Contemporary Perspectives.* San Diego, CA: Academic Press.

Fine, M. J., and Henry, S. A. (1989). Professional issues in parent education. In M. J. Fine (Ed.), *The Second Handbook on Parent Education: Contemporary Perspectives* (3–20). San Diego, CA: Academic Press.

Geasler, M. J., and Blaisure, K. R. (1998). A review of divorce education program materials. *Family Relations, 47,* 167–175.

Gordon, T. (1975). *Parent Effectiveness Training.* Berkenfield, NJ: Penguin.

Guerney, B., and Maxson, P. (1990). Marital and family enrichment research: A decade review and look ahead. *Journal for Marriage and the Family, 52*, 1127–1135.

Harmin, D., and Brim, L. G., Jr. (1980). *Learning to Be Parents: Principles, Programs, and Methods.* Beverly Hills, CA: Sage.

Hildreth, G. J., and Sugawara, A. I. (1993). Ethnicity and diversity in family life education. In M. E. Arcus, J. D. Schvaneveldt, and J. J. Moss (Eds.), *Handbook of Family Life Education: Foundations of Family Life Education,* Vol. 1(162–188). Newbury Park, CA: Sage.

Hof, L., and Miller, W. R. (1980). Marriage enrichment. *Marriage and Family Review, 3*, 1–27.

Jim, E., and Suen, P. (1990). *Chinese Parents and Teenagers in Canada: Transitions and Conflicts.* Vancouver, BC: Canadian Mental Health Association.

Kirkendall, L. A. (1973). Marriage and family living, education for. In A. Ellis and A. Abarbanel (Eds.), *The Encyclopedia of Sexual Behavior,* 2nd ed. (696–704). New York: Hawthorne.

Levant, R. F., and Kelly, J. (1989). *Between Father and Child.* New York: Penguin.

Lewis-Rowley, M., Brasher, R. E., Moss, J. J., Duncan, S. F., and Stiles, R. J. (1993). The evolution of education for family life. In M. E. Arcus, J. D. Schvaneveldt, and J. J. Moss (Eds.), *Handbook of Family Life Education: The Foundations of Family Life Education,* Vol. 1 (26–50). Newbury Park, CA: Sage.

Mace, D., and Mace, V. (1986). The history and present status of the marriage and family enrichment movement. In W. Denton (Ed.), *Marriage and Family Enrichment* (7–18). New York: Haworth.

Meyers, S. A. (1993). Adapting parent education programs to meet the needs of fathers: An ecological perspective. *Family Relations, 42*, 447–452.

Miller, S., Nunnally, E. W., and Wackman, D. B. (1979). *Couple Communication I: Talking Together.* Minneapolis: Interpersonal Communication Program.

Olson, D., Fournier, D., and Druckman, J. (1982). *PREPARE.* Minneapolis: PREPARE/ENRICH.

Popkin, M. (1989). Active parenting: A video-based program. In M. J. Fine (Ed.), *The Second Handbook on Parent Education: Contemporary Perspectives* (77–98). San Diego, CA: Academic Press.

Powell, D. R., Zambrana, R., and Silva-Palacios, V. (1990). Designing culturally responsive parent programs: A comparison of low-income Mexican and Mexican-American mothers' preferences. *Family Relations, 39*, 298–304.

Price, S. J., and Burnett, C. K. (1993). *The Remarriage Inventory Profiles Handbook and Instrument.* Chapel Hill, NC: Intercommunication Publishing.

The Rural and Appalachian Youth and Families Consortium. (1996). Parenting practices and interventions among marginalized families in Appalachia. *Family Relations, 45*, 387–315.

Salts, C. (1989). Group therapy for divorced adults. In M. Textor (Ed.), *The Divorce and Divorce Therapy Handbook* (285–300). Northvale, NJ: Jason Aronson.

Silverman, P. R. (1977). Widowhood and preventive intervention. In S. H. Zarit (Ed.), *Readings in Aging and Death: Contemporary Perspectives* (175–182). New York: Harper and Row.

Stahmann, R., and Hiebert, W. (1987). *Premarital Counseling: The Professional's Handbook,* 2nd ed. Lexington, MA: Lexington.

Stahmann, R. F., and Salts, C. J. (1993). Educating for marriage and intimate relationships. In M. E. Arcus, J. D. Schvaneveldt, and J. J. Moss (Eds.), *Handbook for Family Life Education: The Practice of Family Life Education,* Vol. 2 (33–61). Newbury Park, CA: Sage.

Stanley, S. M., Markman, J. H., St. Peters, M., and Leger, B. D. (1995). Strengthening marriages and preventing divorce: New directions in prevention research. *Family Relations, 44*, 392–401.

Ulrici, D., L'Abate, L., and Wagner, V. (1981). The E-R-A model: A heuristic framework for classification of skill training programs for couples and families. *Family Relations, 30*, (307–315).

Wampler, K. S. (1990). An update of research on the Couple Communication Program. *Family Science Review, 3*, 21–40.

Wood, B. (1987). Survival KIT for the holidays: A grief workshop approach. *Family Relations, 36*, 235–241. ✦

Chapter 16
Family Systems in Flux

Clinical Implications for Life Course Transitions

Suzanne Bartle-Haring
Roy A. Bean
Tina Bedell
Benjamin J. Perry
Ohio State University

It is important for marriage and family therapists or other mental health professionals, to have a way of thinking about families in order to be able to "diagnose" the families that are struggling with life course transitions. The goal of this chapter, therefore, is to offer a conceptualization of families and how they manage life course transitions. A theory or conceptualization must be broad enough to encompass as many families as possible, and providing a theory that is applicable to families regardless of their ethnicity, sexual orientation, or structure (intact, divorced, remarried) is certainly a formidable task. In the following pages we will introduce some general concepts to organize your understanding and our discussion of family development and families in transition. To illustrate the kinds of difficulties that families experience at transition points, we will use the more common types of transitions that families experience and provide suggestions for intervening and helping families negotiate each type.

With just a quick glance at the most recent issues of two of the leading family science journals, *Journal of Marriage and the Family* and *Family Relations*, it is evident that as a field we continue to be interested in the complexities of family transitions. The topics of the articles include caregiving for an elderly parent, caring for disabled individuals, parenting, premarital relationships as couples move toward commitment, adult children's relationship with parents, the effect of physical illness on marital quality, divorce and intergenerational relationships, teen parenthood, early adulthood and attitudes toward childbearing and marriage, the transition to a sibling birth, and children leaving home. All these topics represent a transition point or a change in status for both individuals and families. Any change in status has an accompanying transition period during which individuals and families adapt to necessary changes for functioning in their new status.

It has also been suggested that transitions are one of the most popular topics of research in family studies (Elder 1991). Instead of concentrating on families in particular stages of the life cycle, researchers have shifted their focus to how families move from one stage to the next, exploring such topics as the timing, smoothness, and duration of the transition. Carter and McGoldrick (1988) suggest that family stresses during these transition periods frequently create disruptions to the family that may lead to symptoms and dysfunction. These authors also suggest that such stresses have a continuing impact on families over a long time period. That is, if a disruption occurs in the family because of a life cycle transition (such as transition to parenthood), the disruption may create a "ripple effect" over many years, not just during the transition.

Conceptual Framework: Family System Distance Regulation

We view families as systems and use systems theory concepts to describe the process of distance regulation for families in transition (Broderick 1993). A *family system* is made up of elements or, in this case, family members. Families have a property known as *wholeness,* in which the whole is greater than the sum of its parts (Bertalanffy 1968). As marriage and family therapists, we think about families as more than just a group of individuals tied together by biological, legal, or emotional bonds. Family members stand in relation to one another, so that change in any one person will influence change in all the others.

Although all family systems (which include intact families, remarried families, single-parent families, or any other family form) can be characterized as having this wholeness, tremendous variability exists among families. Families are not all characterized by the same sort of relationships among individual family members or between the family and its greater context (school, work, extended family, and other social institutions). The manner in which family members interact with one another (who talks with whom, who talks for whom, what children can and cannot say, and so on) and how the family relates to its greater context (who is considered a part of "the family") reflect the family's *boundaries.* Boundaries allow information into and out of the family system and lie on a continuum from nonpermeable to highly permeable.

In the same way that gasoline provides the energy for an automobile engine, information is energy for a family system. Children bring information in from the outside, perhaps by talking about what they learned in school or what they did with their friends, or simply by behaving in a particular way that may be different from how they behaved in the past. That information enters the family system, it is processed, and a determination is made as to whether the family needs to respond to the child in a different way. As information is allowed into the family system, the system receives the energy necessary to keep going, because without information or energy the system would die, just like a car engine would stop without gasoline. A family system is believed to have one primary goal, *viability.* Consequently, with new information entering the family from the outside, or the environment/context, the family system learns what it needs to adapt and survive.

As we have mentioned, the permeability of boundaries falls on a continuum, so that some families have highly permeable boundaries whereas others have more rigid boundaries. Those families with highly permeable boundaries may find that any piece of new information leads to some change in response—some new way of being or behaving in relation to their environment. Other families with more rigid boundaries may find that a great deal of new information is necessary to lead to a change in their typical pattern of responding to their environment. The process through which a change in the system's response occurs is known as *feedback.* There are two kinds of feedback: *change-inhibiting* feedback, which suppresses change, and *change-promoting* feedback, which leads to change.

It is helpful to think of the feedback process in families as occurring in loops—actually, endless loops. Information is entered into the system, it is processed, and the system's response to that information (which could be no response) is determined. When the system's response is enacted, it in turn generates a reaction from within/without the system. This then becomes additional information for the system, and another response may be determined. In this complex process, it is essential that the family system know when to change and when not to change if it is to survive and maintain its viability. The family thus has to have a way to be able to watch itself, so to speak. Broderick (1993) proposed that families have a *monitoring function* that allows them to be self-reflective—to think about who they are as a whole, and where they are headed.

Jerry is 14; his brother, Mike, is 12; and their sister, Kate, is 9. Their parents, Michele (34) and Tom (36), both work at the brake production facility for Ford. Jerry has asked several times whether he could get his ear pierced, because many of his friends have pierced ears and so does his favorite heavy metal rock band. Jerry has gotten in trouble with these friends, and his parents are not happy with the crowd he is hanging around. They have said no to the earring. Today, he came home after school with a pierced ear and a diamond stud earring. When his parents returned from work, Jerry was in his room playing video games. They found out about the earring at dinner.

The presence of Jerry's earring is a new piece of information for this family, and it sets the system's monitoring function in motion. When this new piece of information is first analyzed by the family system, several outcomes are possible. It could instigate a change in family functioning, or it could be a part of a preexisting process that does not need to be changed. For example, if Jerry's family has rigid boundaries, this piece of information may be put into a change-inhibiting feedback loop, so that he may be asked or forced to remove the earring. If Jerry's family has more permeable boundaries, this piece of information may be put into a change-promoting feedback loop, so that his new look is embraced and others in the family are encouraged to find their own "look" as well. In other families, this piece of information may be deemed "not important enough" to pay attention to, and no changes in family behavior would result.

Whatever the family system's response, once the primary decision is set into motion, it becomes information for the system to monitor and to make more decisions about. Thus, if Jerry's parents force him to remove the earring, he may not agree with the system's response. This could prompt a fairly violent reaction on his part (he kicks a hole in his bedroom door), which he has never done before. In turn, this is new information for the family system and needs to be analyzed so a decision can be made about what to do about his reaction.

The Balancing of Separateness and Connectedness

The combination of the concepts of *wholeness, boundaries,* and *feedback* contributes to a process called *distance regulation.* By distance, we mean the continuum from *closeness* to *separateness* or *autonomy.* Families all show some combination of closeness to, and separateness from, each other. Also, families have characteristic ways of regulating distances among their mem-

bers and with other systems, such as extended family, schools, work, and so on (Anderson and Sabatelli 1992). Families can promote closeness among their members; distance to other systems, or distance among their members; and closeness to other systems, or to some systems and not others. The process of distance regulation varies across families, but we propose that families are effective or functional when their distance-regulating patterns allow members to feel a sense of connection to each other and to the family as a whole as well as a sense of autonomy or independence that allows them to be individuals in the family (Anderson and Sabatelli 1995).

When individual members of a family have a balanced sense of connection and autonomy, it is believed that they will develop optimally. The balance between connectedness and separateness can vary across families within different contexts as well as across a family's life cycle (Combrink-Graham 1983). There is no one correct combination of connectedness and separateness for all families, or for every situation in which a family finds itself. Finding and maintaining a balance is a dynamic process, as it may shift toward more connectedness during certain periods as in particular contexts, or toward more separateness in other situations. This dynamic balance is sometimes referred to as *homeostasis,* or dynamic equilibrium.

To better illustrate a system's homeostasis, consider the classic example of a thermostat. A thermostat is set so that when the temperature goes below a certain degree, the heater will come on. Then, when the temperature gets above a certain degree, the heater shuts off. Thus, the temperature in a room rarely stays the same because it fluctuates between a lower and an upper threshold. The thermostat is the governor or monitor of the temperature, and it gives the commands for change (turn on/turn off).

Like a thermostat, the family system has a monitoring function that allows it to know when it has reached its upper or lower thresholds. In this case, the thresholds are represented by the family's preference levels for autonomy and connection. For families to know when or how to negotiate a new equilibrium point, however, their distance regulation process must include a monitoring function that can view the family as a whole over time and that has rules about when to change the upper and lower thresholds (Broderick 1993). The typical thermostat doesn't offer this function. Most heating systems can't tell when it has gotten warmer outside and switch to the air conditioner. Families, however, have to have this ability in order to survive in their ever-changing environment. Families need to have rules—about changing the rules, and even rules about changing the rules about changing the rules by which they regulate closeness and distance within the whole and with the outside world. These rules are rarely explicit, but they can be seen by observing family interaction over time. At one level, there are rules that say who can speak with whom and what can be said. At the next level, there are rules about when rules can be broken. At still another level, there are rules about when rules should be changed. And at a still higher level, there are rules about the rules about when rules should be changed.

In the example of Jerry and his earring, let us suppose it is now dinnertime in this household, and mom and dad have just noticed the earring. They both get angry, and a heated argument ensues. If the family system has analyzed this interaction as new information that goes beyond the upper threshold for a child's "different" or independent behavior, it now has to make a choice. The family may decide to continue as before and perhaps discipline Jerry for doing something outside the family's rules of typical behavior, or the family may decide to shift the upper and lower thresholds for a child's "different" behavior. This would then lead them to accept the earring and come up with a new balance of autonomy and connection as a family, while allowing Jerry to assert his independence and personal freedom.

Distance Regulation Over the Life Cycle

Using a systemic perspective of the family, it is difficult to predict just what might create a need to make a shift in distance regula-tion. The context within which the family functions, the family's history, and current ways of regulating distance all influence whether a particular "event" will necessitate a shift in distance regulation. Combrink-Graham (1983) suggests that the dynamic balance looks like a helix across time. During the early part of a couple's relationship, there is a balance toward more connectedness. When an infant child is added, the balance shifts toward more connectedness in the parent-child relationships and more separateness (usually) for the parent-parent relationship. As the child grows, the balance shifts toward more separateness, until the child moves out and has children of his or her own, and the parents begin to age. Then there is a shift in the balance toward more connectedness as grandparents want to enjoy their grandchildren and as adult children assume more responsibility for their parents. The same would be true in a single-parent family where the parent-child relationship would lean toward more connectedness, whereas the parent's relationships with other adults may lean toward more separateness until the child begins to grow and the same processes occur. The key to surviving and thriving is the family system's ability to shift the balance when necessary. Thus, families in transitions need to be able to know when it is time to shift the balance and how best to shift the balance to a new equilibrium point (which may mean more separateness or more connectedness or more of both).

Anderson and Sabatelli (1995) suggest that during each of the transitions or life cycle stages, the family must accomplish certain tasks, with the majority of them centering on distance regulation. Jerry's family, for example, is dealing with the transition to adolescence. During adolescence, families need to renegotiate relationships and allow for more autonomy and responsibility on the part of the adolescent. This renegotiation process requires shifts in parenting practices, as well as in the way separateness and connectedness are balanced in relationship to the child and probably between the two parents. Ultimately, the system must recalibrate its thresholds for autonomy on the part of an offspring and find new ways of connecting with the adolescent.

Donna and Joe have been married for two years and recently had their first child. They are finding this period to be stressful because of the demands placed on their relationship. Joe is feeling as if he is being neglected and sometimes resents Donna's focus on the new baby. Donna is feeling fatigued and sometimes resentful that Joe is not involved with the parenting to the degree that she had anticipated.

This couple is in a life cycle transition known as the transition to parenthood, but they also are continuing to adjust to each other in their marital relationship. In their adjustment, they have created particular interaction patterns and ways of monitoring those patterns. The patterns are fairly flexible in that new pieces of information can be processed, and minor adjustments can be made when necessary without causing stress. The upper and lower thresholds for "different" are set at adequate levels.

However, now a third member of this family has arrived. Infants require intensive care and tend not to fall into sleeping and eating patterns that are particularly convenient for the adults in the family. The presence of the infant is a "big" piece of information that this couple system must accommodate, and it is likely that the system's thresholds for autonomy and connection will have to be shifted or renegotiated. For some couples, the introduction of this information could result in a change-inhibiting feedback loop because they will try to maintain their same patterns of distance regulating despite the arrival of their new baby. This information continues to feed back into the system, and symptoms may begin to occur. For example, if the couple wants to maintain the same late hours or active schedule that they had before the baby was born, the infant may suffer for lack of attention and care, or the parents may suffer for lack of sleep. On the other hand, the arrival of the infant may prompt a change-promoting feedback loop. The couple may start to change their patterns of interaction to include the baby and his or her needs, but in so doing, they may find that they are "drifting apart." The baby is being

well cared for, the parents are getting as much sleep as they can, but they are not talking to each other as much or as intimately as before the baby's birth.

Changes in family life are inevitable because of such factors as the birth of children, the maturation of youth, departure of young adults, and the death of family members. This atmosphere of change suggests that the family system should be flexible yet, at the same time, have a certain degree of continuity and coherence. This illustrates the need for balancing both change-inhibiting and change-promoting feedback, because a family's survival is based on its ability to accommodate these two different and sometimes opposing concepts. If Donna and Joe can work out this balance, their pattern of interaction will change to fully include the child, and his or her needs will be met. At the same time, they will preserve aspects of how they interacted prior to the baby's arrival, which will allow for the continued health of the marital relationship.

Consider a similar example within a different context and different couple. Let's suppose that a gay couple adopts a child. The couple's union is seen as "deviant" in this society, and they may receive little support from their families of origin. Because they are two men, they also receive little employer support for taking parental leave, even though by law, they are entitled to it. To make matters more difficult, only one of the men can legally adopt the child, because legally children can have only one father. Thus, the other man is not legally related to the child. This context creates a different set of burdens on this three-member system. This couple has found a way of interacting as the previous couple has, but their distance-regulating patterns have incorporated other contextual issues such as not showing affection in public, not telling people that they live together, and so on. Thus, this system may have a rigid boundary around it. The boundaries within the system may be more permeable. The dedication and commitment it takes to adopt a child may have already altered the distance-regulating functions in this couple, but the presence of the child will probably create a need for a shift as well.

As you can see, the concept of distance regulation can be used in a variety of contexts and situations. All families, regardless of their particular membership and form, inevitably encounter events or situations that necessitate a shift in distance regulation to avoid or correct problems, and some families seek professional assistance in dealing with these events or transition points. Family problems often have something to do with the way the family is negotiating a particular transition or has failed to negotiate a past transition (Walsh 1983). Indeed, one of the first things to consider when working with a family is whether the family system is providing for the intimacy and autonomy needs of its members. If this is not happening, then more than likely the family is struggling with a life cycle transition or a change in status.

Transition Points: Presenting Problems and Clinical Guidelines

One of the other "trademarks" of being marriage and family therapists is the perspective we bring to symptoms or presenting problems. First, we view problems or dysfunctions as symptoms of the system, not simply of the individual(s) who may be exhibiting the symptoms. Second, we view symptoms as "functional"—that is, they serve a purpose for the system. From the outset, the purpose of most symptoms is to regulate distance within the system. In Jerry's family, for example, his rebellion may be considered the symptom or problem, at least by his parents. If Jerry's family came into therapy, the therapist might observe that when Jerry behaves in this way, both parents work together to resolve the issue. When Jerry does not behave in ways that are too "different," his parents appear distant and uninvolved with each other. One parent may also appear to be less involved with the child, whereas the other seems to be more involved. Thus, Jerry's earring may function to pull the parents together to work on the problem. Jerry's problem thus becomes the system's distance regulator.

It is our contention that the incomplete or inadequate transitioning of families can manifest itself in a number of ways, whether in the form of a parent's or a teen's presenting problems. Problems of all types can be seen as evidence that a change is needed in the system, either toward greater autonomy or toward greater connection. Alexander and Parsons (1982) contend that individual behavior needs to be examined in a context of family relationships. In fact, they suggest that problem behavior can be seen as the vehicle for the family to bring about distance (autonomy) or intimacy (connection) between its members. The problem can be seen as the system's "ingenious solution" to the dilemma of balancing separateness and connectedness at that particular point in the family's life cycle.

For example, substance abuse can often become a problem during adolescence. There is evidence to suggest that the substance abuse is a "solution" for the adolescent's emerging sense of identity and individuality in families where this is seen as a threat to connectedness (Stanton 1979). Drug use and its accompanying culture allow the adolescent some sense of separateness from the family. The drug dependence, however, also leaves the adolescent in a dependent state in the family. The adolescent becomes the "sick one" and needs to stay connected to the family.

To further demonstrate the broad application of this theory of family transitions, we spend the remaining portion of this chapter focusing on general guidelines for intervening in families struggling with transitions as well as with certain "pivotal" events in their life cycle. The events that we address here are those that have received the greatest research attention: (a) the transition to parenthood (e. g., Michaels and Goldberg 1988), (b) the emerging adolescence of a child (e. g., Baumrind 1991), (c) a child's moving away from home (e. g., White and Edwards 1990), and (d) a family member's retirement (e. g., Carter and Cook 1995). Our focus on these particular events should not be construed as ignorance or dismissal of the impact of such transitional events as marriage, remarriage, or the illness or death of a family member. It should also be noted that most of the available research tends to be biased toward white, middle-class, intact families. These same events do occur in families of all ethnic groups and structures, but we know little about their life cycle transitions.

General Guidelines and Rituals

Several general guidelines are applicable, regardless of the particular event, when helping families navigate the challenges of life cycle transitions. For example, it has been suggested that most families cannot return to normal functioning simply by making a small, relatively quick change. A family's problems have developed over time. Distance regulation is a complicated and somewhat unpredictable process; therefore, the therapist and the family should be realistic about the rate and extent of change.

The struggle in accomplishing the tasks of a particular transition may not have an impact in the immediate situation but may be felt later on in the life cycle, perhaps when the child becomes an adolescent or even when that child becomes a parent. A family's ability to navigate the challenges of launching, for instance, is influenced by their history in negotiating distance regulation. Consequently, a careful assessment of past transitions may be necessary, as well as a better understanding of the experience that the adult family members had in their own families-of-origin during the same life cycle transitions.

With the transition to a new life cycle stage comes the inevitable regret or sadness for what is left behind in the previous stage (Breunlin 1983). Depending on the situation, it may be important and entirely appropriate to mourn the losses of the previous stage before moving on to tackle the new stage. Many families do this naturally as they reminisce about the "good old days" before life became involved in full-time parenting or before the children left home.

When families do seem to need help in "closing the door" on one stage before being able to make a successful transition to the next one, it may be helpful to use a ceremony or customized ritual to mark the transition event. Therapists should take care in working with a family to develop a ritual that is meaningful and salient to the family, given their particular situation. Where available, the ritual should reflect the cultural, ethnic, or religious rites of passages or images already available to the family (Imber-Black 1988). Rituals can help make the implicit portion of family functioning more explicit, but only to the degree that the family personalizes the ritual and invests time and energy into planning it. Some examples include having a funeral or a going away party for the life stage that they are leaving, celebrating parenthood by having a pregnancy or postbirth party with friends and family, and making up survival kits for both the children who are leaving home and the parents who are not. A rite of passage to mark the maturation or achievement of family members is especially important for the transitions that are experienced but not celebrated as "graduation events," such as the launching of children and the arrival at adolescence. Rituals should be made to fit the characteristics of the family and its members.

In the next section, we describe several of the more "normative" life cycle events that are accompanied by a period of transition in which a change in status occurs. As we address each transition, we will discuss several points, including (a) the common difficulties or presenting problems of families at each stage, (b) the explanation for these problems from our perspective of distance regulation, and (c) guidelines for intervening and helping the family achieve a more acceptable balance of connection and autonomy.

Parenthood

The diversity that exists among first-time parents is endless. There are young single mothers who became pregnant accidentally, and there are single mothers and fathers by choice, by divorce, and by death of a partner. There are young couples who married because of a pregnancy, couples having their first child later in their lives, couples in second or third marriages having their first child together, and couples from all ethnic and religious backgrounds. The context within which the transition to parenthood occurs has considerable influence on how easily the family adjusts its patterns of distance regulation. Unfortunately, our knowledge of these diverse contexts is quite limited and most of the research available on the transition to parenthood is about white, middle-class, intact couples.

Regardless of the diversity of the context, however, all new parents have some common tasks to accomplish such as altering the family identity, renegotiating relationship boundaries (within the couple, with family and friends), rebalancing the boundary between work and family, and managing added household tasks and new areas of conflict (Anderson and Sabatelli 1995). When couples or single parents struggle with any of these new tasks, a disruption in the transition can occur, which may result in symptoms either in the parent(s) or in the child or both.

With the birth of a baby, a couple, such as Donna and Joe, faces challenges to their established pattern of negotiating the tasks of connectedness and autonomy. Determining the appropriate connection-autonomy balance between two people in any given situation is not a simple process, and with the inclusion of a third family member, the result is an even greater challenge. Where there was only one relationship to monitor in a two-parent family, there are now three (parent to parent, parent to child, and the other parent to child).

The couple's difficulty in adjusting to parenthood can be manifest in any number of presenting problems. Reasons for consulting a marriage and family therapist may include depression, anxiety over the increased responsibilities, conflict over the division of labor, concerns over a decline in marital satisfaction, or less individual and couple free time (Cowan, Cowan, Coie, and Coie 1978).

One adjustment for new parents is the lack of free time (LaRossa and LaRossa 1981). Infants require constant or continuous supervision by one or more caretakers, so time that may have been spent relaxing or recreating must now include the baby. For couples who emphasized autonomy and personal freedom in the past, the responsibility of continuous care can be very troubling, perhaps to the point where one or both exhibits signs of stress or mild depression.

Other problems that may be found in families struggling with this transition can be considered to be relationship focused. First, couples often report a decline in marital satisfaction because they have less time for each other and greater workloads (Grossman, Eichler, and Winickoff 1980). Marital satisfaction can also be affected by a couple's movement toward more traditional gender roles (Cowan and Cowan 1985). Many women quit jobs or take maternity leave to care for their newborns, which may force the other partner to work longer hours to compensate for the change in income. This arrangement may push couples, even those who have had very egalitarian relationships, toward more traditional gender roles.

Second, with greater gender divisions in child care and other household responsibilities, the primary caretaker (usually the mother) often has a much stronger emotional bond with the baby than the other parent. This imbalance is to be expected if one parent spends considerably more time with the child, but it can still lead to symptoms or problems among family members. For example, the lack of personal and couple time combined with inadequate sleep can be related to depressive feelings for caregivers. The depression, while worrisome, can be considered as a part of the system's attempt to regain a balance between connection and autonomy for the family. Grossman and associates found that (middle-class) fathers were more likely to be involved with their children if the mother was unavailable as a result of depression or caesarean recovery or if she scored higher on a measure of autonomy during pregnancy (Grossman et al. 1980; Grossman, Pollack, and Golding 1988). This suggests that when the wife's depression is a presenting problem, it may be the system's way of renegotiating the family distance regulation. In other words, where the depression can be seen as a symptom of the mother not having enough time to herself or with her partner, it also serves a function by getting the partner (father) more involved in child care.

In terms of clinical guidelines, a number of avenues can be taken to help families deal with the challenges and problems outlined here. For instance, the therapist can encourage the couple to work out a way for the primary caretaker to get some more free time, which will not only allow for his/her greater autonomy but provide the other partner with time to form a closer bond with the child. It is important to consider that, when faced with the changes in their marital relationship and their lack of confidence in caring for a baby, some fathers choose to focus on the one duty that has been traditionally defined for them: financially providing for the family. Unfortunately, this practice perpetuates the likelihood that fathers will remain underexperienced in child care, because as they work more at their occupation, they deny themselves the contact with their children needed for them to become more knowledgeable and confident.

In these instances, it may be helpful to assign the father (or the partner who feels the least competent) a particular task to help him or her gain some confidence and "expertise" in a specific area of child care. The second author received a great sense of accomplishment after he gave his daughter her first bath in the hospital with the assistance of a nurse. It was a confidence builder to be entrusted with the care of his daughter mere minutes after her birth and to be able to pass that bathing knowledge on to his wife. This experience helped reduce some of the anxiety about infant care, gave him some professional instruction, and allowed for an emotional bond to begin to form between him and his daughter.

In general, self-education through reading and talking with other families can play a key role in resolving concerns and unrealistic expectations. When new parents can educate themselves by reading books and speaking with close friends and family who have had children, they are more likely to form realistic expectations of what it will be like.

Adolescence

Kathleen and Jim have been married 20 years and have two children, Jennifer, age 16, and Jason, age 15. Both children have been good students and are active in school activities. Recently, however, Jason has been associating with a new group of friends and is becoming increasingly secretive and withdrawn from the family. Kathleen and Jim are concerned that Jason may be involved in drugs and have decided to seek family therapy.

The emerging adolescence of children is often dreaded by families. As a society, we tend to believe that adolescence is a time of conflict with parents and upheaval in the lives of families. This is not always the case; in fact, it is more the exception than the rule (Offer, Ostrov, and Howard 1981). What does appear to occur during adolescence is that friends and peers become more important, which increases the likelihood that family systems will have to deal with information not previously considered or experienced. Of course, the influence of peers, friends, and school authorities can be felt well before the onset of adolescence, but during adolescence these other environmental factors play a greater role in the teen's negotiation of a desired level of connection and autonomy.

Adolescence is a period of increased anxiety for many families as teens work to establish a sense of self, a set of life goals, and meaningful relationships with peers and family. In this process, teens often vacillate between a desire for adult-like rights and responsibilities (autonomy) and the more familiar position of being cared for and protected by parents (connection). This can be a worrisome time for parents, as well, as they watch their children negotiate the challenges of self-discovery and definition.

One of the myths about adolescence is that it is a time when family is no longer important (Youniss 1983). Most research would suggest, however, that adolescence is a time to renegotiate the parent-child relationship so that it becomes less hierarchical and moves toward more equality in order to accommodate the teen's maturation (Youniss 1983). During this life stage the adolescent's increased cognitive abilities allow for a challenge to the family's rules or traditions. Adolescents may want to debate rules and policies. At this point, it is important for parents to agree on what rules and policies they are willing to consistently enforce and which ones may need to be altered. This provides children with strong models for adult behavior and also removes parents from power struggles with their adolescent children. When a family is unable to adjust its upper and lower thresholds for autonomy and intimacy, problems can develop, such as substance abuse, eating disorders, suicide, delinquency, and so forth.

Adolescence prompts a renegotiation not only in the parent-child relationship but in the family's other relationships as well. Thus, adolescence may be a time when parents need to renegotiate their own relationship. With the maturation of their children, they may have more discretion over their free time and may have expectations about how they will be spending that time. Similarly, for the single parent, this life cycle transition may prompt a need to renegotiate relationships with support systems and social networks.

When working with families with adolescents, it is important to consider several important guidelines drawn from the work of Alexander and Parsons (1982). First, as with most models of therapy, it is important to establish a therapeutic relationship with the family. At every transition point, therapists may be presented with issues that challenge their ability to establish a working relationship with families, but the challenge is probably at its greatest when treating families in this life stage. Younger therapists may have a better chance of relating to and engaging the adolescent, but the therapist's youth may prompt the parents to question his or her ability to relate to their own situation. On the other hand, an older therapist who is well past this transition may make the parents feel confident and comfortable but may be alienating for the teen. It can be a difficult process to balance the different goals, values, and developmental levels of both parents and children, but this is one of the most fundamental aspects of treating families in this life stage.

Another important guideline, drawn from the Functional Family Therapy (FFT) model, is that the therapist should examine the relational context of the problem behavior(s). By understanding the types of family interactions that typically precede and follow an incident (fighting, suicide threat or attempt, shoplifting), the therapist can theorize regarding the distance-regulating functions of the problem behavior. The therapist can help the family see that they are headed in the right direction but that they may need to change a few things to move forward. This approach can be helpful in getting the focus off the identified patient and onto the family's need for a better method of reaching their goals of balancing separateness and connectedness.

When treatment objectives allow the function to continue but in a more acceptable fashion, the teen can experience an increase in autonomy while maintaining a connection to the family. At the same time, parents can adjust their relationships to meet their needs without inappropriately involving their children. In simplified fashion, once the family recognizes that they need a different way of negotiating the distance-regulation process, they are ready for what FFT calls the education phase of treatment. During this phase, families are taught communication and problem-solving skills to provide them with alternative methods of interacting and negotiating the autonomy/connection balance.

During the time between the a child's birth and adolescence, the family makes countless adjustments in distance regulation. Consequently, a family's success at negotiating the transition to adolescence may have little to do with the family's situation at that time. If the parents and children have good relationships during the childhood and preteen years, the family is more likely to be able to work things out when a child reaches adolescence.

Launching of Children

The successful launching of children is seen as the primary goal for most families. In most cases, children do leave home, and couples find that they have other activities and satisfactions to look forward to. There is evidence that marital and general life satisfaction sharply increase with the last child's departure from the home (White and Edwards 1990). Menaghan (1983) also found that launching may have a positive influence on marriages, as the equity between husbands and wives was found to increase in the period after the youngest child has left home. However, children may give couples something they can connect to when they otherwise have little in common. When the children are no longer at home to occupy their time, the partners may be less tolerant of their incompatibilities and frustrations with each other.

The distance-regulation process continues to be applicable to this life cycle transition in that couples must adjust to greater opportunities for intimacy and time together. On the other hand, parents do not stop being parents just because their children live somewhere else, so it is advisable for counselors to assess the relationship that they have with their children. This is especially important given the finding that older adults' general life satisfaction is higher when they have contact with their nonresident children (White and Edwards 1990). It is also advisable and may become crucial in reaching treatment goals to invite the whole family into a session.

As children depart from the home and begin to form their own lives, the family must change how they handle the distance-regulation process among adult family members. What the parents want should be balanced with the autonomy needs of the launched children, so that the child's continued development is balanced with the parents' need for a connection with their son or daughter. Alexander and Parsons (1982) give the example of families in which marital or other problems in the adult child's life serve as an excuse for parent(s) and child to get together and enjoy a connection at the expense of the child's other, more appropriate relationships.

Considering the investment that parents make in their children, love and loyalty toward their children is to be expected, but in some cases parents may interfere with the growth of their children because they still want the same closeness they felt when the children were living at home. In these situations, there may be a subtle push or insistence that the child "come home" when difficulty arises rather than try to work things out on their own.

The general lack of research regarding the transition to an "empty nest" makes it somewhat difficult to provide guidelines for treating families at this life stage. Nevertheless, with the parent or couple, the therapist should investigate expectations and planned activities for life without the children in the house. This investigation will allow for a discussion of what parents will do with their time and energy now that they no longer have children residing with them. Unrealistic expectations and discrepancies in expectations will need to be examined and resolved so that the couple can get what they want out of their relationship, whether or not it entails a change in the balance of autonomy and connection. Single parents can also be encouraged to find satisfaction in other life pursuits. Although divorce is less likely among older couples, therapists should be aware that one partner may have been waiting until the children left to seek divorce.

Retirement

Arnett and Barbara have had successful careers and have recently retired. Both assumed that retirement would be an enjoyable period and that they would spend more time with each other, their children, and their grandchildren. They are finding, however, that they miss work, and Barbara, in particular, feels she has lost a major source of her identity. Furthermore, Barbara and Arnett are experiencing increased interpersonal conflict as a result of Arnett expecting Barbara to assume a more traditional role in relation to household responsibilities.

Although the majority of American adults have spent their lives at work, the meaning that they give to work differs. For some, work was a career, whereas for others it was "just a job." The value and importance that a person places on work has a great deal to do with his or her adjustment to retirement. Atchley (1975) contends that individuals organize their life goals in a hierarchy, ranging from most important to least important. Success in adjusting to retirement is more likely when work goals do not have the highest priority or when retirees were able to meet their goals prior to retirement. Other factors predictive of better adjustment in this transition are (1) the modeling of retirement done by one's own parents through planning of finances and postretirement activities, and (2) continued attention to learning and education (Adair and Mowsesian 1993; MacEwen, Barling, Kelloway, and Higginbottoms 1995).

Regardless of the particular situation, retirement can create losses as well as new options for families, as the case in all life cycle transitions. Certainly, the context within which this loss occurs will affect how the distance-regulating function shifts in the system. For those who have been employed their entire adult life in a career they found rewarding, retirement may represent a major loss of identity (Carter and Cook 1995). The individual must renegotiate identity and, with that, relationships with family and friends. These changes may go beyond the distance-regulation thresholds for behaviors that were previously set in the family system. Individuals who went to work for eight or more hours a day now have no particular place to go, and how they spend their time will have a major impact on how their partner spends his or her time. Does the couple renegotiate their relationship so that they spend more time together? Do they continue to keep their distance from 9 to 5 while spending time together in the evening? Do they travel more, see their children more often, or decide to take care of the grandchildren? All these decisions require a shift in distance regulation. If either partner struggles with this new identity, or if the couple struggles with new ways of interacting, symptoms such as marital conflict or depression can arise.

Given the role that activity and learning can have in helping people adjust to retirement (Adair and Mowsesian 1993), it would be important for the therapist to get an idea of the retiree's or couple's typical activities and expectations before and after retirement. Once the therapist understands such things as the nature of the change in activity level, the activities planned for retirement,

the importance that work had for the retiree, and relationship goals for family, he or she can help the couple. If the couple wants an increase in connection, the therapist can help the couple find some activities to share—or more individual activities if they would prefer to maintain a more separate relationship.

Conclusions

For therapists to be truly effective in helping families negotiate life cycle transitions, they must be able to explore and understand the context in which the family and their problems are embedded. Certain families may find it easier to proceed through the transitions because the transitions are clearly marked with religious or cultural ceremonies (Bar Mitzvahs, quinceñeras), whereas for other families, their cultural context may change the transition altogether. For instance, the loss of fulfillment that may be experienced by some stay-at-home mothers at launching is probably a middle-class phenomenom, because poor and working class families often cannot afford to have one parent stay at home until the children have departed from the family home. In addition, among some ethnic or cultural groups, launching is avoided when several generations of the same family live in the same household (McGoldrick 1988). Similarly, retirement may not be a transition of great consequence for some income-level groups, if financial necessity requires them to continue to remain employed at least part time.

By understanding the culture, values, belief systems, and norms that a family utilizes to cope with transitional periods throughout the life cycle, mental health professionals will be better equipped to "diagnose" and formulate culturally relevant ways to help families shift their balance of separateness and connectedness. When working with an African-American family, for instance, it would be important to draw on cultural strengths and resources such as kinship bonds, role flexibility, and religion/spirituality (Bowman 1992). In terms of family therapy, this suggests that extended family, friends, and religious leaders can and should be involved in the treatment of a family's presenting problems.

The challenge of distance regulation is a part of any and all relationships, but difficulties in balancing autonomy and connection are of greatest concern when they take place in couple and family relationships. It is our belief that the theory of distance regulation can help guide the effective treatment and prevention of the many problems that families experience during the transition events in their lives. As therapists assess the family's thresholds for individuality and intimacy among its members, they can use this information to guide the intervention necessary to help the family successfully complete the transition to the next life stage.

Discussion Questions

1. Explain the basic functioning of a family system in terms of boundaries, feedback, and homeostasis.

2. Describe how the illness of one spouse might affect the distance-regulation patterns between the spouses.

3. In terms of distance regulation, why does it make sense for the therapist to help the father gain a sense of confidence in caring for an infant?

4. Is it possible to extend the concept of distance regulation to the relationship between a therapist and a family with an adolescent child? Explain.

5. What are some life cycle issues that would be different for an elderly couple than for a middle-aged couple? How might distance regulation function in these issues?

Glossary

Boundaries Rules about the amount and kind of contact allowable between members of a family system and those outside the family system.

Change-inhibiting feedback Also known as negative feedback; the degree to which family systems minimize change and keep things the same (a mechanism that suppresses change).

Change-promoting feedback Also known as positive feedback; the degree to which change occurs and is accepted by the family system (a mechanism that leads to change).

Distance regulation The process by which families regulate both separateness from each other and outside systems, and closeness to each other and outside systems.

Family system The interdependent parts of a family that make up the structure, organization, and patterns of functioning and the relationships between and among individual members.

Feedback A self-corrective mechanism that serves to temper variations of change to increase the probability of the survival of the system.

Monitoring function A mechanism within the system that allows the system to "see" itself. This mechanism allows the family system to define who it is and how it will function, determining how it will balance separateness and connectedness.

Viability A family system's ability to adapt to and survive change.

Wholeness The idea that change in one element of a family system or in one of the relationships between elements will affect the other elements and relationships that make up the system. Therefore, the whole is greater than the sum of its parts.

Suggested Readings

Anderson, S. A., and Sabatelli, R. M. (1995). *Family Interaction: A Multigenerational Developmental Perspective.* Boston: Allyn and Bacon.

Carter, B., and McGoldrick, M. (Eds.). (1988). *The Changing Family Life Cycle: A Framework for Family Therapy.* New York: Gardner.

Hansen, J. C., and Liddle, H. A. (Eds.). (1983). *Clinical Implications of the Family Life Cycle.* Rockville, MD: Aspen Systems.

Bibliography

Adair, S. R., and Mowsesian, R. (1993). The meanings and motivations of learning during the retirement transition. *Educational Geron-tology, 19,* 317–330.

Alexander, J. F., and Parsons, B. V. (1982). *Functional Family Therapy: Principles and Procedures.* Carmel, CA: Brooks/Cole.

Anderson, S. A., and Sabatelli, R. M. (1992). The differentiation in the Family System Scale. *American Journal of Family Therapy, 20,* 77–89.

Anderson, S. A., and Sabatelli, R. M. (1995). *Family Interaction: A Multigenerational Developmental Perspective.* Boston: Allyn and Bacon.

Atchley, R. C. (1975). Adjustment to loss of job at retirement. *International Journal of Aging and Human Development, 6,* 17–27.

Baumrind, D. (1991). Effective parenting during the early adolescent transition. In P. A. Cowan and M. Hetherington (Eds.), *Family Transitions* (111–164). Hillsdale, NJ: Erlbaum.

Bertalanffy, L. (1968). *General Systems Theory.* New York: George Braziller.

Bowman, P. J. (1992). Coping with provider role strain: Adaptive cultural resources among black husband-fathers. In A. K. H. Burlew, W. C. Banks, H. P. McAdoo, and D. A. Azibo (Eds.), *African-American Psychology: Theory, Research, and Practice* (135–154). Newbury Park, CA: Sage.

Breunlin, D. C. (1983). Therapy in stages: A life cycle view. In J. C. Hansen and H. A. Liddle (Eds.), *Clinical Implications of the Family Life Cycle* (1-11). Rockville, MD: Aspen Systems.

Broderick, C. B. (1993). *Understanding Family Process: Basics of Family Systems Theory.* Newbury Park, CA: Sage.

Carter, B., and McGoldrick, M. (Eds.). (1988). *The Changing Family Life Cycle: A Framework for Family Therapy.* New York: Gardner.

Carter, M. A., and Cook, K. (1995). Adaptation to retirement: Role changes and psychological resources. *The Career Development Quarterly, 44,* 67–82.

Combrink-Graham, L. (1983). The family life cycle and families with young children. In J. C. Hansen and H. A. Liddle (Eds.), *Clinical Implications of the Family Life Cycle* (35–53). Rockville, MD: Aspen Systems.

Cowan, C., and Cowan, P. (1985). Parents' work patterns, marital and parent-child relationships, and early child development. Paper presented at meeting of the Society for Research in Child Development, Toronto.

Cowan, C., Cowan, P., Coie, L., and Coie, J. (1978). Becoming a family: The impact of the first child's birth on the couple's relationship. In W. Miller and L. Newman (Eds.), *The First Child and Family Formation* (296–324). Chapel Hill, NC: Carolina Population Center.

Elder, G. H. (1991). Family transitions, cycles, and social changes. In P. A. Cowan and M. Hetherington (Eds.), *Family Transitions* (31–58). Hillsdale, NJ: Erlbaum.

Grossman, F., Eichler, L., and Winickoff, S., with Anzalone, M., Gofseyeff, M., and Sargent, S. (1980). *Pregnancy, Birth and Parenthood.* San Francisco: Jossey-Bass.

Grossman, F., Pollack, W., and Golding, E. (1988). Fathers and children: Predicting the quality and quantity of fathering. *Developmental Psychology, 24 (1),* 82–91.

Imber-Black, E. (1988). Idiosyncratic life cycle transitions and therapeutic rituals. In B. Carter and M. McGoldrick (Eds.), *The Changing Family Life Cycle: A Framework for Family Therapy* (149–163). New York: Gardner.

Larossa, R., and Laross, M. (1981) *Transition to Parenthood: How Infants Change Families.* Beverly Hills, CA: Sage.

MacEwen, K. E., Barling, J., Kelloway, E. K., and Higginbottoms, S. F. (1995). Predicting retirement anxiety: The roles of parental socialization and personal planning. *Journal of Social Psychology, 135,* 203–213.

McGoldrick, M. (1988). Ethnicity and the family life cycle. In B. Carter and M. McGoldrick (Eds.), *The Changing Family Life Cycle: A Framework for Family Therapy* (69–90). New York: Gardner.

Menaghan, E. (1983). Marital stress and family transitions: A panel analysis. *Journal of Marriage and the Family, 45,* 371–386.

Michaels, G. Y., and Goldberg, W. A. (Eds.). (1988). *The Transition to Parenthood: Current Theory and Research.* New York: Cambridge University.

Offer, D., Ostrov, E., and Howard, K. I. (1981). The mental health professional's concept of the normal adolescent. *Archives of General Psychiatry, 38,* 149–152.

Stanton, M. D. (1979). Family treatment approaches to drug abuse problems: A review. *Family Process, 18,* 251–280.

Walsh, F. (1983). The timing of symptoms and critical events in the family life cycle. In J. C. Hansen and H. A. Liddle (Eds.), *Clinical Implications of the Family Life Cycle* (120–133). Rockville, MD: Aspen Systems.

White, L., and Edwards, J. N. (1990). Emptying the nest and parental well-being: An analysis of national panel data. *American Sociological Review, 55,* 235–242.

Youniss, J. (1983). Social construction of adolescence by adolescents and parents. In H. Grotevant and C. Cooper (Eds.), *Adolescent Development in the Family: No. 22, New Directions in Child Development* (93–109). San Francisco: Jossey-Bass. ✦

Chapter 17

Policy Issues and Families Over the Life Course

Julie K. Kohler
University of Minnesota

Shirley L. Zimmerman
University of Minnesota-Twin Cities

Just as there are many definitions of *family,* there are many definitions of *family policy.* These definitions, which have been the subject of much debate in academic and political circles over the past two decades, have been linked to the debate over "family values" and the role of government in family life. One way that government is involved is through the policies enacted by governing bodies at all levels—federal, state, and local. Although the material presented in this chapter will not address the issues involved in the family values debate or in government's role in family life directly, we hope readers will gain an understanding of these issues through our discussion of policies that affect families at various life stages.

This chapter begins with our definition of family policy and the terminology associated with it. This definition is intended to narrow the scope of this chapter and provide readers with a way of conceptualizing family policy issues. We then present terms that should be useful to students as they begin thinking about the connections between families and government via the policies that are enacted and implemented. Because the

purpose of this book is to provide readers with a profile of important transitions that families experience over their life course, this chapter discusses and reviews important policies that affect families as they (a) form, (b) raise children, and (c) move into their middle and later years. Thus, the chapter is not intended to be an exhaustive review of all the individual family policies that make up family policy as a domain of governmental and nongovernmental activity; rather it illustrates the ways in which various policies affect families as they interact with systems in society: the educational system, the health-care system, the social service system, the workplace, the legal system, and various levels of government. Indeed, we conceptualize families as social systems in interaction with their environment, and we see family policies as the outputs of one of the systems with which families interact: government.

Terminology and Definitions

As we have noted, family policy as a domain is made up of many individual policies that affect families, directly and indirectly. The *family goals* or *objectives* that such policies aim to achieve are sometimes *explicit*— that is, explicitly stated—but most often they are *implicit,* or unstated. Explicit family policies are likely to have *manifest* family content and to obviously relate to families. Implicit family policies lack manifest family content; rather, the family content of such policies tends to be *latent,* or obscure. An example of explicit family policy is federal legislation requiring insurance companies to provide 48 hours instead of only 24 hours of hospital coverage for new mothers and their babies. An example of implicit family policy is state legislation requiring the school attendance of school-aged youth. Appropriation and budget bills are cases of both explicit and implicit family policy in that they contain provisions with both manifest and latent family content.

Regardless of whether they are explicit or implicit, different policies have consequences for families that are both *intended* and *unintended.* Because the family ramifications of implicit family policies generally are not foreseen, their consequences for families generally are unintended. Whether intended or unintended, the consequences of such policies may be positive or negative depending on how such policies are perceived and defined by those families most directly affected by them, by the public at large who may be less directly affected by them, by various interest groups and political elites who have a stake in promoting one particular policy approach over another, and sometimes by researchers attempting to evaluate their effects on families. The possible consequences of implicit family policies usually cannot be anticipated prior to their enactment, because their family connections are often obscure; such consequences can sometimes be foreseen when policies' family goals and objectives are made explicit. For example, the Personal Responsibility and Work Opportunity Act, which was enacted by Congress in 1996, in part to encourage the transition of parents of families receiving welfare to work, could have the unintended consequence of increasing the out-of-home placement of children, because their mothers are working outside the home and unable to care for them. By being able to anticipate such a consequence, researchers and lawmakers can be sensitive to such a possibility and sound warnings to avert its actual occurrence.

The terminology that has been used in analyzing family policies—explicit/implicit, direct/indirect, manifest/latent, and intended/unintended (Kammerman and Kahn 1976)—helps to highlight the multidimensional aspects of policy and suggests that family policy can be defined narrowly or broadly. In its broadest sense, family policy refers to everything that governments do that affect families, directly or indirectly (Zimmerman 1988, 1992, 1995). More narrowly, it refers only to policies that have explicitly stated family goals and objectives. However, because most policies do *not* have stated family goals and objectives or manifest family content (Zimmerman, in progress), defining family policy only in terms of manifest family content or stated family goals and objectives would further obscure

the ways in which many policies affect families over the life course. Just as policy in general attempts to promote the well-being of individuals and social policy attempts to promote the well-being of different groups, family policy attempts to promote the well-being of families. Similarly, just as policy in general is concerned with the problems of individuals in relation to society (Lasswell 1968), and social policy with the problems of different groups (the elderly, children, the poor, etc.) in relation to society (Gil 1973), family policy is concerned with the problems of families in relation to society (Zimmerman 1988, 1992, 1995). In the next section, we will review some of the problems that families encounter in relation to society as they form, raise children, and move into their middle and later years, and some of the policies that aim to address these problems.

Policies Related to Family Formation

Family formation involves the transitions by which two or more individuals form a new family union. Such unions can be formed through a marriage or a nonmarital committed partnership or through the birth or adoption of a child. In this section, we discuss policies that explicitly pertain to problems that some families encounter with respect to both marriage and childbearing—the denial of marriage to lesbian and gay couples and the delayed placement of many adoption-eligible children.

Marriage and the Defense of Marriage Act

Marriage is a cornerstone topic in any discussion of family formation. Marriage has multiple levels of meaning—to individuals, couples, families, and societies—and carries with it certain social and legal rights, responsibilities, and benefits. At a social level, marriage is a public way of validating an intimate relationship and is governed by laws that shape its social definition. These laws extend to income tax deductions, property inheritance rights, social security benefits, the availability of credit, and so forth.

In the United States, states have jurisdiction over who can marry whom. States can establish restrictions pertaining to the ages of the parties involved, the biological relationship of the partners seeking marriage (e.g., whether first cousins are allowed to legally marry), and the sexes of the parties involved. For many gay and lesbian persons, the latter issue has proven to be an obstacle to forming families of their own, ones that are officially and legally recognized and carry with them all of the rights and responsibilities associated with heterosexual marriages.

For many gay and lesbian couples seeking marriage, the problem seems to be one of equity. Because of their sexual orientation, lesbian and gay couples lack ways of socially validating their committed partnerships and may experience problems related to their inability to marry as they interface with other systems in society. For example, gay and lesbian partners do not have the authority to make many "end of life" decisions for a terminally ill partner unless such authority is specifically granted through a living will or other legal document, regardless of the committed nature or longevity of the partnership. Because this responsibility is often granted to biologically related family members, such decisions can lead to conflict or distress if the partner and other family members are not in agreement over the proper course of medical treatment. In extreme cases, the committed partner of a gay or lesbian person could be left out of any medical decisions or be denied access to their ill or dying partner.

The issue of same-sex marriages captured national attention when two gay couples and one lesbian couple filed a lawsuit after the state of Hawaii denied their applications for marriage licenses. Initial court rulings supported the denial, but upon appeal to the Hawaii Supreme Court, the case was returned to the lower court for a demonstration of a "compelling state interest" to justify its discriminatory ruling. Indeed, the Supreme Court ruled that denial of a marriage license to same-sex couples was in violation of the state's constitution and its prohibition of sex discrimination (Freedom to Marry Coalition 1997).

As a result of the lawsuit in Hawaii, the U.S. Congress enacted the Defense of Marriage Act (DOMA) in 1996. DOMA defines marriage as "a legal union between one man and one woman as husband and wife," and a spouse is defined as "the person of the opposite sex who is a husband or a wife" (Section 3). DOMA grants states the authority to ignore same-sex marriages performed in other states. Therefore, same-sex couples could have their marriages invalidated if they moved from a state with legalized gay/lesbian marriages to one that denies them. A number of legal advocacy groups have objected to this provision, claiming that it is unconstitutional, violating the full faith and credit clause that requires states to recognize the "public acts, records, and judicial proceedings of every other state" (Article IV, Section 1). Facing legal challenges, the constitutionality of DOMA will ultimately be decided in court.

Proponents of DOMA, adhering to structural definitions that define families in terms of their childbearing and child-rearing functions, argue that federal and state legislation is needed in order to protect marriage from becoming too broadly defined. Relying on biological arguments to support their position, they have stated that because gay and lesbian couples are not able to have children, they do not fit within the definition of "family" and, consequently, should not be given the same privileges as those awarded heterosexual couples. Others have countered, however, that this argument is flawed, for it overlooks the fact that many heterosexual, married couples are voluntarily or involuntarily childless and that many gay and lesbian couples are now able to become parents via adoption and new reproductive technologies.

DOMA was not the only legislation enacted in reaction to Hawaii's anticipated legalization of gay and lesbian marriages. By June 1997, 25 states had enacted legislation barring marriage to gay and lesbian couples. Such legislation was pending in 11 additional states; similar bills that were eventually defeated or vetoed had been introduced in 12 other states. The governors of two states (Alabama and Mississippi) have issued executive orders barring gay and lesbians from marrying, and in 8 states a ballot initiative or state constitutional amendment disallowing gay marriage is possible. Ironically, in 1998 voters in Hawaii voted not to add an amendment to their state's constitution that would have allowed the legislature to restrict marriage to opposite-sex couples.

Adoption

Another problem that many people may experience in forming families is the inability to bear children. Infertility, typically defined as the inability to conceive or sustain a pregnancy after one year of regular, unprotected intercourse, is estimated to affect 18 percent of all American couples; of those couples diagnosed as infertile, approximately half will eventually conceive (Mosher and Pratt 1982). While many of these couples turn to reproductive technologies and other medical procedures to have children, a number of infertile couples also turn to adoption as a way of building a family. However, the path to adoptive parenthood can be difficult. In addition to the emotional ups and downs associated with infertility, couples may also encounter financial barriers and lengthy waiting periods before an adoptive placement is made, particularly if the couple is interested in adopting an infant.

Although many couples would like to adopt, many children waiting to be adopted languish in foster care for long periods of time, sometimes for years, and thus are deprived of permanent adoptive parents who would love and care for them. These children often have "special needs," meaning they are likely to be in need of special services or belong to a group for whom securing permanent adoptive placements has traditionally been more difficult. Special-needs children include children who are over 4 years old at the time of placement, who are physically handicapped, who belong to a sibling group, who have emotional or behavior problems, or who belong to a minority ethnic or racial group. Older children, many of whom have experienced tumultuous family events early in their lives such as abuse or neglect and many different care situations, may also be difficult to place. They need a stable family life, one that will provide them with adequate structure, love, and emotional support, as well as physical care.

One controversial issue in the family policy domain is transracial adoptions, or the adoption of children of one race by parents of another race. Although a disproportionate number of prospective adoptive parents are Caucasian, many children waiting to be adopted are children of color. However, the number of transracial adoptions has decreased dramatically since 1972, when the National Association of Black Social Workers (NABSW) passed a resolution stating their opposition to the placement of African-American children in Caucasian adoptive homes (Silverman 1993). Much of the opposition to transracial placements is a result of a concern that transracially adopted children will be unable to develop a clear, positive racial identity (McRoy 1988; McRoy and Zurcher 1983), although, interestingly, controversies over transracial adoptions differ dramatically based on the ethnicity of the children involved. Pertinent to this discussion are two policies enacted into law in the mid-1990s: the Multiethnic Placement Act (MEPA) of 1994 and the Adoption Promotion and Stability Act (APSA) passed by Congress and signed by President Clinton in 1996.

The aims of the MEPA are to (a) reduce the time children wait for adoption; (b) prevent discrimination in the placement of children in adoptive homes on the basis of race, color, or national origin; and (c) increase the pool of prospective same-race adoptive and foster parents. The explicit goals of APSA are to eliminate the use of race, color, or national origin as a criterion for adoption placement and to reduce the amount of time that adoption-eligible children spend in out-of-home care prior to their adoption. The goals of these two acts are to be achieved through adoption tax credits. The tax credits, which are adjusted for income, allow individual taxpayers to be reimbursed for adoption-related expenses for special-needs children and are intended to reduce financial barriers to adoption for lower- to middle-income families. Whether these tax credits and the elimination of racial and ethnic preferences in placement decisions will be sufficient to hasten the placement of adoption-eligible children and the formation of adoptive families are questions that remain to be answered.

Possible problematic effects of transracial adoption on the child's racial identity continue to be debated. Research to date has yielded conflicting findings. McRoy and Zurcher (1983) found that a significant proportion of the transracially adopted African-American children in their sample identified themselves as "part white"—a finding which the researchers concluded was a result of the children's predominately Caucasian environments and lack of discussion about race or ethnicity in their adoptive homes. Based on their findings, the authors concluded that transracially adopted children devalued their cultural heritage, which the researchers attributed to the failure of adoptive parents to provide their children with connections to other African-Americans in their communities and the necessary tools to become bicultural.

On the other hand, other researchers (Shireman 1988; Simon and Alstein 1987, 1992) have reported that a majority of transracially adopted youth were proud of and comfortable with their ethnic background. Also suggesting that transracial adoptive placements can be a successful and viable family formation alternative are transracial adoption researchers, reports of normative levels of self-esteem among transracially adopted adolescents and high levels of satisfaction with the family form among their adoptive parents.

Adoption practice in recent years, heavily influenced by the aforementioned research and standards set by such groups as the Child Welfare League of America (CWLA), has tended to take a cautious approach to transracial adoptive placements—recognizing the positive value in finding a permanent loving home for children while still favoring same-race placements for children of color, particularly African-American children. When making transracial placements, adoption practitioners have increasingly considered such factors as the prospective adoptive parents' ability to provide the adopted child with connections to his or her ethnic community. Consequently, APSA marks a dramatic shift in adoption policy, with obvious implications for potential adoptive parents and children of color who are waiting for permanent adoptive homes.

Policies Relating to Families Raising School-Aged Children

Now that we have talked about two problems that people experience in the family formation stage, let us address some of the problems families encounter as they raise children. Both of the problems reviewed in this section—access to affordable quality child-care and family leave time from work—are related to demographic and social trends, most notably the increased number of working mothers with young children. In this section, we will review policy initiatives that relate to these problems. We will also highlight some of the research that has examined the effects of child-care and family leave on various child and family outcomes.

Child Care

The feminization of the paid labor force has led to an increased need for child-care services. In particular, there has been a dramatic increase in the number of women with young children working outside the home. Sixty-four percent of all working women with husbands in the home had children under age 6 in 1995, up from 53.4 percent in 1985 and 36.7 percent in 1975 (U.S. Bureau of the Census 1996). Mothers' employment status varies with their marital status and the age of their children. For single mothers with children under 6, the labor force participation rate was 53 percent in 1995, whereas it was 66 percent for employed mothers who were divorced, widowed, or separated. Recent estimates reveal that nearly 8 million children from infancy to age 5 participated in a child-care or early education program in 1995—60 percent of the total number of children in that age group (West, Wright, and Hausken 1995). The problems that working mothers with young children experience are exacerbated not only by the fact that many are the family's primary wage earner but also by the scarcity of affordable quality day care.

At present, child-care services include a variety of settings: commercial child-care centers; private home care; school-based care; and informal care by family members, friends, neighbors, babysitters, or nannies. Although child-care services vary greatly, policy initiatives surrounding child care have largely focused on (a) child-care subsidies and programs for low-income families such as Head Start, a federally funded preschool program; (b) safety and licensing regulations and guidelines for child-care centers and child-care workers; and (c) the funding of child-care centers.

The issue of affordable quality day care for children has intensified for mothers of young children receiving welfare under the former Aid to Families with Dependent Children (AFDC) program and now under Temporary Assistance for Needy Families (TANF). TANF, created by the 1996 Personal Work and Responsibility Act, limits the provision of financial assistance for poor mothers with young children to two years and to a lifetime of five years. If mothers of these families are to work, affordable child care is necessary for their very survival. One of the provisions of the Personal Responsibility and Work Opportunity Act is that new child-care funding will be combined with the existing Child Care and Development Block Grant (CCDBG), increasing the resources available for child care. Block grants are monies allocated to states by the federal government for specific purposes. Although the federal government stipulates the general function for which states must spend block grant monies, decisions about the funding of specific programs reside with states and local communities. Block grant funds are capped, which means that funding cannot exceed predetermined limits, unlike categorical grants, which are awarded to states for specific programs and are more open-ended (Chambers 1993).

Several advocacy groups, including children's advocacy groups, have raised concerns over the new welfare law, particularly in regard to the ways that new financing formulas will affect child care for low-income families. State receipt of newly authorized child-care funds is dependent on states maintaining their current level of investment in child care and providing new funds. Whether less affluent states will be able to provide the financial resources necessary to obtain federal assistance for child-care programs is yet to be determined.

Although many child-care policies are targeted toward low-income families, other policies are designed to improve the quality of child care for all families who rely on child-care services. The recognition of quality child care as an issue deserving of policy attention has been fueled by a wealth of research in the developmental and family literature since the 1970s, when practitioners (e.g., Brazelton 1985) first raised concern about the possible deleterious consequences of mothers' time away from infants on the subsequent mother-child relationship.

Although some researchers (Belsky and Rovine 1988; Clarke-Stewart 1989; Lamb and Sternberg 1990; Vaughn, Gove, and Egeland 1980) have found a heightened risk of insecure attachment among children experiencing extensive or early nonparental care, other researchers (Roggman, Langlois, Hubbs-Tait, and Rieser-Danner 1994) have found that such risk is not any higher for children receiving early out-of-home care than for others. Other researchers (NICHD 1997) report that attachment problems are associated with a combination of child care and maternal characteristics, not child care in and of itself.

Researchers who have focused on the social competencies, emotional maturity, and intellectual development of children receiving day care (e.g., Clarke-Stewart 1991) report that such children tend to be higher in each of these domains than their cared-for-at-home peers. More recent investigations (NICHD 1997) suggest that although child care that provides positive caregiving and language stimulation is positively related to children's later cognitive and language development, it is not as predictive as a variety of family factors, thus reinforcing the importance of contextual examinations of child care.

Based on a number of studies, researchers have unanimously concluded that the quality of child care has a profound influence on children's subsequent development and relationship-formation patterns. Research on child-care centers in Bermuda (McCartney, Scarr, Phillips, and Grajek 1985; Phillips, McCartney, and Scarr 1987) has pointed to director experience and other indicators of quality care as predictors of children's social development. Recent studies highlighting the less than optimal level of care in a majority of day-care settings in the U.S. have raised serious concerns among researchers and policymakers alike.

In October 1997, President Bill Clinton and First Lady Hillary Rodham Clinton held the White House Conference on Child Care, where they emphasized the importance of quality child care on children's social and cognitive development. Among provisions President Clinton has recommended are federal scholarships for child-care training, a national system of background checks on all child-care providers, a program to encourage businesses to become more involved in child-care policy and provision, and the use of AmeriCorps volunteers in after-school care programs (Brand 1997), all of which could help increase the availability of child-care services for families with young children.

Family and Medical Leave

A problem for all working parents relates to taking time off from work to tend to family responsibilities, such as the care of sick children and elderly parents or the care of a newborn. In addition to finding quality care for their children while they are at work, many parents find that they have limited options when a child becomes sick. In 1984, Congresswoman Pat Schroeder, concerned about the job security of workers who had newborns or were caring for ill children, drafted parental leave legislation that would have allowed such employees 18 weeks of unpaid leave upon the birth, adoption, or serious health condition of a child and up to 26 weeks of medical leave for their own health condition (Elison 1997). Eventually retitled the Family Medical Leave Act (FMLA), the bill was first considered by congressional subcommittees in 1986. However, it did not pass both houses of Congress until 1990,

when it was promptly vetoed by President Bush on grounds that it would interfere with employers' prerogatives. Congress passed the FMLA again in 1991 and 1992, but President Bush, a staunch opponent of FMLA, again vetoed the bill, and congressional attempts to override the president's veto failed each time (Marks 1997). Finally, after the election of President Clinton, when Congress passed the FMLA a fourth time, FMLA was signed into law in February 1993 (Marks 1997).

Although often touted as a policy directed toward families with young children, the FMLA actually applies to families throughout the life cycle. It entitles employees of businesses with 50 or more workers to up to 12 weeks of unpaid, job-protected leave to care for a newborn or adopted child, to attend to their own serious health needs, or to care for a seriously ill parent, child, or spouse (Bernstein 1997). During the debate over FMLA in the 1980s and early 1990s, opponents raised concern over the costs it entailed for business. Although this issue requires more investigation, early evaluations of FMLA do not support this concern, revealing instead that businesses have incurred only minimal costs as a result of FMLA (Women's Connection Online 1997b).

Although proponents of FMLA have touted the act as an example of successful family policy, evaluations of the FMLA have been most critical of its limited scope. Because small businesses are exempted from FMLA, unpaid family leave is offered to only 11 percent of all American businesses and is available to only 46.5 percent of American workers (Women's Connection Online 1997a). Additional concern about the FMLA centers on the failure of many employees to take advantage of medical leave. Early follow-up studies have reported that between January of 1994 and June of 1995, only 2 to 4 percent of employees took leave under the FMLA, and 58 percent of those 2 to 4 percent were women (Women's Connection Online 1997b). Many policy analysts have attributed this finding to the fact that the FMLA offers only unpaid leave time and have argued that many employees cannot afford to go without pay for any extended period of time. In a 1996 report to Congress, the bipartisan Family Leave Commission noted that nearly two-thirds of the employees surveyed cited lost wages as the primary impediment to taking family leave (Women's Connection Online 1997b). Critics have also noted that the United States family leave policy is far less generous than the parental or family leave policies of Western European countries, Canada, and Japan (Scharlach and Grosswald 1997). Sweden, for example, offers 18 months of parental leave to be split among parents at 90 percent of full-time pay, and 18 months of unpaid leave to all employees, even those who do not qualify for benefits (Baker 1997).

Based on these findings, the Family Leave Commission and many women's and children's advocacy groups have led the campaign to expand family and medical leave to include some amount of paid leave (Women's Connection Online 1997a). The Clinton Administration has also called for an expansion of the FMLA, advocating that 24 hours of unpaid leave be offered to employees for the purposes of attending to such family obligations as parent-teacher conferences or routine medical and dental appointments with a child, spouse, or elderly parent. Paid family leave, which was not a component of the president's proposed expansion, is likely to be met with heavy opposition by business lobbying groups. Although this issue remains on the forefront, much debate is expected over the amount and type of expansion of FMLA.

Families in the Middle and Later Life Cycle Stages

Many of the problems that families face in their middle years relate to the squeeze they experience in trying to meet the needs of their young adult children, to save for their own retirement, and to care for their elderly and often frail parents—all at the same time. Although families in all life cycle stages can be faced with difficult decisions regarding the care of a loved one, such as the care of a severely or mentally disabled child or a mentally ill family member, caregiving becomes a particularly salient issue for families as

members move into their later years, often experiencing problems related to impaired cognitive or physical functioning. In this section, we will review one problem that many families in their later years confront—the financial costs involved in the caregiving of an elderly or ailing family member. This problem is affected by numerous policies, including but not limited to Social Security, Medicare and Medicaid, and state or local community-based programs such as adult day care. Pertinent to our discussion of these problems are provisions for reforming the financing of Medicare and Medicaid.[1]

From a historical perspective, caregiving for elderly family members is a relatively recent phenomenon. The vast advances in health care services and delivery have greatly extended the life span, and a greater number of elderly adults are living longer lives and needing care as they become afflicted with acute and chronic illnesses. In the next 30 years, as members of the baby boom generation move into their later years, the number of elderly persons is anticipated to grow by 73 percent. Today, the fastest growing segment of the population is people 85 years and older; this age group is projected to increase by 115 percent in the next 30 years (Urban Institute, 1997). Based on these demographic data alone, a large number of families can be expected to be confronted with problems surrounding the care of elderly parents or other relatives. Adult children will be required to make decisions as to whether or not to care for their parents in their homes, to place them outside the home in a nursing facility, or to draw on an array of services in the community that could enable their parents to remain in their own homes. Because these decisions often require the restructuring of parent-child relationships and other life cycle changes, they are often accompanied by a great deal of anxiety and distress for both adult children and their elderly parents.

Such decisions are often complicated by financial considerations. Although Social Security and Medicare have yielded higher income security and access to regular health care for older Americans (Doty 1992), caregiving for an impaired family member with a chronic illness such as Alzheimer's disease can deplete families' financial resources. Recent reports estimate that annual costs for long-term care in a nursing home facility can exceed $35,000 per person, and long-term home or community-based care runs over $15,000 (Urban Institute 1997). Consequently, medical insurance that covers the costs of this long-term care, which includes an array of health, personal care, and supportive services, is a necessity for most families in this stage.

In 1994, Medicare, a federal program financed through payroll taxes to which people contribute during their working years, covered 32 million seniors (National Academy on Aging 1995). The program is divided into two parts: Part A, a social insurance program subsidizing inpatient hospital care, skilled nursing care or rehabilitation care following hospitalization, home health care, and hospice care; and Part B, a supplementary medical insurance program that allows elderly and disabled adults to purchase outpatient insurance for a relatively small monthly premium, which was $43.80 in 1997 (Schneider 1997). Most long-term nursing home care is not covered by Medicare, requiring families to finance such care themselves through the purchase of long-term care insurance or by becoming eligible for Medicaid. Because Medicaid is designed to serve poor Americans, this option is available only to low-income elderly. In recent years, public concern has arisen over the practice of "spending-down," whereby middle- or higher-income elderly persons disperse their assets in order to qualify for Medicaid long-term-care coverage. Valid data on the rates of affluent elderly who actually "spend down" are lacking, and although some policy analysts and researchers have estimated that these rates are actually rather small, several states have increased their efforts to recover transferred assets in an attempt to prevent this type of fraud (Urban Institute 1997).

The increasing costs to both Medicaid and Medicare have served as the impetus for much of the policy activity related to long-term health care. According to the General Accounting Office (GAO), the costs of long-term care now constitute nearly one-third of the nation's Medicaid budget—85 percent of the increased cost being attributed to long-term care expenditures involving the out-of-home placement of older persons in nursing homes ("Long-term care," 1994). Although the majority of elderly who enter nursing homes reside there for less than a year, the number of people who require long-term institutional care and are unable to finance such care on their own has increased. Although long-term-care costs are currently high, the health care system is expected to face even higher costs as the population ages. Widely discrepant policies have been advocated to address these anticipated problems. Although some analysts have advocated relying increasingly on the private sector, encouraging the elderly to purchase private long-term-care insurance, others (e.g., Urban Institute 1997; Weiner 1996) have deemed this strategy to be insufficient and have advocated expansion or reform of public programs.

Provisions included in the 1997 Balanced Budget Act are likely to have a profound effect on families' ability to provide long-term care for their elderly members. These provisions contain the largest reductions in federal Medicaid spending since 1981 (Schneider 1997). Although Medicaid will remain an entitlement program under the law (rather than be converted into a block grant as some Republican members of Congress previously had advocated), a number of specific provisions related to Medicaid and Medicare could have a dramatic effect on the availability and financing of long-term care and, hence, on the well-being of elderly people and their families.

Legislation pertaining to the public financing of health care, particularly long-term care, is anticipated in the coming years. Although the solvency of the Medicare Part A trust fund has been extended to 2007, concerns remain, and future policy revisions in Medicare and Medicaid are certain. The 1997 Balanced Budget Act established a 17-member Bipartisan Commission on the Future of Medicare to study and propose long-term recommendations for Medicare; however, this commission could not reach a consensus and disbanded. In the coming years, policymakers will be forced to make difficult decisions about what types of and how many health care services to fund. As the need for adequate and affordable long-term care increases, this issue will remain subject to continued debate, with elderly advocacy groups such as the American Association of Retired Persons (AARP), private insurance companies, long-term care providers, and families all having a vested interest in the outcomes.

Conclusion

Through this discussion of the problems that families experience in relation to wider society over their life course and some of the policies that have been enacted or are being debated that aim to address their problems, we hope readers have gained some understanding of the connections between families and government via policy outputs, which are constantly subject to change. Our discussion also highlights some of the complexities involved in attempting to address the problems that many families experience. Such complexities pertain not only to the federal nature of our political system but also to the institutional framework of that system, with different branches of government in different aspects of the policymaking process, the multitude of interest groups that attempt to influence lawmakers to adopt their position on family issues, and political elites who have their own agendas to advance. Students preparing for professional roles in working with or on behalf of families should be aware of these complexities when thinking about the connections between families and government and be alert to the ways in which policies that are enacted may affect families, whether their family goals are explicit or implicit, in order to avert possible adverse consequences for the families they most directly affect.

Discussion Questions

1. How are families and family policies conceptualized in this chapter?

2. What are the goals of family policies?

3. Do the policies illustrated in this chapter meet the goals or objectives of family policies for families at each of the life course stages that were presented? Explain your answer.

4. Select a family issue and review the policies that have been developed to address this issue. Have these policies accomplished their goals? Why or why not?

Glossary

Defense of marriage act (DOMA) An act that defines marriage as a legal union between one man and one woman as husband and wife; under this act, a spouse is defined as the person of the opposite sex who is a husband or a wife.

Family formation The transitions by which two or more individuals form a new family union.

Family policy Everything governments do that affects families, directly or indirectly.

Transracial adoptions The adoption of children of one race by parents of another race.

Suggested Readings

Chambers, D. E. (1993). *Social Policy and Social Programs: A Method for the Practical Public Policy Analyst*, 2nd ed. New York: Macmillan.

Gil, D. (1973). *Unraveling Social Policy.* Cambridge, MA: Schenkman.

Zimmerman, S. L. (1988). *Understanding Family Policies: Theoretical Approaches.* Newbury Park, CA: Sage.

Zimmerman, S. L. (1992). *Family Policies and Family Well-being: The Role of Political Culture.* Newbury Park, CA: Sage.

Zimmerman, S. L. (1995). *Understanding Family Policy: Theories and Applications,* 2nd ed.. Thousand Oaks, CA: Sage.

Bibliography

Baker, M. (1997). Parental benefit policies and the gendered division of labor. *Social Science Review, 71*, 51–70.

Belsky, J., and Rovine, M. J. (1988). Non-maternal care in the first year of life and the security of infant-parent attachment. *Child Development, 59,* 157–167.

Bernstein, A. (1997). Inside or outside? The politics of family and medical leave. *The Policy Studies Journal, 25,* 87–99.

Brand, P. (1997, October 24). Child care is America's "silent crisis." *Minneapolis Star Tribune.*

Brazelton, T. B. (1985). *Working and Caring.* New York: Basic.

Chambers, D. E. (1993). *Social Policy and Social Programs: A Method for the Practical Public Policy Analyst,* 2nd ed. New York: Macmillan.

Clarke-Stewart, K. A. (1989). Infant day-care: Maligned or malignant? *American Psychologist, 44,* 266–273.

Clarke-Stewart, K. A. (1991). A home is not a school: The effects of child-care on children's development. *Journal of Social Issues, 47,* 105–123.

Doty, P. (1992). The oldest old and the use of institutional long-term care from an international perspective. In R. M. Suzman, D. P. Willis, and K. G. Manton (eds.). *The Oldest Old* (251–267). New York: Oxford University.

Elison, S. K. (1997). Policy innovation in a cold climate: The Family and Medical Leave Act of 1993. *Journal of Family Issues, 18,* 30–54.

Freedom to Marry Coalition. (1997). *History of the Lawsuit* [On-line]. Available: http://www.ftm.org/overview/history.html.

Gil, D. (1973). *Unraveling Social Policy.* Cambridge, MA: Schenkman.

Kammerman, S. B., and Kahn, A. (1976). Explorations in family policy. *Social Work, 21,* 181–187.

Lamb, M., and Sternberg, K. (1990). Do we really know how day-care affects children? *Journal of Applied Developmental Psychology, 11,* 351–379.

Lasswell, H. (1968). The policy orientation. In D. Lerner and H. Lasswell (eds.). *Policy Sciences* (3–15). Stanford, CA: Stanford University.

Long-term care home and community-based services. (1994, September 26). *Social Information Legislation Service,* 167.

Marks, M. R. (1997). Party politics and family policy: The case of the Family and Medical Leave Act. *Journal of Family Issues, 18,* 55–70.

McCartney, K., Scarr, S., Phillips, D., and Grajek, S. (1985). Day care as intervention: Comparisons of varying quality programs. *Journal of Applied Developmental Psychology, 6,* 247–260.

McRoy, R. G. (1988). An organizational dilemma: The case of transracial adoptions. *The Journal of Applied Behavioral Science, 25,* 145–160.

McRoy, R. G., and Zurcher, L. A. (1983). *Transracial and Inracial Adoptees: The Adolescent Years.* Springfield, IL: Charles C. Thomas.

Mosher, W. D., and Pratt, W. F. (1982). *Reproductive Impairments Among Married Couples: United States.* Hyattsville, MD: U.S. Department of Health and Human Services, Office of Health Research, Statistics, and Technology, National Center for Health Statistics.

National Academy on Aging. (1995). *Facts on Medicare: Hospital Insurance and Supplementary Medical Insurance* [On-line]. Available: http://gsa.iog.wayne.edu/NAA/medicare.html.

NICHD Early Child Care Network. (1997). The effects of infant child-care on infant-mother attachment security: Results of the NICHD study of early child-care. *Child Development, 68,* 860–879.

Phillips, D., McCartney, K., and Scarr, S. (1987). Child-care quality and children's social development. *Developmental Psychology, 23,* 537–543.

Roggman, L., Langlois, J., Hubbs-Tait, L., and Rieser-Danner, L. (1994). Infant day-care, attachment, and the "file drawer problem." *Child Development, 65,* 1429–1443.

Scharlach, A. E., and Grosswald, B. (1997). The Family and Medical Leave Act of 1993. *Social Service Review, 71,* 335–359.

Schneider, A. (1997). *Overview of Medicaid Provisions in the Balanced Budget Act of 1997,* [On-line]. Available: http://www.cpbb.org/908mcaid.html.

Shireman, J. F. (1988). *Growing Up Adopted: An Examination of Major Issues.* Chicago: Child Care Society.

Silverman, A. R. (1993). Outcomes of transracial adoption. *The Future of Children, 3,* 104–118.

Simon, R. J., and Alstein, H. (1987). *Transracial Adoptees and Their Families: A Study of Identity and Commitment.* New York: Praeger.

Simon, R. J., and Alstein, H. (1992). *Adoption, Race, and Identity.* New York: Praeger.

The Urban Institute. (1997). *Medicaid and Long-term Care* [On-line]. Available: http://www.urban.org/perodcl/prr25_3g.html.

U.S. Bureau of the Census. (1996). *Statistical Abstracts of the United States, 1996,* 116th ed. Washington, DC: U.S. Government Printing Office.

Vaughn, B. E., Gove, F. L., and Egeland, B. (1980). The relationship between daycare and quality of infant-mother attachment in an economically disadvantaged population. *Child Development, 51,* 1203–1214.

Weiner, J. M. (1996). Financing reform for long-term care: Strategies for public and private long-term care insurance. *Journal of Aging and Social Policy, 7,* 109–127.

West, J., Wright, D., and Hausken, E. G. (1995). *Child Care and Early Education Program Participation of Infants, Toddlers, and Preschoolers.* Washington, DC: U.S. Department of Education.

Wolfson, E. (1997). *Anti-marriage Bills 1997: State-by-State Status Report* [On-line]. Available: http://www.ftm.org/overview/state-by-state.html.

Women's Connection Online. (1997a). *Bi-partisan Commission: Family and Medical Leave Is "Tremendous Success" Recommends Exploring Options for Paid Leave* [On-line]. Available: http://womenconnect.com/channels/business/bu50161.htm.

Women's Connection Online. (1997b). *Family Medical Leave: A Report Card* [On-line]. Avail-able: http://www.womenconnect.com/channels/business/bu41661.html.

Zimmerman, S. L. (1988). *Understanding Family Policies: Theoretical Approaches.* Newbury Park, CA: Sage.

Zimmerman, S. L. (1992). *Family Policies and Family Well-being: The Role of Political Culture.* Newbury Park, CA: Sage.

Zimmerman, S. L. (1995). *Understanding Family Policy: Theories and Applications,* 2nd ed.. Thousand Oaks, CA: Sage.

Zimmerman, S. L. (in progress). Political culture and states' family policies in the 1990s.

Note

1. Medicaid also covers low-income families with young children.✦

CPSIA information can be obtained at www.ICGtesting.com
Printed in the USA
BVOW100529290413

319296BV00003B/61/A